Jaunting Through Ireland

Also by Roy Kerridge

BESIDE THE SEASIDE AND OTHER TALES

THE STORE'S OUTING

DRUID MADONNA

REAL WICKED GUY

THE LONE CONFORMIST

BIZARRE BRITAIN

PEOPLE OF BRITAIN

IN THE DEEP SOUTH

Jaunting Through Ireland

☘

ROY KERRIDGE

MICHAEL JOSEPH
London

MICHAEL JOSEPH LTD

Published by the Penguin Group
27 Wrights Lane, London W8 5TZ, England
Viking Penguin Inc., 375 Hudson Street, New York, New York 10014, USA
Penguin Books Australia Ltd, Ringwood, Victoria, Australia
Penguin Books Canada Ltd, 2801 John Street, Markham, Ontario, Canada L3R 1B4
Penguin Books (NZ) Ltd, 182–190 Wairau Road, Auckland 10, New Zealand

Penguin Books Ltd, Registered Offices: Harmondsworth, Middlesex, England

First published in Great Britain March 1991
Second impression April 1991

The quotation on page 16 is from
Country Writings by Geoffrey Grigson,
published by Century.

Made and printed in Great Britain by
Butler & Tanner Ltd, Frome and London
Filmset in Monophoto Ehrhardt 11/12½pt

A CIP catalogue record for this book is available from the British Library
ISBN 0 7181 3246 7

For David Adams, Prince of Bank Managers

Author's Note

☘

When people in Ireland learned I was writing a book, most of them said, 'Leave my name out of it.' The following names, therefore, are fictitious: the Phillarney Tribe, Maher, Percy, Mr and Mrs Harvey-Beaumont, Zelda, Mrs Knelle, Mrs Molloy, Kodiak, June and Pat, Mr and Mrs Clay, Sven Svennsen, Yon Yonson, Mr and Mrs Mulhooley and George Mulverin and Son. Other people mentioned in the book thought I was on holiday. Holford House is a fictitious house name.

Contents

☘

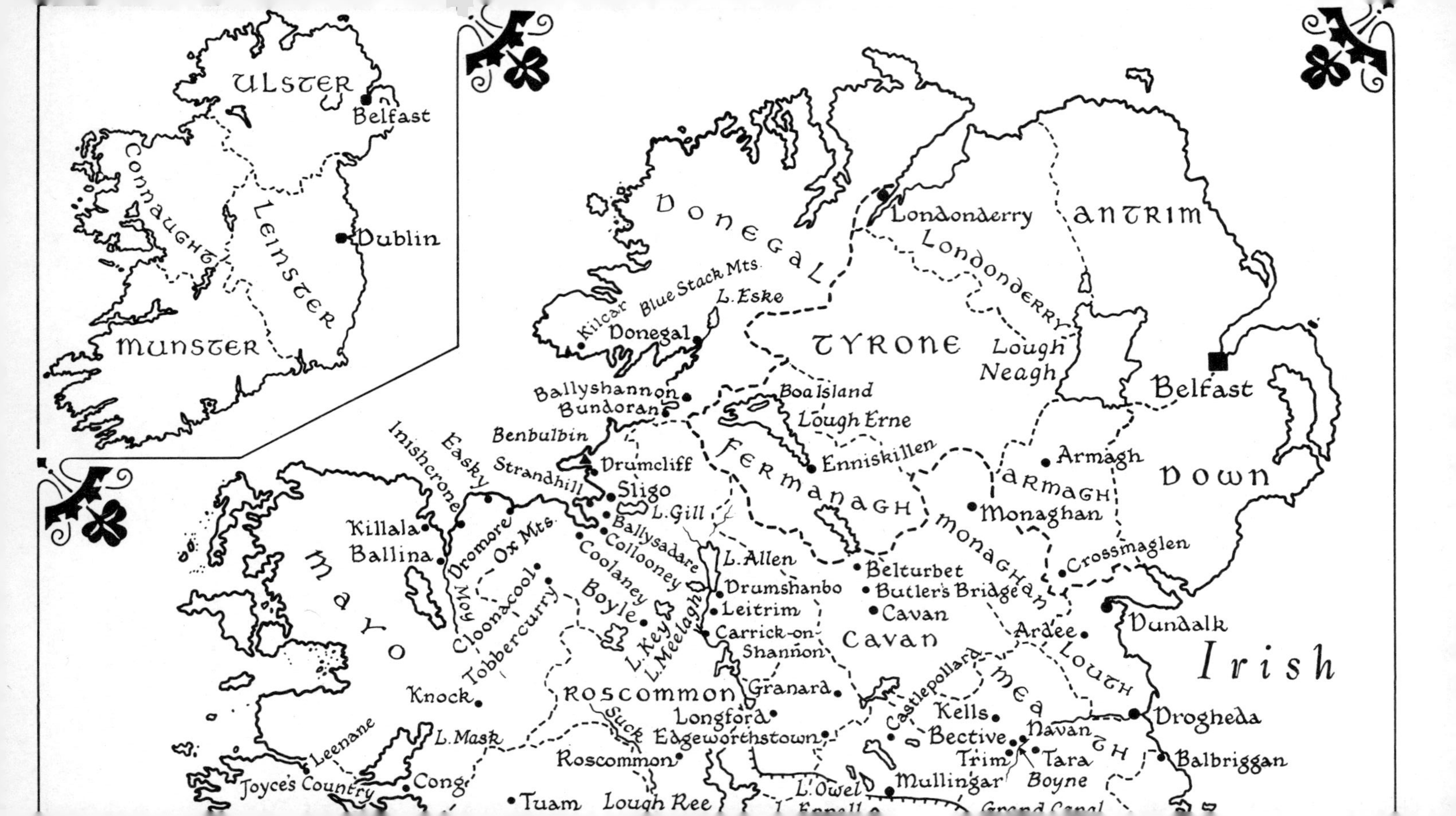
ULSTER
Belfast
CONNAUGHT
LEINSTER
Dublin
MUNSTER
DONEGAL
Londonderry
ANTRIM
LONDONDERRY
Blue Stack Mts.
L. Eske
Kilcar
Donegal
TYRONE
Lough
Neagh
Belfast
Ballyshannon
Bundoran
Boa Island
Lough Erne
Benbulbin
Inishcrone
Easky
Strandhill
Drumcliff
FERMANAGH
Enniskillen
Armagh
ARMAGH
DOWN
Sligo
L. Gill
Monaghan
MONAGHAN
Killala
Ballina
Dromore
Ox Mts.
Ballysadare
Collooney
Coolaney
L. Allen
Belturbet
Crossmaglen
MAYO
Moy
Cloonacool
Tobbercurry
Boyle
Drumshanbo
Butler's Bridge
Leitrim
Cavan
L. Key
L. Meelagh
Carrick-on-Shannon
CAVAN
Ardee
Dundalk
Irish
LOUTH
ROSCOMMON
Granard
Castlepollard
MEATH
Knock
Longford
Kells
Drogheda
Suck
Edgeworthstown
Bective
Navan
Leenane
L. Mask
Roscommon
Trim
Tara
Balbriggan
Joyce's Country
Cong
L. Owel
Mullingar
Boyne
Tuam
Lough Ree
Grand Canal

IRELAND
Sea
Dublin
Dun Laoghaire
Liffey
The Curragh
Wicklow
Anna Moe
Glendalough
Rathdrum
Glenealy
Shillelagh
Wexford
Rosslare
New Ross
Blackstairs Mt.
Barrow
Carlow
Kilkenny
Old Leighlin
Port Laoise
Laois
Kildare
Tullamore
Ballycumber
Ferbane
Taylors Cross
Birr
Clonmacnoise
Ballinasloe
Banagher
Shannon
Lough Derg
Mt. St. Joseph Abbey
Roscrea
Devils Bit
Thurles
Holy Cross
Cashel
Tipperary
Suir
Waterford
Dungarvan
Youghal
Midleton
Cork
Lee
Bandon
Ross Carbery
Clonakilty
Castletownshend
Leap
Skibbereen
Bantry
Glengariff
Caha Mts.
Kenmare
Kenmare River
Bantry Bay
Mizen Head
L. Leane
Muckross
Killarney
Macgillycuddy's Reeks
Dingle Bay
Killorglin
Slieve Mish
Tralee
Kerry
River Shannon
Limerick
Clare
Galway
Galway Bay
Aran Islands
Connemara
0 50 km
0 30 miles
Peter McClure

Acknowledgements

I would like to thank the following individuals for their kind help and encouragement: Diane Flynn, the staff at Kilburn Public Library, Jack Sayers of Cricklewood, Timothy and Angela Price, the North West London Typewriting Bureau, Vicky Hutchings, Richard Addis, Penny Underwood, Mike and Gill Evans, Melita, Sue Millar, Charmaine Gillespie and Buddy, Jane Gaskell, Craigan and Sheena, the Taxi Drivers of Ireland, the Guide Book Writers of Ireland, Michael Wharton, Mr Chisholm, The Protestant Truth Society, the Legion of Mary, Georgie, the staff of the City YMCA, the staff at the Salutation Hotel, Perth, Scotland (particularly Sue in the dining room and June and Pam at Reception) and all at the Old Mansion House, Knighton, Radnorshire.

CHAPTER ONE

Now!

Early on one Sunday morning,
High upon a gallows tree,
Kevin Barry gave his young life
For the Cause of Liberty.

Just a lad of eighteen summers,
And yet no one could deny
As he walked to Death that morning
He proudly held his head on high.

When just a southern English lad of eighteen summers myself, I was absolutely entranced on first hearing my hero Lonnie Donegan sing this song. This experience, together with my discovery of Brendan Behan's writings, marked my first realization that the Irish are a separate people from the English. Quickly I telephoned all my friends, and (although I cannot sing) insisted on singing 'Kevin Barry' to them, verse by verse. Everyone seemed impressed by Kevin's nobility except a Bohemian friend who attended an expensive 'free school' where he spent most of his time folk-dancing dressed as a hobby horse.

Eyes shining behind wire spectacles, I buttonholed him in the manner of a 1950s Ancient Mariner, and sang on.

Just before they hung young Kevin,
In his lowly prison cell,
Black and Tans they tortured Kevin
Just because he wouldn't tell.

'Tell us the names of your companions
And other things we need to know.
Turn informer and we'll free you.'
Kevin proudly answered 'No!'

'Why don't you shoot me like a soldier?
Don't hang me like a dog in scorn,
For I fought to free old Ireland
On that chill September morn.'

To my surprise, my friend burst out laughing. Taking my arm, he steered me into a Moo Cow Milk Bar where he sat down and laughed some more. 'You sound like a typical Irishman!' he said at last. 'You know, an unshaven old tramp reeling about with a whiskey bottle in one hand, shouting abuse at passers-by, threatening to beat them up and roaring "I fought to free old Ireland!" before falling flat on his face.'

'Is that a typical Irishman?' I asked in surprise.

'Of course. They're all mad, and no one knows what they're talking about.'

My mother confirmed that at her university none of the other students could understand the passionate politics of the Irish. Oliver Cromwell came into it, and so did the Potato Famine.

To the socialist intelligentsia of 1950s England, the IRA seemed a noble cause, although nobody quite knew what they wanted. Brendan Behan won instant fame with his autobiography, *Borstal Boy*. I discovered Behan's writings in *Punch*, where his racy accounts of Borstal life looked odd amid mild, jokey suburban essays on broken lawnmowers. When *Borstal Boy* came out, I recognized the *Punch* extracts, and read the whole story, seeing a real-life Kevin Barry in Brendan. Songs peppered the narrative, together with fiery speeches in praise of the IRA and denunciations of the Roman Catholic Church. Later readings of Behan showed him to be deeply ambivalent in his attitudes both to Republican politics and to his Mother Church.

Joan Littlewood, the bawdy-minded theatrical entrepreneur, got hold of Behan and used him in her campaign to depict the Working Man to intellectuals not as a priggishly Revolutionary Proletarian, but as a refreshingly foul-mouthed, honestly dishonest and wholly admirable debauchee. This new fashion swept poor Behan into becoming a parody of my free-school friend's 'typical Irishman'.

Brendan Behan became every Englishman's Irishman. Baffled by the Littlewood-influenced *Hostage*, I read and reread *The Quare Fellow*. Another song of Mountjoy Jail now brought tears to my eyes: 'The Old Triangle'. Brendan's brother Dominic sang this on the radio, but to my indignation the studio audience laughed at the mention of the Royal Canal, as if a canal, like fish and chips, were working class and therefore funny. Much to my surprise, my grandfather, a dignified and cultured figure who sat alone amidst his antique collection, reading Balzac, Conrad and Anatole France, also enjoyed *The Quare Fellow*. He particularly admired the character of a humane warder. Thus encouraged, I romanticized the Irish I had never met, unsure if they were drunk or sober, noble or loveably ridiculous.

'Lonnie Donegan changed the words of "Kevin Barry",' a boy with Irish relatives told me. 'It should say "British soldiers tortured Kevin", not "Black and Tans".'

This made more sense to me, as everyone in our *Daily Worker* circle had heard of 'The British', those terrible people. We all knew of the crimes of The British in India, Africa and Ireland. One day, the *Worker* showed a photograph of The British in Malaya, playing football with a human head. If this were not a forgery, it would at least show that The British had not forsaken their ancient pagan customs, for the game of football itself may have sprung from such a practice. Nobody who spoke so disapprovingly of The British ever connected these British with anyone they knew in England. They seemed dangerous foreigners, over whose depredations we English had no control. If The British were in Ireland, no wonder the Irish were in trouble!

All this while, when Irish songs, plays and stories were seething in the cauldron of my brain, my mother and our Irish neighbour Mrs Kenny were firm friends, and my young sister played at making mud pies with red-haired Rory, the Kenny boy. Mrs Kenny, though born in an Irish house in London, had been taken back to Dublin as a girl, where she had lived in the lively, cheerful district of Rathmines. Here she had learned street songs such as 'Do you want your old lobby washed down, fish-face?' and observed now bygone customs.

'Nearly everyone had a holy water dipper in their house when I was a girl,' she would say, 'and the women sprinkled water all round the room before they went out.'

Pagan friends of my West African stepfather did the same, I

had noticed, but at that time I felt too shy to speak to adults outside the family. I assumed that the only way to learn about people was through books or records. So Mrs Kenny and the Africans went unheeded.

Much later, in the 1960s, my reading habits again drew me towards the Irish. Sitting in Brighton reference library, I discovered and devoured magazines full of non-Communist ideas, *Encounter* and the *Spectator*. One day, in *Encounter*, I read a good-humoured article on the Irish Ascendancy. How far were they surviving as a separate people, the author enquired, and how far were they becoming Irishized, turning Catholic and developing Irish brogues? He came to no firm conclusion, but the article was a revelation to me. I had never previously heard of the Ascendancy at all, only of The British, whom I supposed to have been soldiers to a man and not permanent residents in Ireland. Now it appeared that until recently Ireland had boasted a Wodehousian aristocracy of English descent, with Big Houses, acres of land and horses!

At the same time, my mother discovered the 'Irish RM' stories of Edith Somerville and Martin Ross, and recommended them to me. I took to the RM, or Resident Magistrate, immediately. He seemed to belong to the same comic world, or Golden Age, as characters from stories by Saki, W. W. Jacobs, P. G. Wodehouse, Kipling and G. K. Chesterton, my well-loved Famous Five. A modern novelist, Honor Tracy, also depicted the Irish Ascendancy as a likeable and much-put-upon people. The eighteenth-century novelist, Maria Edgeworth, described a less loveable Ascendancy whose generosity, avarice, cruelty and recklessness derived from the clash between the Irish and English traditions. Two hundred years earlier, in Elizabethan days, the old Irish aristocracy had been fatally subdued and the alien Ascendancy established.

Ireland was beginning to make sense, but I had more reading yet to do. Irish legends of underwater kingdoms in the days when seals were men, as recounted by David Thomson in *People of the Sea*, so enraptured me that I wrote the author a thank-you letter. He replied by posting me a signed copy of *Woodbrook*, the beautiful story of a country house in Ireland where the author had worked as a tutor in the 1930s. Thomson traced the history of the Kirkwood family back to their early days as Protestant settlers in a Catholic land. Unlike some of their ancestors, the present-day Kirkwoods seemed admirable, high-minded people, tricked and beleaguered by a crafty peasantry.

My favourite *Spectator* writer, Tibor Szamuely, wrote a book called *The Russian Tradition*, which I read with interest. It seemed to show that there were, at one time, *two* Russian traditions. Monstrous, sadistic, almost Stalin-like Tsars, whose whims were law, brought into being a half-hidden, half-hearted world of rebellion, whether from peasants, landowners, priests or intellectuals. Martyrs abounded wherever Tsarist suspicion fell. But as the years went by, and the nineteenth century got into its stride, the Tsars began to improve. Like a see-saw, the Tsars grew better while the rebels, with their secret societies, grew worse. In their last days the Russian Royal Family became great-hearted, gracious and Godly, opposed by Stalin-like revolutionaries (one of whom was Stalin).

Was there not a parallel to be drawn here with Ireland, her Ascendancy and her rebels? Serfs had been freed in Russia for generations before the Revolution. Similarly, Irish freedom could be said to have begun just before Queen Victoria's reign, with the 1829 Catholic Emancipation that led to the late-Victorian and present-day Ireland of thriving Roman Catholic institutions. True, thanks to the tragic Potato Famine of 1846, Irish improvement received a severe setback, but the modern Ireland of great Catholic cathedrals, convents and monasteries was well established by the 1890s. By the end of the nineteenth century, with the Land Act creation of a peasantry, Ireland seemed no more or less 'free' than Scotland, Wales or England herself. Why did there have to be a break with the rest of Britain? I began to look on Ireland as an estranged relative who ought to be welcomed back to the bosom of the family.

Without a qualm or a foreboding, I travelled around Northern Ireland in the sixties, but hesitated to enter the Republic. I had one more book to read. This was *In the Wake of the Gods* by Hugh Malet. Travelling the Irish waterways by boat, Malet described a pagan landscape and a pagan Ireland, going far back beyond the Celts to the Fomor and the Firbolgs, a legend for every landmark.

The Celts, or 'wild Irish', who so plagued English settlers in Elizabethan days, were an Indo-European people. Before Christianity, which came early to Ireland, they had enjoyed a semi-Indian way of life, with castes and taboos and pantheons. Like Indian kings, their high chieftains regarded each neighbouring territory as ripe for conquest, as Conquest was the proper occupation for a monarch. Although craftsmen working in gold and other metals wrought miracles that grace museums today, the pagan Irish seemed too wild and daring to form stable kingdoms. Yet thatched huts in compounds, animism and reincarnation, the importance of music for war or celebration, the bossiness of women – all these also suggest West Africa. Although pagan beliefs have been forgotten or Christianized, there is one important similarity between Ireland and Nigeria, one unremarked on by Malet but noticeable to students of African politics. Both Ireland and Nigeria (I realized) are artificial nations made by England, the colonizers riding roughshod over earlier boundaries.

Nigeria did not exist *as one country* until its boundaries were fixed by the English, and conquest or peaceful annexation of various disparate regions had been completed. Ireland was known, before the English came, as a land of five provinces, Ulster, Munster, Leinster, Connaught and the magic heart of Ireland, Royal Meath and the Hill of Tara. The people knew they lived in Ireland, as Africans lived in Africa, but they lived in their own kingdoms on the vast continent of Ireland. Even the provinces were divided and subdivided between different kings and chiefs, and many were the wars and the shifting alliances between these rulers. All the modern counties of Ireland – Cork, Down, Tipperary and the rest – have been drawn on the map of Ireland and imposed by the invading English, conquest by conquest. In just the same way, Gambia, Nigeria, Kenya and Uganda have been drawn on the map of Africa by the English, to the surprise of the various kings and chiefs who lived in different countries with different names in the same places, before the English came.

However, the Irish counties have 'taken', and acquired their own loyalties, the older loyalties half buried, half forgotten but possibly biding their time, along with the ancient gods. Far from being savage enemies of Ireland (and Nigeria) in pre-Independence days, many English rulers were proud of their creations, and sought to help them, even to help them to Independence. The cause of Irish Independence had many English friends in high places, including William Ewart Gladstone, the nineteenth-century prime minister. The non-political majority of Irishmen and Englishmen feel friendly to one another, for the Irish are both foreigners *and* a 'sort of British'.

My stepfather had a friend who mounted a soapbox each Sunday at Speakers' Corner and roared defiance at England, demanding Nigerian Independence. One day, to this man's surprise, a shy, well-spoken civil servant tiptoed down his basement steps in superbly polished shoes and sat down in his shabby kitchen, politely drinking tea from chipped cups and making stilted conversation. Soon the visitor came to the point. He was from the Colonial Office, he had heard good reports of the soapbox orator's speeches and of his following. In short, he would give him Nigeria, as Britain intended to leave anyway. Would he think about it and come to such and such an address next day?

Stunned, the poor Nigerian orator saw his guest up the area steps and then went to bed. There he remained safely ill until he had missed his appointment. Nigeria went to some other claimant.

Nothing quite so absurd happened in Ireland, but the situation seems an Irish one. Would the present Prime Minister of Ireland be delighted if Britain were to hand him Ulster's six counties, Orange Lodges, Dr Ian Paisley and all? This will never happen as long as England and Ireland continue to have goodwill towards one another.

Irish Independence and American Independence, I reflected, gave rise to a new mythology because the rebels *won*. If, in America, the rebels of 1776 had *lost* the War of Independence, American children might now be marvelling that such a traitor as George Washington should ever have had the nerve to exist.

Enough of theory! I must go to the Republic of Ireland, I vowed, and see for myself if rebel Ireland, Ascendancy Ireland and pagan Ireland still existed. So, in 1973, off I went.

Everything was green, even the pillar boxes entwined with Victoria's name. Transformed by paint, she became a Republican monarch, a fitting symbol for this land of contradictions. Entranced, I took a bus from Dublin to Kildare, not far away. It was the month of May, the sun shone, and Ireland was before me.

Soon I discovered the Curragh, an open plain long used for horse racing, with an Irish Army camp on the site of the British garrison. As in the Wild West, settlers of English origin stayed near forts and garrison, daily on the look-out for raids. (In the nineteenth century, the police lived in barracks and seemed in many ways like an auxiliary army.) I arrived on a race day, and stood just outside the official track, with its towering grandstand. Crowds milled around and unofficial bookies took bets from old and young. Children as young as eight years old were placing bets in great delight, chirping out 'four to one' and other expressions that remain a mystery to my unworldly self.

Looking up, I felt a sudden thrill to see the horses suddenly appearing over the rim of the world, circling the great plain beneath craggy blue mountains. Nearer they came, and I could distinguish a jockey on each steed, body bent urgently forward, thong at the ready. Nearer still, and the black horses became chestnut, their flanks shining as they swept by.

The shabby bookies, pockets full of children's silver, grew frantic and began making tic-tac signs with their hands and fingers held high towards unseen accomplices on the 'official' side of the fence. Winnings were paid out gravely.

My first and last day at the races over, I wandered back to town seeing no trace of the prostitute village of furze huts that once had served the Curragh Camp. Next morning was Market Day. Donkeys clattered into town with carts and milk churns, and men sang as they walked along: 'These are My Mountains' and 'The Rose of Arranmore'. One of the stallholders, selling cheap toys, sang out little rhymes as a comment on the passing throng.

'Baby's crying, think she's dying!' he carolled. 'Here, buy her a dummy, my sweet colleen. That's what they call Irish girls in England – colleens!'

'Is it?' asked the mother in surprise.

I entered a dark, cool café, next door to a little shop that sold inanely grinning leprechauns, shamrock tea towels and miniature ornamental bells. 'Now!' said the waitress, the everlasting Irish greeting.

'Could I have a cup of tea, please?' I asked.

'Yes, you could.'

Long pause.

'Well, can I have one, then?' I asked eventually.

'Oh, do you *want* one, is it?' she remarked in surprise, and hurried off to fetch it.

Schoolchildren in uniform, stripy ties askew, filled the little room, talking loudly. Later that afternoon I went to see the Japanese Garden just outside Kildare, a wonder of the world. The winding paths between bowers, under rocky grottos and over little curved wooden bridges beside narrow waterfalls, were said to be of an allegorical Oriental pattern, symbolizing Man's journey through life and perhaps (to allow a more Irish touch) the soul's journeying after death.

Two little girls sat down on the grass and one of them said, 'Let's play at Royal Ladies.' At once they changed their accents to delightful, innocent upper-class tones.

'Oh, *do* have another cup of tea! Are you *sure* you won't have some more bread and butter? Please have some – they are *quite* delicious.'

When I left, twenty minutes later, the refined tea party, with invisible cups and saucers, was still going on. Eyes shining and cheeks flushed, both Royal Ladies were enjoying themselves immensely. Nearby, I admired the National Stud, where fiercely temperamental racehorses rolled the whites of their eyes at me from chestnut-painted stalls. Several other stud farms surrounded the racing town of Kildare. Lord Wavertree, in Edwardian times, had founded both the National Stud and the Japanese Garden, yet the happy make-believe of the little girls formed the best memorial to a vanished aristocracy.

Some aristocrats remained, and on the way to County Clare I met a dreamy-eyed contented boy of sixteen whose only job was to walk round and round a demesne (estate) wall with a kitchen knife, prising weeds and ferns from the cracks between the stones. He spoke well of his landlord, and told me that 'the Major' owned a famous South African diamond. In another town, the former Big House, on a hill above the village, was an extraordinary ivy-covered ruin, not a stone or a chimney pot uncovered by the dark green blanket. French windows gaped strangely, black caves in the foliage.

'Who lived there?' I asked two teenage girls.

'No one! It's always been like that,' they replied, bursting into laughter.

Walking near Lough Derg in County Clare, I met a dark-haired woman who told me of the terrible days of 'the landlords'. At that time, when in England, I had lived near the estate of the Duke of Norfolk, a man then regarded by his tenants almost as a god. Coming from a land where 'everyone loves a lord', the haunting-eyed woman's words seemed unfamiliar and strange. She in turn seemed surprised to hear of a people who could admire a great landlord.

Later I learned how English colonizers, from Elizabethan days to Georgian times, had enclosed vast tracts of land and then demanded rent from the people who had always lived there in huts and cabins. It was an earlier version of the same process whereby Englishmen in Southern Rhodesia had coolly built ranches and ranch houses on local chieftains' land and declared the Mashona in their thatched huts to be 'squatters'. In any case, the Irish, declaring that the Earth had been given to them by God, deeply resented paying rent.

The Irish cry of 'No rent!' has echoed in English ears over the centuries. Although both the Irish cabin-dwellers and the Ascendancy became as Irish, or as English-speaking, as one another with time, they were still 'foreigners' by religion – Catholics in cabins and Protestants in castles. Usually the cry of 'No rent!' was heard only faintly by the landlord in remote England, and fell more plainly on the ears of an unjust steward.

Like a 'call and response' pattern in a Negro church, the cry of 'No rent!' was answered by the call of 'Rent or eviction!' and so Irish history wore on. Even when 'tenants' were dying of hunger with blighted potatoes or grass on their lips, in the 1840s, their gasps of 'No rent!' were often answered in the traditional fashion. Irish history is one of resistance to the Rent Man, whether the rent was there to pay or (more usually) not.

Memories of Ireland ... I was walking along a country road in County Clare, in the west; it was one of the few Irish roads which did not hide behind high banks, but lay open to the fields, bounded by low stone walls. A gaunt man was raking the ground, and I asked him for the time. Without a word, he threw the rake violently down, leaped over the wall on long legs, raced across the road and ran into a cottage on the other side.

'Maureen, what does the clock on the mantelpiece say?' I heard him shout urgently.

She told him and they both appeared in the doorway to tell me. I was reminded of a 'Wet-Dry' couple in a barometer cottage. Maureen, who wore boots, apron and a headshawl, gave me a motherly smile.

I could have done with a barometer myself, for a shower had left me soaked to the skin. In a tiny wayside pub, I was served with a pot of tea on a tray. Big men sat around me drinking and listening to a radio broadcast from Dublin. In hushed tones, the solemn announcer was describing a visit the Irish President was making to St Patrick's Cathedral in Dublin. Organ music and choir singing filled the dingy bar, and the gnarled countrymen listened reverently.

'It'd be funny if someone threw a bomb in there!' one of the men said suddenly. Everyone roared with laughter, slapping their knees with huge hands, and the sounds of their merriment echoed around the room. A glass of rum finally dried me out, served by a sprightly barman of eight years old. He and his brother of nine seemed to be in charge of the bar. Both were more than capable, measuring out the amount of spirits per glass with a meticulous eye.

Had Irish irreverence to authority, the trickster-versus-landlord mentality, survived Home Rule to bedevil democratic Republican Ireland?

In 1982, while travelling through Northern Ireland once more, I made a foray across the border from the City of Armagh, County Armagh, to Monaghan Town in County Monaghan. A friendly young man from Armagh sat beside me on the bus, adding 'so it is, so it is' to the end of every sentence.

'Here's the Border, so it is, so it is,' he remarked as we bowled along a country road. I looked out and saw a man in shirt sleeves, head lolling on one side, sound asleep on a kitchen chair beside the hedge. He was guarding the Border. Without a pause, the bus rattled on into Monaghan in the green Republic once more. I stepped out alone into the hot square, where scowling young men sat, bandit-style, on the steps of the one hotel. The battered town hall still boasted an extravagant Lion and Unicorn over the doorway.

The Republic seemed to have changed since my previous visit, though admittedly I had not been to Monaghan before. Nobody sang as they walked, a habit that lingered in Ireland for a decade after its disappearance in Wales and three decades after its disappearance from England. Old ladies in long black shawls, rarely seen in the seventies, had now departed from Ireland altogether.

In the middle of the square stood a large wooden shed marked 'Café'. Inside it was clean and neat, the bill of fare, posted up on the wall, consisting only of 'Meat, Tea, Bread and Butter'.

'Now!' said a big woman, facing me.

'Could I have meat, tea and bread and butter?' I asked, forgetting my Kildare experience.

'Yes, indeed you could.'

Pause.

'Oh, is it after *wanting* it that you are!' the woman exclaimed.

Nothing in Ireland had changed after all. 'Meat' proved to be just that, a warm slice of beef with no vegetables. In a few days' time I would be on my way to Wales. Just supposing I could one day return to the Republic of Ireland, and spend three months there instead of the mere three weeks I had spent in the seventies. Just suppose . . .

Dreams became reality, and in 1988 I made plans for a lengthier visit to Ireland. The Republic had grown expensive since the Irish pound had separated from the English quid, but I worked out a route that would take in every County except Kildare, Clare and Monaghan, here described. Still a lover of Ireland, I now felt disenchanted with Kevin Barry, whose black tie I had earlier seen in a glass case in the museum of Kilkenny. Far from being the 'merry ploughboy' who joins the IRA in the Irish song, and far from being a curly-haired blue-eyed broth of a boy like young Brendan, the martyr of Mountjoy turned out to have been a *student*. Nowadays I am tolerant of students, but in my Kevin Barry and Lonnie Donegan-haunted youth I had hated students and their swanky 'more working-class than thou' ways with a deep and bitter hatred. Kevin, you have let me down!

Nevertheless, here I was, off to Ireland where I might learn more and better songs.

Now!

CHAPTER TWO

☘

Floating Round Cork

On a fine summer evening I set off from my house in London's Kensal Green in high spirits, swinging my clock, pyjamas and electric razor in a plastic bag held at a jaunty angle. I was off to Ireland! Down the Harrow Road I went, to the top of Ladbroke Grove, where a slope leads down to the towpath of the Grand Union Canal. I am very fond of towpaths, even this one, where the white concrete underbelly of the Westway overpass curves overhead like the underside of a whale. Joggers, cyclists and playing children passed me by as I headed determinedly for Paddington.

For a moment, I stopped in surprise as I noticed an ornamental holiday barge with the name of *Scinflint Kerridge*. How had they known I was coming? Near a timber yard and a Pentecostal shop-front church I left the towpath, crossed a roundabout or two and entered an unprepossessing semi-derelict lane behind Paddington Station. This was North Wharf Road. Ducking beneath a barrier, I found myself in a little-known corner of London, the domain of Slattery's Coaches. A hardened taxi driver, well steeped in 'the knowledge', later told me that he had never before realized that this coach station existed. Slattery's is an Irish secret.

From this unlovely rubble-strewn flattened-out bomb site, rows of orange, grey and white coaches leave every evening, at half past eight, for destinations all over Ireland. Fares, whether single or return, are astonishingly cheap. I showed my tickets to the cubby-hole office girl in the long shed used as a waiting room, and she pointed out my coach. Luckily I was early, and able to grab a window seat, as the coach soon filled. Most of my fellow passengers were young people going home to visit relatives. Girls in slacks chattered to one another (sometimes in London accents), but ignored the few older people. A quiet middle-aged woman from Kilkenny sat next to me. She said that she had been visiting her aunt in Leeds.

As my coach pulled out, bound for Cork, I felt as if I were already at sea. Slattery's yard faces a jetty, and seagulls wheeled, crying plaintively, before a background of wharves, gaily painted longboats and the Grand Union water glowing in the evening light. We would be travelling all night.

At half past one in the morning we entered Pembroke Dock, a ghostly, sleeping town in West Wales. We were told to disembark and to take our luggage to a bleak waiting room, whence we were eventually shunted on board a ferry. Our coach boarded the same ferry boat by a separate entrance. I found a comfortable seat in the warm bar, stretched out my legs and fell asleep. Most of my fellow passengers did the same.

I awoke to find a calm morning sea outside the porthole, a lighthouse on a rock and a dark line of coast on the horizon. Ireland already! That had been easy. Hurrying down the gang-plank at Rosslare Harbour, I recognized the orange Slattery's coach by the picture of a tiger on the front. When everyone was aboard, we were off once more, past the unpainted grey-brown houses of Rosslare to a land of small, low-lying fields where horses grazed.

Before long we were in Wexford, a town with a ha'penny harbour or semi-circle of sea biting into the streets, ringed by links of chain. A long bridge stretched across a corner of the bay, but we took a different road, to New Ross, through fields golden with August wheat, the Blackstairs Mountains in the distance. Rooks, now scarce in England, were common here, and swaggered on the verges in their ragged black knee-breeches.

Heading south, we soon reached the lovely waterside town of Waterford, on the River Suir. Ocean-going vessels lay at anchor beside the river promenade. Here we stopped for half an hour, and I hurriedly admired narrow shopping streets with lanes running down to the water, and a Church of Ireland (Anglican) cathedral among eighteenth-century houses. Modern factories surrounded the town. Among them was the famous glassware factory, seen as we pulled out of Waterford, on the grassy outskirts of town.

At Dungarvan we reached the sea once more, and before long we arrived in Youghal, a beautiful holiday town full of happy people. Many of the towns had rows of 'cabin suburbs', which also exist here and there in Wales. In the latter country, as in Ireland, nearly everyone has left his isolated stone cabin to crumble into ruins on the hillside. *Country* cabins are no longer in use as homes, but some cabin *terraces* remain in the towns. Although these are as small and as picturesque as the old country cabins, with three tiny rooms apiece, they are acceptable because they adjoin a motor road, among shops and neighbours. On my 1973 visit to Ireland, some town cabins had been thatched, but now their roofs were of slate or (more usually) corrugated iron.

From Youghal, we passed through Midleton, and our tiger-coach came to a final stop beside the wide River Lee in the famous City of Cork, capital of County Cork. As I stepped out on Irish soil, I could hear the bells of Shandon ring out the hour of noon.

I found myself facing a wide bridge over the river. To my left, I could see docks, cranes and boats. To my right I could see fine buildings stretching along the shore and high up to a hilltop on which was perched an enormous church. Ahead of me, traffic streamed into the town centre, with rows of smart shops as in London's West End. Nowhere looked very promising of accommodation, so I turned round and walked up the hill behind me, swiftly espying the smart, slate-roofed Ashley Hotel. This was posh by Kerridgean standards, but I was too tired to search for Bed and Breakfast. Sinking into my comfortable bed, I fell fast asleep.

It was evening when I awoke, the whole day wasted! From my window, I looked out on to a delightful curved street of tall shops, one painted bright crimson in colour. Faint country and western music wafted from a bar, and a very smart public house attracted streams of well-dressed customers. Some stood outside in groups on the pavement, while light streamed from the open doorway. I caught a glimpse of a large chandelier inside. Perhaps a dance was being held there.

Above the tiered rooftops that ascended a steep hill, the tower of St Anne's, Shandon, rang the quarters. The bells boomed from a curiously shaped steeple crowned by a black iron weathervane in the shape of a long fish. I set my clock right by Shandon's Big Ben.

This famous Cork landmark has been celebrated in verse by Father Prout:

The bells of Shandon
That sound so grand on
The pleasant waters
Of the River Lee.

On my previous visit to Cork, in '73, I had climbed up to see the huge bells, and banged my head on a beam.

Seating myself in the Ashley's elegant dining hall, I ordered roast beef, now a favourite dish in Ireland, and gazed out of the window on the street outside. That smart pub seemed to be *very* popular.

Suddenly I noticed a thin lady in a blue hat with a long blue veil, and I realized that I had been looking at a funeral parlour! I had forgotten the importance of funerals as a social occasion among the Irish. Sure enough, before long I saw strong men carry a flower-bedecked coffin out through the thronged pavement to a waiting hearse. Cloth-capped men, not smart enough to enter the parlour, stood aside respectfully. Apparently the reception was held *before* the funeral.

It was dusk by the time I stepped out into the streets of Cork. At the corner of the road, a drunk man sat on a doorstep, brandishing a bottle and roaring a tuneless song. Unshaven drunks, lurching and breathing nonsensical speeches on Old Ireland over startled passers-by, may be seen as 'typical Irishmen' in England, but in Ireland itself they are very rare. The poor man on the doorstep had probably spent some time in Leeds or London.

Shabby-genteel Georgian houses with cracked and blistered façades and steep basement areas stretched uphill, many of them solicitors' offices. Green pillar boxes bearing Royal insignia stood on occasional corners. However, the dismal grey shabbiness of Cork (and indeed all the Southern Irish cities that I had seen on my previous visit) had all but vanished. True, ruinous houses and unpainted terraces could be seen here and there, but Cork had been freshened up with new paint and plaster. So, I was to find, had most other Irish cities.

In *Country Writings* Geoffrey Grigson had written: 'Towns have been imported by the English and foisted upon a tribal, rural Irish, who did not know and still have not learned how to conduct them or live in them.' Reviewing this book in the *Field*, I had remarked that, 'of the country Irish, Grigson is properly respectful.' For some reason, this had appeared as 'properly regretful'. No Irishman complained! Perhaps, as Grigson stated, the Irish have never founded a commercial city, an honour given to savage Viking invaders. However, during the English Dark Ages they built many *holy* cities. If holy monastery towns such as Glendalough and Clonmacnoise had not been destroyed by Vikings, English invaders and Irish enemies of Christendom, they might now be the Oxfords and Cambridges of Irish civilization. But it was not to be.

Although I had dined well at the Ashley, I popped into one or two of Cork's many Chinese restaurants in fruitless search of my old friend Carol E-Wing Kao. Nobody had heard of her, yet in 1973 this flamboyant woman had presided in queenly fashion over Cork's only Chinese restaurant. Her waiters, scurrying anxiously to obey orders, had been young pinch-faced Irish lads.

When I had finished my sweet and sour pork, back in '73, I had left not only a tip, but a newspaper addressed to Chinese Christians. I had picked it up while admiring the Bells of Shandon.

'Is me! Is me! I am Chinese Christian!' Miss Kao had exclaimed in delight. With eyes shining, she told me that missionaries had brought her up, and had later smuggled her out of Communist Shanghai in a small boat, where she had hidden under the seat. After many dangers and vicissitudes, she had arrived in Ireland. 'Bring this man beer!' she shouted, clapping her hands at a brush-haired boy.

The poor lad was so nervous that he stumbled and spilled the glass over my head. Aghast, he mumbled apologies.

'This man doesn't mind! He's a Christian!' Miss Kao assured the youth imperiously, and I gave a sickly grin. That unexpected shower was one of my most vivid memories of Cork in 1973.

Next morning I set out for a quick look at Cork. It was a fine day, sunlight sparkled on the ripples of the Lee, and soon I stood once more on the splendid stone bridge. On the other side, some wharfside buildings were being pulled down, others remodernized, in imitation of the 'development' of dockland in London and Liverpool. England's old docklands are now redundant, and may as well become pleasure gardens and expensive flats, but Cork is still a centre for merchant shipping. Never mind, England must be imitated, come what may, for such is the creed of modern Ireland. Perhaps Cork's Merchant Quay rejuvenation scheme will be a success worthy of that lovely city.

Just now, boarded up with red-painted planks, the pavements

replaced by a narrow wooden walkway, the half-completed work made an unlovely entrance to the shopping streets of Cork. When the scaffolding had been left behind, I found myself upon the wide pavements of fashionable St Patrick's Street. Narrow Continental-looking streets of shops and bistros snaked their way between tall grandiose buildings. At the entrance to one of these little streets, the pavement widened, and two pavement artists kneeled hard at work.

Both young men, they were using powder paint to create an impressive Biblical scene – David slaying Goliath. White clouds drifted across a pale blue sky shading into pink on a pastel horizon behind the two Old Testament heroes. Passers-by stopped and dropped money into an upturned hat.

'That's very good!' I said to one of the artists, a slim tufty man with a mouth-corner moustache. 'Back in London, I used to be a pavement artist myself.'

'Is that right?' said the young man, standing up. 'We always work at this corner, doing Christian pictures. This one should last till there's a rainy day. Sometimes we do nursery rhyme pictures for a change. The paint washes off, and we start again. We photo our work before it gets spoilt – look, here's our collection.' So saying, he displayed a shiny booklet of photographs in cellophane pages. Modest Virgins, eyes downcast, were followed by fervent, fiery-eyed angels as the young man flipped the pages. 'We always pray before we begin,' the artist continued. 'Sometimes I get so excited when I've hit on a picture to do, that I begin straight away, without praying. Then I remember and pray halfway, like.'

Not all the Cork people were as God-fearing as the two artists, for a notice outside a side-street McDonald's read 'No Soliciting'. I did not see the sort of person warned off by that sign, but smartly dressed indifferently good young people filled the pavements of Cork and of every Irish city I was to come across. Ireland seemed plagued by the young, whose self-centredness and self-possession overwhelmed and threatened the old easy-going ways of kindly, out-going and talkative Ireland.

A new and magnificent Waterstone's Bookshop beckoned to me from across the road, and I plunged gladly into its shady depths. Table after table of books about Ireland suggested that the Irish like to read about themselves. Eventually I reached the back entrance of the lengthy shop, which faced on to another shopping street. Looking out of the door, I was amazed to see St Anne's

Church, Shandon, once more, complete with bells and impaled fish on high. Yet I had left it near my hotel, on the other side of the river! This one must be a replica, I decided.

Retracing my steps to St Patrick's Street, I followed the smart shops up to Washington Street. There, beside a patriotic monument, I found a little bridge that crossed a tributary of the River Lee. I walked along the quayside, for the rivulet had been canalized, and found that a new brewery of shining aluminium had been erected on the far bank since my last visit.

Across the street towered the tall, grey broken walls of the seventeenth-century Elizabeth Fort, its ragged ramparts hung with ivy. A hill rose steeply from the far side of the wall. Once a visible sign of English power, the fort had made a grim and fitting home for Oliver Cromwell, who had wintered there with his men in 1649. He raised the walls by an additional fifteen feet. Cromwell's name is a curse and a spitting in Ireland, as he raged around the unhappy island putting Roman Catholics to death wherever he found them, which was everywhere. During the later war of 1690, glorified in Ulster's Orange folklore, William of Orange's men (Protestant) broke down the walls that Cromwell had made, in an offensive against James II's men (Catholic). Nevertheless, a barracks remained in the fort until Home Rule this century. During the Civil War that followed Home Rule, the fort had been burnt by the Anti-Treaty Forces, the men who would not accept the Treaty with England that guaranteed the Union of Protestant-dominated Ulster with Britain. Anti-Treaty forces took Cork ('the Rebel City') and many citizens were evacuated before peace was finally restored.

Ever since the invasion and settlement in Ireland of English Protestants in Tudor times, there has been conflict between Protestants and Catholics. Instead of using Ireland as an example of the evils of holding a religious faith, it should be understood that the English and Scottish colonizers were Protestants and the Irish who found themselves colonized-upon were Catholics. It is as if England were invaded by Iran, and the conflict were described as a superstitious quarrel between Christianity and Islam.

Leaving Elizabeth Fort to its sombre memories, I trotted on and soon stopped in admiration at the sight of a golden angel gleaming in the sun. This vision hovered behind iron railings, fixed to the side of St Finbarr's Cathedral of the spiky towers. Since my last visit, the cathedral had been scrubbed free of grime.

A Church of Ireland (Anglican) cathedral, St Finbarr's had been built in 1870, a long way from the town centre. It was named after a seventh-century missionary who had helped to bring Christianity to Cork in the Dark Ages.

Like Dublin, Cork City had been founded as a Viking settlement. Again like Dublin, most of its glorious architecture had been raised by the eighteenth-century Anglican aristocratic Ascendancy, of largely English descent. Many Irishmen simply describe the Ascendancy of pre-Home Rule days as 'the English'. This is misleading, for not only had most of that class been born in Ireland and had imbibed Irish qualities, but they had been joined by Irish social climbers and by lordly Irish chiefs who wished to safeguard some of their power. Many such well-to-do people renounced Catholicism and threw in their lot with 'the English'.

Do I contradict my earlier statement that Protestants are of non-Irish stock? I must have acquired the Irish ability to think two opposite thoughts at once! Nevertheless, the Irish Protestant ideal *began* as an attempt by outsiders to transform and take over Ireland. By the Age of Enlightenment, many Protestants had come to the conclusion that since so much blood had been spilt in war and mixed in marriage, the best thing was to live side by side with Catholics and try to agree to differ. Over the years, the Protestants, whether Trinity-educated Anglicans or canny dock-working Presbyterians, have been continually *associated* with mainland Britain, the Catholics with 'native Ireland'. Nothing is proverbially quite as simple as it seems.

On my last visit to St Finbarr's, I had met a chipper little dark-haired Dean with a mischievous sense of humour. Unable to find him (he is probably now a bishop), I retraced my steps to the Fort, past shabby little terraces in need of paint and repair.

Crossing the great bridge once more, I wandered along MacCurtain Street. A long street of shabby, sleepy grey terraces, little shops and green pillar boxes, MacCurtain was bounded on one side by the docks and waterfront and on the other by stone steps leading up to further terraces perched one above another on the steep hillside. In 1973 I had been shocked by the squalor, but fifteen years later I had either grown hardened or else MacCurtain Street and its tributaries had improved. Professional people, in Ireland, prefer suburbia to nineteenth-century town centres, and unloved houses are abandoned and fall down where they stand. Luckily for Cork, the docks have remained in use, and so have most of the houses in MacCurtain Street. Old people stood gossiping by open doorways.

Modern Irish cities remind me in places of London in the 1950s (a fairly decent, innocent decade), with its drabness, bomb sites and propped-up dwellings in need of paint or repair. There were no air raids on Republican Ireland, of course, yet many Irish ruins owe their fate to the 1940s, when rates were unbearably high. Today rates are abolished in Ireland, leading to more municipal decay as the pendulum swings from one extreme to another.

That night in the Ashley dining room, opposite the crimson shop and the funeral parlour, I was given soda bread along with my evening soup.

'Now!' the waitress announced herself.

Next morning I set out to solve the mystery of the two Shandon churches. I walked through Waterstone's, resisting the temptation to browse, and out of the back door once more. Soon I found myself facing the real St Anne's, Shandon, with the river between us. St Patrick's Street was more bow-shaped than I had supposed, and the river had been hidden from view, hence my mistake. Crossing by another bridge, I set out to re-explore the delightful hillside neighbourhood of Shandon.

An enormous white neo-classical building, labelled '1832', faced the quayside on the Shandon shore. At first I thought it must be a town hall or a customs house, but no, it proved to be St Mary's Roman Catholic Church. It had been erected shortly after the complete emancipation of the Catholic faith, obviously with great jubilation. The church was associated with a nearby Dominican friary, and funds had doubtless been raised from Catholics abroad.

By the side of St Mary's, steps ran straight uphill, past rows of brightly painted front doors of tiny stone cabin-sized houses. I found myself in a maze of miniature streets and toytown houses, like nothing to be seen in mainland Britain. Obviously the web of lanes and alleyways had been cobbled once, the stones now coated with uneven layers of cement and tarmac. Contentedly, the homes of Shandon baked in the sun. Cork is a city of hills ringed from top to bottom with streets of terraces.

St Anne's, Shandon, Church of Ireland (Anglican), had been museumized, and it cost one pound to go in. I saved my money by peeping between dark velvet curtains at the rows of neat pews in the shady interior. Services were still held there for a shrinking congregation. The church had been built in 1722, in the heyday of the Ascendancy, and now looked in need of repair. A window in the tower had been broken, but the Fish of Shandon on top seemed as fresh as ever.

Moving on, entranced, I admired houses with one door and one window each. There were no gardens here, but the little doors, half-doors, and window frames were painted mauve, yellow or purple, flowers in themselves. Tiny bars and dark corner shops abounded. Here and there, pointy dormer windows poked from roofs which were almost at eye-level. Owning such a house must be far more satisfying than having a small flat with the same amount of room.

In a wide open courtyard amidst the alleys, I stumbled on the huge domed Butter Market (1849), and a similar unnamed neo-classical building beside it. Now I remembered that I had been there before. My waking memories of these strange buildings and alleyways were real after all, instead of being places visited and revisited only in dreams, as I had supposed. Even the pretence of calling the Butter Market an 'art centre' could not break the magic spell. Cabin terraces, steps and alleys led me around the Roman Catholic cathedral and Murphy's Brewery to Leitrim Street and then Coburg Street and the Ashley Hotel once more. Then I retraced my steps to the Dominican church where my walk had begun, and fell into conversation with a stout old lady who was nailing thick wire netting over her two windows.

'I've had eight break-ins recently, and I can't stand living in fear,' she told me. 'It's young men who do it, in need of drink and drugs.'

Trouble in Paradise. Later, in a park off Grand Parade, in the town centre, I saw some of the peculiar punks of Cork. Clad all in black, and strung with bondage chains, these young men sat on the grass or slouched on walls, talking in loud, excited, curse-filled voices. All of them had identical up-ended carpetbrush hairstyles standing starkly on top of shaved domes. It was impossible to tell if they were out-of-work ruffians or posing Polytechnic students.

By chance, while roaming around, I came across the Cork art gallery, a magnificent building that was almost empty of pictures, except for some 'modern' daubs and splashes. However, the gallery café was crowded with well-to-do housewives all talking at the tops of their voices in refined Cork accents. Here I found the best picture in the gallery, a German study of cheerful wild boars in the snow. Judging by all the names on office doors, a healthy art bureaucracy must flourish in Cork.

In one of the sidestreets nearby, I was startled to see a smirking IRA man, or so I thought, at first. A big good-humoured man, he stood at ease in the centre of the pavement, wearing a black beret, dark glasses, and a camouflage suit, a rifle under one arm.

'They must be moving money at the bank, that's why they need a soldier,' a man told me, observing my surprise.

Later I learned that Provisional IRA raids on banks had become so frequent that the Irish Army was sent for whenever bullion was moved. Obviously the Irish Army had combined two traditions, that of the Royalist regiment and the freedom-fighting rebelry. Just as in England; for our modern army derives not only from regiments raised by noblemen but also from the Cromwellian forces who later declared their loyalty to Charles II at the Restoration.

That evening I returned to the hillside alleyways of Shandon, to find them alive with children playing intensely with balls, carties and BMX bikes. It was an ideal neighbourhood for hide and seek, and the air was filled with merry or indignant shouts. I walked up the steepest hill I could find, thinking it might be the one I had seen earlier, with a great church on top. I was mistaken, and seemed to remember making the same mistake in 1973.

Nevertheless it was pleasant to walk back downhill in the growing dusk, as lights went on in the terraces and children were called home for tea. A large family party, mother, father and five children, walked down the hill behind me, on a cosy excursion to a pub along the way. Pubs in Ireland, usually known as 'bars', are places for all the family and serve tea or coffee without a qualm. Deeply soothed, I reached my hotel in time for supper.

On my last day in the City of Cork, again a fine one, I set out for St Finbarr's Cathedral and Elizabeth Fort once more, determined to walk across the city to the place where the fields began. In St Finbarr's, I admired a stained glass picture of Adam and Eve, well clad from head to foot in leaf suits. They looked aghast at the appearance of the angel with his stern message: 'No Dress Only.'

In Barrack Street, which ran steeply uphill (as usual), I found the entrance to the ruined fort. Tall, thick stone walls opened on to yards of levelled rubble, and steps led up to a rampart wall with a fine view of the city. Directly below this wall stood the last remaining military buildings, now used by the Garda or Irish police. Genial policemen in caps greeted one another on what once may have been the parade ground.

Until their mass destruction at the onset of Home Rule, barracks were a feature of almost every Irish town of any size. Disturbances would be quelled, fairly or unfairly, by soldiers loyal to the British Crown, from Tudor times until Home Rule. Many of the soldiers were Irishmen, of course, yet the line between a country kept in peaceful order and a country kept under foreign occupation must often have seemed a thin one.

The traditional Irish method of keeping the peace was very different. Young people from chiefly families would be commandeered by the local high chief or king, and held in semi-captivity in the thatch-roofed court. Although they might pick up skills or refinements from bards or master-craftsmen, they were hostages, held to bind their home settlement over to good behaviour. Should their tribesmen disobey the king, the hostages would die. All law is said to boil down to force in the end, but in Ireland a light boiling is often all that is needed.

Leaving Elizabeth Fort behind, I walked up Barrack Street, along Bandon Road and into Glasheen Road, up cabin-terraced hill and down suburban-hedged dale. Where pebble-dashed cabins gave way to leafy suburbs with rolling green hills of open countryside in the distance, I paused at a wayside pub. It was full of big jovial workmen shouting to one another through a haze of smoke. Television has Anglicized Irish speech, yet these men exceeded English workmen by the sheer amount of 'fecks' or 'feckins' they could cram into each sentence. Never let it be said that the Irish are 'feckless' . . .

Here, at the head of Glasheen Road, at a recreation ground and council estate called Sandymount, the fields began, and I had reached the very edge of Cork. Boys played at hurling, the ancient Irish form of hockey, banned in olden times as un-English. Now it is more popular than ever.

While looking around the housing estate, I suddenly noticed an enormous grey stone reposing in the centre of a suburban crescent. It looked like a thunderbolt, as big as a house, and with an eerie quality, as if Bronze Age men had sacrificed slaves to appease its power. Had glaciers left it there, or had the devil hurled a bolt to smash a nearby church and missed his mark?

As I neared the great boulder, I noticed that one end of it had been hollowed out and a flower garden planted around it. Within the hollow stood a meek figure of the Virgin Mary in blue and white, a sweet sad smile on her face. A notice stated that a bishop had blessed the figure and had formally opened 'the Grotto'.

Wonderingly, I walked around the rock. On the far side, away from the Virgin, the boulder looked rough and frightening once more, with bushes for hair. A group of children, dominated by a red-haired girl of eight or nine, played beneath the shadow of the rock.

'How did that big rock get here?' I asked them.

'They call it "the Grotto", but it used to be called the Devil's Rock,' the bold ginger-haired leader replied at once.

'I love the devil,' said a smaller girl sentimentally.

'No, don't love him!' a tiny boy reprimanded her. 'He takes you down underground and tortures you with fire. Once the devil came out from under that rock, all with blue fire . . .'

'I love the devil and I love witches!' the girl insisted. 'I lick the ground. I do that 'cause I love the ground, I always lick it. I lick fences, too.'

'You should say, "I love God Almighty",' protested the boy, visibly distressed – and no wonder.

'No, I lick the ground, and I lick dirt! *She* loves the devil,' Dirt-Licker added, pointing at the tiniest child of all.

'No, I do *not*!'

'My Dad's in the Garda!' the red-headed girl suddenly announced, with the air of capping an argument.

Everyone fell silent, and I hurried away before her father could arrest us all.

Obviously, the families who had moved into the new houses had been alarmed to find their front doors facing the Devil's Rock. To exorcize the devil, a holy grotto had been made and blessed by a bishop. Yet to the children (and so it seemed to myself) Our Lady owned half the rock and the devil had the rest, an awkward and unpleasant neighbour.

Musing on such mysteries, I caught a bus back to the Ashley Hotel.

Cork Bus Station stands beside the docks on the side of Merchant's Quay. After admiring the battered trading vessels at anchor, I caught the bus for Ross Carbery, a little seaside town in West Cork. This is the corner of County Cork made famous by the 'Irish RM' hunting stories that my mother had admired. Like most Irish buses outside Dublin, the West Cork bus was a single decker. As if in parody of America's Greyhound buses, it had a picture of a lolloping Irish setter on the side.

Past Cork's gold-domed town hall the bus went, past fine churches and elegant houses and into a gorsy, scrubby countryside. 'No Temporary Dwellings', a notice declared, aimed at Irish tinkers (or 'gypsies') and their caravans. Nevertheless, two trailers stood within sight of the notice, and tinker men dragged milk churns of water up to their doors. On my previous visit to Ireland, the tinkers had lived in bright painted barreltop wagons with enormous wheels, their piebald horses tethered nearby. (Nomads often love piebald horses, as students of Red Indian lore will testify.)

In the narrow shopping street of Clonakilty, we got stuck in an enormous traffic jam. Shoppers with baskets milled around the stationary cars. Everyone in the bus began to talk.

'So I met him on the way to Mass, and he said "How are you, at all?"'

I told the stout, elderly lady in front of me where I was going. 'Have you heard of the Missin' Head?' she asked me.

'No, what missing head?'

'It's a place, the Mizen Head, beyond Skibbereen.'

And so I chatted with the lady from Mizen Head, who knew I was English without having to ask, until the driver called out 'Ross Carbery'.

CHAPTER THREE

Ross Carbery

I stepped down from the bus and glanced up and down the main village street and market square of Ross Carbery. It was a cold, drizzly day. Before Home Rule, I later learned, a police barracks had stood at the foot of the hill, long since burnt down. An angling shop, with a window full of rods and nets, sported a 'Bed and Breakfast' sign. I thought it would be fun to live over an angling shop, but it was not to be.

'We're full up, but head down the street, go round the corner on your left, and ask at the post office,' I was told.

It was a small dingy post office with a melancholy postmistress, who led me up narrow steps to my room. Aspidistras and other non-flowering plants sat quietly in pots on every shelf and window sill. Every inch of wall, up the steps and along the landing, was hung with pictures. Most of them were of religious themes, but some showed scenes of Ireland and two showed maps of England, painted on cloth and framed, with Union Jacks and pictures of 'our dear Queen' at her Coronation.

'My sister made those,' the postmistress said in an expressionless voice. 'She lived in England. Now this is your room and here is your key. Always put it in upside down, as the lock and keyhole were fixed on upside down.'

Pocketing the large iron key, I waited until the landlady had returned to her postmistressly duties, and then sauntered around looking at the pictures. Most of them had been painted or printed in the nineteenth century, some with green Irish lettering around the borders. St Patrick, like the nineteenth-century concept of a Druid, held a crozier, and stood beside a cross that resembled a standing stone, as he banished a bevy of small brown adders.

Another picture showed the saint as a youthful slave, herding pigs for a rich Druid. This was historically accurate. Another picture showed a Mass held in a cave during the Penal Times, with look-outs in eighteenth-century dress warning the priest and people of approaching redcoats.

The seventeenth-century Gunpowder Plot in England, the work of Papists in league with England's Continental enemies, caused English suspicion to fall on Roman Catholics in Ireland. For over a hundred years thereafter, all Catholic worship in Ireland had to take place in secret, for fear of barbarous punishment. Such were the Penal Times, still a living grievance and talking point in Ireland itself, but unknown to rabble-rousing 'professional Irish rebels' in England and America. For some reason, displaced rebels of all nations who live in England and rail against England tend to concentrate on small or wholly imaginary grievances. Those that are Marxists cannot make sense of religious issues. However, just because they talk nonsense about England's 'crimes' does not mean that England has been blameless.

Strangely enough, the Penal Times drove Irish Christians back to the pagan shrines of their forefathers. Bronze Age altars on lonely moors, large flat boulders with ancient scoop-marks, became Christian altars for the outdoor Mass. Figures of the Blessed Virgin were hidden and worshipped in caves, just as Earth Mother goddesses, excavated as 'Venus of Willendorf' statues, had been adored by cave men of the far-off Stone Age. Renewing these links that were never quite broken must have been immensely satisfying for the country Irish. The threat of discovery by the red-coated soldiers of England must have given the worshippers a loyal sense of togetherness, tinged with thrills of excitement. Instead of being wiped out in Ireland, the Roman Catholic faith grew stronger than ever, the chants and choirs of Mother Church swelled by ghostly voices from the days when Irish tribesmen worshipped aspects of Mother Nature.

Looking back at the narrow staircase that led down to the post office, I gave a start, for I suddenly noticed that the wall beyond the steps opened out to show a life-size tableau of a young girl kneeling and pointing towards an enigmatic Virgin within a dark cave. Perhaps the two plaster statues represented St Bernadette and Our Lady of Lourdes. Thick sheets of crumpled paper, painted dark grey, resembled the eerie rock formations of a holy grotto. All over Ireland I was to find outdoor artificial grottos of real rock beside the roads or in private gardens, always depicting Our Lady in a cave.

The Willendorf Venus, or cave goddess, is all body and no face, a fertility goddess. Venus of classical times, often worshipped in a cave temple, was the goddess of love. Our Lady, the Queen of Heaven, represents purity, the goddess in the cave moving daintily from earth towards Heaven. I do not mean to imply that Mary is a myth, for Jesus must have had a mother. But the *idea* of Mary draws some of its strength from the far-from-ignoble pagan past. Why do people pray to Our Lady of here or there, if there is no connection with animism and the Gods of Place? I gazed on the post office Virgin with awe.

More pictures, flowers and cottage scenes, hung in my tiny room. I lay on my bed and looked up at a bowed ceiling of brown creosoted planks, as if I were living under a boat. After a refreshing sleep, I set out to explore Ross Carbery. Before I went, I looked in at the post office to ask the landlady what time the door was locked at night. Lion and unicorn symbols were neutralized by green paint, and a faded box on the counter contained very little 'Money for Africa'. My question alarmed the postmistress.

'Why, do you drink?' she asked, looking shocked.

I assured her that I did not, and made my escape, heading for the main village pub. As I went, I heard her laughing with regular customers, so she was not as solemn as she appeared. In Nolan's Bar, I ordered black coffee, for I had not misled the postmistress. A stout barman was being helped by a small, alert blond-haired boy, who would dart forth from the counter and collect empty glasses. Most of the time the little boy sat on the bar amid customers' pints and looked angelic. There was a cheerful family atmosphere. German voices rose above the local banter, and one old couple talked spasmodically in Irish and English by turns.

A banner hanging outside proclaimed that Ross Carbery's carnival would begin next day (a Friday), and last through till Monday night. This was good timing on my part, or would have been, if I had known about the carnival. Already an outdoor stage was being erected for the singers and musicians.

From my somewhat sepulchral post office, the hill sloped down towards the bay. On the map, Ross Carbery was a seaside town, but I could see no signs of the sea. Another hill towered over the village, crowned by the vast Gothic edifice of the Sisters of Mercy's convent. Two gangs of ten-year-old boys were fighting in the lane leading up to the convent, hiding behind trees, running low beneath hedges and sometimes cutting across a corner of the Sisters' garden. Rooks cawed noisily in the trees above them. Half-play, half-earnest, the battle seemed to consist largely of ambushes.

A chubby-faced boy emerged from a hedge, soon followed by a friend. 'Did you see a lot of other boys just now?' he asked me.

I pointed out the way they had gone, and the two boys set out prudently in the opposite direction. The warriors were all sons of holidaymakers who had come to West Cork from various other parts of Ireland.

Returning to the path that led downhill from the post office, I saw caravans in a muddy field and men erecting stalls and roundabouts for the fair on the morrow. In one of the quick changes of weather for which Ireland is famous, the sun came out and the grey sky turned blue. Beyond the carnival field, I could see the sharp spire of the Anglican cathedral pointing skywards. At the bottom of the field, on the far side of a narrow road, stood a delightful garden of New Zealand fern-like palm trees.

No house was attached to this long strip of garden, which was separated from the road by a log stockade. Similar logs had been used to build an Uncle Tom's Cabin which stood below tall evergreens that shielded the magic garden from the sea breezes of a lengthy waterway. An old-fashioned kitchen range, a fireplace on its own, stood among the flowers, with various black pots and pans hanging from hooks. Even Nature had been improved upon, for a rhododendron plant had been grafted on to the stem of a palm. On the far side of the garden, a great causeway carried the motor road over a wide estuary inlet, a crooked finger of sea between sandbanks and gorsy dunes, with no view of the ocean. Anglers sat here and there on the sea wall. I was reminded very much of Portmadoc in North Wales where a stone wall and road hold back the sea yet have not prevented the creation of a leaked-in backwater, a marshy lake used by duck-shooters.

I crossed the Ross Carbery sea wall, frequently stopping to admire the birds that dabbled in pools among the damp stretches of sand on the seaward side. They were birds I had often seen at estuaries in Wales and Devon – herons standing still and then suddenly jerking into movement, pacing curlews, black and white oystercatchers, little whistling sandpipers with pointed wings and bouncing, aggressive jackdaws. Hooded crows, black in brown waistcoats, added a purely Irish touch. Ireland seemed a good place for the crow tribe.

Desolate, overgrown forestry plantations stretched along the peninsula on the far shore, then came marshes and dunes, and at long last, quite unexpectedly, I reached the sea. Happy families were sitting in isolated clumps on the yellow sand, and a small boy patted a large sandcastle into shape with his spade. Cliffs curved round the beach, and a steep path with a rickety bannister rail climbed steeply among the gorse. High on the cliffside path, amid furze and sea pinks, I met an old man with a Jack Russell terrier. When the man heard my accent, he at once launched into stories of his visits to England. Near Keswick, he had seen 'a fierce big lake', and in Bristol he had arrived on the day when a policeman had stopped a bank robber's bullet with his strong front teeth. 'There's no work in Ireland now,' the old man added.

Returning to the beach, I saw, from the cliff top, a cloth-capped man driving a long-shafted chariot, holding the reins of a high-spirited trotting horse and tearing along the sand at a tremendous pace. His carriage seemed to be all wheels and no middle save for a tiny step-like seat.

Back at Ross Carbery, I climbed the hill into town, this time passing the cathedral. Alone in the churchyard stood a single arch, hung with dog roses, a relic of the medieval cathedral which had been demolished. A children's party was taking place in the former schoolhouse next door, and I could hear the cheerful sounds of an accordion wheezing above the general uproar. An outraged boy who had been locked out pounded angrily on the schoolhouse door.

Nearby, I found a white-painted 'village' of sharp-cornered modern cottages, all named after trees, with silhouettes of rural figures painted on some of them. The new cottages were let out to holidaymakers. A few more steps took me to the market square from whence I had set out. After a bite to eat in a restaurant bar, I headed for bed, taking care to obey the sign pinned up by the postmistress: 'Be Careful of Your Fore Head'.

In the morning, the postmistress showed me to a table in the conservatory annexe of a large, dark dining room. I breakfasted with heavy sombre cutlery amid potted geraniums and window-sill statuettes. A large family from Dublin occupied the main table.

'It's the twentieth anniversary of the day the British Army went into Dundalk!' a young man remarked loudly.

No one quite knew what to say to this, and all avoided my eye.

It was a dull morning when I at last emerged from the post office side door. I decided to pay my respects to the nuns up at the convent on the hill. On my way, I noticed an old village pump with a shiny dripping tap attached, and I later passed hydrants with similar taps. Perhaps some of the gaunt terraced houses had no water supply connected.

Up on the hill, where the boys had been fighting, I walked around the mansion-like convent, and found myself on a terrace with views down to the fern grotto, fairground and causeway below. After admiring the garden and tennis courts, I turned and rang the bell of a brown wooden door, highly varnished, like a sticky bun.

A nun dressed in blue and white opened the door and looked on me wonderingly. I asked if I could look round the convent.

'Of course. We are the Sisters of Mercy, and I am Sister Redemption. Come inside. There is not a great deal to show you, for the girls are all on holiday now.'

'Oh, are you a school?'

'Yes, we take girl boarders up to the age of eighteen, and also a few day boys. No, this was never a stately home. It was built as a convent in 1894. It seems very quiet and empty now! Look at that fine picture up on the wall. That is our Founder, Catherine MacAul.'

I gazed with interest at the oil portrait of a nun with a calm, kind face, while Sister Redemption spoke.

'She first of all founded a convent in Bagot Street, Dublin, after the Great Famine. You know, she didn't want to be a nun. Originally she just wanted to help poor children and prostitutes, but the Call came and could not be denied. Now they say she may be beatified.'

I was led through corridors of varnished pine, and shown into highly decorated little parlours unchanged since the nineteenth century. A small organ in a corner resembled a writing desk, and pictures on the wall, painted by former nuns in Japanese style, showed swans, flamingos and graceful deer. Only the Chapel was marred by a lurid stained glass window of modern design. Lay helpers and a big hefty nun were preparing a meal in the spacious kitchen. Politely shaking my hand, Sister Redemption at last showed me out again through the terrace door.

Back in town, I decided to explore the cathedral, St Fachtna's.

This saint founded a monastery and school at Ross Carbery in AD 590, and the village itself grew from this foundation. St Patrick had not evangelized in County Cork. The great missionary had stood on a mound near Limerick and blessed all the land to the west. The blessing had great effect, and sailors putting into Cork harbours brought the news of Christianity. Fachtna, who came along much later, from Youghal, had been a pupil of St Finbarr at the city of Cork.

My mind awhirl with saints, it seemed only natural to approach a robust pink-cheeked young man in a dark clerical gown. He stood talking to a parishioner in the garden of a large cosy house, 'The Deanery', that faced the entrance to the cathedral. The Dean of Ross (for such he proved to be) was a big sunny-looking man who spoke in soft Oxbridge tones with a trace of New Zealand thrown in, and looked one squarely in the eye. His friend left, and the Dean gave all his attention to me. I explained that I was a writer at a loss in Ireland.

'Please to meet you! I'm afraid I can't ask you into the Deanery at the moment, as we've got rather a lot of visitors. People are always staying here! However, I'll be glad to show you around the cathedral. Was there anything else that you wanted to know? My name's Townley, by the way – Robert Townley. I've been Dean here since 1982.'

'Well, er, I wondered how the Anglican Church was managing in these days of Home Rule. It has rather the name of being the Ascendancy Church, as I understand.'

'We survive by lying low! Now, here in Ross, only four per cent of the people are Protestant, but all of that four per cent go to church. So our attendance compares favourably with the Church in England. This is the Diocese of Ross, and when the Anglican Bishop of Cork comes here, he becomes the Bishop of Ross! As for being 'the Ascendancy church', well, we pray each Sunday for the President of Ireland. No reasonable person could say that we were the same as the Catholic clergy in Northern Ireland, who won't co-operate with the state.'

'No, but people *aren't* reasonable.'

'True . . . there was some trouble here in the Civil War, in the early twenties.'

'Really? It seems strange to think that people once were killing each other in a peaceful spot like this.'

'Well, just over there was once a house where two elderly ladies by name of Whitley lived. They did a great deal of good in the town, but nevertheless their house was burnt down just because they were Ascendancy. However, they both escaped alive. Since the late eighteenth century, many of the English who ruled Ireland were reformers, trying to put matters right. By the turn of the last century, the peasants were getting land, often their old ancestral land. If you had been here a hundred years ago, you would have seen country people in little thatched huts with the smoke finding its way out through a hole in the roof. Things have been getting steadily better for the Irish people, especially since the last Land Act. Even the Great Famine, terrible as it was, did some good, as the survivors could expect more pay, as workers had become so few.'

'Like the Black Death in medieval England!' I chimed in.

'Oh, is that right? I'm a little shaky when I'm away from Irish history. Come on, I'll show you around the cathedral.'

A light airy place of whitewashed stone, the cathedral door opened on to a large anteroom. Two statues of local grandees stood near the entrance to the cathedral proper.

'That fine marble statue is of John Evans Freke, of Castlefreke, a local philanthropist. It was brought here from the great hall of the castle, when the Frekes left. Castlefreke is a ruin now. All our old gentry have gone, the Frekes and the Hungerfords. This way . . .'

As Robert Townley showed me around, he enlarged on local history, as described by many a tablet and inscription on the walls. Apparently the monastery that had first occupied the site had been sacked first by the Danes, and then by the Waterford Norse, Vikings who had settled down at their Irish base (now the city of Waterford), yet still went pillaging once in a while. County Cork, until the late Middle Ages, had been the home of warring tribes such as the Corcalee, and the monastery had been built on land donated by the tribesmen. The first cathedral had not been built until 1195.

'See that stone head up there on the wall?' the Dean asked, pointing. I looked up and saw a well-worn mask of St Fachtna, looking impassively down at me. 'People here think that if you kiss St Fachtna, he will cure you of toothache. You would have to go up on the gallery and lean over.'

Outside in the churchyard, the Dean showed me the Hungerford Tomb and discursed on the Penal Times when the Roman Catholic

Mass had been held secretly in private houses and under hedges around Ross Carbery.

'That would have been in the early eighteenth century. Anything else?'

'Yes – who made that lovely garden down by the water, with the palm trees and miniature log cabin?'

'Ah, that's the work of a local man, Jack Keohane. He lives in the white cottage opposite the garden, called "Angler's Rest". Why don't you go down there? He'd love to talk to you. Meanwhile, if you ever decide to come to Ross again, let me know in advance and I'll give you a bed in the Deanery.'

Shaking Robert Townley's hand, I hurried down to the Angler's Rest and knocked on the door. It was a long low single-storey white cottage that had probably housed several families in bygone days. A sprightly teenage girl answered the door, and I asked her about the beautiful garden.

'My Dad made that!' she answered with a smile.

'Really! Why, it serves as a stately park for all Ross Carbery. I thought at first that the council or some great landowner had planted it.'

'No, my Dad is the culprit! Come back in a couple of hours and you'll find him.'

Grey clouds parted and an Irish sun shone through, so I decided to go for a walk in the country. I headed up the village street, past Nolan's and the angling shop, and soon found myself walking beside the crumbling demesne wall of an old Ascendancy estate. Later I was told that the girl who became Mrs Bernard Shaw had once lived there.

Climbing over a gate, I crossed a field, keeping by a hedge of furze, and soon reached a high point where heather bloomed among the rocks. A rolling, hilly landscape of small fields and furze bushes met my gaze. From somewhere nearby I could hear the persistent cry of a corncrake, remembered from a Sussex of long ago. The bird is now extinct in England. When I climbed over the next gate, I found myself among Friesian bullocks, who stared at me hard and then began to lumber towards me. In England they only do this if I have a dog. I flew for the gate, followed by thundering hooves, and just climbed over in time. Mooing for blood, the desperate beasts pressed against the sagging rusty gate, and I made my getaway.

In the stone-walled country lane that led back into Ross Carbery,

I encountered another group of children. 'Remember me?' a boy asked.

It was the chubby-faced boy I had seen at the fight near the convent. He had short brown hair and short trousers in the English 1950s style.

'Would you like some rabbits?' I asked innocently, and whipped out my trusty sketch pad.

Sitting down on a stone, I drew google-eyed rabbits, a knack I had picked up when a boy from copying the *Mickey Mouse Comic*. The other children, freckle-faced girls and jug-eared boys, looked keenly over my shoulder.

'My name is Dermot Rafter,' the boy told me. He spelled 'Dermot' in the Irish way, which I cannot. 'I'm on holiday here. My home is in a place called Grange Bective, just outside Navan. You can't miss it if you ever go there. It's got cream walls, a black gate and big stones outside the door. That's in Mead – I mean County Meat. But not the sort of meat you eat.'

'Oh, County Meath. Here, show me on the map.' From the depths of my plastic bag I produced a tattered map of Ireland, torn from my atlas at home.

'There's where I live. Now I'll show you where my uncle has his farm. Oh! Where's Leash?'

'Leash', or County Laois, was nowhere to be seen. In its place was Queen's County, as my map was pre-Home Rule. It was not the first time my atlas had let me down. When planning a trip to America, I had been puzzled to find a Liverpool in Texas that wasn't on most other maps. Looking further, I noticed a large chunk of America marked 'Indian Territory', and realized that my atlas had been overtaken by events.

'I've got five uncles who are farmers,' Dermot continued. 'Their farms are all over the east of Ireland. One of my uncles was a bank manager, and his bank was robbed by Des O'Hare, the Border Fox. That's a famous robber. I love farms! I'm ten now, but when I'm grown up I'd really like to be a farmer. I'll be a dairy farmer with my own milking parlour!'

Dermot's eyes glowed as he described his vision. I too felt enthusiastic, for at that time I vaguely supposed a milking parlour to be a place of high-backed Victorian chairs with antimacassars, little tables for the tea things and framed miniatures on the walls. Quite how cows could fit in, I wasn't sure, unless they sat in the chairs while Dermot delicately milked them into cream jugs. Later

I discovered that a milking parlour was a horrendous hygienic and technological place, where unfortunate cows had electrode-like suction pads placed on their udders, which caused their milk to be forced out of them at a great rate and sent bubbling upwards into enormous containers that looked like giant test tubes. All most unpleasant. My farming friends in Wales, the Prices, always use a stool and bucket, as do my Pennine farmer friends, the Gospatricks. Ireland seemed ahead of Wales and England, unless, as I suspect, I am merely good at picking farmers.

I drew more rabbits and a wolf for Dermot, who looked at me curiously. 'Are you a Pioneer?' he suddenly asked.

'No, what is it?' I enquired, memories of *Soviet Weekly* tales of Russian boy scouts stirring in what passes for my mind. In England during the last war, the Pioneer Corps had offered a refuge for idiots and intellectuals, who stayed in Britain and dug latrines. In modern England, the Pioneers are the young Jehovah Witnesses who give Bible lessons in the homes of the faithful.

'It means someone who has promised not to drink. They give you a medal.' Later, I saw a notice in a shop window: 'Renounce Drink, Join the Pioneers', and a little later still, I learned that the Irish Pioneers had been formed by Father James Cullen of Dublin. Good for him! Teetotalism is a much-maligned cause.

'Oh, so that's what a Pioneer is.'

Promising Dermot and the other children that I'd see them later, I returned to the Angler's Rest (good name for a pub, that – P. G. Wodehouse used it in his Mr Mulliner stories) and at last met the gardener himself, Jack Keohane. He was a big curly-headed man in orange boots.

'It's very good of you to make a garden for the town like that,' I said.

'It is!' he agreed candidly. 'That's our old kitchen range out there, and the fern with the rhododendron on comes from my father's garden.'

Music and laughter from behind his house heralded the opening of the funfair. Pocketing a photograph of the fern (or palm) garden which Mr Keohane kindly gave to me, I hurried to the fair field. Children were simply *pouring* into the small funfair and swarming all over every rideable object in sight. After admiring their energy for some minutes, I climbed the hill back to the market square. Musicians were unloading equipment and placing it on the small outdoor stage, which was protected from the Irish weather by a fairground stall-type awning. I returned to the post office for a well-earned nap. When I emerged, it was early evening, and the concert was about to begin. Taped Irish songs were already booming from loudspeakers hung about the square, and I hurried eagerly towards the stage. A young country and western group, the Beach Combers, were ready to start playing.

Cars filled the market square, with families inside many of them, awaiting the concert in passive American drive-in style. Children and young people stood expectantly below the stage, and so did I. Most Irish country and western groups play country 'n' Irish, two American songs and then an Irish song. The instruments used may not be Irish, but the rhythms are traditional to Ireland, England, Scotland and the American South. It is misleading to call modern Irish traditional balladry 'Celtic', for the tunes would have been well-known to English fiddlers at country fairs all over eighteenth-century England. Two songs in the repertoire of every Irish singer, 'The Bunch of Thyme' and 'My Bonny Lad is Young But He's Growing' have been collected time and again from pub singers in Norfolk villages well into this century.

A lilting male tenor voice from the loudspeaker sang out the spine-tingling rebel ballad, 'The Croppy Boy'.

> It was early, early one morning in Spring,
> The birds they did whistle and sweetly did sing,
> Changing their notes all from tree to tree,
> And the song that they sang was: 'Old Ireland Free'.

I can scarcely hear this song without tears forming in my eyes, yet I am a good English patriot for all that, as the first three lines of this stirring ballad of the Penal Times were known to minstrels in the medieval English greenwood. They may have been used to introduce a lay of Robin Hood, surely the spiritual ancestor of the Irish Croppy Boy. (Cropped hair was once the sign of an Irish nationalist.)

Now the Beach Combers, with jangling guitars and rattling drums, were away with a cheerful rendition of 'Jambalaya', mangling the words a trifle, as well they might, for the song is an American parody of the pidgin-French spoken in the swamps of Louisiana. Young people jived in front of the stage, and then, as Irish tunes made their appearance, jigged and waltzed melodramatically. Heads poked from car windows everywhere. Three personable young men, the Beach Combers consisted of a drummer, a singer and a guitarist. In the background, a stout old accordion player sat in the shadows and waited his turn. Wherever there is a frolic in Ireland you'll find a fat old accordion player in one corner or another.

'Lay down your Galway shawl, my dear, I swear it is no joke,' sang the Beach Combers, 'While I tell to you the story of the Old Dungarvan Oak.'

According to the song, unless you take your hat off to the Old Dungarvan Oak, the oak will fall and Dungarvan Town will tumble into the sea, which it might well do if the oak's roots were only long enough. Mothers threw down their cigarettes and danced with their small children. I was struck by the Welsh accents of the local people. It was an accent that belonged to no particular part of Wales, yet the Welshness in the tones I heard was unmistakable. Most of the old races of Wales were in Ireland too, but Wales lacks Ireland's Viking influence. Few Vikings can have left their mark in West Cork, however, for the local farmers and their wives and families looked as Welsh as could be. The real Welsh lost their traditional music in the Methodist Revival.

At last it was the turn of the accordion player, who looked deceptively slow and sleepy until he began to play, the accordion jerking into life and spilling out jig after frantic jig as the children danced. All over the world, the accordion is replacing the fiddle among traditional musicians. The old man's tunes were age-old fiddle music, yet as new and rhythmic as rock and roll in their appeal to Ross Carbery's young people. While the Beach Combers rested, with glasses handed up to them, the accordion player sang ditties I knew by heart from the Irish pubs of London – 'The Irish Rover', 'Where the Three Counties Meet' and, of course, 'The Bunch of Thyme'. Finally he launched into a somewhat banal jingle, and everyone joined in.

> I'm off my trolley
> For Irish Molly,
> My Irish Molly, O.

With that, the Beach Combers returned and played a country and western song, 'A Ring of Fire'. This title inspired a lively group of little girls to join hands in a ring for some Kerry dancing. The good people of Kerry, the next county to West Cork, are known for their ring dances. Perhaps they are akin to fairies – certainly the rest of Ireland regards them as 'fairy kissed' or slightly mad.

Musical contests were taking place in the pubs, meanwhile, so I crossed the bunting-hung square, paused for a hot dog with onions, and then squeezed into the Rossa. This crowded pub was named after Ross Carbery's own rebel hero, O'Donovan Rossa. O'Donovan had been a shop assistant in nearby Skibbereen, until one day he joined the Fenian Brothers, gun-happy rebels against the Crown who carried a price on their heads. For belonging to an illegal organization, O'Donovan Rossa had been sentenced to life imprisonment in 1865 and pardoned soon afterwards. He went to live in America, and a long time later a pub in Ross Carbery was named after him. More rebelry took place in Ross Carbery in 1921, when latter-day Fenians (the IRA) carried an eighty-pound mine to the police barracks and blew a hole in it. Sergeant O'Shea and Constables Borlas and Reynolds were killed and nine other officers were injured. A bomb left behind by mistake blew up next day and killed two farmers.)

Meanwhile, in the 'Rossa', I struggled towards the front of the crowd that surrounded a microphone. A succession of young women in jeans were singing Exile songs, sentimental ballads of Irish emigrants in Australia or 'Amerikay' who dreamed of returning to their home towns yet were jerked back to cruel reality as the cock crew and they awoke. Songs of exile are growing ever more popular among Irish singers, particularly in Ireland itself, and new ones are being written every day. These songs *do* strike me as being Celtic in spirit, for the 'dream' of most such songs is really a journey of the soul, the dreamer sadly noting changes made in the old home town since he or she set sail for Philadelphia. A freckled girl in ringlets pitched her voice in a strange, archaic tone, the Irish ancestor of the high-pitched hillbilly voice, as she sang of a dream-visit to Bantry. Tears filled my eyes – could it have been the onions? I struggled out into the square, weaved my way in and out of the parked cars, and came to rest at Nolan's. A newly parked car hit an empty vehicle quite hard, but the parking driver smiled and said, 'Not to worry.'

I parked my body against the outer wall of Nolan's Bar and fell into conversation with a large man in rimless spectacles. He told me that he was in the textile business, and he gave me the sad news that Lister's Mill in Bradford had closed. Lister's, once the pride of Manningham! Where would my Pakistani friends work now?

'I live at a place called Grange Bective,' the big man added.

'Oh really? I met a boy called Dermot who came from there.'

'Yes, that's my son. I'd like to thank you for drawing him that picture. I think he's down at the funfair now.'

Surprised, I spoke to Dermot's father for a while, and then wandered back towards the post office. A little gang of children were coming up from the fair. One of them, a dark, serious-looking girl, called out to me.

'Will you draw us some pictures, please?' she asked gravely.

'Ah, I remember you – you watched me drawing for Dermot, didn't you?'

'I know who you mean, yes. My name is Geraldine McCarthy, and these are friends of mine.'

'Where can I sit to draw for you?'

Geraldine and the others led me to a tiny grocer's shop, full of rows of tins. The grocery counter stretched to the rear of the little shop, and there became a bar, where Geraldine's parents poured drinks and sold tins of food. A big man sat in a snug whose walls were tins, tipped back his Guinness and departed. I took his seat, surrounded by children. Mr and Mrs McCarthy were not at all taken aback by this, but greeted me kindly in Welsh accents. She was talkative, with glasses and dark hair, while he was gruff and kindly in a reassuring protective manner. I could easily have been in a Welsh farmhouse. The grocery-pub was called the Star. Until the 1940s, most Irish country pubs were also shops, for plush bars with music are a modern innovation.

A boy and two girls, friends of Geraldine, were on holiday from Kilburn in London, very near to Kensal Green where I live. They were 'London Irish', but more Irish than London. The others spoke often of their potato shop, for all seemed to be in the potato business. As google-eyed rabbits and donkeys flew from my pen, the children held them up to show Mrs McCarty, who cried, 'Oh fancy!'

Finally I feared that I would be locked out of the post office for the night, so I put away my paper and made ready to leave.

'Come to our shop and draw pictures for us there in the morning,' the potato children begged. 'You can't miss it – it's a yellow shop, just down past the lake of anglers, by the bridge.'

I didn't remember seeing a shop near the Causeway, but I said that I would see what I could do.

On Saturday morning I rose early, for I wanted to go to Castletownshend for the day, the home of writers Edith Somerville and Martin Ross. Another, even larger, Dublin family had main possession of the breakfast room. One of the ladies had been singing in the Rossa the night before, so I congratulated her on her voice and we all became quite friendly.

Down at the Causeway, I could see no sign of a shop. Looking round, I noticed a man energetically shaking potatoes out of a sack on to the ground. He stood beside a yellow hut in an open field by the road. There were the girls I had met from the Star, setting up a board that advertised fresh greens and potatoes. Another of the children sat up at a Punch-and-Judy-type counter in the shed.

'That's not a shop!' I complained to them. 'It's a kiosk.'

'Well, we call it a shop. We're all cousins. That's my uncle, there with the potatoes.'

Uncle Potato gave me a businesslike 'Morning!' and took no more notice of me as I sat outside and tried to draw, the wind fluttering my notepad.

'Ah, here's my father and my brother,' said one of the girls, as a boy and a man appeared, carrying a sack. They stood watching me civilly as I drew more rabbits and donkeys. Soon my bus would leave, so with a final wonky donkey I was off. The potato family bade me a cheerful farewell. On the Causeway, a golden Labrador ran dangerously among the traffic, its owner unconcerned.

'Skibb?' asked the bus driver, as he took my money, and I nodded.

Skibbereen seemed to be the nearest place to Castletownshend that I could reach by bus. We drove through gorsy countryside, and soon reached the village of Leap. Or so it was spelled on the official sign.

'Lep!' shouted the driver, and I remembered a phrase from Somerville and Ross: 'She lepped like a hare.'

Later I heard that the village had acquired its name from an O'Donovan who was pursued by the devil one day, and escaped by a mighty Leap (or Lep).

At Skibbereen, I alighted to find myself in a bustling town of narrow bunting-hung streets full of holidaymakers. Nearly all of them came from different parts of Ireland. Coming straight from a small place like Ross Carbery, I felt dazzled by the big city and stood gawping and bewildered. Fortunately I soon found a gap between houses in the High Street and found myself in an instant among green fields where swallows skimmed and black cattle waded in the River Ilen. Returning after a while to the crowds and the traffic, I walked up and down the vivacious town admiring the many brightly painted houses. House paint in vivid colours, red, pink, blue or yellow, is one of the great inventions of the modern age. In the forties, when I was a boy, there was only distemper paint, usually grey, and often poisonous to the poor souls who applied it.

In a brown cosy little bar, I enjoyed a splendid lunch of cabbage cut small, bacon cut thick and rough-looking boiled potatoes in torn jackets. Big men tapped their feet to taped fiddle music while anxiously watching the Curragh horse races on the television.

One or two people, including a bus driver, assured me that there were buses to Castletownshend. Others assured me that there were none. After waiting for a while in the hot sun, I realized that the pro-bus party had only been trying to please me. So, having found the right road to Castletownshend, I walked along it hitchhiking. Within minutes a curly-headed farmer stopped his car and drove me for a mile or so, his little daughter by his side.

'I get out here, but it's only a mile to Castletownshend,' he promised me.

A mile didn't seem worth while hitching for, so I walked with thumbs down and stopped to admire two small village schools in the middle of nowhere. Stonework writing proclaimed them 'National' schools.

Just then, a man poked his head out of an ice-cream-type van marked 'Soft Drinks', and offered me a lift. I hopped in beside him, and asked about the schools.

'One of them's used, but the other one now, 'tis desolate,' he said.

I was glad the fizzy-drink man had offered me a lift, as it seemed a very long way to Castletownshend. Obviously the farmer had told me it was a mile simply to please me once more. Finally I emerged in a long narrow Clovelly-like street of old grey houses that led straight downhill to a harbour. Thanking the soft-drink vendor, I set out to explore.

Skipping downhill, I passed several charming cottages and prosperous pubs, and at length reached the end of the road. Here, as if in a fairy-tale Place of Three Choices, I encountered a harbour, the gates of a great castle and a church towering on a sudden hill.

First of all I went to look at the harbour. Various young Ascendancy-types, augmented by English from England, played around with yachts on the blue sea and curving quay.

Then I went to look at the castle. This was now a guesthouse, as I had been forewarned. However, it was still owned by one of the Townshend family who gave Castletownshend its name. Seventeenth- and eighteenth-century English colonizers in Ireland very often gave their names to the places where they settled. These became village names, just as most English villages are called after the original Saxon colonists of the Dark Ages. Both these waves of English settlers were dominated by men who had no patience with unpronounceable old Celtic place names, and swept them aside.

Castle Townshend was still impressive, with an avenue leading up to the guesthouse, sweeping lawns and ancient trees. It was not a medieval castle, but in a dangerous country like Old Ireland there is no such thing as 'mock medievalism', for great Ascendancy houses were in a sense forts until the end. I had not taken two steps along the pathway when a car stopped and a woman in glasses poked her head out of the window, and said, 'You can't go in!'

I sensed correctly that this was Mrs Salter Townshend, and asked if I could have a look at her castle from the outside, so as to be able to describe it in a book I was writing.

'Just a quick look!' she warned me.

Castle Townshend is a long grey castle, with a Gothic tower at each end and a gabled former rectory in the middle. Visitors seemed to be chosen from the same background as family guests, and looked very much at home, with Dalmatian dogs racing to and fro across the lawn. Castletownshend seemed to be a rich man's playground.

My Third Choice was the church up on a hill. Being so near the castle, it was, of course, Church of Ireland, like the cathedral in Ross Carbery. It was a steep climb, the castle-like church tower among green trees beckoning me onward. Cool, shady stonework and gold- and red-stained glass made Castletownshend's church well worth the climb. Most hilltop churches are dedicated to St Michael, a great saint for replacing pagan gods, but this church belonged to St Barrahane. As usual in Ireland, a Norman church on a nearby site had been replaced by an eighteenth-century building with no Roman connections.

Normans, coming from England, had settled on the coast of West Cork, and in many other parts of Ireland, without being regarded as conquerors of All Ireland. They had been of the same faith as the Irish chieftains, they soon intermarried with chiefly families and became chiefly families themselves. Scarcely accountable to the Norman rulers of England, they swiftly grew Irish in their ways. Soon they became regarded almost as renegades by the more austere Normans whose alien rule fell hard on the English shires. In Ireland today, such Norman families are known as 'the *old* English'. Acceptance came easily to them, as the Irish chiefs expected other chiefs to conquer them, for were they not always plotting to conquer other chiefs? Normans, or *old* English, built castles and churches of stone in Ireland as in England, replacing the wooden buildings of Celts and Saxons. The English Conquest that shook Ireland to the core and altered the island's destiny was the Protestant Colonial Invasion of Tudor times. St Barrahane's was its monument. Many of the old English joined the *new* Ascendancy and became Protestants, but they seem to this day to be regarded with some affection by the old Irish.

According to the guide book, I had climbed fifty-two steps to the church door, one for every week of the year. A lifeboat oar from the *S.S. Lusitania* stood on the porch, in memory of the dead who had been taken ashore at Castletownshend when the enemy sunk the ship in 1915.

Beside the private pew of the Townshends (or Townsends) an enormous family history had been engraved on three stone 'pages' that dominated an entire wall, standing side by side, a triumph of the stonemason's craft. Few mentions of things holy intruded here, but battlefields where Townsends had distinguished themselves featured prominently.

'To the Glory of God and in record of Eight Generations in Direct Descent from and including the founder of the Townshend family at Castletown, County of Cork . . .' I skipped here and there, for the writing was small and the lines closely packed. '. . . His only sister, Henrietta, is unmarried . . . It is a received tradition in the family that . . . This memorial is presented to the Church of her immediate ancestors by Geraldine Henrietta Townsend Mundy, Lady of the Manor of Bridgetown, Easter, 1903.'

Easter! Alas! For it was another Easter, an unlucky thirteen years on for the Townshends, that spelled the end of the Ascendancy Raj. Now every Irish schoolboy and girl learns of the Easter Rising of 1916, when rebels in Dublin seized the main post office and, 'mid stamps and postal orders, changed Ireland's history once more.

Another memorial tablet on the wall, small and unpretentious, struck me with greater force than the mighty tablets of the Townshends. Paid for by American lovers of literature, it depicted an easel, a lyre and crossed quills over a scroll. Here were commemorated Edith Somerville (1858–1949) and Violet Martin Ross (1862–1915). Even if you violently disapprove of fox-hunting, the theme of most of their stories, I urge you at all costs to read the *Experiences of an Irish Resident Magistrate* in all its glory. These so-called *Experiences* and *More Experiences* are in fact a series of short stories. They describe a bygone West Cork that resembles in many ways an antebellum American South where, in slave folklore, humble tricksters always get the best of Ole Massa. Not many foxes are killed, and those that are would surely have died of old age by now anyway, if they weren't fictional.

When I had finished admiring the interior of the church, I walked around the outside, reading the headstones on the graves. At the rear of the church I saw a strange battered standing stone amid the grass, and wondered if perhaps the church had been built on a pagan site after all. I rested my hand on the stone, expecting it to be icy to the touch, as most uncanny old pagan stones seem to be. Instead, it was pleasantly warm, and seemed to fill me with kind thoughts.

A long time later I learned that the stone stood as a memorial beside the grave of Somerville and Ross.

Back at the harbour, I reflected that none of the Three Choices had resulted in any magic happening. A loud voice suddenly boomed, 'Isn't that Roy Kerridge?' It was Jeffrey Klinke from Memphis, Tennessee!

CHAPTER FOUR

☘

Enter Jeffrey Klinke

For a moment I didn't recognize him. Yet how could I forget that tall, broad-chested, talkative young man with his brown suit, shoes and leather bag, his clean-shaven looks and determined jaw? I knew him not from Tennessee but from the office of the *Spectator* magazine in London, where he had been editing the travel anthology, *Views from Abroad*. Later he came close to fighting a duel with another editor over the same anthology.

Jeffrey is a Southern aristocrat, and the American Civil War looms large in his life. One of his forebears had just invested in forty new slaves when the war broke out. After the Late Unpleasantness, or War Between the States, Jeffrey's great-grandfather wisely decided to abandon cotton for dairy farming. Klinke's Ice Cream is now a prosperous concern in the South. So few 'Southern gentlemen' exist that Jeffrey's accent is unidentifiable outside Dixie. It is not Good Old Boy 'y'all come back here' talk, and it is most certainly not Yankee American (perish the thought). A slight Canadian accent, softened and made musical, would be nearest the mark. Displaced outside Dixieland, he now seemed to have found his niche with the Irish Ascendancy.

'I've been here since February,' he told me, talking rapidly as is his wont. 'Let me show you round!'

'Well, can you do it quickly, as I have to hitch back to Ross Carbery tonight?'

'Of course! I know pretty well everyone here. Let's go to Mary Ann's bar first.'

At Mary Ann's we sat in the garden, while the pub dachshund, Clea, frolicked around. Cries of 'Dahling!' floated on the evening breeze, for it appeared that Castletownshend, with its yachting club, was a centre of Ascendancy Bohemianism, with visiting *Spectator* writers in abundance. One of them, Richard West, had apparently been greatly amused by the Townsend history in the church. Having read the whole thing, he had burst out laughing over the realization that an eminent Townsend (or Townshend) had changed sides at various times during seventeenth-century skirmishes, depending on who was winning at the moment.

'In most parts of Ireland, the Ascendancy live scattered about,' Jeffrey explained. 'But here at Castletownshend, they live side by side. The great thing here is to visit Drishane, the Somerville house at the other end of the village. Yes, Somervilles are still here. Edith Somerville played the organ in the church for seventy years – she went round across the fields to avoid the fifty-two steps. I always attend this church, as they retain the traditional prayer-book service. The Irish Ascendancy *now* are like Southern planters used to be in the 1920s – going to seed, but still there. I'm reminded so much of attitudes of my boyhood – it's quite fascinating here! The interplay of new and old orders! It's like the South in the old days, as they haven't had so long to decay.

'There are two different grapevines for gossip, the Roman Catholic and the Protestant. The Roman Catholic gossip is often based on wild guesses and faulty interpretations, so it's by far the most interesting. There are all kinds of rumours about boats smuggling in cement mixers, at the moment. All the Roman Catholic gossip takes place at Creameries – the dairy co-ops – and after Mass.

'Before I came to Castletownshend, I was staying in a remote part of West Cork, and in the local fishermen's bar the television showed IRA supporters in Andersonstown, Belfast, tearing British soldiers to pieces with their bare hands. To my surprise, the fishermen were laughing and rejoicing and slapping their thighs.

'"We remember the Black and Tans,"' they told me.

'Yet here at Castletownshend you can hear Stan Gebler-Davies, who stood as a Unionist (anti-Home Rule) candidate for West Cork, holding forth in the pubs at the top of his voice. He's as popular with Roman Catholics as he is with Protestants, for he's a good talker and an excellent drinker.'

Skill in the drinking arts counts a lot with Irishmen, though not with Irish women. An Irish friend in London, who wanted to compliment me, said that I was a great drinker, though actually I scarcely touch a drop. Well, I'll maybe have the one. Meanwhile, in Mary Ann's, I could overhear other patrons discussing who could, or could not, expect to be received at Drishane.

Jeffrey Klinke went on to tell me of Admiral Boyle, Edith Somerville's brother, whose memorial I had seen in the church. A well-loved old boy, he went out of his way to help local unemployed young men to join the British Royal Navy. This was in the 1930s. In 1936 the IRA gunned him down on his own doorstep.

'Almost all the Roman Catholics in Ireland heap praise on the *old* IRA, of the Troubled Times in the twenties,' Jeffrey told me, 'yet most of them, the fishermen apart, pour scorn and hatred on the *modern* IRA. So Sinn Fein – that's the IRA political wing – have brought out a pamphlet to show that the crimes of the *old* IRA were just as mean and underhand as those of the modern lot. It's an extraordinary book – you must get hold of it. I thought at first it was an exposé or indictment of the IRA, but no, they wrote it themselves to show that shooting people in the back, or in bed, is perfectly justified in a war, in the twenties as now. It certainly destroys the myth of the good *old* IRA. But let us talk of happier things. Let me take you to see Peter Salter-Townsend. He lives right here in a small house in the village.'

We found young Salter-Townsend entertaining a golden-haired young lady at dinner. She had a humorous face, but something in Salter-Townsend's expression told us we ought to leave. He too had long yellow hair in the hippie fashion. Jeffrey blurted a request for a guide book, which Peter curtly handed to him, and we found ourselves outside. I was pleased, as dusk was falling, and I can't abide hitchhiking at night.

Much later, all was explained. An apologetic Peter Salter-T. explained that he had just been about to propose to the humorous lady. When we had gone, he got on with it, and was accepted. Congratulations!

'Don't worry about hitchhiking – I'll come with you!' Jeffrey Klinke kindly offered. 'Everyone knows me here. I'd love to see the Ross Carbery Carnival. The Bord Fàilte, or Tourist Board, arranges the village carnivals so that when one ends, another begins.'

'It gives a lot of work to Irish musicians,' I said, 'and I'm fond of Irish music.'

'So am I. Last week I got a lift from a fiddler on the way to a wedding, and I stayed for the wedding.'

I mused on Tourist Boards, with whose aims I am not always

in sympathy. In Wales, hypocrisy has left the Chapel and taken over the so-called Tourist Industry. Although this drastic change of religion has left many chapels redundant, those that are left are Purified. A modern Caradoc Evans, or Welsh satirist, would certainly write about tourist officials, not preachers. *Fàilte*, in Irish, means 'Welcome', not 'Faulty' as you might suppose.

Jeffrey Klinke, meanwhile, was talking of Knockdrum Fort, an Iron Age fortress that was not far out of our way. He led me up a rocky hillside and over a stile to a perfect ring of loose stones around a circular hollow, with a walkway around the rim. I could scarcely believe that an Iron Age fort could have lasted so well, and no wonder, for I found out afterwards that one of the Somerville family, in the nineteenth century, had imaginatively 'restored' the fort almost from scratch.

A yachting couple from England sat on the wall and admired a glorious Celtic view of coves, bays and cliffs. Around the other side, among darkening mountains and moors, Jeffrey pointed out the Four Fingers, two tall Neolithic standing stones pointing at the sky. The third Finger, which had toppled over, could be seen nearby, but where was the Fourth Finger?

'One of the Townsends dug it up and moved it to the castle,' Jeffrey explained. 'It's a very long stone, lying on its side.'

Soon we were swinging along the road, I with my plastic bag and Jeffrey with a leather cricket-type bag, which he was never without. It usually contained the works of Shakespeare and a bottle of wine.

'Farmers here get up at nine thirty, not at dawn like farmers everywhere else,' Jeffrey said. 'Some Germans have settled here, but it takes them time to appreciate the Irish character. They bark orders, go away and come back from Germany months later to complain that an annexe has been built in the wrong place. The Irish won't take Prussian discipline. But for the most part, the Irish and Germans get on very well.'

I feared that the Irish were beginning to look outside Ireland towards the EEC for comfort and inspiration. Perhaps Ireland would lose its independence in the European Economic Conglomeration.

Just then, a car stopped and a bearded Englishman with an Irish girlfriend, both friends of Jeffrey Klinke, told us to hop in. The Englishman came from Kent, and had bought a house near Castletownshend.

'You got your car back from the Customs, then?' Jeffrey enquired solicitously.

'Yes, but it took *ages*!' the man replied ruefully. 'You would never think the Customs had the right just to seize something.'

'People round here think you're a drug smuggler!' Jeffrey explained, cheerfully offering a choice fruit from the Roman Catholic grapevine.

'Is that so!' exclaimed the bearded man, who was actually an antique dealer. 'So *that's* why they confiscated my car! I could have sworn they'd taken it apart, as now it doesn't work properly.'

'That's nothing!' Jeffrey continued. 'They think *I'm* a spy from the CIA. You see, Russian fishing fleets are offshore some of the time. Occasionally the men come ashore, shepherded by a KGB type. The first time I went into a shop in West Cork they asked if I were Russian. An American used to come here on holiday for a time, and then stopped. Then *I* came along, and they think I'm his replacement. It seems obvious to them that the CIA would pay special attention to West Cork. I'm supposed to have radio equipment in my leather bag so I can contact the White House or Pentagon. It makes no difference to the way people treat me – everyone is perfectly charming.'

The ersatz drug pedlar drove around numerous inlets of the sea, for Ireland teems with miniature narrow fjords, across a bridge over a watery gap between mountains, and set us down on a country road where we began hitching again. Jeffrey never grew despondent and talked all the time. Soon it was completely dark.

'At Skibbereen they roped off the main street for hours for terrier racing. That was good sport. In the lanes where I used to live, outside Castletownshend, people went road-bowling, pitching great bowling balls along the backroads. One day a car got damaged, and nobody would own up as the culprit, so they stopped road-bowling. Ah, here's a car.'

A pleasant-faced middle-aged couple, who looked like Welsh country people, stopped and let us in. They too were going to Ross Carbery for the Carnival.

'Are you farmers?' Jeffrey asked politely.

'Yes, we have a dairy farm over at Bandon.'

'Bandon, where even the pigs are Protestant!'

'How did you hear that?' asked the farmer, amazed, but Jeffrey smiled and said nothing.

I told the farmer and his wife how much I had enjoyed exploring Castletownshend.

'Yes, you'll find many English admirals' graves at Castletownshend churchyard,' the man said, with a half-smile. Then they pulled up at Ross Carbery market square, and we climbed out with thanks. In a way, the teeming undercurrent of gossip in Ireland reminded me of tales I had heard from West Africa, where villagers believe in witches and water spirits, and ascribe supernatural intentions to the inscrutable doings of foreigners.

Carpenters had been hard at work in the car park square, and we found a see-saw going at full tilt, beneath a lengthy awning held up by wooden props. Young men and girlfriends were the riders, and the object was to see who could see-saw longest before falling off exhausted. Spectators were invited to donate to charity. Thirty or so sees and saws were all that most couples could manage before boredom set in, though one girl tore off her coat in mid-air, threw it down and told her partner that they were out to beat the record.

On the stage, a third-rate country and western group plunked on. Jeffrey plunged into Murphy's Bar, where a ballad competition was taking place. It was so crowded inside that I found it unbearable. Song after song, glutinous or lugubrious, was met with roars and cheers. Some good Exile songs were sung, but most applause went to an open-shirted young man who sang of Fiddlers' Green, the sailors' paradise where whiskey and women are free and pork chops grow on trees.

'I'm sure that girl is American,' Jeffrey suddenly cried, pointing to a giggly maiden yards away in the crush. 'She has a tan, and the native Irish don't tan, by a genetic quirk.'

'I'll never find you again in the crowd,' I said. 'How will you get back to Castletownshend?'

'Oh, I'll hitchhike back when the bar shuts, and I'll hitch back here again in the morning. If you attend morning service in the cathedral, I'll see you there.'

Thankfully I escaped from the Welsh uproar of the bar, and found the same couple still see-sawing away. In the bar-restaurant, I said hello-goodbye to the party from Dublin who were staying at the post office. 'I'll see you in the morning,' I mentioned.

'Please God!' the mother added, with a look of great alarm.

'Yes, in the morning, please God,' I hastily amended. I had forgotten that to the Irish, understandably enough, nothing is certain. You cannot say 'I'll see you' without challenging God, Who might then make it quite certain that you *won't* see that person. If you add 'please God', that makes it all right. 'Take nothing for granted, but thank God for what has been', might be the Irish motto.

And so to bed.

In the morning, I saw the Dublin family safe and sound, and then went to the cathedral, or 'Church' as it was known in Ross Carbery.

All over Ireland, the local Roman Catholic church is always called 'Chapel' and the Anglican church is 'Church'. Again Wales comes to mind, where the nonconformist churches are called chapels, as they fulfill the same function as the Catholic churches of Ireland – worship of God and opposition to the Church of England in any of its guises. Considering how some Welsh chapel preachers fulminate against 'Rome', it is odd for a travelling Englishman to hear the Roman church described as a chapel. Many Irishmen visibly shuddered if I mistakenly referred to their local Catholic church as a 'church', and I was usually corrected at once – 'That's the Chapel.' In the wider sense of a world-wide community of believers, however, the word 'church' was used. None of these distinctions cross the Irish sea, for Anglicanism is irrelevant to the Irish in England, and the Roman Catholic churches of Kilburn are free to be Churches.

Late as usual, I tiptoed into Church and sat timidly at the back. At once I saw the huge figure of Jeffrey Klinke in a front pew, almost blotting out my view of the Dean. The small whitewashed cathedral was half full, and it was a pleasant service, marred only slightly by modern rituals.

'Let us pray for the safety of British security forces everywhere, particularly in Northern Ireland,' the Dean concluded his sermon.

After the service, the Dean shook Jeffrey's hand joyfully. 'I never thought I'd see you here again!' he exclaimed.

'I did vow that I would never worship under this roof until the old prayer book was reintroduced,' Jeffrey said. 'But as my friend from England is here, I broke my own rule.'

'Well, I'm glad that you did! You must come again.'

Jeffrey and I walked down towards the sea, and he told me of a neighbouring Roman Catholic priest who had urged his surprised congregation to go inside old Protestant churches to admire their fine architecture. 'After all, they used to be ours!' he had joked.

Somehow the priest's innocent remarks, when the tangled RC grapevine had finished with them, had become interpreted as a bold plea to seize the Protestant churches and hold them for the Old Faith. 'There was a lot of fuss about that,' Jeffrey added.

'Was that girl in the pub an American?' I enquired.

'No, she was a Yellow Protestant. That's what they call a tanned person of English descent around here. But having introduced myself, I thought I ought to stay and be agreeable. It was two a.m. before I began hitching back, but I was in bed by four this morning.'

We walked far out on a headland, the sea below us and gorse all around us. Jeffrey pointed out ruined Castlefreke in the distance across the water. On the yellow sands across the bay, children played at ball. At that moment I saw a big grey seal poke its enormous head out of the dark blue waves. It spread its nostrils and hare lip and snorted vigorously, then rolled over and swam away upside down. Jeffrey insisted that it was a walrus, and would not be dissuaded from this view.

Taking long strides, he climbed up the hillside, stepping over drystone walls that sometimes resembled rows of grey teeth, at other times miles of stacked grey tea trays. I followed as best as I could.

'All I want in this Creation/Is a pretty little wife and a big plantation', he sang blithely, a nursery rhyme from his childhood.

As we walked over gorsy hills and along the edge of cliffs, he told me of Southern songs and singers, of the Gandy Dancers, the Negroes who heave and ho in work gangs to straighten out buckled 'railroad lines' on little forgotten 'freight-carrying' branch lines in Mississippi.

'When I was last down there, a few years ago, they were still singing those wonderful old songs and choruses to help with the work,' he told me. 'On most of the bigger railroads, they line the tracks with machinery now.'

Irish navvies in England sang worksongs in my boyhood. I wonder if any still do so. Jeffrey would be unable to stay for the music and singing in Ross Carbery that night, as he had to meet someone in Castletownshend. Before he left, he gave me his opinions on Irish history, this time striding downhill and stepping over slabs of wall.

'In the eighteenth century the rulers of Ireland denied the existence of a Gaelic civilization, although it was all around them,' he said. 'Now, in the twentieth century, the new rulers of Ireland deny the existence of English civilization, although it's all around them.'

'To my mind, the eighteenth century was to Ireland what the eleventh century was to England,' I put in. 'There's a Kipling poem that describes the Norman invaders as putting England on the anvil and painfully beating her into shape. Nearly all the Irish landscape, the cities, stately homes, parks, mills, little towns, cathedrals, canals and so much of what you see is the inspiration of the Ascendancy, however harsh they may have been to the Irish who did the physical labour of it all.'

'Not here, though. These fields are Gaelic. The pity of Home Rule is that it came about with such violence. England had put Home Rule on the agenda when the First World War broke out. So the Irish were told to wait until the war was over. But in 1916, when the war was still going on, armed rebels seized the Dublin General Post Office.

'After many casualties, they were arrested, and public opinion was against them. The ringleaders were hanged, and received opinion now is that this made them martyrs and helped the rebel cause. But I think public opinion changed over to the rebel side when the Irish saw that England was indecisive.

'Ireland became ungovernable. England sent the infamous Black and Tans to try to crush the rebels, then Home Rule was granted and the Irish Civil War began, between those who agreed with the Treaty that guaranteed British citizenship in the six counties of the North, and those who called it a betrayal. The two main Irish political parties now, that go in and out of office, are based on the two sides in the Irish Civil War.'

'I must say, the Irish Civil War doesn't have the romantic image of the English or American Civil Wars,' I said. 'No one will write paperback love stories about it. Instead of having a "wrong" side that everyone loves, all lace cuffs and chandeliers, it conjures up an image of hard-faced men in wire spectacles and old macs, riding bicycles along narrow lanes in the pouring rain in order to hide behind hedges and shoot identical hard-faced men in macs on bicycles. No film such as *Cromwell* or *Gone With the Wind* can be made of it. It was an unpoetic war.'

We had now reached the road to Castletownshend, and Jeffrey Klinke shook my hand, firmly seized his leather bag and walked hitching along the road, an enigma to all who saw him.

Much later, I came into possession of the Sinn Fein booklet Jeffrey had recommended: *The Good Old IRA*. As he had said, it sought to prove that the *old* IRA, part of Ireland's new heroic folklore, used the methods of the modern IRA and was right to do so.

It made curious reading, being a list of killings year by year, during the 'Black and Tan War', from 1919 to 1921, the fighting that preceded the Civil War. More than half of those killed, it was easy to see, were innocent Roman Catholic Irishmen who had been suspected on slender grounds of being 'informers'. Again and again, the condemnation of this violence by godly Roman Catholic priests was repeated with a sneer, as if to say 'all priests are traitors'. Most alien to the English mind was the way that so many killings were headlined with humorously-intended puns.

> FOOTBALL RESULT: At Bandon on May 14th, a soldier of the Essex Regiment who was protecting police and soldiers playing football, was shot dead. Two civilians were wounded. One of them, Cornelius Sooney, an elderly man, died later.
>
> UNLUCKY THIRTEEN: Patrick Briody, a shoemaker of Mullahoran, County Cavan, was taken from his house and shot dead on Monday morning, May 23rd. Thirteen bullets entered his body, attached to which was a piece of paper with the inscription, 'Convicted spy. Executed by the IRA.'
>
> DEAD LETTER: Private Letter of the Machine-gun Corps, stationed at Ballyvonare, County Cork, was shot dead at 7 p.m. on July 10th. He was unarmed.
>
> HAIR-DO: On the night of April 16th, a number of armed and masked men visited the house of Mary Gallagher aged 56, of Derrybeg, and cut off her hair, apparently because she had reported a neighbour to the Crown forces for 'having poisoned her dog'.

Knowledge of all these horrors yet before me, I had a bowl of soup at Nolan's Bar and went to see the official opening of the Carnival, which had been delayed until today (Sunday) when the Carnival was nearly over.

This was a lucky time of year for the carpenters of West Cork, who were sawing off the rough corners of a large stage near the red see-saw. No sooner had they finished than a ludicrous assembly of local notabilities in tight suits took their portly places in rows upon it. It was pleasant to see proper councillors once more, after having been ruled or misruled for so long by hippies and ex-squatters in my home borough in London. Music no longer played, the see-saw ceased to saw, the cars disgorged their tenants; all Ross Carbery stood gazing at the platform in respectful awe as the Chairman of the Carnival Committee arose to speak. I had never seen anything like it, but I stared with the rest.

First of all we were welcomed to the Ross Carbery Carnival, delights of which would include not only music, singing and dancing, but 'the Famous Rag and debating in the bar of the Carbery Hotel'. What was the Famous Rag? It sounded like a piano tune.

'We have a celebrity here today to open the Carnival – Larry Tompkins, the Gaelic football star! In addition, here to speak to you are the spiritual leaders of our Two Communities – Father Walsh and Dean Robert Townley!'

The whole square clapped and cheered as Larry Tompkins, the Roman Catholic and Anglican priests all bowed their heads. With a start I recognized the man whose sermon I had enjoyed that morning, looking pink and sleek among the raw, red faces. Surveying the standing crowd sternly, like the leader of a successful Latin American revolution, the Chairman launched into a long catalogue of the woes of Ross Carbery.

'Crime will surely spread here from Dublin! Already we have had vandalism last night!'

Everyone looked at their neighbour in surprise. Who had done what? In a hollow doom-laden voice the Chairman announced that more, much more, must be done to attract the British tourist and to solve the curse of unemployment. Father Walsh was then called upon, not to give the Last Rites to Ross Carbery, but simply to speak.

First of all the Father made an announcement in slow, carefully articulated Irish, obviously the result of much hard work and rote learning the night before. Everybody cheered at such cleverness. Irish has replaced Latin as the Mystery Language of Ireland, held in great veneration whatever it might mean. Having got that over with, Father Walsh relaxed with a smile, fell into West Cork English and cheered everybody up with some well-chosen words on Carnivals.

Robert K. Townley, the good Dean of Ross, then stepped

forward with a modest air and condemned the 'violence in the North'. 'Here our Two Communities are a lesson in peaceful co-existence. [Cheers] We Church of Ireland Clergy are often accused of talking at great length, so I'll now end.' [More cheers. The Dean seemed popular.]

Taking his cue, the Chairman spoke at much greater length on 'our Two Communities'. 'Not all of the money raised by the Carnival see-saw will be spent on local charities,' the Chairman concluded. 'We are donating a large sum to the Zambian village of Chinoke in Africa. There the people will be asked to identify their own problem, find their own solution and then get the money to solve it.'

I did not join in the cheers that followed this recipe for discontent. Chinokians in Zambia might well be leading idyllic lives with no problems whatsoever until the dread intrusion of the Ross Carbery see-saw into their world. If the sum raised were large enough it could lead to a Civil War.

Finally, to great applause, Gaelic footballer Larry Tompkins took the microphone and declared the Carnival open. A tough young man, seemingly with a broken nose, Tompkins read haltingly from the paper in front of him. The Carnival was open, the dignitaries stepped down, and a band consisting of two guitarists and an accordionist began to play. As the crowd thinned, children appeared from between their legs and began to dance. Adults made for the bars, and so did I.

In Nolan's I met the Potato Uncle from the shoreside kiosk, a sharp-faced horse-dealerish man with black sparkling eyes.

'How's the potato business?' I asked, feeling very grown-up.

'Fairly good. I grow 'em all on my own farm.'

Exile songs, American country songs and English folk songs rang across the square. Ireland cannot be said to have folk songs proper, unless all the songs are folk songs, as her traditional music is still alive. Our English concept of a folk song derives from the intellectual movement to revive an extinct music. Traditional music is never as extinct as people think it is, but movements to rescue it do a great deal to seal its coffin. Songs that in England are 'folk songs', and confined to intellectual circles, are often taken up with glee by Irish traditional singers and become traditional. This goes not only for genuine old songs rescued by folklorists, such as 'House of the Rising Sun' (a Ross Carbery favourite) but *imitation* traditional songs composed and sung by Marxist socialists such as Ewan McColl.

To my chagrin, I emerged from Nolan's to see half Ross Carbery go wild with excitement over Ewan's fearful ditty, 'Dirty Old Town'. I regard this song as a personal enemy. It was a great BBC favourite in the early sixties, and seemed to lead directly to the destruction of many grimy but lovable Northern towns, cobbles, terraced villas, factory chimneys and all.

After describing a particularly delightful Northern English town, with a gasworks wall and an old canal, the singer suddenly roared, 'We'll tear you down and build a new town!' to great applause.

And so, in England, it was done, and while everyone now complains of 'high-rise flats', 'concrete monstrosities' and wonders where the market has gone, Ewan McColl stays silent. Fortunately, at Ross Carbery the singer-guitarist next launched into an Irish song, 'The Town I Loved So Well', with its poignant lament for the old gaswork walls of Derry where children once had played before Progress, this time in the form of soldiers and terrorists, had torn it all down.

To return to my theme: intellectual folk singers in England and America have invented a new music, derived from traditional music, and they call it 'folk music'. This folk music is parasitical on traditional music. When the host is strong, as in Ireland at present, it can bear the parasite, but where the host is weak the parasite kills it and then replaces it, as has happened in England with morris dance.

A blare of bagpipes, sign of Gaelic vitality, jerked me from my mournful reflections. A large pipe band, mostly consisting of children in kilts, assembled and then marched off around Ross Carbery, led by a calm self-assured little girl of eight who expertly twirled her baton. The Famous Rag had begun! Like a Brighton Polytechnic College Rag of old, it consisted of comic floats, driving round and round the square, pulled by vans or by tractors.

Many of the floats had political themes which I could not understand. Too much public interest in politics always jars on me. Local jokes, concerning men dressed up as comic priests, also left me cold. One float consisted of a 'nun' (played by a man with hairy legs and dark glasses) and a 'priest' riding up and down on a see-saw. Even I, however, had to smile as a caravan containing a slatternly family of 'tinkers' paraded round, pulled by a small open lorry with a cloth-capped boy in the back insolently drinking from a beer bottle. High jinks were going on inside the caravan, where a real fire burned beneath a cooking pot, a dog sat on the step and disorderly characters roared and brawled at one another and chased each other round and round. Perhaps this was a protest against a proposed 'itinerants' site'.

A children's band of capable fiddlers and guitarists came next, and then a Protest Float called 'Flight of the Small Farmer'. Two tiny little boys dressed like American farmers in straw hats and blue overalls, accompanied their father who drove a tractor adorned with this message on a placard:

> We're small farmers,
> What are we gonna do
> In the years ahead
> After 1992?

I had heard that Irish farmers feared that they would lose their special privileges in the EEC if that organization should become quite standardized or if Turks were to be considered a still more worthy case for bounty.

Somehow, straw lying in the path of the floats caught fire and blazed quite fiercely until a bucket of water and several stamping boots put it out. 'It was a spark from the hot dog stand,' someone said.

I sat on a bench outside Nolan's, next to the stout and lugubrious barman who usually served me with soup. Like everyone else, he was enjoying himself intensely, in his quiet way. A huge, immensely fat man in a black suit rolled up and squeezed me to the very edge of the bench. 'I'm a stranger here,' he observed.

'Where are you from, then?' I asked.

He replied in song, dirging away for some minutes at a ballad of his native town. I couldn't understand a word, but I praised him politely.

'Ach, I cannot sing in the bar as I have no teeth,' he lamented.

Meanwhile, the float went round a second time and the see-saw see-sawed on.

Next morning I said goodbye to the postmistress and stepped out into the pouring rain. The rain did not worry me, as I was clad from head to foot in plastic oilskins. No, I was more concerned about catching my bus to Killarney, in County Kerry, my new destination. There was only one bus a day, and the journey seemed rather erratic.

When the bus was already twenty minutes late, and I was going frantic, the barman from Nolan's beckoned to me from across the market square. Terrified that the bus would sail by, I picked up my bag and galumphed across.

'Wait in my doorway where it's dry,' he said considerately. 'Ah, the bus won't be ages, yet.'

After I had waited a moment he suddenly pressed some silver into my hand. 'Run along back there and buy me a *Cork Examiner*,' so I dashed across the square and back, and then back again as the bus appeared. My glasses were now so wet that I could hardly see.

'I nearly left you here,' said the curly-headed driver as I got on. 'You see, I thought of by-passing the town. What's the way out of the square?'

A summer driver, he took several wrong turnings on the way to Killarney, usually corrected by Irish passengers. Most of the passengers were Continental youths with enormous knapsacks, all gabbling away. Before long they had filled the entire single decker bus, and covered every inch of space with their laid-down burdens. Luckily I had a window seat, even if the view was rather watery.

Gorsy hills gave way to wild mountains with great boulders tumbled about. We entered a tunnel with a jagged entrance curtained by a rushing cataract of rain, and came out the other side, to enter an Ireland of fjords and headlands, with occasional bridges. Strange archaic-looking potato patches began to appear, the earth heaped into enormous furrows with fresh green plants sprouting from them. These round-cornered oblong patches of earth and potato seemed to be draped over the hummocky hillsides like handkerchieves. They were few and far between, and always with a house close by. Giant boulders in rows did duty as hedges or fences.

At a seaside town called Glengariff, a sign advertised 'Boats to the Italian Gardens on Garinish Island', but all I could see was rain. I formed the watery impression that Glengariff was a lovely place when dry, with a touch of the late Victorian resort about it. It stood near the head of a 'fjord' called Bantry Bay.

Now we were crossing the Caha Mountains, vast brown-green flanks sweeping up to craggy pinnacles. Far less of the flanks were cultivated than would have been the case in England or Wales. Little chains of bright green fields bounded by dark hedges hung here and there on the dark moorland. Sunbeams now peeped through chinks in the austere heavens, picking out gems of emerald and gold among the tiny fields on the great mountains. Some little pieces of field were detached from the others, as if a necklace had broken. Round-headed rocks and boulders loomed up as in Chinese paintings.

Inside the bus, Norwegians over six feet tall, in tightly pressed rows, loomed over *me*. We stopped at another fjord-town, Kenmare, and the Norwegians struggled from the bus. Wild and desperate rows of Continental youths, who looked as if they had been waiting for hours, charged towards the entrance of the bus. Twenty or more were left behind, evidently to wait by the roadside until the same time next day. By a miracle, a nun in a grey habit sat next to me, someone I could talk to.

'All the time we pray and pray for peace in Northern Ireland,' she told me earnestly. 'The people up there are very good. All the churches, Catholic and Protestant, get together and pray for peace.'

'It must work in the end,' I said.

'Yes, it must work in the end.'

Her words reminded me of an account I had read of slaves in the Southern states of America in the old days. 'We prayed and prayed for Freedom to come,' an old Negro lady had been quoted as saying. 'Year after year we prayed, and oh! it seemed like slavery would never end. Why were our prayers so slow to be answered? Yet we prayed on and on, and then Freedom *did* come.'

Now a new drama was taking place, for the driver announced that he had taken a wrong turning and we were lost 'somewhere near Killarney'.

I was glad of this, as God had granted us a tour of Macgillycuddy's Reeks, gloriously wild mountains and rushing rivers that plunged over the cliffsides. Foam and spray sparkled in the newly discovered sunshine. Sheep stared down at us from overhanging slabs on tall ridges, as our bus purred on its uncertain way.

At long last the bus stopped outside the Great Southern Hotel near the Victorian railway station of Killarney. All change!

CHAPTER FIVE

♣

Blarney in Killarney

Why was I staying in the Great Southern Hotel, the grandest place in Killarney? It was to remind myself of all the adventures I had enjoyed there, back in May 1973. Now, Killarney isn't an ordinary town at all. It is a resort, set by great lakes, with pointy mountains visible over rows of dormer windows and crooked chimney pots. Narrow grey streets of souvenir shops, cafés and musical bars vie with jaunting cars, resembling the horse-drawn landaus of Blackpool, for the holidaymaker's attention. Only names of alleys, such as Pawn Office Lane, show that long ago Killarney must have been a workaday town where poverty was not unknown.

On my previous visit, very many of the holidaymakers had been American. These Innocents Abroad had brought out the worst in Killarney people – servility, greed and above all, Stage Irishness.

I made my way up the wide steps, past great white columns and into the vast coffee-table-strewn hall of the Great Southern. Most of the holidaymakers were now Irish. Humorous grey-eyed girls in immaculate uniforms were flitting to and fro ministering to their wants. Contented families with enchanting children, all Irish, were sitting comfortably around dining tables whose gleaming cutlery reflected the chandeliers above. Foliated columns supported a magnificent domed ceiling.

After dinner, I set out to explore the town. Irish music, either taped or played by skilled musicians, swirled from every third doorway. Soon I discovered a 'Beer Garden' that had not been there before, a large circular glass-walled restaurant with a high-beamed barn-like roof, a bit like a giant bandstand. Family parties sat at tables, while bold spirits danced on a polished floor to the music of a trad jazz band. Outside, a mock street sign read 'Bourbon Street'.

After a time, the jazz musicians stepped down, and an accordionist and electric guitarist took over, playing jigs and reels. More and more adults and children took to the floor, dancing and leaping around; similar scenes were taking place in bars all over town. Bourbon Street is a good name for the centre of Killarney. The original Bourbon Street is the heart of New Orleans's tourist quarter, and it too is an unreal place, half fake, half genuine. Instead of fake Irishmen, such as I had met in Killarney in the seventies, fake Southerners abound in Bourbon Street. In both places it is impossible to tell who is being their real selves and who is putting on an act, and who is doing both – for many musicians play for their New Orleans friends when no tourists are around, but put on a false Southern accent whenever a tourist approaches. Both Killarney and Bourbon Street are obvious magnets for traditional musicians who come from hundreds of miles around to work in bars packed with holidaymakers. In both places, souvenir shops of extraordinary vulgarity stand cheek by jowl with fine restaurants and elegant dress shops.

Roaming around Killarney, I encountered a few tramps and unsavoury characters, inevitable in a town devoted to Pleasure, where crowds surge from one neon light to another and the music of bar tills ringing almost drowns the ceilidh (pronounced Kayly) bands. However, the streets seemed very safe, thanks to the Garda, tall men with a slight swagger to their military bearing. Unlike the police in Northern Ireland, they were unarmed, soft spoken and very helpful.

I also found many churches – chapels, sorry – and a public library almost exactly like its English counterpart. Nearby I admired a statue of a comic-looking rebel or patriot, with a big head on which perched an even bigger top hat.

'Positively No Spontaneous Singing Allowed', one pub sign proclaimed. This may have been to prevent fights breaking out over rebel songs or (Heaven forbid) Ulster Orange songs, or to avoid foreigners being scared to death by IRA songs.

I paused outside a bar door, whence fast and frenetic fiddle-playing spiralled from a ceilidh band. A ceilidh means a party, or social get-together, with food, drinks, singing and story-telling. Ceilidh bands consist of fiddles, melodeons and accordions, together with optional instruments, such as flutes, spoons, and a banjo or a *bodhran*. The bodhran is a tambourine-like drum, sometimes made of goatskin. It is held upright like a tambourine without bells. A little wooden two-headed drumstick is used, bounced to and fro in one hand. Yoruba tribesmen of Nigeria and some of their West Indian descendants play similar drums in little back-street churches in London and Liverpool.

Commercial ceilidhs were taking place all over Killarney, the bodhrans thumped and the fiddles flew, while singers carolled out many a 'Tooral-y-ooral-y-ooral'. One de-luxe band boasted not only a girl harpist but also a young man playing genuine old Irish bagpipes. The bellows-like pump under his arm swelled out a bag of red velvet. Holidaymakers with dreamy eyes hummed jigs to themselves as they wandered from bar to bar, sampling beer and bodhrans.

Now, as I recalled my earlier visit to Killarney, it is time for a flashback. All of a sudden, the scene grows all wobbly, it shimmers, dissolves and reappears in 1973, as revealed in my diary of that year.

MAY, 1973:

In the comfortable train from Limerick Junction, I found myself sitting next to a bright sixth-form schoolboy and a merry-faced nun. The nun told me that she had just come back from a long stay at a convent in Mexico. 'Our Mother Superior was such a lovely lady – she came from Ireland too, so. The water there was bad – sure, we couldn't drink it at all. We had to drink tequila instead. It made us tipsy all the time, but if they had no water, what could we do? When the Mother Superior was examined by the doctor, he was shocked. "Holy mother, your blood is sixty per cent alcohol," he whispered. "Never fear, I won't tell anyone." "Tell the world!" she shouted, with a laugh. "It had to be done, as God knows, because of bad water."'

I told the boy how strange it seemed to me to see street names, public notices and road signs in the Irish language while the people all spoke English and used the old unofficial English names for everything. He seemed to think the Irish language was ridiculous, and rejoiced that it was no longer necessary for many important jobs.

'What I like about Ireland is that the ancient monuments and ruins are just *there*, where you find them, covered in ivy, with no official explanation-board or postcard-stall. It makes the past seem part of the present day,' I added.

'Yes, we don't believe in advertising our heritage,' he said, gratified.

'Oh, is it a policy?' I asked, disappointed. 'I thought ruins were unadvertised, with no car parks or ice-cream kiosks, simply because no one had got round to doing anything.'

'Well, that reason applies as well,' he reassured me.

At Killarney Station, where geraniums hung in baskets, I was besieged by boarding-house touts who tried to seize my suitcase. I took no notice of them at all, for I had seen a Vision. This was the Great Southern Hotel, a beautiful white Georgian-style mansion with a coat of Irish ivy. It had been named after the old railway company who had made such a good job of building the gracious station. Lord Kenmare, landowner in the 1850s when the hotel was made, is said to have sold the hotel site to the railway company on condition that his regular train would always wait for him.

Inside the hotel, I found myself in a light airy world of plush carpets, great ceilings and classical columns. A bit of luxury would do me no harm, I decided. At the Great Southern, my fellow guests were Irish businessmen and German holidaymakers. Coach tours, from the hotel's own fleet of buses, had been laid on for them. I preferred to ride around in one of the small sight-seeing minibuses operating from a shop in the High Street.

Although Killarney would have been a charming old town if tourism hadn't been invented, it was now coated in a blancmange of Blarney from which the real Ireland was hard to extricate. In a frenzy of greed at the sight of Americans, the Irish of Killarney were all acting as stage Irishmen. They did not actually put shamrock in their hats and carry plastic shillelaghs, as the rows of leprechauns in the shop windows did, but they sat in the driving seats of horse-drawn jaunting cars and sang roistering folk songs, interspersed with brogue-laden invitations to passers-by to come for an expensive ride.

My first minibus trip took a group of young people and myself high into the mountains, along a narrow looping road. I looked down and saw a blue lake set as a jewel amid wildly rumpled grey-green velvet, sweeps of mountainside and open desolate moors. We stopped at a cottage tea shop, the sole building in an empty land, the garden wall made of huge boulders rolled in a line. I was the only Englishman in the bus, and the cheerful tea girls asked me eagerly if I had been to Birmingham or Manchester.

'All our relatives are there, working in pubs,' one freckled girl with long auburn curls told me. 'We go to both cities every year for our holidays! It's like Paradise after being stuck in these empty old mountains here.'

Our driver, a big florid-faced man, had cast himself in the role of a jovial ould rascal, and kept cracking jokes and singing the same line from an ould ballad again and again: 'It was not for the want of employment at home.' Caught off guard, talking to another driver, he seemed a sour and cynical person.

At one point we passed a peat bog, a vast expanse of dark brown nothingness, churned into further oblivion by enormous yellow bulldozers. Peat is now big business, and all Ireland is seemingly being churned up and taken away with the peat. At the edge of the road, beside this moonscape, a man stood next to a donkey, with a spade and bundle by his side. He was pretending to be an old peat-digger, or 'turfman'. If at one time he had actually *been* an old peat-digger, this made his pretence all the more pitiful. By pre-arrangement, with many winks, the driver stopped and encouraged us to alight and admire the turfman. The man whistled, a little fox terrier jumped on to the donkey's back, and everyone showered the digger with money.

My next tour was advertised as 'The Ring of Kerry', and our driver on this occasion was a neat young schoolteacher with glasses. A fervent Republican, he gave a jerk of the wheel and nearly crashed when I casually told a pair of young Americans that the reason Ireland was so like England was because it had once been part of England. Gritting his teeth and saying nothing, he drove on, taking us Westward to a dreamy, sub-tropical land where grey stone walls were crowned with scarlet fuchsia hedges. A bright red and white stoat ran across the road, called a 'weasel' by the driver, as real weasels are unknown in Ireland.

Our driver had promised us a rare treat. We would, if we were lucky, meet someone who actually spoke Irish. Glowing with pride, the young man stopped by a roadside cottage and ostentatiously greeted a woman in the Irish language. She replied loudly and clearly, seeming a little embarrassed, as well she might be. Then we paid our entrance fee for the Oratory Field and she thanked us in English. A little paddock was covered in stone igloos or beehive huts, the dwellings made in Ireland by holy saints and hermits while England was enduring the Dark Ages. I had heard, from a friend, of a modern Anglo-Irishman who had learned how to make these ingenious oratories. For fun, he used up all the stones from his stony fields and made an oratory village. To his surprise, he found tourist-coaches stopping near his house and drivers giving speeches about ancient Holy Ireland. I wondered if these were the same igloos. There was no way of telling.

Next day, in the street, I fell in with another young American couple. We had stopped to admire stone chess sets in a shop window, one set depicting Alice in Wonderland characters, the other Reynard the Fox and King Lion's medieval court. Grimalkin the Cat and Isengrim the Wolf caught my fancy, while the Americans seemed drawn to the White Rabbit and hookah-holding Caterpillar.

Mrs America was a short forceful girl who described herself in self-mockery as 'a New York Jewish princess from Queen's'. Her tall devoted husband wore a mouth-corner moustache and short hair and trousers. After talking for a while, I found myself acting the part of a stage Englishman, exclaiming 'The deuce!' and 'What-ho!' After that, I could not blame the Irish for their fall from grace. Americans have such a compelling yearning for the phony, that they 'will' every non-American to comply and give them what they want. Real Englishmen and Irishmen have abolished themselves out of admiration for America, and now we pretend to be what once we were, to please the nation for whom we have sacrificed ourselves.

'Ho, jaunting car!' I cried in rich Victorian tones, and soon we were jogging along towards the deep blue lakes of Killarney, where crumbling Ross Castle stands among oak trees overlooking Lough Leane. This time our jarvey, or driver, proved to be a young boy of fifteen, who held a long looped whip. The best driver yet, he spared us the blarney and spoke chiefly to the horse. While I gave the American couple a garbled account of Irish history, he didn't even flinch.

'We've had our Revolution,' the princess told me. 'That's how I met Dick, my husband. We were fighting the cops side by side on campus.'

She went on to speak of their socialist ideals, as the driver swung past Muckross House and its knobble-headed red stag among the cattle. All of a sudden, the heavens opened and released a fearful cloudburst. Both Americans insisted on going inside the stately home, leaving the boy waiting outside, drenched to the skin. I went in after them and tried to hurry them up, but they took their time. A bare, empty Ascendancy house, Muckross sported a sad Folk Museum of butter churns and other relics of a lost civilization. The boy was still in his seat when we returned, his clothes clinging to his body and his horse waterlogged. He made light of my apologies.

'I'm a fine and fresh boy!' he bragged, and we were soon trotting homeward.

Back at my hotel, I gave him a tip and urged him to drink 'something hot with something strong in it'. His face broke into a grin, for I evidently spoke his kind of language, though without the tinge of Welsh that I could trace in the Killarney accent.

I invited the Americans back to the Great Southern for tea. A Buttons in scarlet and gold uniform greeted us, and a man who looked like a Victorian bishop's butler showed us to a table in the lounge, beneath a huge chandelier.

Over tea, the princess loudly told me that she had been urging every Irish person she met to use contraceptives, which are officially banned in the Republic. She was a champion of Women's Lib. 'Do you know what they told me?' she complained. '"Go home and have children." God, I hate Catholics!'

Her husband looked wistful. Suddenly the princess noticed a grand piano nestling among potted palms. Leaping on to the stool, she began to play the blues, screeching out erotic lyrics at the top of her brassy voice and wiggling her body about. Dick gazed at her as if she were a real princess and he an unworthy frog. The other guests were very nice about it, and no one threw us out. At last I managed to shoo my new friends away, saying I would see them later in a musical pub. Outside they were shocked to find that a yellow flag on a pole had been stolen from their chained-up bikes. An Empire of their own, they used to raise the flag wherever they pitched their tent. I promised I would look out for it.

Back in my room at last, I turned on the bath tap a little too forcefully. It came off in my hand, and a Niagara of water burst into the room from the pipe. In terror, I ran down to Reception.

'Something terrible's happened!' I cried, and the girl called the bishop's butler, who came running.

Gasping and wrestling with the plumbing, this noble white-haired old man succeeded in stilling the angry pipe with a towel.

The tables were turned, and I found myself addressing this superior man as 'sir'.

'You can do it, sir!' I urged him, and sure enough, he fitted the tap back on and turned the water off. What is more, he refused a tip.

At last I hurried to the pub, where I found a cheerful crowd of Dubliners dancing to a show band. The band leader played a glorious liquid clarinet in the style of a fiddle, and sang:

> Come down the mountain, Katy Daly!
> Come down the mountain, Katy do!
> Come down the mountain, Katy Daly,
> And give us some of your Irish mountain dew!

In a corner I found the American couple, held enthralled by a fat unshaven squint-eyed man with greasy black hair. He was putting on the Irish for them.

'This man says that if we come back tomorrow night, he'll introduce us to three authentic members of the Provisional IRA!' the princess shouted.

'Sooner you than me,' I muttered.

'Ah, you're right, sorr!' the man said, turning to me and adapting his opinions to mine. 'Some of the boys are chancers, they say they're collecting money for guns and all the time it goes on drink.'

Later that evening, having said goodbye to the Americans and their hanger-on, I headed back to the Great Southern. On the way, I passed some boys who were playing at medieval jousting, charging one another on bikes and holding poles as lances. One of the poles had a yellow flag attached to it. I told the knight that the flag belonged to a princess, and he surrendered it with apologies, saying he had found it on the ground. It was an enormous flag, and they stared in the hotel when I strode in carrying it. However, the bishop's butler stowed it away in a locker, as I didn't know where the Americans had gone.

For all I know, it's still there, exhibited to other Americans as the personal standard of Brian Boru. Killarney is a Land of Make Believe.

The screen of my memory shimmered once more, and I found myself standing outside a bar, back in 1988. A guitar and accordion band played inside, so I stood in a corner and watched the dancers. Well-dressed men and women of all ages whirled around, faster and faster, as the accordionist's hands plied to and fro. As he played, he loudly sang the same two verses again and again, faster and faster.

Some say the divil's dead,
Divil's dead, divil's dead,
Some say the divil's dead
And buried in Killarney!

More say he rose again,
Rose again, rose again,
More say he rose again,
And joined the British Army!

Those who were not dancing, clapped and cheered the musicians.

I continued on my way, pub crawling for music, not for beer, just as I had done in the real Bourbon Street long ago. I was about to return to the Great Southern, when the sound of ceilidh band fiddles and melodeons lured me into a little pub where someone was singing a country and western song I had heard in Ulster: 'Oh Lord, it's so Hard to be Humble When You're Perfect In Every Way'. Speeded up by an Irish record industry, Irish music is going through as many changes as jazz and rhythm and blues have done in America, but underlying all these superficial changes was the ceilidh band, the place where it all began – the blues of Ireland.

After singing an Irish-Australian ballad about gold-digging, the band slowed down and played the introduction to the loveliest of Irish songs, 'The Spinning Wheel'. This should really be sung by a girl harpist, not an all-male ceilidh band, but it is a song that is hard to spoil. In its present form, it belongs to Georgian times, when the ancient music of Irish harpists, noted down in the late eighteenth century, inspired sophisticated composers to write new words and take the music from the street corner and the beggar's cup to the drawing room and the family gathering at the harpsichord. With the banishment of Irish kings and chieftains, harpists who played Celtic melodies became wandering beggars instead of court musicians, just as in Scott's romance, *The Lay of the Last Minstrel*. Fortunately their music was preserved, albeit imperfectly, and with English words added found its way back to the fashionable society of Bath and London.

Thomas Moore (1779–1852) is the most well-known of the Drawing Room Bards, as they are often called. He was the son of a Dublin grocer, but 'The Spinning Wheel' was the work of an Irish lawyer, John F. Waller (1809–1894). To understand the tune, you must imagine the steady rhythmic stepping of a foot on the pedal of an old-time spinning wheel. So, by a paradox, the oldest, most Celtic form of living Irish music has the most sophisticated English lyrics. I like to think that the tune is as old as the spinning wheel itself, going back to the Iron Age and beyond. This is the tune that Grania the Fair played and sung on her harp to soothe her daughter Fandy, in the novel *Druid Madonna*, which I wrote myself.

I was stepping from the pub when the song started, so I stood outside beneath the Killarney stars and listened. When the song was over, the pub pretended to shut. Doors were locked and curtains drawn, but the bar remained open. So the song was my farewell to Killarney.

Mellow the moonlight to shine is beginning,
Close by the window young Eileen is spinning,
Bent o'er the fire her blind grandmother sitting,
Is crooning and moaning and drowsily knitting.

Merrily, cheerily, noiselessly whirring,
Swings the wheel, spins the wheel, while the foot's stirring,
Sprightly and brightly and airily singing,
Thrills the sweet voice of the young maiden singing.

'Eileen, a chara, I hear someone tapping',
''Tis the ivy, dear mother, against the glass flapping.'
'Eily, I surely hear somebody sighing',
''Tis the sound, mother dear, of the summer winds dying.'

There's a form at the casement, the form of her true love,
And he whispers with face bent, 'I'm waiting for you, love.'
Get up on the stool, through the lattice step lightly,
We'll rove in the grove while the moon's shining brightly.'

Lazily, easily, swings now the wheel round,
Slowly and lowly is heard now the reel's sound;
Noiseless and light to the lattice above her
The maid steps – then leaps to the arms of her lover.

Slower and slower, and slower the wheel swings,
Lower, and lower, and lower the reel sings;
Ere the reel and the wheel stopped their singing and moving,
Through the grove the young lovers by moonlight are roving.

CHAPTER SIX

The Year of the Missing Crown

Every year on 10 August, a three-day Puck Fair is held at Killorglin, a small town near Killarney. On the opening page of *At Swim-Two-Birds*, a novel by the great Irish writer Flann O'Brien, it is stated that a 'Pooka' is 'a member of the devil class'. Killorglin's 'Puck' is in fact a billy goat, with spiral horns, traditionally caught in the mountains that surround the town. As the climax of the fair, which draws thousands of exile Kerrymen and tinkers to Killorglin each year, the captive wild goat is crowned King with great ceremony. Dancing in the street and merry-making follow.

These carryings-on suggest a pagan origin for the fair, the goat a sacrifice to be slain and eaten in honour of a bygone god or goddess. Many people *do* claim the fair is pagan, dating back to pre St Patrician days. Others say the goat's coronation first took place during the Cromwellian terror, when a wild goat fleeing from the mountains into Killorglin alerted the townspeople to the enemy approaching over the hills. The people had time to hide, and ever afterwards crowned a goat in gratitude. Still others claim the tradition began in 1804. A law had prevented landowners from charging toll at fairs devoted to the selling of pigs, horses and cattle. So in 1804 a goat fair was declared, and toll collected, a billy goat held high in a cage for all to see.

No matter. However the fair had begun, it has taken a pagan form, perhaps thanks to folk memories lain dormant for hundreds of years. Killorglin is known as a pagan place, for each February the Biddy Boys parade begging up and down the main street. These are masked figures on tall stilts, and their appearance strongly suggests West African pagan masqueraders. Ostensibly the Boys are honouring St Bridget, but in folklore the saint herself has taken on many of the aspects of Bridget or Bride, a popular goddess of pagan days. Perhaps the saintly Bridget, once Abbess of Kildare, had been named after the goddess.

Jack Sayers, an Irish friend who lives in the 'Kerryman Quarter' of Cricklewood, London, first told me of the Crowning of the Goat. 'You know that pub in Kilburn down the road, where you go to hear music – The Black Lion? Well, one year the landlord, who was from Killorglin, held a Puck Fair in the bar. He had a goat up there on scaffolding, in a corner of the bar, but the old RSPCA burst in and closed the fair. They took the goat away with them.'

Another Irish friend told me that a Killorglin man who owned a goat staged a Puck Fair in Boston, USA. 'And when the fair was over, d'ye see, all the thousands o' Kerrymen began to fight one another with bottles. Sure, the streets of Boston were running with blood! So the authorities made sure there was niver a Puck Fair held in Boston again.'

These stories had whetted my appetite, and I was agog with excitement as the bus carried me from Killarney to Killorglin, about twelve miles away, on the day before the Fair. We travelled through idyllic scenery, beside the River Laune; a tall stretch of mountains, the Macgillycuddy's Reeks, dominated the horizon. At last I was set down beside the great stone bridge that crossed the Laune and led to Killorglin. On the far bank I could see a gaunt grey town whose main street climbed a tall hill, in familiar Irish style.

Before crossing the bridge, I noticed that the road into a housing estate had been barred by a row of oil drums linked by a line of string. Small crop-headed boys were tying knots or pushing earth, stones and rubble into the heavily filled drums, supervised by a schoolmistressly woman in glasses. 'There's a pagan fair in town tomorrow,' she explained to me, 'and if we didn't do this, the travellers would invade our estate.'

By 'travellers' she meant Irish tinkers, gypsy-like people who travel the roads of Ireland. Most of them are of pure Irish, non-Romany stock, unlike English gypsies, and nobody really knows why their ancestors took up a roving life. The Puck Fair is also a horse and cattle fair, and it is at horse fairs that tinkers, like gypsies, come into their own.

Before exploring such mysteries, I had to find a place to stay.

A signboard by the roadside advertised Oslan House, a newly built guest house up on a rise overlooking the river. A winding path led me to the front door, and the young housewife who answered my knock said I could have a room. Everything in the house was stripped pine, glittering and modern, with the exception of a ragged stuffed stoat (or weasel) beside the stairs. My large, bright bedroom looked out on a glorious view of river, mountains, green forests and meadows.

'There's clothes hangers in the press,' the housewife told me. 'See you in the morning, so.'

My Trinidadian friend, Priscilla Blackman, always used the Elizabethan word 'press' for 'cupboard', so the word made me feel at home. After a rest, I set out to explore the town.

First of all, I had a look at the housing estate behind the barricaded road. A crumbling stone wall surrounded an overgrown, melancholy Roman Catholic cemetery. In the centre, a ruined chapel stared with empty window sockets on to sunken stone vault houses which had become modern versions of Bronze Age cromlech graves. Mounds of earth had been heaped over the stone slabs, coarse grass and bracken had grown from the earth, and the graves had become tussocky hummocks, almost turf cabins, with their stone-rimmed doorways. Somewhere inside each one, coffins presumably lay. Inside the ruined, roofless chapel, recent graves had been dug from the rubble-strewn floor. On the crumbling stone altar, I found a loose rusty crucifix. Beside a gravel path, the graves were more orthodox, with bright artificial flowers under glass-like plastic domes. In a back yard that met the cemetery wall stood two great heaps of dark rolled-up peat. When used for burning, peat is known in Ireland as 'turf'.

Leaving this sad, strange place, I crossed the bridge and walked up the street into town. Fairy lights, as yet unlit, had been strung above the bridge and up the main street. Pausing only to admire a large heron that waded along the banks of a wooded island in the river, and white gulls that swooped squawking over the waters, I followed the fairy lanterns. At the top of the street, in a wide square, I saw a large tower of wooden scaffolding, painted blue and white, with a dance-floor platform of boards in the middle. A derisive-looking dark goat head, complete with crown, looked down from the Poc Bar, one of the few Irish pubs with an English-style inn sign. Wild goats are not native to Ireland, but ran away from farmers hundreds of years ago, and took to the hills.

Like a shanty town outside Killorglin, the tinkers' camp spread across a wide field covered in litter, with wild dogs and wilder children everywhere. Many of the tinkers, both men and women, appeared to have ferocious tempers; the skit on 'travellers' at Ross Carbery Carnival seemed not so wide off the mark.

Continuing on my way, past scattered bungalows, I came across yet another 'desolate' school of grey stone, with the rafters burnt and fallen in. Peeping through the window, I saw that all the wooden desks were still in place, inkwell holes and all, rotting where they stood. The last traces of sums or maps had been washed by rain from the blackboard. Weeds and tall flowers, bursting from the broken floorboards, did duty as pupils. A less ruinous part of the school was in use as a costume store by an amateur dramatic society, and I spied gowns and masks through the dusty window.

'That school's in limbo,' a passer-by told me.

Between bramble hedges, a narrow footpath snaked its way around and over bumpy ridged countryside. Feasting on blackberries, I followed the path. Every now and then, at gaps in the hedge, I came across abandoned stone cabins, tiny one-storey cottages, often with a room, or stall, at one end, for cows or pigs, under the same roof. The farmers who had lived here evidently still owned the properties, as barns stacked with hay had been built against the cottage walls. Sometimes a cabin wall was knocked away to allow entrance to a tractor. One tiny house, still intact, had been filled with hay, which pressed against the glass windows. A stone trough for horses or donkeys was now dry, but a deep-furrowed potato patch remained in use. Over a hedge top, I saw a blue expanse of water, with tall mountains beyond. Excited, I pressed on, songbirds swooping away as my less melodious singing disturbed them.

By and by, I came to a lonely crossroads, where the path met a motor road and reappeared on the other side. I wondered if fiddlers and dancers had once met here. Before the era of dancehalls, which preceded the modern era of musical pubs, Irish musicians had played out of doors at country crossroads on summer evenings, while young people clapped and danced. If the local priest heard of such 'sinful' goings-on, he would hurry there as fast as he was able. When the people saw him, they would run away, lepping like hares over the hedges, the fiddler grasping his instrument by the neck. The fiddle was particularly associated with the crossroads and with the devil. Slave fiddlers in the American South learned some of these attitudes from Irish overseers, the Irish folklore perfectly meshing with scraps of half-remembered West African pagan beliefs. When the guitar replaced the fiddle as the Southern 'devil's instrument', the powerful myth of the musician who sells his soul at the crossroads gained a new lease of life. In slavery days, the crossroads fiddler of legend had been called Balaam, while today he is guitarist Robert Johnson (a real person). Several records (some by Johnson himself), and a film have been made of the devil at the crossroads, a myth that reached America from two widely separate sources.

Treating the crossroads warily, I walked on, past barking dogs and intently playing children outside a house that had been made from a former three-cabin terrace. A strip of green grass did duty as a white line along the middle of the narrow 'made' road. Soon the whole path became trodden earth below brambles swaying under the weight of singing finches. These little Irish lanes, which go on for ever, are called 'boreens'. Some boreens are tarmacked, with a green line as nature returns, others are kept alive by foot, hoof and tractor wheel.

Leaving the boreen, I followed a footpath that led to a grassy ridge above a landscape of reedbeds, creeks, pools and small sloping fields with high hedges. In one of these fields, haycocks stood in rows beside a tractor. Some of the waterways looked as if their banks had been artificially improved long ago, with paths along ridges and crisply cut-away land at the water's edge. Reedbeds, impassable without knee boots, meandered down to a wide stretch of calm mysterious water, tall mountains rising from the far shore.

I turned and saw a farmer standing beside a bicycle, eyeing me genially. Greeting him, I asked him the name of the lake I saw before me.

'Lake! That's the sea!' he said, shocked. 'I think they call it the Laune estuary.'

Later, I looked at my map and realized that I had stumbled on the innermost point of fjord-like Dingle Bay. The mountains I could see were the Slieve Mish on the Dingle Peninsula.

'Have you always lived here?' I asked the farmer. He was a lean old man, with crimson patterns on his cheeks and smiling blue eyes.

'All my life, but I have relations in London and America. That's my house and farm, way over there. I am seventy years old, boy, and my name is Jim Houlihan.'

Inspired by the Welsh swing of his accent, I told him that he ought to visit Wales. He agreed that perhaps he ought, but grew more animated when I said I was staying at Oslan House.

'Have they got a small girl by name o' Tara?'

'I think so.'

'Aha, 'tis a small world, for all them people are relatives of mine!'

Before parting on the most cordial of terms, he told me that I could walk anywhere in the fields. Gingerly, I climbed down sloping broken paths and entered a strange land of sedgy creeks, walking beside reeds as tall as myself. A curlew flew crying overhead. After a time, I turned back, and crossed the field with the tractor. Now it had purred into life, and as I approached, a big man stepped down, gave me a wave, and began tossing the yellow-green hay into neatly cocked heaps with a pitchfork. Rows of haycocks, like little hay tents or igloos, are one of the sights that symbolize all that is best of Ireland.

Later, having safely recrossed the crossroads, I set out to explore the bars around the main square of Killorglin. Music poured from open doorways, while a loudspeaker on the scaffolding boomed out a Kerryman's lament: 'Cricklewood, oh Cricklewood, 'tis cruel you've been to me.'

A complete ceilidh band played in one bar, the musicians tough, stout men in their thirties. Most of the Puck Fair musicians seemed less polished than their counterparts in Killarney, unless that impression was given by the bars themselves, made for farmers' muddy boots, with no carpet in sight. Lack of polish is an asset to traditional music, as often as not, and I felt I was in for a treat. The bodhran player had a selection of small hand-carved drumsticks, and rattled away with a will. I could hear traces of Scottish tunes in the endless Irish medley that swirled around the room: 'Cock o' the North', 'A Thousand Pipers' and 'The Barnyards of Delgaty O'.

In the Kingdom, the premier Killorglin pub, many of the customers were raffish tinkers in slouch hats, mutton-chop whiskers and marvellously expressive puckish faces. I wouldn't like to be on the wrong side of a horse deal with one of them.

Irish families, complete with children, were also crammed into the bar, as were several tourists of the Scandiwegian variety. Steps led up to a small dingy brown room with benches and a row of amplifying devices. Three grey-haired musicians, two fat and one thin, sat on three stools and played age-old Irish tunes with a steady foot-tapping beat, supplied by a drum machine. All the benches were packed, and whenever the music stopped, the customers would begin a roar of conversation, often requesting favourite tunes. Portentously, an old head-shawled granny nursed a glass of bay rum, while her daughter chatted animatedly with the accordion player. A dark-haired bird-faced young farmer was shouting excitedly in what seemed to be the Welsh language, but was probably English with a strong Kerry accent.

The instruments, apart from the drum machine, consisted of electric keyboard, banjo and accordion, the accordion player singing in loud and vigorous tones that scarcely needed amplifying. All the while, the organist (or keyboard player) played notes exactly like those of an accordion or a lilting fiddle. Perhaps the banjo player was paid by results, for he was the thin man of the trio, and could hardly play at all. Lank grey hair hung down the sides of his cadaverous face, he wore a grey suit to match, and produced a monotonous 'plunk' every two minutes, continuously, from song to song. His face wore a perpetually gaunt, lugubrious expression, even if the accordionist's song was richly comic. It was not an Irish face, but belonged in eighteenth-century England. In the age of knee breeches, he could be any Tom or Dick, but not Harry. Harrys, even in those days, were fat, jolly, vulgar and usually somebody's uncle. This banjo player should have been called Tom Lackpenny or Dick Starveling.

Meanwhile, the accordionist sang Exile songs, sounding very much like an eighteenth-century fiddler. Popular Irish songs seldom sound older than that, as earlier ditties which have been preserved are in the Irish (or Gaelic) language, and are no longer widely understood. Most consist of hymns, love songs and songs about chieftains and fighting, instead of journeys of the soul to the old home town.

'One night as I lay dreaming in Philadelphia town...' 'On Connaught's mountains drear...' 'Dear old Ballinasloe...' 'Alone at an old country crossroads...'

Everybody in the room clapped at the end of each number. Eventually I tore myself away and returned to Oslan House along the rainy street. Cafés and restaurants were doing good business, although it was ten o'clock at night. From my bedroom I could see the illuminated big wheel at the fairground merrily turning. Tomorrow would be the day that they crowned the goat.

A dull, damp dawn greeted me, with flecks of rain on the window pane. Nevertheless, I donned my plastic oilskins in glee and hurried down the rough zig-zag driveway to the road below. A tinker caravan blocked the driveway as it joined the road, but I sidled round it, watched by an alert, friendly Alsatian on a short chain. Inside, a Darby and Joan old couple looked out on the road with kindly eyes. Traffic streaming into town was reflected on their highly-polished copper coal scuttle, perched on the step.

Slowly I walked across the great stone bridge, savouring the scene. The first day of the Puck Fair was known as the Gathering. Grim, tall farmers, in ones and twos, led or dragged horses across the bridge into town, tugging at ropes roughly tied to the bridles. Most of the horses were huge, black and bony. Some clattered along in the shafts of traps, their mackintoshed owners sitting in style. Today was Horse Day, tomorrow would be Cattle Day. Sheep and pig days had been abolished. On the far side of the bridge, a barrier of hurdles had been raised, and young men in 'Fair Marshal' badges directed the horses round a back lane.

Stalls, hawkers and hucksters filled every available inch of the main street. Street musicians squeezed into the occasional gaps. I could have been in medieval London. More people were arriving every minute. King Puck would not be crowned until evening, so I had plenty of time to explore the strange world in which I found myself.

A straw-haired girl in an apron tried to sell me a basket of knitted hazel branches, a bowed-branch handle at each end. Another hawker nearby was trying to sell lobster-pot-like containers made of hazel.

'New! Whole Pig Roast!' read the banner over one stall, but the white-haired pig man was still trying to light his fire. Piggy stood nearby, ready for roasting, his head removed.

Three spotty punks in dark glasses, strumming on guitars, struck a more modern note. Behind stalls selling cheap toys, anxious Church of Ireland people unlocked and then locked the gate to the churchyard, to let a hearse through and to keep the tinkers out. A funeral was taking place in the midst of the Puck Fair.

At the top of the street, past the scaffolding, an old scold of a tinker lady had set up a hoopla stall, the pegs with ten-pound notes and wristwatches draped round them. Seven rings cost twenty pence, but you had to stand well back before you could throw. Determinedly, a boy of thirteen had go after go, but could win nothing. Sometimes he would go off to find his father and borrow more money, then come back and lose it again. When the horrible old woman turned her back, I quickly put a ring over a peg with my hand. Utterly scandalized, the woman jumped an inch in the air and screamed out, 'Sure, you shouldn't do that at all! Get right away from here, get out!'

'I win ten pounds *and* a watch,' I claimed fruitlessly, before leaving.

Now beginning to enjoy myself, I headed for the funfair. On the kerbside, a fat man sat at a small drumkit, whacking out a rhythm on the horizontal drums, while a tape recorder played Irish jigs beneath his camp chair. More taped music blared from the closed dancehall, a shabby 1930ish building beside the funfair, where on the previous night Jim McCann and his Band had played till the small hours. Part of the village hall was given over to an 'Historic Puck Exhibition', but I stepped over mud and puddles and entered the funfair, where most of the amusements were still closed. One old horse-drawn wagon stood among the showmen's trailers.

In the narrow space between the roundabouts and the village dancehall, the horse fair was beginning to take shape. Donkey dealers were the first to arrive, the patient mokes standing on gritty islands between puddles and tyre-ditches. Gentle grey animals with tall ears, they blinked innocently from white-rimmed eyes. A black donkey stood out from the rest, and so did a donk with zebra-striped legs.

Outside the fairground, more stalls were being erected against a crumbling stone wall with 'Dangerous Wall' painted in large whitewashed letters upon it. The Catholic church was locked, but a flourishing horse fair, complete with bargaining sessions, had been set up in the gateway. In the narrow lane on the far side of the fairground, horses stood for sale alongside bridle and leather stalls, fortune tellers' caravans with garish placards in the windows, a cobbler with an enormous mound of gigantic hobnailed boots, spilled all over the ground, and a small caravan advertising 'Dr Blood's Menagerie of Freaks'.

Inside the Freak Show, I admired a stuffed two-headed calf and winced at the sight of a case of mutilated dolls covered in blood, with knives stuck into them. A Sleeping Beauty waxwork, with chest rising and falling, had been hastily changed into a vampire with fangs to suit the age of horror videos. A small case contained a Jenny Hanniver, a freak commonly shown in the days of Frank Buckland, the great Victorian naturalist. Just as described by Frank, the Hanniver, a stuffed skate, stood upright, its fins cut to resemble arms and legs, its tail a devil tail. The underside of a skate looks devilish at the best of times, the gills resembling slit eyes and the mouth curved in a fatuous smile. I was surprised at the amount of freaks squeezed into such a small caravan. There was no sign of Dr Blood, unless the young girl selling tickets in the doorway were she.

Now the sun came out, I stepped fully clothed out of my oilskins, which I rolled up and put in my plastic bag, and strolled over to the edge of the tinker camp. More horses were on sale here, their bridle ropes held not only by big men in cloth caps but by youths in cloth caps and small boys in cloth caps. There seemed no immediate danger of the Kerry farmer facing extinction. Some of the horse dealers sat on the ground beside their living wares, their backs resting against the shop fronts. One of them popped his young son on a horse and let him ride bareback, holding the bridle rope and leaning backwards in gypsy style. An old tinker lady with a basket hobbled among the throng, selling shawls.

A bright freckled cloth-capped boy of twelve stood alone beside his black pony, a rope around its muzzle doing duty as a bridle. The end of the pony's tail was tied in a large knot, a Killorglin fashion.

'What price are you asking for your pony?' I enquired.

'Two hundred and twenty five pounds.'

'Is it a boy or a girl?'

'It's a horse.'

Well, it made sense. I should have asked 'Is it a horse or a mare?' Throughout the day, I kept meeting this well-mannered boy and his pony Black Beauty.

Inside the Historic Puck Exhibition, the walls were covered with old photographs of previous Puck Fairs going back to the nineteenth century. Patrick Houlihan, the owner, took my money at the door. A stout, bluff friendly man, he was helped by his wife and children, and took great pride in the exhibition. On a centre table stood a model of Puck on the scaffolding and a carving of a tinker caravan, gypsy-style again, made by the tinker himself in imitation of his old home. This tinker had once been a regular accordion player at the Fair.

Brown Edwardian photographs pinned beneath cellophane showed that in earlier times the ceilidh bands had played in the streets, not inside bars. Wild Appalachian-looking fiddle-players were supported by a banjo-player, perhaps Dick Starveling in his younger days. I was pleased to see this, as it proved the banjo had come to Irish music by way of the seaside minstrel show, and not through country and western or revived folk music. A more recent exhibit showed that the Puck Fair had nearly died out in 1970, due to lack of organizers.

Thanking Mr Houlihan for an enjoyable time, I walked out to run the gamut of three-card tricksters, wheel of fortune operatives and men selling rabbits in tiny hutches from the backs of vans. My destination was the Roast Pig Stall. A delicious aroma of hot pork and apple sauce led me on to the stall 'neath a blue awning where piggy lay in a long pan, the florid-faced white-haired pig man continually basting him in his own juices. Criss-cross chunk-marks had been sliced all over the pig's body, and each customer received a chunk in a bun, with all the stuffing and apple sauce you could eat. I've seldom tasted anything so delicious. Other people thought the same, and piggy was rapidly vanishing before our eyes. An assistant was roasting a second pig at a roaring flame in the back of the small tent-stall.

'At a fair like this, the public eat two to three pigs a day,' the man told me.

Crowds gathered around Cockney hucksters who demonstrated vegetable-peeling devices, with much banter. Three peeling-men, with demonstration vegetables, worked the fair, and so deft were they at peeling that the demonstrations looked like conjuring tricks.

'I'm from Watford, myself,' a cheerful curly-headed young peeling-man told me, as he slipped some money into a leather pouch strapped to his waist. 'After this fair, I'm off to Tralee for the Rose of Tralee beauty contest and festival. Orright, mate?'

This last question was addressed to another young peeler, or vegetable-shaver, and they were soon animatedly discussing holidays they had enjoyed in Morocco and Gibraltar. Kindly-faced women passed through the crowds selling raffle tickets for holy charity. For a time, I escaped from the throng and wandered the side streets. Glimpses through windows and open doorways revealed Victorian drawing rooms, full of ornaments, dark wooden furniture, framed texts and large wall mirrors. Flute music piped from a bar doorway.

In the High Street, I saw a strange old building which vividly brought a bygone age to life. 'John and Denis Mangan, General Store', the large fancy gold lettering on the wide shop front read. Healthy weeds and small shrubs grew out of the chimney and guttering, and inside the shop Victorian shelves were covered in dust and fallen plaster. Like a gigantic chemist's shop, Mangans' Stores was a mass of wooden drawers in dark wooden cabinets, but, unlike a chemist's shop, the drawers and shelves stretched far back into the dingy rear of the shop, then turned a corner and vanished. Long sturdy counters, like bars in Wild West saloons, lined both sides of the store, the shelves and drawers fixed to the walls behind them. One old man with white hair, obviously John or Denis Mangan, tottered about his duties. He looked as if he had been tall and strong once, and there was plenty of life in him yet. As I peered through the dusty window, I saw him holding up a large roll of lace for the inspection of two housewives. The stores seemed to sell items of lace, linen, wool and cotton, sheets and pillowcases. One of the two brothers had obviously invested in an enormous amount of stock back in the 1920s.

Only another hour or so now, and the goat crowning would begin. Restlessly I wandered into the Kingdom bar again, where a stout man and a girl, both with accordions, were joined by a fiddle player who introduced himself easily, sat down and joined in the playing. Conversation grew silent as a tough beer-bellied middle-aged man stood up and roared out the opening verse of 'The Dying Rebel'.

> My only son was shot in Dublin,
> A-fighting for his country bold!
> He fought for Ireland and Ireland only,
> The harp and shamrock, the green, white and gold.

Many Irish people fought in the two world wars. During the last war, the Republic was neutral, but where there's a will there's a way, and countless Irishmen joined up and fought bravely. However, the boy in the song fought for Ireland only, during the Troubled Times. Traditionally, the Irish flag ought to be St Patrick's Cross, extricated from the Union Jack. The Tricolour of green, white and gold (actually orange, but you can't say 'orange' 'cause of you-know-who up there in the North) was based on the

French *tricolore*. Much Irish rebelry was inspired not by Irish wrongs but by the anti-clerical revolutionary French of 1789. Later, more Irish rebelry was inspired by Marx and Lenin. Revolutionary leaders are often intellectuals fired up by ideas learned from books. If they notice oppressed people at all, it is as cannon fodder for a Cause.

Still restless, I left the bar, where the singer was being warmly applauded, and returned to the tinker camp. On the way, I passed the boy with Black Beauty, and he gave me a nod. Some younger boys leading a horse were jeered at and pushed roughly by malevolent-looking tinker children.

At the edge of the camp, I admired an ancient lurcher with a touch of Irish wolfhound in him. He was tied to an off-white trailer. Smaller dogs and grubby children raced around noisily, cursed at by adults. A lean, morose farmer surveyed the camp solemnly.

'These tinkers shouldn't be here at all,' he opined after a time. 'They make a dreadful mess, they've been there a month now, and it's supposed to be a children's playground. Still, they have to live somewhere, I suppose. Lots more have come for the fair, and every con man in Ireland is here today.'

Tinkers can be disconcerting people, as I had found time and again in England. On one occasion, I had grown friendly with an elderly shock-haired tinker, who played the harmonica and sang of the Wild Colonial Boy, a Kerryman turned highway robber in Australia. The next time I met the singer, he was in a pub with a heavily bandaged hand. 'I grew so angry that I put my fist through the juke box,' he informed me. He closed his eyes and there was a long pause.

'Yes? Yes? And then?' I asked, eventually.

At once his face froze into a mask of hostile dignity. 'What is this, the Inquisition?' he enquired, and never spoke to me again.

Merry little tinker girls from a Kilburn camp once told me that they came from Belfast. Suddenly they realized that they had carelessly told me the truth by mistake! 'That's on the Isle of Wight,' one girl hastily remarked.

'We're really rich,' her friend added. 'We can talk Posh, and English too.'

Next day my brother rescued an old lady who was being savagely robbed and manhandled by ragged tinker boys. They ran away with her handbag.

All in all, I decided I had better get to know the tinkers the safe way, by having my fortune told. I retraced my steps to the 'Dangerous' wall by the fairground, where a fortune-teller was plying her trade from a trailer. Her name, like that of all fairground fortune-tellers, was Gypsy Rose Lee.

'Come in, deary,' she said, opening the double door of the poky trailer and closing it carefully after me.

I sat down and looked at the gypsy, who was a blousy staring-eyed tinker lady with her head in a shawl. Beside her sat two hefty crop-headed blonde daughters in jeans, on the wall-bench opposite me.

'It costs three pounds, deary.'

Here was a quandary! The Irish pound had been cut off from the English quid, with disastrous results for the Irish economy, and had remained a note, not a coin. In order to pay the gypsy, I had to take a large roll of ten-pound notes from my jacket pocket, find and then peel off three oncers. All three women gave a start as I fumbled and rustled with the cabbage patch of notes. Their eyes brightened and their noses and hands seemed to turn into the hooked beaks and talons of birds of prey. The money had to see me to Wicklow or Carlow; I could ill afford to lose it. Besides, I don't even *believe* in fortune-telling.

I paid the woman and the reading began. A small crystal ball was produced. The glass had a purple sheen. 'Make a wish,' commanded Gypsy Rose Lee. 'Your wish has now been answered,' she added, before I had time to think. She made several passes with her hands and eyeballs. 'Your sweetheart will be for ever faithful to you and marry you in six!' she continued mysteriously.

'Six?'

'Yes, six! Either weeks or months.'

'Or years or decades,' I added mentally. One of the two blonde girls casually rose and sat next to me, moving nearer until she was squashed against me.

'Do you want a girl tonight?' the gypsy asked suddenly, as if coming to the point.

'No.'

'No?' echoed the gypsy in amazement, reeling slightly at this reversal of the natural order of things. Stunned for a moment, she rallied and gave a nod to her daughter, who leaned on me heavily. 'You like excitement, don't you?'

I wasn't sure that I did, as from the corner of my eye I observed the blonde girl gently lift the flap of my tweed jacket pocket and put the tips of her fingers inside. Quickly, I turned to face the girl, and her hand was out in a moment. Everyone laughed, as if there had been a minor breach of etiquette, such as yawning.

'No, I *don't* like excitement,' I said decisively.

'I don't mean excitement, deary, I mean fun.'

At the word 'fun', the girl's fingers crept cautiously into my pocket once more. I gave a jump, and stood up.

'Ah, that's too bold!' the mother remonstrated with the girl.

'I think I'd better leave,' I said, and opened the door. Then I opened the bottom half of the door and jumped out. To my enormous relief, my wad was intact. Ashamed of my rudeness, I popped my head in again.

'Thank you very much indeed,' I said. 'It was very interesting. I'm only sorry I had to leave, due to certain circumstances.'

All three women seemed very touched and pleased by my little speech, and waved goodbye with happy smiles.

In order to steady my nerves, I decided to buy a woollen pair of long johns from John or Denis Mangan at the General Store.

Inside the gigantic and totally ramshackle shop, I told John or Denis what I wanted. Mangan was a kindly old man, rather deaf and with very bloodshot eyes. When he understood my message, he began to take down box after dusty box from the shelves and to examine the contents. While he did this, I examined the shop. At the rear, round the corner, the rafters were open to the sky, the shelves and dusty wall mirrors streaked with bird droppings. Nearer the front door, a counter covered in empty cardboard boxes also contained rows of fresh jam in sparkling jars. Still Mangan searched, never giving up, talking good-naturedly all the while. I grew nervous, as the goat procession had been due to start half an hour ago. When at last Mangan found the long johns, he could find no change to give me, and wandered off somewhere in search of silver.

Leaving him to it, I hurried outside. A lorry loaded with turf (or peat) edged its way through the crowds at the top of town, followed by a donkey with a cart. Horse and donkey carts were in general use in Ireland until the late 1950s, and seemed the emblem of the country. People who left Ireland before 1950 fondly ask me if donkey carts, and even (in Cork) goat carts, are still to be seen everywhere. When I say 'No', they look astonished. Donkeys pulled turf, and goats used to pull milk churns. Returning a nod to the boy who was still trying to sell Black Beauty, I looked in at Mangans' to see how the hunt for change was getting along. He had found some, and seemed relieved to see me.

'How are things in London?' he asked. 'Do look in again before you leave.'

Just then, a surge of bagpipe music and a crash of drums told me that the Coronation procession had begun! Up the main street marched the Valentia Island Pipe Band, clad in red and black tartan, blowing Scottish bagpipes. A long line of little girls in green danced behind them, followed by still younger boys and girls from the Sports Club, in white shorts and tunic. Crowds parted and a triumphant float came by, on which sat the Queen of the Fair, twelve-year-old Kerry O'Sullivan, accompanied by her Lady-in-Waiting. Kerry, the Puck Queen, was a pretty red-headed girl with a pleasant smile. She wore a gold paper crown and a white cloak embroidered with Celtic symbols from the Book of Kells. Her Lady-in-Waiting, Michelle Melia, wore a green cloak.

They swept by, and were helped on to the stage. Behind them came the goat. The future King of the Fair was a medium-sized white billy goat, with twisty kudu horns. Looking bewildered, and pressed in by crowds on all sides, he stood in a blue box on a float, with just room to turn around. Soon he was placed, in his box, on the platform beside the Queen and the Lady-in-Waiting. A confident Master of Ceremonies took over, wielding the microphone with aplomb. He was a young man with glasses and a gift for public speaking.

'Ladies and Gentlemen, welcome to the Puck Fair! Do we have any Irish here today? [Roars.] Do we have any Americans here today? [Murmurs.] Do we have any *English* here today? [Me: "Me!"] Well, wherever you are from, welcome to the Puck Fair, the time when the goat acts the king, and the people act the goat. Can anyone tell me: What's a Hindu? A hin do lay eggs. What was Gandhi's first name? Goosey goosey!'

Having set back Irish–Indian relations by a thousand years, he proceeded to welcome representatives from the committees of two other great Irish fairs, Ballinasloe (October) and the Ould Lammas Fair of Ballycastle (August).

'Greetings from North Antrim,' said the Ould Lammas man in gravel Ulster tones that you would need a breadknife to cut. 'I invite youse one and all to see oor fair up at Bally-cassel. In spite o' the troubles in the North, I am proud to co-*op*erate wi' the organizers of ither fairs, and I truly admire your organization of Puck.'

There were murmurs of Irish approval. I had been to Ballycastle, though not at fair time, and I knew the old song:

> Oh, the Ould Lammas Fair, boys, were you ever there?
> Were you ever at the fair at Ballycastle-O?
> Did you treat your Mary Ann to dulce and yellow man
> At the Ould Lammas Fair at Ballycastle-O?

'Dulce' is edible seaweed and 'yellow man' is yellow candy floss, a speciality of the Ould Lammas Fair.

'We have a pure white goat for '88!' the Master of Ceremonies announced proudly.

Actually, the goat was pure white save for a light fawn beard that gave it a faintly Assyrian air. The poor animal looked utterly bemused, as well it might. According to the MC, it had been caught in Macgillycuddy's Reeks. He missed the chance of a joke by neglecting to say that no wonder they're called Reeks, with all those goats there. Perhaps jokes based on the Irish language cannot lightly be made.

A stray sunbeam made an aura of light about the Queen's curly head as she stepped forward boldly to the microphone and recited a speech in Gaelic which no one could understand. In the same tones of reciting a parrot-learned poem at school she repeated the welcome in German and then in French.

'There now!' came cries of admiration from the crowd, who believed it the height of patriotism to speak words that no one could understand.

Visibly relaxing, the Queen began again in English. 'Noble friends, I welcome you to attend the Coronation of Ireland's only King!'

Two goat-minders soothed the animal, while the Queen delicately placed a green cardboard crown upon its brow and tied a string around its horns to keep the crown in place. It looked like a party hat. Queen Kerry stepped back to admire her handiwork while the crowd roared and cheered. I was just thinking that the scaffolding with wooden platforms and trap doors looked very like a gallows when the same thought occurred to the MC, who cracked a joke about it. He then paid tribute to the two goat-lifters.

'For the past several years, these skilful men have been hauling King Puck up to this platform overlooking the whole fair, using all the latest equipment, a rope and a chain!'

Using this equipment, fixed both to pulleys and to the goat box, the skilful men hauled King Puck up into the air. His Majesty swayed from side to side in his box, but made no attempt to jump out. In this way he was transported from the wide ground-floor platform to the more narrow middle platform, and finally to the high pinnacle of a platform at the very top of the wooden-ribbed tower. Four flags flew around him, one at each corner. One was Irish, the other three Continental or Scandiwegian.

A purple cloak was tied around the goat's shoulders by the two men, who soothed the animal and put down some food and water. King Puck turned his crowned head here and there, looking absurdly innocent and not at all Puckish. He had to struggle in the small space in order to lie down. Drops of rain fell from the sky, so the men fixed a protective white howdah roof over His Majesty, and then descended by ladder and trap door to the ground. Fifty feet aloft or more, the goat sat looking up at the sky. He was to remain in that attitude for two more days, a resigned Philosopher King.

'Puck is now declared King of the Fair! [Cheers] I now present Noel Tuohy and his Music, who will play for you while the step dancers get ready!'

Noel Tuohy, and a companion whom I suppose was Mrs Tuohy, ascended the ladder and sat on the middle platform with a large accordion and an electric keyboard apiece. After some test squeezes and wailings, Noel launched into a lilting ditty, 'The Galway Shawl'. His voice was melodious and easy on the ear, but he kept breaking off to announce a forthcoming line for the benefit of singers-along.

> She wore no jewels, nor costly diamonds,
> No paint or powder, no, none at all.
> [*Spoken*: She wore a bonnet!]
> She wo-ore a bonnet
> [With a ribbon on it!]
> With a ri-ibbon on it,
> And round her shou-oulders a Galway Shawl.

A genteel Coffee Shop adjoined the goat-tower. I sat inside, facing the window, and watched the rest of the proceedings in luxury. Others had the same idea, and soon the place was packed, the harassed waitresses struggling to and fro. School after school of step-dancing children, aged from seven to nine, took their places on the ground-floor platform outside, accompanied by teachers. Sometimes they wore green, sometimes white. Nearly all the girls had dresses embroidered and sometimes sequined with Book of Kell-tic designs. Noel Tuohy and his consort played jigs and reels, and the children capered like organized fairies, very prettily. Most of the dancers were girls, with proud mothers not far away. For some reason, all the girl dancers stood stock still at the beginning of each dance for ten seconds after the music started. They then leaped into action. What went through their minds during those crucial ten seconds?

All the little girls of Kerry must have been mustered for the fair, as dancing went on for hours, and was to continue for the next two days, the girls coming and going in relays. Noel Tuohy was kept busy. When he paused for a break, a loudspeaker-and-tape took over and bawled 'So we'll shout Hooray for the IRA!' almost in the stoical goat's ear. This was followed by 'The Old Triangle', the poignant song of Mountjoy Jail in Dublin.

I left the Coffee Shop, roamed around for a while, then entered a crowded, rowdy restaurant for my supper. A villainous-looking man with black bushy eyebrows sat opposite me, squinting at me in a disagreeable way. After a time, a clean-shaven fat-faced young man came and sat next to him.

'God, I hate the English!' growled the first man.

The second man nodded appreciatively at this remark, and then began to stare at me also. Finally he spoke. 'You're not eating the skins o' them boiled potatoes, are you?' he asked me.

'I certainly am,' I said, making short work of them.

'Don't you know them things are covered in poisonous sprays and chemicals? He's eaten the skins, look! He'll never see another Puck!'

Seeing that they had failed to frighten me, both men ate up and left, and a decent Dubliner sat down and told me that Ireland was growing more poor every day, thanks to unemployment. Even so, it seemed to me a richer country than the shabby Ireland I had seen in 1973.

It was dark when I stepped outside, and loudspeaker-music had replaced that of Noel Tuohy. Mangans' shop was still open, and in the dimly lit window I could see the old man serving customers. Someone pulled at my sleeve. It was the freckled boy, now without the pony Black Beauty.

'I sold him!' he said.

'Did you get your price?'

'I did.'

'Good man!' I said. 'Don't waste your money, now.'

To illustrate my meaning, I took out my sketch pad and drew a picture of a gullible farmer handing over all his money to a grasping tinker lady whose crystal ball lit up with the message 'Welcome, Sucker!'

Looking pleased, the boy pocketed the drawing and disappeared into the crowds. Don't do as I do, do as I say.

Inside the Kingdom, an accordion wheezed away and a group of enormous weatherbeaten farmers sang lustily. To my great joy, one of them sang the prince of Exile songs, 'Spancil Hill'.

Last night as I lay dreaming of pleasant days gone by,
My mind being bent on rambling, to Ireland I did fly.
... I thought I heard a murmur and I think I hear it still,
It's the little stream of water that flows down Spancil Hill.

I went to see my neighbours to see what they might say.
The old ones were all dead and gone, the young ones turning grey.
I met with Tailor Quigley, sure he's bold as ever still.
He used to mend my breeches when I lived at Spancil Hill.

... The cock he crew that morning, he crew both loud and shrill,
And I woke in California, many miles from Spancil Hill.

This song is often sung at fairs, and the narrator shows a fine sense of priorities when he awakes bitterly disappointed to be in the sunny El Dorado of California instead of Spancil Hill, wherever that may be.

Back at Oslan House, I had some difficulty in circumnavigating the tinker caravan in the darkened driveway, but at last I was safely in bed. It had been a long day.

Cow Day dawned with a chilly mist. Nevertheless, there was a fine mountainous view from my window. Three lines of Macgillycuddy's Reeks could be seen. The dark row of mountains in the foreground, their heads hidden in the lowering clouds, swept down and up again, the gaps filled by white mist in which other mountains could faintly be discerned. Beyond these could be seen ethereal mountains, castles in the air which belonged to a nebulous world where clouds could be mountains and mountains could be clouds.

At breakfast I told the young landlady that tinkers had lodged in the driveway, their dog tied to the Bed and Breakfast signpost. She looked alarmed, obviously afraid that if she spoke harshly to them, they might curse her. 'I don't like to cross them in any way, or be against them at all. The dog does no harm.'

On a gravel bank in the river, a heron hunched up its vulture shoulders and stood shivering in the rain. Up in the town, children were enjoying themselves with great gusto at the funfair and along the stalls, despite the weather. To my surprise, the cattle sale was being held in the street, in a long gloomy lane of hardware shops, grocery-bars and terraced houses that stretched away from the stalls of the fair. Dour, docile cows and oxen stood in clumps along the kerbside, each little herd watched over by a big farmer in cap, boots and a dirty green-brown coat. Few of the farmers had dogs, but most had sticks; their gale-ravaged faces were a study. Laconic, lugubrious or ludicrous, they stood in rows to be admired. Many were ribald, even leering, like wicked Toby jugs. Young farmers and child farmers wore the same uniform, their curly hair springing up and setting the cloth caps at a jaunty angle, their faces pink and innocent.

Now and again the cattle grew restless, and had to be shouted at, with much waving of sticks, but on the whole they were remarkably docile. A grey and white calf, frisking and twirling its tail, was a playful exception. Two patient grey donkeys were also offered for sale. Grocery-bars were full, and farmers and dealers were clearly drinking themselves to the point where a sale might be made over a glass and a handshake. Pavement, road and gutters ran with green cow ordure.

Round the corner, near the goat scaffolding, a lone heifer sat down calmly in the doorway of a jeweller's shop. Any minute, I expected to see a bull in a china shop. Some of the black or dun-coloured cattle were well on the way to being mature bulls, but they were as well behaved as the rest.

King Puck still sat on high, although his crown had vanished.

He was eating something, perhaps the crown itself. Noel Tuohy, beneath the throne, began to set up his Music equipment. Unusual music swirled from the Kingdom – an Irish under-arm bagpipes pumping away while an accordion player sang. Suddenly a farmer shouted, 'We don't want no more o' your Dublin songs, we're in Kerry now!' Seizing the microphone, he sang 'In the Dear Old Kerry Hills'.

That night, fairy lights lit up the scaffolding, and at the top of it the Goat King stood erect and proud, as if surveying his domain. Drunks weaved and swore around the stalls, the cattle had all gone but the farmers were still singing in the Kingdom. I reached Oslan House in safety.

My last full day in Killorglin was known as The Scattering, the day when the goat was dethroned, the stalls put up and taken down for the last time, and everyone went home. The weather had improved, and I stood amid a great crowd by the scaffolding, waiting to see King Puck lifted down. Hoarsely, the sound of singing wafted from the open door of the Kingdom, which had been open all night. Gamely, though worse for wear, the big farmers drank, threw their heads back and sang on, to an ever changing relay of musicians.

Noel Tuohy was soon on his platform seat, joggling his accordion on his knee, while middle-aged waltzing couples and uproarious ring-a-rosie Kerry dancers cut swathes through the crowd. There was a clattering sound, and Queen Kerry came running down the road, her cape flying behind her. With her ran the green-caped Lady-in-Waiting, flashing apologetic smiles at the crowd for being late. The Master of Ceremonies, the same man who had introduced the goat on the first day, had turned up again, and helped the two girls on to the stage. Meanwhile, a procession came up the street, consisting of emerald-clad boy scouts and the Canoe Club with a boat on a float.

Four able-bodied men were needed to bring King Puck down from his perch. Two ladders took them to the top, where they raised a tall wooden tripod above the goat-in-a-box. A rope and tackle were fixed to the tripod, and the howdah canopy was lifted from the goat and handed down to ground level. King Puck was then stripped of his cloak, and strapped into a harness which was also connected to the sides of the box. With a rope on the harness, he was swung down and placed on a green float, the back of a small lorry. With the Queen and the Lady-in-Waiting by his side, he drove away, followed by a line of scouts and canoe-clubbers.

'This is the first time in living memory that the goat has had no crown for the Queen to strip from him!' announced the MC. 'What has happened to the crown? Ladies and gentlemen, we don't know. Nineteen eighty eight will go down in history as the Year of the Missing Crown!'

Noel Tuohy packed up his Music and quietly left. As the procession moved away, a swarm of ragged tinker children leaped on to the stage and began to run round and round, climbing the scaffolding and triumphantly picking up cigarette ends.

Hurrying after the procession, I caught it up at the bridge over the river, where Queen Kerry and her Lady-in-Waiting jumped down and waved the others goodbye. Scouts and canoeists also dispersed, but the goat travelled on and was taken into a builder's yard on the outskirts of town. Standing at the gate, I watched as the goat in his box was lifted on to the ground. The four strapping young goat-lifters then made ready to go indoors. At that moment, two punky young English girls scampered up, shouting 'Coo-ee! It's us again!'

With smiles, the men asked them into the yard, and I discreetly followed. The girls made a great fuss of King Puck, a king who was surely very glad to abdicate.

'Oh, pooky, pooky, who's a good boy, izzums? Ah, look how poor pooky's tied up!'

To my surprise, the goat was shackled. Deep inside the box, invisible from the road, a tent peg had been fixed in each corner. Strong ropes were tied around the goat's hooves, and each hoof was tethered by a cord scarcely two inches long. No wonder the goat could only sit or stand. He could not turn around, much less run away. An untied sure-footed mountain goat would have been down that scaffolding before you could say 'Macgillycuddy'. But was he a real mountain goat, caught wild for the occasion?

Giving me suspicious looks, the men reappeared and lifted the goat-in-a-box into the back of a van. Squealing and giggling, the girls jumped in too.

'What are you going to do with the goat now?' I asked one of the men.

'Set him free in the mountains!' he answered shortly, and they all drove away.

Logically, by pagan rules, the goat king should now be roasted and eaten, but in my opinion he was either set free or returned to the farmyard from whence he was borrowed. Off went King Puck, most guileless of goats, and I never saw him again.

That night there was a dance in the village hall and spontaneous dancing in every pub in town. In the Kingdom, old men in heavy suits danced frenetic jigs, their unbuttoned jackets flapping up and down. At the fairground, the Big Wheel turned, and at the roast pig stall, business was brisk. Savouring every morsel of hot pork, apple sauce and stuffing, I walked down the hill to Oslan House and said goodnight to the glass-eyed weasel (or stoat) for the last time.

A blackberry lane led me out of Killorglin; I kept stopping to pick and eat the luscious berries as I hitchhiked fruitlessly but not berrylessly along my way. It was one of those strange Irish days when the sun shines brightly for half an hour, then the rain pours down and then the sun comes out. For much of the way, my road kept close to the River Laune and the tall mountains beyond. Cows grazed in meadows, and through a gap in the high-banked hedge, I could see the mellow stonework of Ballymalis Castle. A woman pulled up and offered me a lift, talking of her relatives in Kilburn, and before I knew where I was, there I was, in Killarney.

My train to Cork did not leave for two hours, so I went to the Beer Garden, where to my surprise I discovered a Transport Museum. I walked around looking at old cars and listening to a radio commentator shouting in great excitement as Larry Tompkins excelled himself on the Gaelic football field. I remembered having seen Tompkins at the Ross Carbery Carnival.

Crowds of French, Scandinavian and German youngsters were sitting on the ground beside their knapsacks at Killarney Station. A long train roared by on a far-off line, then backed into the station. We all climbed on board. The train seemed to be made of big, thick iron slabs painted orange. When it picked up speed through the thistly countryside, you could hear pieces falling off.

After spending the night at Cork, I set off for Dublin, where I spent a happy fortnight relaxing at O'Brien's Hotel in Lower Gardiner Street.

CHAPTER SEVEN

☘

Dublin Interlude

Roaming around Dublin one day, I came across Parnell Street, a long road of shabby second-hand shops, greasy take-away places and newsagents, that ended near the patriot statues of smart O'Connell Street. Mild, shabby people ambling to and fro matched the mood of the flyblown street. Yet leading off from Parnell Street were delightful rows of Georgian dwellings, with bow windows and spike-railed basement areas, just as at Islington in London. Like Islington in the 1950s, the old houses of Upper Gardiner Street, leafy Mountjoy Square and environs, did not know that they were aristocratic. Like princes and princesses stolen at birth and brought up by peasants, they had humble manners and they were the abodes of many humble people. Some of the houses, unfortunately, had been boarded up as 'slums', a very 1950s touch.

Mountjoy Square suggested Mountjoy Prison, where Brendan Behan and Kevin Barry had both briefly stayed. Further clues soon showed themselves. On one corner stood a pub named The Auld Triangle, the name of the song composed, or perhaps collected, at Mountjoy by Brendan. Another corner boasted a pub named The Big Tree, presumably the gallows tree on which Kevin Barry had lost his life in 1920.

Soon I came across toytown streets of red-brick cabin terraces, one door, one chimney and two windows apiece. Here there was a pleasant, relaxed atmosphere, and all the tiny houses were well kept. At the end of one row stood a Virgin statue with downcast eyes, alone in a grotto garden. Wherever poor people live in Ireland, delightful sights such as this may be seen. Emerging from a cabin avenue called Valencia Row, I saw on a signpost that I had reached the semi-mythical neighbourhood of Phibsborough.

Phibsborough was once the seat of the Phibbs family, whose most well-known modern representative is journalist and 'Conservative Activist' Harry Phibbs. The Phibbs family came to Ireland as soldiers of fortune in Elizabethan days, probably from Shropshire, and stayed to found Ascendancy dynasties. Harry's mother Antoinette is the Miss 'Tony' Kirkwood of *Woodbrook*, as described by David Thomson in his poignant book of that name.

David Thomson was a kind, lovable man with a thousand friends, and *Woodbrook* was a flawed masterpiece. However many of the Phibbs (and the Kirkwood) family think otherwise. A Phibbs has composed a ringing denunciatory poem addressed to Thomson. It begins 'Iscariot...'

There is little sign in Phibsborough today of the glory that was Phibbs, but it seems a pleasant neighbourhood. However, the most prominent building there is Mountjoy Prison. There is now no death penalty in Ireland, but the gallows on which Kevin Barry hung has been preserved as a shrine. Suddenly, from peering at cabin terraces, I found myself staring at a great grey and white building, of castellated design, with a portcullis-style doorway.

A driveway, with flower beds, led up to the main gate of Mountjoy. Now and again, a van drove through, with uniformed officers at each gatepost, and I caught a glimpse of an open yard and the great warehouse-like cell blocks with rows of Pentonville windows. Though large, it lacked an aura of tragedy, at least from the outside. Good men had doubtlessly been executed there once upon a time, but nowadays Mountjoy, with dubious characters such as myself hanging round the great door, evoked the lazy, resigned, cynical humour of criminals forced to spend a spell 'inside'.

Singing 'The Old Triangle' and 'Kevin Barry' softly to myself, I looked Mountjoy up and down, and wondered how the inmates were getting on. Thirty years ago, when I was devouring the works of Frank Norman and Brendan Behan, and singing 'Kevin Barry' at the top of my voice, I often pictured myself in a condemned cell about to be hung. The romance of execution has a great appeal for some young men, and Rebels Without Causes were fashionable then.

Since Mountjoy was one of the places where my dream-hanging took place, I gazed at the prison's solid walls, with a feeling akin to nostalgia. A small door within a giant door, like an Oxford college entrance, opened and women visitors with prams left unobtrusively. Then the main door opened to admit a minibus full of resigned cynical young lads. Officers in black uniforms held the doors back, and a barred portcullis closed on the hopes of the young people. Small houses for warders and their families adjoined the driveway. One of the entrance lodges was labelled '1896'.

Musingly, I retraced my steps to The Auld Triangle, where I popped in for a lemonade. It was an interesting pub, full of old-fashioned snugs and cubby holes, a maze of high settle benches and chairs. Until recently, according to the barman, it had been called The Four Seasons.

However, I couldn't stay long, and next spent an uncomfortable hour getting my heavy bag on to the bus for Wicklow Town. At last, with my usual feeling of mounting excitement, I gazed out on the sprawling suburbs of Dublin as the bus headed for the countryside. It was a countryside of ruined estates, broken demesne walls and tumbledown gateways. England is a country that supplies mansions and Anglican churches for the rest of the world to neglect or put to non-English purposes. The Wicklow Mountains had been plainly visible from the centre of Dublin. Close to, as seen from the bus, they were covered in forestry plantations. Past hills and cornfields, close to the coast, the Red Setter bus ran, until at last bus and I parted company outside the Wicklow Hotel.

CHAPTER EIGHT

Wicklow and Carlow

Wicklow Town, as glimpsed from the bus, seemed to consist of one long grey shopping street, with innumerable side streets leading to the countryside or the sea. My bag, a new one, full of Irish acquisitions, was so heavy that I couldn't search long for Bed and Breakfast. I settled instead for the grand Wicklow Hotel. A tall, gaunt red-brick hotel, standing apart from the row of shops, it had been modernized since the troubled days of 1920. In that year, the IRA had shot one of the hotel porters, William Doran, a family man, for the crime of being an ex-serviceman. Now the hotel boasted a conservatory-style dining room, with windows that looked out on to a rockery pool with fountain.

My bedroom had a fine view, for just across the way could be seen the broken towers and arches of a Franciscan friary. Surrounded by palm trees, they towered like crooked standing stones behind the high wall of a private garden. When I had unpacked, I set out to look at them.

According to a plaque on the high wall around the ruins, the friary had been founded by the Norman Fitzgeralds in the thirteenth century and used by Irish and Normans alike. Since its dissolution, it had been used as an armoury, a prison and a courthouse. After that it fell down.

On the seaward side of the main street, the town looked crumbling and desolate. A long stretch of inland water, Broad Lough, ran parallel to the beach. I crossed a bridge and found myself at the seaside. It was a warm summer evening, and I enjoyed a pleasant walk to the end of the jetty. Here, on a wall, a flock of swallows sat looking out to sea. Never before had I seen swallows sitting on a flat surface. However, they did not stay there long, but skimmed away on my approach and played with the waves, flicking their wings over the top of the breakers. A long black boat, like a motorized *curragh* (or Irish coracle), swept around the bay in a curve, the bow high out of the water. Three big men sat on board. After a while, the swallows returned, flitting past my bat-like ears and resuming their old seat on the wall.

Nearby, I found a mouldering harbour with derelict buildings around it, and another jetty. On a rocky headland, a dark ruined castle rose defiantly from the surroundings crags. I recrossed the Broad Lough, and met my friends the swallows again. This time they were sitting and twittering in rows along telephone wires that connected the slate rooftops of a narrow terraced cottage street. Africa was in their minds.

Near the green-domed Anglican church, I walked down a brambly lane where house martins swooped overhead, and emerged at the railway station. A path led beside the line to the lough and the sea once more, through a strange semi-industrial wilderness, with coarse grass, heaps of gravel, and the green dome of St Thomas's rising above the forest on the horizon. Mud flats at the loughside were picked at by curlews and sandpipers, wading birds who trod delicately, making arrow footprints.

Soon I was back at the dilapidated prom, where wheatears flew from rock to rock along a wall of rough boulders. What did wheatears sit on before men invented walls and fences? As dusk fell, the birds vanished. I walked along the harbour jetty, towards a lighthouse, where I could hear more birds twittering out at sea. A dark-haired girl stood staring out at the waters towards a rock with a cormorant on it. 'The salmon are jumping and skimming over the sea,' she said.

In the morning, I awoke to find Wicklow enshrouded by fog. Hills far away were half hidden by black fog, those nearer by white. Over the sea, where the swallows had been, bright sunlight pierced the clouds and the sea changed from deep green to sky blue, then experimented with brown and purple.

I walked into the narrow shopping street, and soon encountered a white wall ornamented by the message, in huge black letters, ACAB. Four scowling youths, also in black, leaned against the wall beside the letters as if posing for a photograph. More usually seen tattooed on the knuckles of someone who is hitting you, the letters

ACAB stand for 'All Coppers Are Bastards'. Round the ACAB corner stood the Unemployment Office.

These youth apart, the people of Wicklow, shoppers and shopkeepers alike, were friendly and courteous. In a wide-open space, on top of a small hill, stood a gigantic pinnacled Roman Catholic church, with a primary school by its side. Outside the church, a statue of Jesus was dwarfed by a greater statue of His mother wearing a crown. I gazed up at her goodness and beauty appreciatively, remembering a quotation from Nathaniel Hawthorne given to me by Joan Barry of the Legion of Mary.

> I have always envied the Catholics in that sweet sacred Virgin Mary who stands between them and the Deity, intercepting somewhat of His awesome splendour but permitting His love to stream on the worshipper more intelligibly to human comprehension through the medium of a woman's tenderness.

Strangely framed by white fog, the Catholic church of Wicklow seemed to stand at the very edge of the world.

'Can I have a look around the school?' I asked a young teacher in jeans.

She told me to return at two o'clock, so I rejoined the shopping street and found, on another corner, a huge deserted prison tightly enclosed by a high stone wall. A small public library had been built against this wall.

'There used to be another prison beside that one where the prisoners of 1798 were kept,' the librarian told me, with a sharp look to see if the martyr's year of '98 meant anything to an Englishman. 'But it's been pulled down now.'

At the end of the town, behind grim terraced houses, a cargo ship was anchored in the gloomy docks. With clatters and roars, excavator-trucks were busily scooping up golden sand from an immense heap and loading it on to a perpetual conveyor belt that dumped it into the ship's hold. On the other side of the quay, mountains of Swedish planks had been stacked.

Through lightly spitting rain, I walked across a field where goats were tethered, along a footpath that led to the offshore castle on its craggy peninsula. An archaeologist might have described it as 'a promontory fort'. Roughly hewn steps led up and down the gap where the drawbridge might have been. According to legend, St

Patrick had landed on the beach near here, on the first of his missionary journeys.

I scrambled over the boulders into the grassy castle keep, where jackdaws wheeled around, shouting 'Jack!' and staring at me with mad pale blue eyes. Broken towers and ramparts, none very high, lay all around. A plaque told me that the castle had been built by the Fitzgeralds, under the direction of Strongbow, Norman conqueror of part of Ireland. Medieval England, under the Normans, owned a large chunk of Ireland around Dublin known as the Pale. Wicklow Castle had marked the southernmost limit of the Pale. 'Beyond the Pale', according to the Englishmen who coined the phrase, were the barbarians.

At Wicklow, the barbarians were the O'Byrnes, led by ferocious chieftains who had stormed the castle many a time, and cut many an English or Norman throat. The surname Byrne is still common in Wicklow. In 1500, after many rebuildings, the castle had been allowed to fall into ruin.

When I finally returned to the school and Catholic church, I found children everywhere, for the lunch break had not quite ended. There were no school dinners, and the pupils went home or brought sandwiches. Big boys soared around the Virgin Mary on skateboards. Two little girls took a tiny white puppy into the church. Solemnly, they prayed first before a figure of Our Lady and then before a figure of Our Lord, all the while keeping a careful eye on the puppy, which kept trying to run away.

Soon it was time for me to go to school. Cheerful boys, aged from five to eleven, played boisterously outside the long, low modern RC school, St Patrick's Primary. There were no girls in this school. That would not have suited *me*, for I was far more romantic as a seven-year-old than I have ever been since. All the boys wore crimson jerseys, the school uniform. A boy showed me to the headmaster's room. On the way, I paused to admire a case of faded stuffed birds, obviously quite old.

'Come in!' a mild, benign voice called out in answer to my knock.

Soon I was shaking hands with a gentle, elderly priest in a black robe with two white cards joined to his dog collar. Bald, beaming and bespectacled, he was the complete opposite of the roaring ogre-like headmaster of my romantic days. As in America, the Head was called 'the Principal'. Showing me to a seat in his small cluttered study, he told me a little about the school and education in Ireland.

'This school, and the college for older boys, is run by the De La Salle Christian Brothers. Most schools for boys in Ireland, apart from private schools, are run by the Christian Brothers, the girls by the Sisters of Mercy. Usually, girls and boys are taught separately.'

'Are most of the teachers here monks?' I asked.

'No, no. Once they would have been, but now almost all the teachers are lay people. The schools are free, but parents have to buy the books. Now, let me show you the new extension to the Infants.'

The Head led me along a corridor decorated with holy pictures to a classroom. 'This class is Religion, and the boys are nine years old,' he said, as he knocked and entered.

A fiery, forceful and freckled young lady teacher was writing in Irish on the blackboard. The Head proudly told me that she came from a Gaelic-speaking family in the West of Ireland.

'This gentleman is here to write a book about our school,' the Head introduced me. 'Let us greet him in song. All stand.'

All stood, while the dear old curly-bald Headmaster conducted with both hands and led the singing in a pleasing tenor.

> Let's all sing together, together, together,
> Let's all sing together, wherever we may be.

He then gestured towards me, and I found that I was expected to address the class.

'I'm very pleased to meet you all, and I'm very glad you're studying Religion,' I said. 'Can anyone tell me the story of Jonah and the Whale?'

All the boys looked mystified.

'No? Well, does anyone know the story of Noah and the Ark?'

After a long silence, a tousle-haired boy put up his hand and gave a garbled account of the legend. Everyone else looked at him in amazement. The Head looked stricken, and with a guilty pang I remembered that I was in a Roman Catholic country where the Bible was not considered to be important. Doubtless the boys knew legends of the saints, but as I didn't, there wasn't much I could say. Legends and folk tales, which to the heartless scientific mind are errors and untruths, are as important in imparting Christian belief as they are in teaching history (Alfred and the cakes, Bruce and the spider, and so on). They contain the spirit of the subject, and give the child a rung to climb on, upwards to mature faith or historical knowledge.

Before I could say another word, the freckled teacher rushed towards me and began to shout earnestly: 'It's disgraceful! Disgraceful! There's thirty-eight children in this class! Thirty-eight! How can I be expected to teach them properly? It crushes their individuality! There's no individuality about any of these children!'

'Oh dear!' I said, noting that the mortified Headmaster had fled the room altogether. I wanted to please one of the boys by putting his name in this book. 'Who is the star pupil in this class?'

'We don't believe in competition here!'

Saved by the bell! The lesson ended, and as the Head was nowhere to be found, the freckled teacher from the West kindly took me to a class of twelve-year-old boys. They were studying Geography under a Mr Murphy, a big friendly boyish man with glasses.

Here I did much better, lecturing the class about cowboys I had seen in Texas. In perfect discipline, the boys put up their hands and asked intelligent questions about lariats and six-shooters. Star pupil: David Maher.

When the lesson was over, I found that the Headmaster had materialized once more. He was full of apologies.

'Look, there are many Biblical posters on the walls,' he said. 'Children learn the Bible in church, not here. Here, Religion means learning to be kind and to help one another. That boy who knew about Noah's Ark is not the cleverest boy in the class at all. He's from a Remedial class, and he's a very poor scholar in natural lessons. Clever children are shy, and don't put their hands up like brash children. In this country, we have a different attitude to Education than they do in England. In England they say "Here is the subject, we must teach it," but in Ireland we say, "Here is the child, we must let it learn." We believe children should be happy.'

Just as we were shaking hands in farewell, the Head saw me looking at the glass case full of birds. 'That case has been with us since we were founded in 1919,' he said. 'It's been carried from building to building through the school's history.'

'That's a fine example of a boat-bill heron,' I remarked.

'What! You know the birds' names? People always ask us, and we know none of them. Now you can do *us* a good turn! Wait while I fetch pencil and paper! Once we know the names, we can have labels made.'

Feeling very much the good boy of the class, I reeled off bird names. Eagerly, the Headmaster wrote them down. I left school in a glow of pleasure and star pupil conceit.

By now the fog had lifted and the sun was shining brightly. At the Wicklow Hotel, I asked the Receptionist to phone for a taxi, as I wished to see the remains of an ancient religious city founded by St Kevin in the sixth century – Glendalough.

Over a hasty snack, I scanned the literature given to me by the Head. Obviously, Irish education had changed completely since the days when not-very-Christian Brothers and Sisters of little Mercy had tormented children by physical and psychological punishments, recorded in myriad autobiographies. Nowadays, Brothers, Sisters and most lay teachers seemed to drip with the milk of human kindness. Boys and girls, I gathered, now received a gentle, woolly but not intellectually vigorous education.

> Parents of young boys seventy-five years ago [I read] would never have heard of television and computers, space shuttles and cassette recorders, let alone rock bands and drugs... All of these are now commonplace, and expected and even demanded by young people.
>
> Second year at school... Their study of number will extend gradually to ten... Shopping experiences will be extended in line with the children's competence in the field of number.

Mind you, schools and teachers in England are scarcely more sensible than this. My seven-year-old nephew's teacher wrote the following sum in his book: 'I buy five packets of crips, and give away two. How many have I got left?' 'Crips' was the teacher's way of spelling 'crisps'. My nephew wrote 'Four crips left' as his answer, and received a tick and the comment 'Well done!'

Mr Dolan the taxi driver interrupted my reverie. He was a garrulous red-faced man with white tufty hair. To my surprise, he led me not to a car but to a blue minibus full of children. 'So we meet again!' one of the small boys from the Religion class announced boldly.

I squeezed in beside rows of freckled young girls of nine, with glowing blue eyes and names like Siobhan, Eileen and Tara. They screamed and held their eyes when it seemed likely that a small dog would get run over, but the animal escaped. Soon all the children had been delivered except a little girl who devoutly crossed herself whenever Mr Dolan passed a chapel. She lived in a pink manor-like farmhouse at the head of a drive. With a wave she was gone, and Mr Dolan headed for Glendalough.

'I used to be a coach driver in Somerset,' he informed me. 'Ah, now that was a good job, that was. You see all these forestry plantations? In poor times, people would sell their land to the Forestry. Now they wish they could have it back.'

We drove over the hills to Glenealy, then to Rathdrum and down into the beautiful Vale of Clara, below the Wicklow Mountains. At one village, Mr Dolan drove up and down the main street to show me how neat and tidy it was. 'We Irish are a very houseproud people,' he said with satisfaction. 'This is a very good country to live in, if you have work.'

Finally we dived down through dark woods and came to rest beside steps leading towards two grey archways, one behind the other. Before we parted, I took Mr Dolan's business card and asked him to call for me at the Wicklow Hotel next day and take me to Carlow. On my own once more, I climbed the magic steps, walked through the two archways and entered Glendalough.

I found myself in a strange flowerless garden, where yew trees grew amid rockeries of ancient masonry, a broken wall here, an incomplete arch there, with paths and steps winding up and around, and a great pointy-topped Round Tower reaching for the sky. This Round Tower dominated the monastery gardens, and could be seen from miles around. Round Towers were made as refuges from Viking attacks during the Dark Ages. Like tall factory chimneys made of blocks of stone, or giant sharpened pencils standing up-ended, they always have an open door, resembling a window, fairly high up. Often the Round Tower was also a bell tower. According to legend, the monks (who would have attracted the Christ-hating Vikings' wrath) would climb a ladder into the belfry or upper storey, and then pull the ladder in after them and wait till the raid was over, like Londoners sheltering from the Blitz. Why the Vikings didn't knock a hole in the base of such towers, light fires and cook the monks alive is not known. Perhaps they didn't think of it.

Ireland is famous for such towers, and Glendalough has two. The second one poked through the roof of a small empty chapel known as St Kevin's Kitchen, perhaps because it resembled a bakehouse with the bell tower as the chimney. Glendalough's main tower, standing alone, slender as a wand, was most impressive.

'Glendalough' means 'The Glen of two loughs' (or lakes), and this was where St Kevin had first settled as a hermit, some time in the mid to late sixth century. The two lakes lay further along the valley, and according to Mr Dolan, the saint had a hollow cut away from the side of the mountain, facing a lake. This was known as St Kevin's Bed. Ardent young disciples came to learn wisdom at St Kevin's feet, and a monastic community arose. Stone beehive huts gave way to square stone dwellings and a church. After St Kevin died, in AD 618, the monastery was moved to a more sheltered spot, the place of the Round Tower which I was now exploring. A cathedral had been built, now roofless, and various alms buildings for the poor.

By the eighth century, a holy city, Ireland's lost contribution to civilization, had arisen. Vikings, who founded Ireland's present mercantile cities as places in which to divide their loot, attacked and burned the holy city, which they approached from the river valleys; and wild Irish tribesmen swept down from the mountains, also burning and looting. Patiently the monks restored and rebuilt. The 'wild Irish' of the mountains belonged to the Clan O'Toole. By the twelfth century an O'Toole had been ordained Abbot of the Glen, and he made many improvements to Glendalough. Norman soldiers became the new menace to the city, and their final raid in the year 1398 put paid to the glory of Glendalough. It has been a ruin ever since.

Although the Irish cheerfully use stones, bricks and tiles from ruined Ascendancy mansions for their own purposes to this day, holy sites for them always remain holy. The very soil is sacred, and ruined monasteries nearly always become graveyards. Sometimes against official opposition, people bury their loved ones there, where the deceased can enjoy the company of saints who may lift them up to Heaven. So it was here at Glendalough, and it was impossible to tell which of the many crosses dated from monastic times and which were relatively modern. Graves on the cathedral floor dated from the eighteenth century. One person had died aged 102, another 106. Modern graves, with bright plastic flowers in bubbles of cellophane, adorned the walkways and shrubberies outside. Pleasant-faced family parties walked admiringly around, greeting one another beneath the Romanesque archways and Celtic crosses of the unusual gardens.

As I intended to hitchhike to Wicklow, I was fearful of darkness, and decided to walk quickly to the lakes along the motor road. Savouring every moment in this enchanted place, I gazed at the grey roofs, towers and ragged walls, which, though grand, were dwarfed by the magnificent Wicklow Mountains that loomed high above the glen on every side. Soaring to spiky peaks or rounded hill tops, their flanks were clothed with black conifers or romantic greenwood of oak, ash and beech.

At the base of the Round Tower I gazed upwards at the clouds drifting past the pinnacle, and wondered how stone could be cut and fitted on to stone to make a tower so rounded. Modern graves nearby had logs placed round them as markers. A family called Cullen had headstone dates beginning in 1860 and continuing up to 1986. The tower, like the unique double archway at the garden entrance, dated from the tenth century. Curiously enough, it had *three* openings, one perilously near the ground.

Worship among the ruins continued until the Penal Days of the early eighteenth century. In 1714, the High Sheriff received information that Catholics were gathering at Glendalough for 'superstitious worship to St Kevin'. Soldiers broke up the meeting, scattered the worshippers and pulled down crosses. Fortunately, tall St Kevin's Cross, under which the saint is said to lie, still remains upright. O'Toole, a Popish schoolmaster, was arrested. Later, sporadic services resumed, the last one recorded being in 1810.

For the last time, with many respectful backward glances, I left the monastery garden by the double archway and walked along the road, beneath chestnut trees, towards the lakes. First of all I passed a long marshy lake lying close to the mountainside. Then I reached the magnificent Upper Lake, whose shores had been spruced up for visitors, with shaven lawns, a driveway and small car park. However, St Kevin's Bed, the cave on the mountainside, had been closed to the public.

By the grey pebbles of the lakeside, I stood and marvelled. A heron flapped lazily across the blue lake, a lake hemmed in by hills and mountains whose flanks swept down to the lapping water itself. Strangely shaped crags seemed to rise from the lake, clothed in thick oak and beech forest, although seemingly too steep to retain earth. Brown hills, cut away so the lake (or a glacier) could pass, wore scraggy crowns of dead white pine stems, just as I had seen in the Canary Islands. Further down, the same hills wore sleek black conifers like soft mink wraps. On the furthest shore of the lake, directly in front of me, a sugar loaf hill reclined among pointy peaks. (Incidentally, has anyone now alive ever seen a sugar loaf, a large saccharine loaf-size lump from which the grains of sugar were scraped in olden times?)

Already the sky was aglow, in readiness for dark, the lake reflecting the molten gold. Unable to leave a spot of such beauty, I followed a path into the oak woods, where water from a hidden spring trickled down over the boulders. Soon I found the levelled walls of Rhefeart Church. Back at the lakeside, the remains of beehive oratory huts could be seen. Here St Kevin would have walked and worshipped. Known as 'the burial place of the kings', Rhefeart is said to have grown from St Kevin's original oratory, and to be the oldest church in Glendalough.

A few drops of soft rain cooled my head, and I hurriedly retraced my steps to the place where I had left Mr Dolan. The great Round Tower suddenly became visible among lush lakeside pastures. To my surprise, a coach with driver stood by the roadside.

'Hop in!' said the driver. 'I'm going back to Dublin, but I'll drop you off at Anna Moe near Wicklow.'

Through unfamiliar wild woods the coach sped, and below a bare brown mountain. Finally I was put down in a forest beyond Anna Moe and told to take the road through the trees.

It was still light enough to see, the evening breezes caressed my two tufts of hair and I felt carefree as I jogged along. I passed an old farmhouse by the side of the road. A mock-Gothic castellated doorway had been added to the old house, a grandiose touch somewhat nullified by the corrugated iron roof painted scarlet. With a creak the front door opened and an old man, in cloth cap, boots and weskit, emerged and gave me a nod. Opening two gates, he herded his Friesian cows across the road to pastures new, guiding them with loud hummed shrieks, his mouth tightly closed.

A little further on I came to a prosperous farm, with cattle grazing, set on a rise not far from the lane where I was sauntering. Mature trees led in an avenue to nowhere, probably the place where an Ascendancy house had been. Another path led to the bungalow where the farmer lived.

Suddenly, without any warning, a huge yellow flash of lightning ripped across the blue sky in front of me. It was followed by a roar of thunder, and all the farmer's cattle stampeded with their tails up. As my way ahead led through wilderness, I decided to seek sanctuary and ran to the bungalow.

A young lady answered my knock, and politely saw me into the front room while she phoned for Mr Dolan. I greeted an elderly man, the farmer himself, and sat down. He was a big man, with a face heavily lined about the jowls, and a genial yet serious air. Putting down his newspaper, he began to cut a block of tobacco and put the pieces in his pipe. Meanwhile, I could hear the girl earnestly assuring the Dolans that a former passenger of theirs was stranded.

'That's my granddaughter,' the farmer proudly informed me. 'She's a clever girl, she's always winning cups for sprinting. Last year she won the Queen of the Festival trophy. That's it, on the mantelpiece, made of Connemara marble. Been to see Glen*dal*lock, have you? Now that's an interesting place. Kevin had a stone bed on the mountainside, though I've never seen it. There's a hole leads from his cave down into the lake. Now one day the saint comes home and there's this woman, Kathleen, looking for him. He never cared for women, not at all, so he hid and watched her. Finally she looked down the hole, so he crept behind, gave her a shove and she fell down into the lake and drowned! So he was rid of her.'

'I don't call that much of a saint!' I said indignantly. 'I'm a better saint than that, and *I'm* no good.'

He seemed amused by this response. I declined tea, as the taxi was coming. Outside, no mighty storm but thick darkness fell. Someone knocked at the door. To my surprise, it was *Mrs* Dolan, whom I had never met before.

'I'm sorry I didn't come before, but I thought it might be a hoax,' she said. 'We get hoax calls that take us out to lonely spots like this.'

Mrs Sadie Dolan drove me through the woods in the rain, and told me of the awful times Wicklow had suffered a year or so earlier, when Hurricane Charlie had paid a visit. She and her husband had been called out to rescue people stranded by floods and could not reach them for the fallen trees.

Back in my room at the Wicklow Hotel, I leafed through a guide book I had bought at Glendalough. It listed many charming legends once told about St Kevin, concerning wild geese, a Glenda-Lough monster, blackbirds, wild boars, ravens, skylarks and an otter which retrieved a book he had dropped into the lake. Tactfully, the writer phrased the legends in a way that would not offend believers. Yet in all my Irish travels-to-be, the one legend told to me again and again was that St Kevin had drowned a lady who had been pursuing him amorously. This the guide book angrily refuted. St Kevin did not drown the lady at all, it firmly stated, but merely beat her up with a bunch of stinging nettles. The guide book went on to say that the saint's 'Bed' had recently been found to be of prehistoric pagan origin. Perhaps the saint took up abode there to defy paganism, the writer suggested. I wondered if human sacrifices to the Lake Spirit had once occurred there, and been confused in the folk mind with the later incumbent, St Kevin. Surely a monastery of such beauty could not have been founded by a misanthropic murderer!

What does the ballad say?

> In Glendalough there lived an old saint,
> Renowned for his learning and piety.
> His manners were curious and quaint,
> And he looked upon girls with disparity.
>
> The saint he was fishing one day,
> A-catching some kind of a trout, Sir,
> When Kathleen from over the way
> Came to see what the saint was about, Sir.
>
> 'You're a mighty fine fisher,' says Kate.
> ''Tis yourself is the boy that can hook them.
> But when you have caught them so neat,
> Don't you want some young woman to cook them?'
>
> 'Be gone out of that,' said the saint,
> 'For I am a man of great piety.
> Me character I wouldn't taint
> By mixing with female society.'
>
> But Kathleen wasn't going to give in,
> For when he got home to his rockery
> He found her sitting therein,
> A-polishing up all his crockery.

He gave the poor creature a shake,
Oh, I wish that the peelers had caught him!
He threw her right into the lake
And she sank like a stone to the bottom!'

'Fish! Fish!' shouted raw-faced fourteen-year-old boys in Wicklow High Street next day, selling black-eyed codfish from a wooden box on the middle of the pavement. Mr Dolan drove up, I collected my bag and we were off to Carlow, county town of County Carlow, a very small county indeed. My journey from Dublin so far had been directly southward. Now we would be veering south-westerly away from the sea.

It was a sunny day, and after driving though idyllic scenery, Mr Dolan stopped at a bridge, near a new and particularly hideous Craft Shop. 'This is a famous place, so it is, the Meeting of the Waters, where three rivers join. There was a poet wrote a song about the place. You might like to get out and take a look,' he explained.

White concrete steps and walkways cut swathes through the grassy river bank, where the Avonbeg and Avonmore rivers were supposed to join the River Avoca. Beyond the rushes, amid tangled woodland, a flowing stream bubbled its way into a larger river, the Craft Shop looming over all. Beside the bridge, a concrete tablet displayed a few lines of Thomas Moore, the Drawing Room Bard, author of 'Believe Me, If All These Endearing Young Charms' and (more pertinently) 'The Meeting of the Waters'.

There is not in the wide world a valley so sweet
As the vale in whose bosom the high waters meet;
Oh, the last rays of feeling and life must depart
Ere the bloom of that valley shall fade from my heart...

Sweet vale of Avoca, how calm could I rest
In the bosom of shade with the friends I love best,
Where the storms that we feel in this cold world should cease,
And our hearts, like thy waters, be mingled in peace.

It is just as well that Thomas Moore never knew his verses would spoil the place he was versifying about, or he would not have written them in the first place.

A man, showing his wife the place where he used to play as a boy, stared around in surprise. 'When I knew this place, they didn't have all this concrete!' he exclaimed.

Meanwhile, a coach full of tourists with cameras pulled up, and Mr Dolan struck up such a strong friendship with the driver that I thought I would never get away. However, we finally set off once more, Mr Dolan's accent growing ever stronger, so that I had to concentrate hard in order to understand him. We drove through the village of Shillelagh, but he firmly assured me that the place had no connection with shillelagh clubs.

'There is a pub near here, mind that's just a wee stone house all out on its own, and every night the owners go up a ladder into the loft above the bar, where the beds are. They bring the takings up to bed with them in a bag, and pull the ladder up after them. Nothing's ever been done to that pub since it was made. There was a Swede near here heard about it, and told his landlady he'd like to go there.

'"You'll never get in there without a dress suit," she said, playing a trick on him.

'So he believed her, and hired a dress suit with a top hat and all. It was me he hired to drive him there. When I saw how he was dressed, I cautiously remarked on it; I heard his explanation, but I said nothing. Everyone else in the pub had cloth caps on, d'ye see? The Swede got served, but he felt uncomfortable, and complained afterwards to the landlady, only she wouldn't stop laughing.'

We drove into the sprawling, unlovely environs of Carlow Town, below a bridge and up to a railway station. On a neat suburban house, I saw a Bed and Breakfast sign, and told Mr Dolan to stop. We parted with many civilities, and he headed rapidly back to Wicklow for the school minibus run.

A polite soft-spoken young housewife showed me to a pleasant bedroom with a net curtain view out on to school playing fields. Several modern schools with large playgrounds stood side by side. I unpacked and set out to explore.

Once I had got clear of the suburbs and newly widened roads, I found Carlow to be a delightful old grey town of narrow slate-roofed shopping streets and terraced houses, beside an unsung Meeting of the Waters, the wide rivers of Burren and Barrow. There was something faintly mournful about the place, but it was soothing and interesting, like Carmarthen in Wales with a touch of Cardigan thrown in. The shops were very bustling. Most of them were small, but there was also a modern shopping centre. I found a bank in the Old Potato Market and drew out some money. Now that I knew that Irish parents had to buy all their own school books, I realized why there were so many bookshops in Carlow and other Irish towns.

Irish history, as taught in secondary schools, seemed to leave something to be desired, judging by the books I glanced at. Some of these were in cartoon form, each episode introduced by a comic man in a bow tie, whose face registered Manic Glee or Heavy Gloom, depending on whether the news was good or bad. Balloon-speech emerged from the mouths of cartoon historical characters. Irish and English history were mixed, a bit of one and then a bit of another, with no great anti-English bias. Karl Marx and Lenin were introduced as great heroes. France did not exist, apparently, until her Revolution suddenly showed her to be of fit stuff to stand with Irish history. Russia, too, lay invisibly dormant until *her* Revolution. Each chapter ended with question and answer boxes to tick. Where history is still taught in English state schools, books far worse than these are doubtlessly used. Thanks to the buy-your-own-books rule, Irish education was on display for all to see.

Marvelling at all I saw, I drifted from shop to shop. Outside the Allied Bank stood a naïve statue, not very old, showing a man and a woman each riding on a pike, the fish glaring horribly. The little man held a stumpy arm aloft, his fist where his elbow ought to have been. Behind the new shopping centre, where much of Old Carlow seemed to have been flattened for car parks, I saw the broken towers of a Norman castle in the distance. I browsed on until I came to the Catholic cathedral, standing in a wide open space. Built in 1833, it was an extraordinary grey building of turrets and towers, like a spiky castle in an Arthur Rackham picture. A large white statue of Mary, Queen of Heaven, stood above the front entrance. I stood in the entrance hall and listened to the priest's kind, melodious and thoughtful voice, as he addressed a vast congregation. Soft lights from a stained-glass window cast gentle patterns on a column. 'Whatever cares you may have, turn to Mary, for she will not fail you. Today we are asking Mary to ask for us . . .

Continuing on my way, I crossed into another shopping street, and came to the public library, the former Assembly Rooms, once owned by Bernard Shaw. Many curious little shops, alleyways and terraced cottages later, I emerged from a narrow street to see the gigantic courthouse, like a Greek temple taken over by the military. It stood in its own park, and many rooms seemed to be unoccupied. This courthouse shouted 'British power' so loudly that I was surprised not to see the Union flag still flying. Pikes of a different kind could now be seen, as the railings around the courthouse had been made in the form of these weapons. A cannon from the Crimea guarded the doorway.

I heard later that the plans for the eighteenth-century courthouse had been mixed up with those intended for the city of Cork. Carlow had Cork's gigantic city courthouse, while poor Cork had to make do with Carlow's smaller courthouse. Similar mix-ups must have happened when standardized Norman rule was imposed on Saxon Britain.

Early in the nineteenth century, an English traveller had been surprised to see decayed heads impaled on spikes outside Carlow courthouse. They belonged to the rebels of 1798, and had stood sentinel since that fatal year. By moonlight, they created a strange and eerie impression on all who saw them. In that rebel year of '98, both French revolutionary ideas and actual French revolutionaries swept over Ireland. The common people, who wanted the true freedom to indulge in Roman Catholic worship, did not always see eye-to-eye with their Frenchified leaders. Anti-clericism, part of the French revolutionary package deal, was precisely the oppression the Irish wanted to be *rid* of. Their Protestant rulers were often as anti-priest as any French revolutionary. Nevertheless, peasantry rose everywhere, fought guns with pitchforks and lost their heads to the axe and not to the guillotine.

In the *late* nineteenth century, English officers and explorers in West Africa had been shocked to find the kraal-like courts of some African kings to be decorated by human heads swaying in rows upon spiked branches. Sir Harry Johnston, the artist-explorer-administrator, carefully sketched African impaled skulls to show his critics in England the kind of barbarians he was dealing with. Yet only eighty years earlier, rows of skulls with tufts of hair and gaping sockets had stood impaled in rows in Irish towns, placed there by officers of English descent. Barbarism and civilization sometimes walk hand in hand. Carlow Town, now so peaceful, had been the scene of fighting and massacre in '98.

Earlier on, near my Bed and Breakfast, I had seen a road sign that pointed out of town towards a dolmen. A dolmen is a prehistoric grave, formed by raising a huge flat boulder above several smaller ones, like a giant lop-sided table, and then covering all with earth and grass, to make a hollowed-out tomb. Usually a chief or someone important was placed inside, with a few belongings. Nowadays the dust of the Bronze Age chiefs has flown, the earth covering has blown away and the bare stones of dolmens stand in the middle of moors and fields for all to see.

Off I set after the dolmen, and walked and walked. It was a *very* long way out of town until houses began to be replaced by fields. At one corner I read these words, deeply etched into the stone wall: 'Here We Meet. Pal's Corner.' No pals could be seen.

Half an hour later, I came to a farm where a black mule grazed. It hated me on sight, and advanced braying with ears erect. Luckily a fence stood between us. On the other side of the road, a tall demesne wall of a long-broken-up Ascendancy estate blotted out the view. Finally, to my relief, I espied the dolmen in a field. The footpath leading up to it, and the dolmen itself, were enclosed by wire netting. This was unsightly, but held the farmer's cows at bay. By now, the sun had begun to set, and this increased the sense of mystery there.

Three tall upright stones supported a gigantic boulder which leaned heavily on them, pressing them into the ground. A fourth stone stood apart, looking on. One side of the boulder rested on the ground, the other reared blindly to the sky. It seemed as if the underside of the boulder had been hollowed out, perhaps by human hands. Until the stones had become a Site of Historic Interest, stories must have been told about them, how they moved or danced or were people turned to stone, with a special role for the lone magician or musician who stood aside from the rest.

Standing as far away as the wire mesh allowed, I gazed at the stones and the streaks of yellow in the darkening sky behind them. Sadness, melancholy and a mournful sense of loss hung over them. Words like Dolmen and Site of Historic Interest had obscured the fact that I was looking at a grave.

How cosy and merry did Carlow Town seem after my sepulchral excursion! It was a warm twilit evening, lights shone in bar windows and accordions played within. I set out in search of the castle, and found it at last by the river. I stood on the bridge and gazed out at two castle towers, on facing banks of the Barrow. The nearest and most eerily misshapen tower was adorned with luminous statues. No road led towards it, but at last, in the darkness, I found an archway entrance to an alley that opened into a builder's yard. Towers loomed above the yard wall, and I saw that the shining 'statues' were actually human-shaped windows, broken at odd angles, with the last light of day shining through them. There was no roof and no sign of rooms in the castle. It grew too dark to see, so I returned to my room, tiptoeing upstairs past rooms where cheerful laughter told of a contented family.

At breakfast next day, I admired the framed jigsaw over the fireplace, said 'hello' to the jolly schoolgirls of the house, and then left for the riverbank to see Carlow Castle by daylight.

I had a surprise when I did so, for the 'castle tower' on the far bank of the river proved to be a huge disused mill, about a hundred years old, with a faded sign 'Animal Feeds' on the wall. I walked along the tow path below the mill, where the River Burren met the Barrow, in a dramatic Meeting of the Waters. The introduction of one river to another was effected smoothly by the means of a long slanting weir that crossed the wide expanse of water and once, no doubt, helped to turn a mill wheel. Having admired the turbulent waters, I returned to the archway and alley to have another look at the castle.

Castle, yard, archway and alley all seemed to be owned by Corcoran's, the fizzy drink people, a sleepy old firm whose minions took no notice as I trespassed here and there. The Normans, when they settled at Carlow, built the castle on the site of an Iron Age fort to protect themselves from the ravages of the Kavanaghs, kings of Leinster. Dublin, Carlow, Wicklow and Wexford are all part of the ancient Province of Leinster. Today the Kavanaghs are not kings but poets, and their works are well worth reading. Cromwell's men destroyed Carlow Castle as a fort, but it remained a respectable ruin until the nineteenth century.

On one evil day in that time, so I later learned, a doctor bought the castle and decided to convert it into a lunatic asylum. He decided to thin the walls down a bit, and enlarge the windows. Amassing an enormous heap of dynamite, he placed it inside the castle, lit the fuses, and stood a long way away with his fingers in his ears, like a cartoon character. There was a terrible explosion, and the whole castle fell to bits! There was not enough left for a lunatic asylum, so the good doctor sadly and slowly put on his top hat, picked up his doctor's bag and quietly left the town. Many of the charges had been placed beside the windows, which explained the odd shapes of the latter, shapes I had piously mistaken for the gleaming statues of saints.

Around the bridge and the castle, among whitewashed cottages, Carlow seemed to be at its best. Cloth-capped old men yarned together on seats or leaned against bridge parapets. Inside an old pub, a young mother fed her baby on spoonfuls of ice cream. At the back of a sweet shop, a dark room with rickety tables did duty as a café, and I had an enjoyable lunch of (to quote the menu) 'Roast Beef and Accompaniments'.

'Now, so! Apple tart, is it?' asked the waitress, when I had finished.

It was. Diners called to one another across the tables. 'There does be a big crowd at the market today.' 'Ah, it is you, Patrick, is it not? I didn't see you there.' 'Did you not? You didn't see me till you looked.'

After listening to such pleasantries for a while, I set out to walk to a nearby village, Old Leighlin (or Locklin). There I hoped to see an interesting cathedral. One of the reasons why I liked Carlow Town so much, I realized, was that the place had not been discovered by young Continental holidaymakers with knapsacks.

I followed a lane near the old mill, and soon found myself walking along a narrow motor road out into the open fields beside the lazy River Barrow. An old tinker caravan stood by the roadside, but there was no one at home and no horse grazing nearby. By a crumbling stone wall, below the trees, an archway stood on its own in the weeds, a remnant of an Ascendancy garden. Another archway leading nowhere, sad relic of the Lost People, stood nearby. Rushing water drew me to a lock in the canalized river, where an old man leaned meditatively on a wall. He told me that Old Leighlin was further than I had supposed, so I decided to hitch-hike.

Almost at once, a car stopped and a friendly young man asked me to hop in. He was a soldier in the Irish Army, stationed at Kilkenny, and now he was going back to the Old Place to see his parents. His particular Old Place was a farm high on the hilltop above Old Leighlin, so he could take me all the way there. We swung out of the lane on to a busy motorway-style road with steep banks, then along another enchanting little lane that climbed a hill through lush farmland, until we reached a small grey village perched on the hillside. This was Old Leighlin, and I could see the cathedral gates beside the road. Somewhere near here, the

Kavanagh kings of Leinster had held court, but no trace of their stone palaces remained.

A path led down to St Laserian's Cathedral, a thirteenth-century building, of church size, nestling in a hollow. In the seventh century, a monastery had been founded here by St Gobban. When Gobban died, Laserian succeeded him as Abbot. With my yearnings for the vanished Celtic Church, the church that preceded the standardized rule of Rome, I am not sure that I should altogether approve of St Laserian. Son of an Ulster nobleman, he had been trained at Rome and ordained by Pope Gregory the Great. Arriving at what is now Old Leighlin in AD 632, he championed the Roman style of worship and the Roman method of dating Easter, an important talking point in those days.

However, both the monastery and St Laserian's tomb perished by fire in the eleventh century. Almost a hundred years later, Donatus, Bishop of Leighlin, ordered a cathedral to be built on the spot, and it has been there ever since. Before the Potato Famine, the neighbourhood would have been heavily populated, and before Home Rule the cathedral provided worship for landowners and their families. Now it seemed to be stranded in the middle of nowhere. When I tried the door, it was locked.

'Try at the Forde cottage', the lady in the tiny grocer's shop advised me, pointing across the way.

I knocked, and a polite eighteen-year-old youth, Liam Forde, produced an enormous iron key, walked down with me and let me in. He declined to enter, and returned to his cottage. Two medieval fonts reposed in the dark interior, one with carvings and one plain. The plain font may have been salvaged from the monastery. Everywhere were monuments to the once vigorous Vigors family, the former landowners.

After nosing and snuffling around for a while, I locked the cathedral and returned to Forde's Cottage. Again the polite youth came out, I returned the key and enquired after the fate of the Vigors family.

'There's still a Vigors knocking about here somewhere,' the boy said innocently. 'But he hasn't got any land.'

The sun began leisurely to prepare for retirement, but before returning to Carlow, I couldn't resist looking in at the village pub, a dark little bar presided over by two more polite open-faced young men. To please them, I drew pictures of donkeys and weasels.

'Ah, you've been to art school,' one of them said, as if that explained everything.

Outside the grocer's, I tried to use a grey phone box, as I wished to phone a farmer uncle of a London friend. I could make no sense of the phone, which had a peculiar chute for the money. Through the glass, I could see a round, cheerful girl standing in the middle of the road bidding a lengthy goodbye to a jovial old farmer. I opened the door and beckoned to her. She soon showed me how to work the phone – each coin waited in the chute until its time had come, and then it slipped into a slot quite naturally.

'You're ahead of us here – we haven't got these phones in England yet,' I said seriously. However, the idea of Ireland in general, and Old Leighlin in particular, being ahead of England tickled the girl's funny bone, and I could hear her laughing until she was out of sight. Having invited myself to tea on the following week with a bemused farmer's wife in Tipperary, I trotted briskly down the hill to Carlow.

It was a golden evening, the shadows of trees barred my path, the countryside smelled sweetly and a small combine harvester purred across a field. A ragamuffin tribe of small blond-haired brown children sat in the trailer and cheered and waved as I marched by. At last I reached the thunderingly busy and dangerous main road, and here my troubles began. The more I thumbed, the less people stopped. Dusk turned to darkness to pitch darkness on a road without a vergeside path, where blinding lights of lorries and cars swung out at you from every direction. I felt like a ball in a pintable machine, hurled here and there amid sudden noises and flashes of light.

Soon I grew very alarmed, then I fell into despair and wondered if I would survive. Two hours of dazzled and bewildered torment had passed, and there was still no sign of Carlow. With exaggerated caution I crossed the road and tried to read a signpost in the blackness. A friendly man with black curly hair and sideboards stopped his car and asked me if I wanted a lift. Did I! Exhausted, I fell into the seat beside him.

'I used to live on a farm up on the hill,' he said conversationally. 'It was really wild and rugged up there, but unfortunately I had to leave when I got married. Now I live in Carlow.'

He dropped me off at the centre of town, and I walked up and down amazed to see lights burning and citizens cheerfully greeting one another, after the lone desperation I had endured. Somehow

I felt that it ought to be four o'clock in the morning, the streets empty yet full of menace. Instead of which people were singing and laughing in the bars, men in cloth caps gathered at various Pals' Corners, youths sat on walls with legs dangling and newsagents and chip shops were still open. I felt like falling down and kissing the pavement, and I feel a great affection for Carlow Town to this day.

A bunch of the boys were whooping it up in Ned Lennon's Lounge and Real Estate House. I went inside and listened to a group of red-faced young men who swayed in a circle, arms tipsily about one another's shoulders, singing lustily, in the crowded bar room. Outside the circle, another young man played the spoons with machine-gun rapidity. Were it not for the song – 'Whack fol de Daddy-O, there's whiskey in the jar' – I could have been in South Wales, where farmers and miners sing drunken barber shop harmonies in exactly the same manner. Subordinated to the Carlow style, ordinary pop songs and American plantation melodies quickly became Irish. 'House of the Rising Sun', originally a blues sung to the tune of a spiritual, 'Balm in Gilead', reverted in no time at all to the old ballad 'Bonny Barbara Allen' which had probably inspired the American composer in the first place.

I crossed the road and walked back towards my Bed and Breakfast, pausing at the bar where I had heard music on the night before. Inside, I found that the dark old place had been divided into sections, snugs and hidey-holes by the maze-like use of settle chairs, tables and old wooden shelves for pint pots. Earthy old men nodded appreciatively as a small group sat at a beer-stained table and played energetically. There was a guitarist who sometimes had to peruse a misspelled ballad book, a bodhran player with thimbled hand and a spirited accordionist who played fast jigs with a touch of the rhumba to them; an excellent musician, with his own style.

A little later I tiptoed up to bed in my room near the station. In the morning I sat at breakfast and listened to the agreeable sound of a mother hustling children off to school. It's agreeable if you are not one of the hustled children, that is. Soon I boarded a train at the nearby station, heading for Cashel, County Tipperary. Farewell to mellow Carlow Town!

CHAPTER NINE

The Rock of Cashel

To my great joy, I was now able to satisfy a long-held ambition and stay at Grant's Castle Hotel, a genuine grey castle tower built by a long-ago warlord and incorporated into Cashel's prosaic main shopping street, sandwiched between nineteenth-century shops. About the size of a large lodge-house tower, the castle was only half-a-house higher than its neighbours, but with its ragged, broken ramparts it looked haunting and strange. A large neon sign, 'Hotel', hung aslant over the battlements, some of the letters lit up, others not. More neon signs were displayed further down, as the owners held the castle's historic value in blithe disregard.

I paid a bland Reception girl for a four-day stay, and toiled up the narrow wooden steps with my bag. Corridors twisted here and there like indoor boreens, with pictures of the Pope and other holy subjects on the walls. My little room was pleasant enough, but a room on the landing above (which I explored) contained a weird and wonderful ebony dressing table, covered in little mirrors and shelves, all highly polished. A stained-glass window on this room's door depicted two red-bearded bandits with long feathers in their caps. What a blessing that I hadn't asked for a room with a shower, or I would have been put in the modern wing and missed all this!

Snuggling down on my bed for a nap, I could hear the staff and their small children laughing and playing in the yard outside my window.

'I'll huff and I'll puff and I'll blow the castle down!' somebody shouted, answered by shrieks of laughter. I knew I was going to like it here.

On my first morning in Cashel, I discovered a room where the proprietor's stout little son and curly-headed daughter sat watching Bugs Bunny videos. They greeted me solemnly, so I sat beside them and learned, among other things, that the Castle was haunted by a man who had been hung there in the olden days.

'I'd like a pusheen,' the little girl said. 'I mean a baby cat.'

'Do you mean a puss-een?' I asked.

'No, a pusheen.'

Musing on pusheens and boreens, I stepped out into the main street of Cashel. A fountain stood across the way, dated 1842. This was an early water supply for Cashel, with jets still gushing into a clean trough from the mouths of stone lions. 'Ryan's the Harnessmaker's' shop nearby had a window heaped with saddles, bridles and harnesses, all looking as if nobody had touched them, or swept the shop, since 1923.

Cashel had fallen into decrepitude, but not uniformly so. A grand house or shop would have an uninhabited ruin as a neighbour. A mansion, the eighteenth-century Bishop's Palace, dominated the long, narrow shopping street. It was now an hotel, glittering with opulence. A little further on, rows of empty, grey, boarded-up cottages, shops and terraced houses gave Cashel the look of a ghost town. Smartly painted houses and business-like shops co-existed with dismal squalor. Beside the eighteenth-century Anglican cathedral, with its graceful spire, stood an abandoned farm: house, stables and barn, all crumbling away unregarded. Evidently Cashel's last heyday had been in the eighteenth century, though its greatest glory had shone from the holy Rock in the medieval Age of One Faith.

Crossing a strip of suburbia, I soon came to a place where old cottages had been cleared away, leaving a few standing in isolation, the better to allow access to the Rock. In reality, 'the Rock' is a steep top-heavy hill, girdled with sharp ridges of stone. It is more grassy than Edinburgh's Castle Rock, and resembles one of the strange hills to be seen in Brueghel paintings, with ruins on top.

Suddenly, from the plain, the Rock towers heavenward, a jagged mass of boulders rising almost vertically, a well-worn path leading up to the summit. Once the Rock had been crowned by a scrubby tableland, the Fairy Ridge, but now the top was ringed by a high wall that seemed to grow naturally from the surrounding stones. A Rapunzel tower and broken turrets peeped over this wall. I was standing directly below the Rock, so I walked around it for a time before ascending, perfectly recapturing the wonder I had felt when first I saw it, fifteen years earlier. Outside Cashel, the Rock sloped to a grassy mound, separated by a narrow road from the open fields. From here, the empty cathedral, castle and Round Tower could best be admired.

In ancient times, the Fairy Ridge was probably a place of worship, sacred to Bronze Age men and to the later-coming Celts. A sacred stone, perhaps one of Ireland's Stones of Destiny, stands there to this day. Corc, King of the Province of Munster in which Cashel lies, had his castle built beside the stone in AD 370. From then on, until the twelfth century, Cashel of the Kings was the Royal seat of Munster. One of these kings was Brian Boru, named High King of Ireland, although his rule no more covered All Ireland than did King Alfred's rule cover England. Both kings are also comparable in that they fought back the invading Danes.

When I add that St Patrick arrived at the Rock in AD 448 and there baptized King Angus, a former pagan, it can be seen that All Ireland seems concentrated on Cashel, the Rock a ghostly equivalent of England's Westminster Abbey. St Patrick's Cross, hewn from a single stone, was placed atop the Stone of Destiny in the Middle Ages. So could Christ be said to triumph over paganism. But I prefer to admire Stone and Cross as the sign of Christ *complementing* paganism, or finishing a half-completed tale.

At the beginning of the twelfth century, King O'Brien decided that Cashel was too good for Royalty such as himself, and should belong to God. In all humility, he handed over his palace to the Church, and the Rock became seat of an Archbishopric. Hitherto, bishop-kings had sometimes ruled from Cashel, but now the Fairy Ridge had danced full circle and became a sacred site alone. Cardinals from Rome climbed the steep path to the palace. St Patrick's Cathedral rose beside the pointy-topped Round Tower where men had once sought refuge from the Danes.

Cashel's Golden Age ended when Cromwell's men attacked the town in 1647. They were led by Lord Inchiquin, whose ambition it was to be President of Munster. Cromwell granted him this title. The Rock was attacked with cannon and fire, the priests and friars butchered as they fled. Then Inchiquin's men set to work with a will, and burned Cashel to the ground, killing almost all of the three thousand inhabitants, sparing not even the smallest child. ('Nits will be lice.') A melancholy still hangs over Ascendancy-rebuilt Cashel. Eventually the cathedral was repaired and became

Anglican until de-roofed. Most of the killings had taken place inside it, as townsfolk sought refuge there.

Inchiquin is said to have become a Roman Catholic in old age. Some years ago I met an old man who had been a British officer during the Troubles of this century in Cork. His wife told me that he had shot Irishmen from his bedroom window, and chased people all round the town for breaking curfew. He too became a Catholic when old. If only such people would turn to Rome when *young* we might all be spared a lot of trouble. But then, I suppose, they might kill Protestants. Young manhood is often a time of blood.

I climbed the path to the Fairy Ridge, but received a shock when I reached the top. A modern entrance hall and Interpretative Centre had been built, with a turnstile. Once I had surmounted this obstacle, I made straight for St Patrick's Cross and the magical stone. They stood among tussocky grass, just as I had remembered them. Yet something was wrong. On my previous visit, cross and stone had struck me with rapture, and I had stood entranced before them for several minutes. This time I felt nothing. Looking down at the inscription, I saw to my amazement that I had been looking at concrete replicas. The real cross and stone had been placed inside the entrance hall to protect them from the elements.

Retracing my steps, I faced the real cross and stone once more, bathed in electric light, and tried to summon up a proper sense of awe. Bronze age axe and spear heads lay nearby, with neat new pinewood shafts and their heads touched up with gold paint. A stone slab lay against the wall, adorned by a carving of a pig-snouted and boar-tusked elephant and castle. A griffon, a frequent symbol at Cashel, stood on top of the castle.

I had always admired the way the Irish left their ruins alone. Nowadays, when people do anything sensible, it is usually for want of money. Give them money and they will be as mad, or progressive, as anyone else. Someone had spent a fortune on tidying up the Rock of Cashel. This disappointment aside, the Rock was much the same as ever. The open Romanesque doorway of the cathedral faced the entrance hall, and I walked once more through carved stone halls whose only roof was the sky. One vast gravel-floored room had a domed ceiling, yet outside, a square tower could be seen above it. Castle and cathedral merged, in fact and in my memory, both equally fine and equally ruined. Families of holidaymakers enjoyed themselves by climbing up tower staircases and poking their heads out of openings. On a wall, I discovered the figure of a grinning wolf with outspread paws, a wolf-like lion and two tiny griffons.

Plastic flowers lay on modern graves on the cathedral floor. Moslems in India also like to bury their dead in the holy soil of ruined mosques so that they can hitch a ride to Heaven on the shirt-tails of the saints.

On the far side of the castle, a lawn sloped upward, studded with graves, to the perimeter wall. Beside this wall, a tall broken cross depicted the life of Patrick in square panels. Looking back, I admired the pointy-roofed Round Tower, with noisy jackdaws flying in and out of the openings.

Beyond the wall, a grassy precipice swooped down to the plains of Tipperary. To my left were high mountains bathed in shafts of sunlight, to my right, gentle hills rolled away. A fertile plain stretched before me, where horses and cattle grazed. More ruins, grey and haunted-looking, stood in the middle of a marshy field facing the Rock. This was Dore Abbey, destroyed in the Reformation year of 1541. Where else but in Ireland could you look from one ecclesiastical ruin to another, in a trail of devastation that covers the land? Yet the Catholic faith is livelier than ever, and the Tipperary farms seemed prosperous.

Two neat little girls of eight or nine lay on a grave near the wall, basking in the sun. After some moments, they arose and looked over the wall down towards the town.

'I'm tired of speaking in English, let's speak in our own language,' said one, loudly and clearly. For several minutes, with great assurance, they spoke to one another in Irish, pointing out sights of interest in the town below. I pretended to be enjoying the view, and overheard them whispering instructions whenever one of them got stuck. Aloud, they spoke in bell-like tones. 'Shall we say "hello" to that man?' I overheard a whisper.

I said it first, and asked in wonderment if they had really been speaking Irish.

'Yes, we learn it at school,' one of the girls answered politely. 'Our parents don't speak it at home. We were only messing, pretending it was still our language.'

'I'm so pleased to hear Irish spoken, I'll give you a present,' I said, proffering coin. 'It was the English who stopped the language in the first place, so I ought to give compensation.'

Both girls thanked me most politely, then *ran* to the sweet shop at the foot of the Rock. 'Teach it to your children when you grow up!' I called after them.

'We will!' one of them shouted, looking over her shoulder as she ran.

Why did I do it? I knew better than anyone of the dangers of Gaelic Revivalism, yet I had felt impelled to reward the girls. Such is (or was) the dilemma of the imperial Englishman.

Turning back to the Round Tower, I saw no more jackdaws but a pure white dove perched in one window, perhaps a sign that I had done the right thing.

That evening I admired the Rock floodlit in splendour against the night sky. In town, the gushing fountain was beautifully illuminated from underwater. I dined in a neo-Gothic Methodist chapel, Chez Nous, that had been sumptuously restored as a restaurant, with wood panelling, paintings on the wall and a roaring fire. People greeted me as I walked through the quiet streets back to the centre of the town. Merry bands of children, boys and girls together, roved the streets in cheerful innocence.

A different sort of Rock of Cashel could be found at the Castle Hotel, where loud pop music blared from the bar and a crowd of young people roared and brawled. A fight broke out as I ascended the narrow stairway and I heard girls shrieking with laughter. Feeling glad that I was no longer young and obliged to enjoy myself, I prepared for bed.

Next morning was Sunday, and the dining room was crowded. Breakfasting youths relived the glories of the night before.

'Did you see him kick you in the face? . . . Yes, Shane's on heroin now.'

I went to St John's Anglican cathedral in town. Many cars were parked outside, and several of the congregation looked like well-to-do farmers. The Alternative Church of Ireland prayer book listed prayers for the Queen 'if in Northern Ireland', and 'Our President' if in the Republic. When the prayer came along, 'Our President' sounded insincere, and everyone's eyes seemed to turn wistfully to the 'If in Northern Ireland' paragraph. If you *are* in Northern Ireland, you must not confuse the Church of Ireland's Anglican Protestants with the Presbyterians of the Loyal Orange Lodge. The latter are the ones who play flutes and go on marches. Southern Irish Catholics often confuse the two, as for them a

Protestant is a Protestant, and they say, 'Of *course* Catholics can get on with Protestants.' At St John's, a collection for bomb-damaged St Colum's of Londonderry brought forth a salad of notes into which my coins disappeared as if into a well.

Just as if I were in a Church of England, no one spoke to me after the service except a forcedly bright upper-class lady who hoped I had enjoyed myself. Children poured out of the Sunday School, held in the portrait-hung vestry, happily clutching crayoned pictures.

Outside, I saw crowds of people walking through one of Cashel's many alleyways. I followed them, and I found myself facing Cashel's Roman Catholic Church, a bright wedding cake of a building, with an ornate grotto. Half the population of Cashel, or more, were streaming towards the church gates along a narrow road. Newsagent-grocers were doing a roaring trade along the way, with oranges, apples and English and Irish Sunday papers sold from pavement tables. Headlines concerned the homosexual affairs of the famous. Happy-looking people, some in large family parties, others alone, poured through the narrow gate of the churchyard. As if checking that all were there, the priest stood at the gateway, a tall, lean man in black robes.

A few yards away, at intervals, stood mean-faced shabby men, also with tables. 'Labour Party', their placards proclaimed. Many who passed dropped a handful of coins into their collecting bowls, deference paid to this world and the next. 'We have no connection with the English Labour Party,' was all they would tell me.

In contrast with these beggarly specimens, the priest looked proud and self-satisfied, as well he might. At last he decided that his entire flock was inside, and turned to follow them. I looked after him yearningly, but lacked the courage to go in. Supposing it was discovered that I couldn't genuflect? Although I readily go into any kind of Negro church, and pick up the rituals instinctively, I am not at home with the High Civilization of Roman Catholicism, even though this civilization accommodates every kind of magical belief. I feel ignorant and afraid of doing something wrong. So I mooned away an hour or two in town, and then returned to the church (or chapel) when it was empty.

Inside, the statues grimaced so horribly, like South Sea idols in a museum, that I could scarcely bear to look at them. Posters advertised the holy resort of Knock, where the Virgin is said to appear. Attractions included candlelit processions and the services of numerous marriage brokers. An inscription in modern English, below a statue, had been rendered Biblical by somebody's pencil. 'Have' had been corrected to 'Hast' and all the 'Yous' had been replaced by 'Thous.'

It was absurd that here I was in Ireland and had not yet succeeded in Catholicizing myself a little. So, as the sun had now reappeared from behind the clouds, I decided to hitchhike to Holy Cross Abbey, several miles from town. According to a pamphlet I had picked up,

> Holy Cross Abbey was a Cistercian Abbey founded in the twelfth century, restored in the fifteenth century, a decaying ruin for four hundred years and restored again between 1971 and 1985. It is now a restored national monument, a centre of prayer and reconciliation. It is visited by thousands of pilgrims each year. Holy Cross Abbey took its name from a notable Relic of the True Cross enshrined within it when it was founded in 1180. It is situated eight miles north of the Rock of Cashel.

A Relic of the True Cross! That was worth hitchhiking eight miles to see, so I set out without delay. Near the Rock of Cashel, I found a 'Lady's Well' by the road. This poor well attracted no pilgrims, for it was full of dirty leaves and rusty tins. 'Do Not Drink', a superfluous sign proclaimed.

Soon I was swinging along a straight road leading directly through the lush plain I had seen from the Rock battlements towards Holy Cross. The idea of restoring a ruined abbey, in medieval style, appealed to me. Would the True Cross still be on view?

With the sun at my back, I walked beside hedges and grass verges that rustled with rats. Every now and then I saw one. For a long time, a pretty red-haired girl walked along behind me. I was fearful that she was a hitchhiking rival, but eventually she passed me with a smile and turned beneath overhanging trees into a farmyard. Shortly afterwards, a farmer stopped and took me all the way to the Abbey, crossing an ancient stone bridge over the River Suir. 'There's been a big Gaelic football match, Cork versus Meath,' he said. 'To everyone's surprise, it was a tie.'

No sun shone over Holy Cross, and the great Abbey seemed unnaturally cold. There was no service going on, no priests or abbots around. Outside, the Abbey had been given a new roof, and inside were new tiles, pine flooring and long bleak white walls. Although no modern architectural styles had been used, the Abbey seemed far from medieval, its spirit not yet recovered. At heart it was a dismal ruin still. I entered through broken stumps of grey cloisters, parts of which had been repaired in the 1920s. A small door led into the great empty Abbey.

Where were the throngs of pilgrims, kneeling and chanting? A few dispirited-looking family parties wandered around, lost in the vast coldness of the Abbey. No one seemed interested in the True Cross. At last, in a glass case, I found the casing which once had contained the relic. Itself in the form of a small cross, the exquisitely jewelled silver casing depicted a winged donkey, a dove and what looked like an Indian god. Below these, a cross-shaped locket lay open, revealing nothing. Lunatic metal lightning zig-zagged around the case, evidently modern art.

Round the corner, on an altar, I discovered the Cross itself. Bright lights shone upon a small glass case which contained a tiny wooden cross, scarcely visible. It could fit upon your little fingernail, and if it slipped, might enter your finger as a splinter. I felt moved to think that five successive English kings, in the Middle Ages, had kneeled before this cross.

Nowadays, the Abbey visitors glanced at it as if it were in a museum, registered a mournful 'Oh yes?' and passed on. Never did the thought that it might be *real* occur to them. In my heart of hearts I too felt it must be an imitation, but a very old one, surely a relic in its own right. It had been presented to the Abbey by Pope Pascal II not long after the building had been completed under the auspices of King O'Brien.

After the sixteenth-century Reformation, the Abbey fell into the hands of the ubiquitous Butler family, who removed the Cross. The Butlers allowed some of the monks to stay on in a corner of the Abbey. For a time, the fragment of Cross was lost sight of, until a Butler unearthed it in 1625. From then on it had various Ascendancy owners, who may or may not have believed in it, until now it had been restored to Mother Church.

I mused on the bygone passion for relics, and on the vigorous, materialistic Protestantism that in England had emerged from the Age of Faith.

When the Reformation began, the Holy Roman Catholic Church seemed to lose a lot of its holiness, as if stunned to find that rival modes of Christian thought might exist. From symbolizing Eternal Truth, it became a faction among factions, often perpetrating great cruelties. Catholics and Protestants can match martyr for martyr.

In 1555, John Hullier, the Protestant vicar of Babraham, Cambridgeshire, was condemned to death by the Bishop of Ely under Mary Tudor. On Maundy Thursday, 1556, he was burnt at the stake on Jesus Green, Cambridge. To the last, as the flames rose higher, he lectured on Protestantism to a sympathetic crowd of bystanders. He laid great emphasis on the wrongful superstition of venerating relics. When the fire had been put out, and the soldiers had departed, the martyr's skeleton was found to be intact, bound upright to the stake. At once the Protestant crowd rushed forward and seized his bones as holy relics. The urge for relics had proved irresistible.

When Protestantism had been reestablished in England, England's enemies in France and Spain had the perfect excuse for a conquest – restoring England to the True Faith. So much of English anti-Catholicism was justified in those days. To be a Protestant was to be an avowed patriot, loyal to the English Crown, while to be Catholic was to be a suspected spy, in league with a Continental enemy. Poor Ireland was tarred with the same brush as Spain, and was more easily available for vengeance.

Americans today fear Communism, as they associate it with the enemies of their country. Substitute 'Catholic' for 'Communist', and you realize what fears, real or groundless, the English Protestants once entertained. Ireland was a thorn in their side, as she might so easily ally with the Continental Catholic enemy and bring about the downfall of proud Protestant England.

English Protestantism's great age, from sixteenth-century Elizabethan days to the eighteenth-century Enlightenment, was robust and by no means entirely ignoble. It has its champions, historians such as J. A. Froude in Victorian times and the late Sir Arthur Bryant today. In my mind it is associated with roast beef and hanging, the good and the bad together. The new faith, not always very Christian, sent fire through men's veins and inspired great feats of conquest, seaworthiness, exploration, piracy and trade, including slave trade. Again and again, parallels with the rise of Mohammedanism and the great days of the newly-inspired Arabs come to mind. For two and a half centuries, fierce Protestantism symbolized England. Monks and abbeys were soon forgotten, and our medieval ancestors were scornfully dubbed

'Goths', or barbarians. Every true-born Englishman cursed the Pope. Severed, with evident relief, from a United Europe of Roman Catholicism, the English felt more English than ever before. Englishmen and Irish-born Protestants in Ireland sought to make Ireland more English too.

These Protestant ideas survive in Northern Ireland, where they make exactly the same sense as they did in England long ago. Catholicism is associated with an enemy outside who seeks to conquer. In this case, the enemy is not Spain, but the Republic of Ireland, whose government has never relinquished its claim to the Six Counties. Some Irishmen, who deplore the activities of the modern IRA, still have a 'sneaking regard' for the Provos. They are known as 'sneaking regarders'. I too am a 'sneaking regarder' for Northern Protestants who keep alive the old ideals I associate with Yorkshire pudding, gravy and piracy on the high seas.

Freethinkers of the Enlightenment in late eighteenth-century England, in my view, paved the way for an English reappraisal of Roman Catholicism. Christianity was debunked, and the age of Triumphant Protestantism came to an end. France had a violently anti-Catholic revolution. England, feeling less Protestant, wondered what all the fuss about anti-Papism had been for.

The beginning of Victoria's reign almost coincided with Catholic Emancipation and the abolition of slavery in the British Empire. Soon afterwards, in England, came a rehabilitation of the Middle Ages: Young England, the 'Gothic Revival' in architecture, the Anglo-Catholic or High Church movement, Anglican monks and nuns and Pre-Raphaelite art. Men of talent flirted with Rome, and much that we warmly associate with 'Victorian days' owes its beauty, whimsy or delightful absurdity to the nineteenth-century rediscovery of the Roman Catholic Middle Ages.

In Ireland, the Anglo-Irish Ascendancy of Victorian days felt the pull of the same ideas. To their surprise, they found the peasants of the Middle Ages, faith and folklore intact, at their very doorstep or serving them tea. Gaelic Revivalism was born, and a love affair began between some of the Ascendancy and the Ascended-over – Ireland Rediscovered. It was a somewhat one-sided love affair that led to a new wave of proud Irish nationalism, one that eventually merged with Marxist thought. The 'Young England' movement attracted romantic and impractical lords, but the 'Young Ireland' movement attracted romantic and practical rebels. A justified love of Irish folklore and the Irish language led many members of the Ascendancy to seal their doom, and helped to bring about the Dublin of 1916, when marches of armed men of no known cause, with strange flags, seemed not unusual.

All these thoughts, and more, flowed through my mind as I stood before the True Cross in a place where an attempt had been made to restore the glory of the Middle Ages.

Outside Holy Cross Abbey, I found a tawdry Garden of Meditation with badly-planted roses. The Abbey grounds reached to the banks of the River Suir, where a restored water-wheel stood motionless. A weir, which once had directed the water to the wheel, in mill days, spouted two waterfalls with a dry ridge of pebbles between them. Grey wagtails waggled and wobbled amid these pebbles.

A warm riverside pub, with a wood fire, was a great deal more cosy than the Abbey had been. I enjoyed a pot of tea and listened to the ribaldry of a large family, small children, buxom women and wizened men.

When I emerged, I found, to my horror, that dusk was setting in. Would I have to relive my nightmare walk back from Old Leighlin, when I had been dazzled, terrified and nearly run over as I tried to hitch back to Carlow? Yes, I would. Soon it became pitch dark, no car would stop, and headlights from two directions gave me that familiar pinball feeling as I weaved despairingly along the road. In the ditches, the rats grew bolder with darkness, and crashed around like baby bears. Trees from Snow White's forest loomed over me with outstretched arms. At long last, when all hope was lost, I saw the Rock of Cashel standing illuminated in the sky like a fairy castle far away.

'Begod, you'll not wanting to be out on a road like this,' a voice called to me from a miraculously passing car. I was so surprised to hear an Irishman say 'begod' in real life that I didn't know what to say. However, my companion had talk enough for the two of us.

'I'm a security guard for a well-known horse trainer,' he told me. 'It's fine, flat, lush, fertile country here, that's good for horses. Been to see Holy Cross, is it now? The bishop of these parts organized to get Holy Cross restored. It was his life's work, and when he retired he went to live there.'

Safely back in the main street of Cashel, I found myself surrounded by lively, happy boys and girls from the football match, wearing headbands and waving scarves. Their innocent faces reassured me, and as the dining room at the Castle was shut, I had a meal in Ryan Jewellery, a plastic-leprechaun souvenir shop which also did duty as a café, with tables and chairs in odd corners. It was next door to Ryan the Harnessmaker. The same tape of traditional Irish music played again and again.

'Don't you ever get sick of Irish music?' I asked the woman at the counter.

'Oh, terribly sick of it!' she cried with feeling. 'But it's what the tourists want.'

'Never mind, you'd be worse off in England, as there it's all rock music,' I comforted her.

Afterwards, I followed the Gaelic football fans to a small bar where a country and western guitarist played. I squeezed inside in time to hear his last song, 'On the One Road', the unofficial Irish anthem, a vastly popular Hibernian hit.

> We're on the one road, sharing the one load,
> We're on the road to God Knows Where!
> We're on the one road, maybe the wrong road,
> But we're together now, who cares!

To the knees-up rhythm of the rebel song, the young men danced wildly, holding up Confederate flags! Such flags, blue and red, with stars, belonged to a different kind of rebel, the diehard White Southerner of Jeffrey Klinke's USA. In England, too, disaffected young men wave Confederate flags or wear them as denim emblems, without knowing what they mean. Southern country and western has become the music of the International Working Class (white variety) and the Confederate flag is its emblem even in Ireland.

That night I nestled cosily in my bed at the Castle, while young Irishmen and Germans fought one another in the disco downstairs.

Next day I waited anxiously outside Ryan Jewellery for a bus that was to take me to a Tipperary farmhouse, home of the Phillarney family.

'All the Irish side of my family are rich farmers,' a London friend told me carelessly, giving me an address. 'Just phone Tim and Nancy Phillarney when you get there, and they'll look after you.' When I had phoned them, from the call box in Old Leighlin, Nancy had answered and invited me over for tea. 'We live way up on the mountain,' she had added.

A small bus with shabby paintwork arrived, already half full, and I showed the stout, cloth-capped driver the address. It was too Irish for me to pronounce.

'You'll be after walking five or six miles from where I put you down,' he warned.

As the bus rolled on into the country, stopping at a farm here or a bungalow there, it soon filled up completely. Everybody talked cheerfully, women knitted, and healthy children with brick-red cheeks ran up and down. Rain streaked across the windows, and the hills were obscured by mist. When we neared my destination, I asked the man next to me if he had heard of the Phillarneys. He was a canny-looking old fellow with a flat cap and wiry eyebrows.

'Which Phillarneys is it you'll be wanting? Sure there's Phillarneys all over the mountain, and that's the truth. Tim and Nancy? Now, did the old man die?'

'I don't think so.'

'Tim Phillarney died four years ago,' a woman behind me volunteered.

'Is it Fox Phillarney he's after?' a man shouted, several rows back.

I hoped not, as that sounded like an outlaw name, 'The Border Fox'. However, I later learned that the original Border Fox, Des O'Hare, had been captured and was doing forty years. Soon the whole bus was involved in the controversy.

'What can that gentleman want with the Fox?' a boy loudly asked his mother.

'Don't be so bold!'

'It is all Phillarneys up that lane,' the driver said, as I disembarked.

At first I felt rather daunted, especially as there were no more buses back to Cashel. But in a few minutes I cheered up, as the rain stopped and the sun came out for the first time that day. Twisting and turning between steep banks, the long lane climbed steadily upwards, and so did I. Finches swooped among the brambles, and I feasted on blackberries as I walked. Very soon the mist rose, and the sun shone with watery clarity. The range of hills before me, and the fields behind me, glowed with luminous, magical light green colours.

After a steep climb, the lane levelled out and curved around the towering mountain. Here I discovered a modern bungalow, where a large, lively family, led by a young mother with long brown hair, were climbing into a car. 'You're on the right road, keep on!' she urged me.

So on I went, beneath the brow of the green wet hill, passing stone cottages and an isolated shop, which was closed. By and by, I came to a tiny Catholic church, and beside it, carved out of the mountain, a large rocky grotto where once again St Bernadette discovered Our Lady at Lourdes. Inside the church, a mural above the altar depicted Christ beside an Irish Sea of Galilee, speaking to Irish fishermen. Outside, the rain began anew.

A little further on, I came to a gate in the hedge that overlooked the long sweep of pasture that led down to the main road, miles below. The name on the gate was the same one I had shown the bus driver. But where was the house?

Then I saw, below the hedgetop, the tiled roof of a large farmhouse, or rather, several roofs, as various bits of house had obviously been added on over the years. All were old. Instead of a path, the gate opened to steep stone steps, that glistened in the rain. These steps led down to a stone-flagged farmyard and the small wooden front door of the Phillarneys' home. An Old English sheepdog rollocked around me, barking excitedly.

'Ach, Mr Kerridge, I thought you wasn't coming,' a small woman observed, opening the door. She was thin, in her sixties, and wore an apron. Irony and caution flickered in her eyes, but she was not unfriendly. The door opened to a dark kitchen, with a table, several chairs around a comfortable log fire, and a new-looking wooden staircase. There had been a fire some years before, and so few of the wooden fittings were old.

'Yes, my friend in London said to be sure to call on her Uncle Tim and Aunt Nancy,' I prattled, as tea was prepared.

'My husband Tim died four years ago,' she said. 'My children and grandchildren help me with the farm. I've got cousins and relatives on farms all over the mountain. Sure, we're an old family in these parts.'

To my surprise, I learned that my friend in London had not been back to see her aunt and uncle for eight years, and no one on the farm knew her address. This address was in Hampstead, for my English-born friend, of peasant stock, had been born confidently upper-class by a magic fluke, and had soon attained her rightful position in life. So I gave Nancy Phillarney all the gossip ('*How* many husbands? Is that so?') and we were soon friends.

The cream poured in my tea had a buttery look, and I asked if the farm had many cows.

'We have some, still, and a bull on loan at the moment. But my brother had a share of the farm, and he brought us into debt by gambling. We had no *idea* he gambled, for he kept it secret, d'ye see? So two years ago, we had to sell the main dairy herd and the milking parlour to settle his debts. It would have killed my husband, if he'd lived to see it, as he spent all his life building up that herd. It's hard work on a farm. I blame the English landlord, no offence, of course. We used to pay rent to the agent from the Castle, but that's gone now, thank Heaven, there's not a trace of it.' Her face darkened, then lit again joyously, as a pixyish little girl in jeans ran into the room.

'I've shut away the cows, Nan!' she cried.

'This is my granddaughter Colette,' Nancy told me proudly, visibly softening and relaxing. 'How old do you think she is?'

'Nine,' I hazarded.

Colette looked like a miniature adult, and I could easily have mistaken her for a boy, with her short blond hair. She looked at me with alert blue eyes.

'Six!' said her grandmother triumphantly. I could scarcely believe it, as Colette obviously did half the work on the farm with no trouble at all.

I told Colette about England, and mentioned that I had seen two half-thatched houses, with pegs and ladders, from the bus window that day.

'*Our* house used to be thatched,' Mrs Phillarney said, sending Colette off for the photograph album. 'We have an old photograph that shows it. What is more, and that's the truth, there used to be an even older house on the site of this one.'

Many of the old photographs showed men in uniform, and I looked at them quizzically.

'We are an old IRA family,' Nancy Phillarney said proudly. 'When the police came, we would hide the guns under the table. Father sent us girls up on the hill when he heard the Black and Tans coming. In them days the Black and Tans had the only motor transport, dirty big lorries and that's the truth. My brother was killed in the Civil War by his own side. Ach, that happened all the time.'

From the back of the book, she lifted a loose photo in a white cardboard cover with serrated edges. With great emotion, sorrow, pride and pity, she opened the cover. I dared not look her in the eye in case I saw tears.

I saw a pale, brooding young man, with dark hair, dark eyes, high cheek bones and doomed good looks. He wore a smart uniform, with an officer's peaked cap. Below the photograph, in spidery writing, was his Battalion Number and the letters 'IRA'. Had he been shot, on no good evidence, as an informer? It did not seem wise to ask, and the photograph was put away again.

With a clatter, two young men wheeled bikes into the kitchen, greeted me cheerfully and wheeled the bikes through into a back room. They were Matthew and Michael, two teenage grandsons, slightly built and with open candid faces. Michael had never been outside Ireland, and listened eagerly to my stories of London. He was a curly-headed boy, with spectacles, and he seemed to know all about farming.

'Ach, Michael, show Mr Kerridge the farm,' Mrs Phillarney requested. 'Colette, show Mr Kerridge where the boots are, for its after being fearfully wet out there. Now, Matthew, have you seen your uncle the Fox the day?'

In a narrow, dark hallway, I struggled into a pair of boots, then sploshed across the farmyard behind Michael, who seemed pleased at the chance of showing me round. Drizzle fell steadily, so I did not pause to examine the barns and outhouses, which seemed to be full of old-fashioned equipment. A wet iron gate opened on to even wetter tussocky pastureland, sloping steeply. The first field was full of sheep – 'cross-bred', Michael called them – and the second field was full of cattle. Friesian cows grazed with calves by their sides. A mild-eyed bull watched us without comment.

'He's on loan,' said Michael. 'Don't worry, he's a gentle bull. He's done his duty, and tomorrow he goes back. We once had our own gentle bull, and one day he caught sight of Dad's red tractor and he went mad! He charged at Dad, who jumped up on the tractor and drove off, with the bull chasing him! Dad drove the tractor level to the fence, then jumped off it, straight over the fence, and so he escaped. Now, this one is my favourite field.'

So saying, he opened another gate and we entered a very steep field indeed, that sloped up to the hedge and the lane I had walked along. Two white goats watched us curiously. We climbed for a while, and then encountered a brown and white nanny goat, tethered to a stake. Michael seemed pleased to see her. 'She's a Toggenburg,' he announced proudly, and began talking to the goat in affectionate squeaks, stroking her brow between the horns.

Up beside the hedge, we discovered three young goats, almost kids, who had got their three separate chains tangled up into one knot. As a result, all three were lashed together in a bundle, facing each other's tails, like my dogs when they get their leads tangled. It took Michael nearly half an hour to separate them, while I stood foolishly by. The goats wriggled and ducked their heads under loose-hanging chains, tangling themselves worse than ever.

'You're a divil, a divil, d'ye hear me?' Michael good-humouredly accused a particularly awkward goat. In between talking kindly to the goats, he told me of his life on a hilltop farm.

'There's a fierce old view here on a nice day. When I've finished with these divils, do you want me to take you up on the ridge, above the road, and you can see a fine rabbit warren? Last night I saw a hare up there.'

'No, it's too wet and misty,' I said firmly. 'Do you shoot rabbits?'

'Do I? Not at all. I set snares for them, on their runways, and when I catch them, I break their necks, so. I can't afford a gun. That's the trouble with Irish farms – no money.'

'Is there fox-hunting here?' I enquired.

'Here's how the farmers hunt foxes up in these hills – one man drives a Land-rover with a hole made in the top. The other man looks out of the hole, with his gun, and shoots the fox when he sees it.'

'You seem rather a bloodthirsty lot. Do you have badger-baiting?'

'No. I heard a badger bark the other night. Once I found a badger foot in a trap, where it had chewed it off to get free. There's a lot of cock-fighting here, the district's known for it. There, free at last! I'll move their stakes further apart, that's the best. They like eating thistles and whitethorn branches from the hedge.' (In England, we say hawthorn, or May.)

As we walked back to the farmhouse Michael told me, 'I'd like to see a city, but otherwise I think it's grand living here. All my relatives live all around. There's music, talking and company. You have to go to Mass, is the only thing, or the people look down on you. Maybe when I'm older, I'll come and see you in London, just for a holiday.'

'Why, how old *are* you?'

'Fifteen. I have to go to school, it's a real pain, when I'd rather be on the farm.'

I had thought him to be eighteen or nineteen years old. It appeared that Phillarneys matured quickly. It seemed absurd, a keen farmer like Michael kept chained to a desk like one of his own goats on a stake. Perhaps Michael could read my thoughts, for when we returned to the kitchen, he asked his grandmother if he might not leave school early.

'I can't say about that, but schools aren't what they were,' Mrs Phillarney replied. 'It used to be wonderful, with the Christian Brothers and Sisters of Mercy telling you all about the blessed saints. Now it's all lay people and the vocation has been lost. Education is a wonderful thing, but it's more important to have Jesus in your heart.'

At that moment, the door burst open, the sheepdog barked and in came Nancy Phillarney's two brawny sons, in outdoor clothes. One of them wore a slouch hat and a dark bushy beard.

'Daddy!' Colette cried, and ran up to him to be held on high.

Soon afterwards, Colette's mother arrived from work, a neat young brunette, and we all sat around the kitchen table for an enormous supper of boiled bacon, huge potatoes boiled in their jackets and mountains of cabbage. Nancy Phillarney had done us proud, and we all got on famously. All the conversation was about a funeral the family were looking forward to attending.

After the meal, everybody except Mrs Phillarney and myself trudged into a back room. I caught a glimpse through a crack in the door of a large fascinating room, lined by old cabinets and gigantic chests of drawers. It was an awkward moment, as my hostess clearly didn't want me to follow, but I couldn't resist it and went. Immediately I began telling ghost stories to Colette, making myself indispensable, so Mrs P. made the best of it and sat down too.

Obviously, a hundred years ago, perhaps, this large room had been an immaculate parlour. It was still furnished as such, with cabinets, horsehair sofas, solid wooden furniture and Victorian chintzery. All over the middle of the room, however, lay the debris of family life. Michael and Matthew's large bikes lay on their sides, and you had to step over them to reach the sofa. Boots, buckets, books, newspaper and other oddments lay scattered around. It was a pleasure to be with an Irish family who were not houseproud.

'... And I've been to that very haunted house myself!' I finally concluded, as Colette stared into my face. 'But on my way home, I had a sad accident and what do you think it was? I trod on a nail, and the nail bended, and that's the way the story ended.'

It was now pitch dark outside, and as I had hoped, Colette's bearded father offered to drive me back to Cashel. Colette and her mother would come too, for the ride. At this news, Colette gave a skip of ecstasy and began to sing.

We're off, we're off, we're off in a motor car!
Sixty police are after us, and they don't know where we are!
I fell, I fell, I fell in a dirty well.
Sixty police are after us, and they fell in as well.
Walking round the corner, eating up the pies,
Along came a policeman and punched me in the eye.
I went to tell my Mammy, my Mammy wasn't in.
I went to tell my Daddy and he chucked me in the bin.

Finally we were really off, and I said goodbye to Nancy and the boys. Somewhere on the way, Colette's father parked in a deserted, moonlit village street and went into a bar for cigarettes. The street was deserted, but the brightly lit noisy bar was full. Somebody inside was playing the bagpipes, and the loud eerie sound followed us down the road as we departed.

'What songs do they sing in the playground at your school?' I asked Colette. With great verve, she sang once more.

Ibble abble uptree,
Ibble abble out,
Turn your petticoat
Inside out!
Not because it's dirty,
Not because it's clean,
Just because it's the fairy queen.

'There's a fairy tree near our house,' she added brightly.

'How do you know it's a fairy tree?'

'Because it's got fairies on it!'

Well, there's no answer to that. At long last we reached the Castle Hotel in Cashel, and I bade the Phillarney Tribe farewell. Then I took out a specially borrowed enormous iron key, let myself in and tiptoed up the winding stairs to bed.

Once more I stood nervously outside Ryan Jewellery waiting for a bus, but this time I had my heavy red, white and blue bag with me. For now I was leaving Cashel, and heading up to Roscrea, in Tipperary's North Riding.

'Sit a while, the bus is always late,' advised the kind-hearted Ryan lady, the one who hated Irish music. She pointed to an ornamental plastic chair outside her shop. So I waited for the Roscrea bus in luxury.

At last it arrived, and bowled through Thurles with its two cathedrals, skirting the Devil's Bit Mountain. Some of the old farmhouses on the way still had pumps with handles in their yards, unpainted and disused. Finally the bus stopped at the gateway of a tall grey ruined castle.

'Roscrea!' the driver shouted.

CHAPTER TEN

☘

The Pathe Hotel

Dragging my bag from the bus, I found myself in the gateway of Roscrea's ruined castle, high walls and tall grey towers. A shabby Queen Anne mansion stood in the middle of the castle grounds. My hotel was directly across the busy road. Jackdaws called from the ragged battlements, and the castle courtyard was covered in loose stones and slabs, some of which had fallen from the walls. On my last visit, in 1973, the mansion, Damer House, had been boarded up and seemed on the point of collapse. Now it had been repaired, with glass in all the windows, and called itself 'Roscrea Heritage Centre'.

Roscrea still preserves some of the atmosphere of its heyday as a coaching town on the Dublin to Limerick road. That was its *last* heyday, for the town has had several. Edward II, of England, granted the medieval castle to a member of the Butler family, and Roscrea had belonged to the 'old English' Butlers until 1703, when one of them sold it. Town and castle were shortly afterwards resold to one John Damer, who built the mansion. Then came the mail coach, and Protestant prosperity. In the nineteenth century, the Army were garrisoned in the castle yard, and Damer House became a barracks. Roscrea's *spiritual* heyday must have been the fifteenth century, when a Franciscan Friary had flourished. It was to Roscrea that I had come, fifteen years ago, to stay for several days' acclimatization before setting off to travel the rest of Ireland.

Then, as now, I stayed at the Pathe Hotel, a square flat-roofed building with rows of tall windows. The Pathe first opened as a coaching inn in 1725.

'Yes, we can give you a room, I'll be thinking,' said rascally Gerard Horan, still the landlord. So once more I bumped my bag up those historic stairs. Once more I paused at the quaint Reception Room for local farmers' societies, with its heavy curtains and furniture and sporting prints on the walls. An hotel of robust Irish character, the Pathe may have been named after the Pathé newsreels of the forties and fifties. In the late fifties, these newsreels were replaced by Pathé Pictorials, introduced by a ghastly technicolour woman in a top hat sitting on a porcelain rooster. But the Pathe Hotel remains the same as I remembered it, complete with gossip-laden bar.

As I reached my small, neat room, with its view across to the grim castle, I recalled the poem I had written at the Pathe long ago.

> A man at the Pathe Hotel
> Said 'I've a fine racehorse to sell.
> He can go with a bound,
> And for one extra pound
> I'll throw in the milk-cart as well.'

I soon unpacked, and strolled musingly around the Pathe, before crossing the road to Damer House. At the top of the stairs, a gentle old man welcomed two German tourists and myself.

'Sharon!' he called over his shoulder, and a quietly spoken ginger-haired girl appeared to show us round. Various knick-knacks reposed in draughty rooms, the floorboards creaked, and in spite of the magnificent hand-carved staircase, Damer House had a forlorn look, unlived-in and not yet museum-like.

The lacemaking exhibit showed photographs of doughty old lacemakers of Roscrea, together with examples of their work. Apparently lacemaking had been brought to Roscrea by a nineteenth-century Countess of Aberdeen, whose husband had been a great landlord. When she came to Roscrea, the Countess had been appalled at the wretchedness of the cabin-terrace side streets, the homes of the poor, set on unpaved roads full of filth and mud, with TB and other diseases rampant. Opening a School of Lacemaking may seem a curious response to such horrors, but the Countess sought to make the poor women of Roscrea independent and self-supporting. She supplied them with thread and showed them how to work it. Soon, the women (whose husbands may have been unemployed or drunkards) began to make a good living selling lace, and so were able to move into better houses. The side streets remained, and bits of them are still there today.

Another interesting room at Damer House contained the diaries written by a local farmer and his son, Thomas and Hubert Kelly. These covered the first seventy-four years of this century. Young Hubert Kelly was still writing his diary when I had first unpacked my bag in the Pathe Hotel. No national news was recorded, just the day-to-day life of a Tipperary farm. Pathetic relics from the farmhouse were preserved in glass cases.

Sharon showed us an enormous lump of Bog Butter, said to be a thousand years old. It had turned hard, and looked like a mouldy cheese boulder. A Fomor or a Firbolg or some other breed of Early Irishman had sunk his butter supply in a bog for safe-keeping and then forgotten about it. Turf-diggers had unearthed it in our time.

Finally, Sharon led us outside and showed us the castle towers. The energetic Germans rushed up and down the narrow stone stairs. A laughing team of young men ran out of an outbuilding, calling out to Sharon. They were on a work-training scheme, led by an indulgent-looking craftsman-restorer in a safety helmet. For a time, I wandered alone around the sad overgrown courtyards, with tottering ruins that echoed the days of the Butlers, the Damers and the British Army. Then I returned to the house to say farewell to the old curator.

'So you're from London,' he said mildly. 'There's lots of Heritage in London.'

'Yes, piles of it.'

'So I have heard. You would need a week or more to see all the Heritage that's there.'

Saying goodbye to Heritage with some relief, I stepped out into the lively shop-lined streets of Roscrea.

Outside the Pathe Hotel, a stand on the pavement advertised 'Briquettes of Peat', shiny black bricks used for fuel. If hand-dug they would have been called 'turf', but they had been factory processed in some way. New Factories and industries had encroached somewhat on the greenery of Roscrea since my last visit. It was a grey morning in Roscrea, and the housewives had sarcastic, pinched, narrow-eyed expressions. After a time, the long shopping street developed into an even longer street of council houses, the glory of Roscrea. I remembered these pre-war council houses with affection. All of them had been made in the style of Swiss cottages, with wooden shutters, high gables and all the trimmings. They stood in a long unbroken terraced line on either side of the road, front steps facing the pavement. More enchanting council houses I have yet to see, although they may have been a little dark inside. A derelict side street showed the houses they had displaced, empty shed-sized cabins with corrugated iron roofs. One was still inhabited. If lived in and regarded with love, these cabins too could have been enchanting. In 1973, only half of them had been empty, and some of the roofs had been thatched.

Eventually the Swiss row ended at the enormous firm of 'Roscrea Bacon', which must have employed half of the tenants. It is here that the Roscrea Sausage, famous in Ireland, is made. Rough, swaggering men were emerging in twos and threes, walking into town for their beer break.

Back in the more opulent, older end of Roscrea, near the Pathe, I was pleased to see that the Italian fountain was still playing in a little square bounded by shops. It had been noticed in Italy by an enterprising councillor, bought and set up in Roscrea. Not far from here, I found a funny little pub, a building standing on its own, with curtained windows. It was called The Hogan Stand. Hearing music, I went inside and walked straight into an impromptu dance, men and women jigging as an accordion player shouted out 'Dicey Reilly!' This is a Dublin song.

> Poor old Dicey Reilly, she has taken to the sup,
> Poor old Dicey Reilly, she will never give it up...
> She walks along Fitzgibbon Street with an independent air,
> And then it's down to Summerhill, at her the people stare...
> She owns a little sweetshop at the corner of the street,
> And every evening after school I go to wash her feet...

Everyone in the bar looked happy and rosy, and reminded me once more of the old Roscrea. I remembered the first and second times I had entered a bar in Roscrea. I am not a 'pub person', and always enter pubs with trepidation. However, I walked into a smart Roscrea pub, where as usual everyone stopped drinking to stare at me. Whereas in England everyone looks annoyed, and finds it hard to start talking again, at Roscrea I had been swooped on eagerly by a sandy-haired man who looked like a solicitor, or at least a solicitor's clerk. His bright, knowing eyes were half closed, surrounded by creases. With seeming innocence, while talking of other things, he asked me endless questions until he had found out everything he needed to know. Fox Phillarney could have taken lessons from him on foxiness.

'We are looking for an Englishman to produce our opera, *Oklahoma*,' he had told me. 'Irishmen can sing like angels, but they won't obey one another. That's why we need an Englishman.'

When I had made an excuse and left, everyone in the bar had wished me 'goodbye'. On the following day, I again entered the bar, and nobody spoke to me, all averting their eyes, including Foxy. I had been expecting this. *Hotel* bars are quite different, and the Pathe never disappoints.

On my previous visit to Roscrea, I had been enchanted by the sixty-foot Round Tower, then the first I had seen. It had been eighty feet high once, but the top was lopped off in 1798. (Vikings had ravaged Roscrea in the sixth century.) The tower stands opposite the Anglican church, near the Tower Hotel, one side enclosed by a ramshackle garage. The friendly garage people had allowed me to admire the broken tower wall inside their premises. Now the garage had closed down, but the Anglican church, which had been kept locked in 1973, was open. It was as bare and featureless as I had remembered.

With great trouble, I had found the vicarage, fifteen years earlier, and the vicar had come out, unlocked the church and shown me round. Like almost all Church of Ireland vicars, he was an extremely pleasant person. However, I had been utterly stuck for complimentary remarks about his church, which rather disappointed him. 'Very nice' was the best I could think of.

A short way away, the ruins of the Franciscan Friary, far more substantial, form an entrance to Roscrea's enormous Roman Catholic church, set in woodland with a stream running between steep mossy banks. In 1973, I had been entranced to see dippers, like dark robin whitebreasts, fly below me over the tinkling waters, or perch boldly on stones in the midst of the little waterfall. Now the wood seemed smaller than I remembered, but the dippers were 'as bold as ever still'.

Walking quietly along, I looked down and found I was standing directly above a dipper, which perched on a stone and stared at the rushing eddies. It was absolutely motionless, a sleek dark brown bird, intent only on seeing and capturing a water insect. From a tree on the bank opposite, a brown kestrel with pointy wings swooped down over the dipper and myself, and flapped into a patch of long grass, where it began tussling with a mouse. Still the dipper didn't move. Soon the kestrel flew back into the tree with its prey. *Still* the dipper didn't move. Finally the bird turned its head rapidly right and left. Feeling somehow relieved, I walked on. Chestnut trees, with twisting mossy branches, dropped conkers on my pathway.

That night I dined at the Tower Hotel, along with several local couples enjoying a quiet night out. A big hairy-armed man walked in, scowling like a bullock and swinging his whole body from side to side. He was unshaven, with tufty eyebrows, and seemed docile. All the waitresses greeted him, but I felt nervous in case he had come to reclaim his butter, now in a case at Damer House.

Over my meal, I glanced through a magazine called *Hot Press*, Ireland's answer to the *New Musical Express*. In other words, it catered for the Rock Intelligentsia, cynical schoolboys, students and ageing hippies, and contained arts reviews and political articles as well as pop music news. In England the Rock Press often seems above the law in its approval of drugs and casual use of swearwords. The Irish *Hot Press* in its turn seemed free to ridicule religious belief. Writers and readers seemed greatly tickled by the reported apparitions of the Blessed Virgin Mary. They referred to her as the 'B.V.M.' and affected to believe that she was a pop singer leading a group and playing surprise venues all over the country. When people gathered in hope of seeing an apparition, and none came, the *Hot Press* would lament 'How much longer is the B.V.M. going to disappoint her fans?' It seemed to be a running joke in the paper.

With interest, I read an article about the town of Tullamore, to the north of Roscrea. *Hot Press* dubbed it the 'Entertainment Capital of the Midlands'. I had already made arrangements to go to Tullamore, all unaware that I was heading for an Irish Las Vegas.

At breakfast in the Pathe Hotel next morning, I saw with resigned disappointment that the waitresses were just ordinary women. In 1973 they had been laughing Tipperary country girls, merry and innocent, reared on cream and butter, fond of a joke yet morally inviolate, in the bloom of contented youth. It always amused me to see that when they had finished serving delicious lunches, they would rush to the Tower Hotel for their own lunch, although the food there was exactly the same. In the company of the young Pathe barman they would transform their lunch break into a feast of merriment, away from the eyes of their supervisors.

Looking back, May 1973 seems almost a golden age, when Ireland's lush neglected pastures were yellow with buttercups and water iris blooms, gilded lilies indeed. My diary pages are covered with drawings of little animals and comic Irishmen labelled 'Farmer Maloney' and 'Paddy O'Rourke, He's Nothing But Talk.' But what does the writing say?

MAY 1973:
Today there was a great wedding at the Pathe Hotel. The dance hall, where a Reception Buffet was being served, was out of bounds to the uninvited, but nearly all the Reception took place in the lounge bar. Continuous Guinnesses were being handed through the hatch, dripping with foam. Confetti covered the hotel, from the front steps to the hall and into the bar. I peeped past the stern ushers into the ballroom, and caught a glimpse of the bride and groom, both in their late thirties. He was red-faced in a silver grey suit and brown Beatle hair, and she was in white and blushing. All the guests came in family parties, with lots of tow-haired children. Soon the children began to amuse themselves by flicking beermats through the air.

The smoky air of the bar lounge quickly filled with skimming beermats. One bounced off my head. Adults gave slight curses when hit, as if stung by a gnat, and then went on talking and drinking. Matters were very soon brought under control by a practical young lady with a page-boy haircut and kindly grey eyes. I guessed at once, quite correctly, that she was the local schoolmistress. Within minutes she had gathered all the children around her, an accordion on her knee. This she played expertly, singing loudly and urging the youngsters to join in the chorus.

> There was an old woman and she lived in the woods,
> Waley waley wire!
> There was an old woman and she lived in the woods,
> Down by the Banks of the Suir!

Mention of the River Suir reminded me of Suir Ice Cream, Ireland's finest. I fell into conversation with a family who had never been to England, with the exception of an Auntie Bridget, a woman with long dark hair and a thirst for whiskey. She had lived in Kilburn and knew London well. All the family seemed open, innocent people except for Auntie B., who was sarcastic and cynical. Meanwhile, the schoolmistress and the children sang on cheerfully.

> She stabbed him with her wee pen knife,
> Waley waley wire!
> She stabbed him with her wee pen knife,
> Down by the Banks of the Suir!

All at once, a huge swag-bellied man in a waistcoat stood up, and called for quiet. 'Shhhh!' all the adults admonished the children at once. 'Patriot songs!' Eyes closed, the big man sang in a rich, melodramatic tenor, song after song, with all eyes upon him. The flow of Guinness continued as a whispering undercurrent.

> Oh, I remember well the day
> Kilkenny's pride went down...

'I was dere, boys, I was dere,' a tiny old man interrupted emotionally, in an indescribable croak.

Next, the singer, obviously a well-respected man of local fame, sang a song of the Wild Geese, the aristocrats who fled Ireland to offer their services as fighting men to Continental monarchs of the seventeenth century. Almost sobbing, he told of a girl's sweetheart who 'has gone to France, to wear the Fleur de Lys...'

Finally, with the same passionate emotion, he sang a Percy French ditty, unaware that the song was supposed to be comic. Percy French (1854–1920) came of Ascendancy stock, and wrote of 'native Irish' matters with great affection. Wildly popular all over Ireland, he sang, told jokes and played the banjo in a one-man show. His most famous song must be 'Abdul the Bulbul Ameer', which he failed to copyright.

'Come back, Paddy Reilly, to Ballyjamesduff, Come back, Paddy Reilly, to me!' the singer lamented, wiped the tears from his eyes, and sat down. A moment later he sprang up again as if inspired, and sang the most patriotic song of all, in his rich marvellous voice, slowly sinking to one knee and singing on in that position, with one hand on his heart, as if proposing.

> Here's to the flag of Ulster's boys,
> Our flag is theirs also...

Lesser men then took his place, and we were speedily treated to popular hits such as the 'Cliffs of Dooneen' ('Farewell to Doneen, farewell for a while') and 'I'll give you a daisy, a daisy – I'll give you a daisy a day.' Meanwhile, an electric organ rang out from the dancehall stage, augmented by yet another accordion, and all the invited guests hurried in for the dancing. I wasn't allowed in, but stood in the doorway.

To my incredulity, an apparently serious IRA song was sung, to great applause, by a hairy-legged man in a skirt and lipstick, dressed as a policewoman. Waltzes were then played, to favourite old tunes, 'Daisy, Daisy', 'Cockles and Mussels', 'On Top of Old Smokey' and 'Loch Lomond'. Whenever the music stopped, people changed partners in quick grabs and were off again, leaving the less quick-witted as wallflowers. In the midst of all this hilarity, the bride and groom slipped away. A little later, I did the same.

It was a glorious day, and I walked out of town to see the fish farm. I had never seen a fish farm before. It turned out to be three newly dug ponds in a meadow, each one boiling and leaping with trout. After admiring them for a while, I retraced my steps to a monastery I had seen, a huge stately building set in park grounds, obviously ex-Ascendancy. I got talking to a group of young Irishmen on holiday, and they said that they were staying in the monastery guest house. Apparently, if you know your monasteries, you can have monastery holidays all over Ireland.

So ended my diary entry on the memorable day of the Pathe wedding. Throughout all the intervening years, I had regretted not having stayed in that monastery. I was now about to set matters right. Finishing my breakfast, I strolled down to the Catholic church, on my way to the monastery once more. It was a grey, gloomy day, very different from May, 1973.

Steeply wooded slopes led up from the church to the graveyard. I clambered through these woods, caterpillars on threads and all kind of creatures taking up abode on me. A neat strip of graveyard among trees and undergrowth contained rows of black iron crosses where nuns were buried. After a while, I descended to the dipper stream once more, and followed it out of the churchyard to a crossroads with a tiny faded grocery-pub. Here the stream passed underneath small, stone Burcoo Bridge, dated 1898.

I did not know it then, but the Burcoo Bridge is a local landmark for tinkers, who gather outside Roscrea to beg for alms from the monks. A sarcastic old tinker lady stood on it, regarding me closely. She was accompanied by a small girl with the aged face of a changeling. With a distant nod, unacknowledged, I walked past them and on to the road which led through fields to the monastery. Brown rats with young, inexperienced faces hopped about in the roadside verges. Children's voices could be heard from a tinker caravan in a narrow side lane.

Eventually I reached the great monastery gates, with a brightly burnished golden eagle on the pillars at either side. Chestnut trees leaned over the demesne walls. Playing in the road in front of this grandiose gateway was a ragged, grimy tinker boy with warts all over his hands and the tip of his nose scraped off. 'What have you got in your bag?' he asked me conversationally.

I showed him, and he waved me on in the manner of a blasé customs officer. So I entered Mount St Joseph Abbey, home of Cistercian monks.

The great building that I had supposed to be the monastery back in 1973 proved in reality to be a select boarding school for boys, who were taught by the monks and by lay teachers. From the path, I could see thirteen-year-old boys being led through doorways by monks in brown robes. Large hurling fields surrounded the school, and much of the parkland was given over to pasture, where friendly Friesian cattle grazed. A large flat prehistoric-looking stone had been wired off from the boys and cattle. *All* stones are prehistoric, but you know what I mean! It was balanced on another stone, with a white cross beside them.

My path curved around a farm, and I then beheld a gaunt, grey cathedral-sized church with a tall steeple. Steps led down to the great church, but my path continued beneath trees, up terraced gardens and so to the doorway of Mount St Joseph. The Mount was a cream-coloured building, a former 'gentleman's residence'.

Inside, I found myself in a highly-polished hallway, with a tall ceiling and religious pictures on the walls. There was a Reception desk in the hall, and behind it was a pink, merry-faced innocent country girl called Mary, the very image of all the long-lost waitresses of the Pathe Hotel.

'I'm only just started here today,' she informed me. 'We do accommodation, but the best is, if I fetch Father Gilbert.'

Father Gilbert appeared, and listened benignly while I explained my reasons, both spiritual and literary, for wanting to stay in his monastery.

'Our Bursar is a literary man,' he observed. 'Father Walsh has written a book about the man who once lived here, Richard Heaton. You will meet the Bursar shortly, and he can arrange about your room. Meanwhile, why don't you have some tea?'

So, waited on by smiling Mary, I tucked into an enormous pile of bread and butter and drank quantities of tea. An extraordinary brown beetle, shaped like an historic musical instrument, perhaps a squat violin, emerged from my clothing and walked across the table. Its head was the violin handle, and the snapped-off strings formed its legs.

After tea, I sat in the long, stately lounge, with its large windows overlooking the gardens and oil paintings of bearded priests on the walls. I found that the house had been turned back to front for the monks, and the front door had at one time been the back door. A monk called Father Gabriel pointed out an eighty-two-year-old monk to me, one of the older Fathers. He was outside, gravely feeding a donkey. Most of the monks were in late middle age. 'We hand out food and clothing to the tinkers, and that makes us a bit unpopular with the farmers,' Father Gabriel said. 'The tinkers often graze their horses in the nearby fields.'

I told him about my visit to Damer House, where I had seen the Kelly diaries.

'Our Bursar knew the Kellys well, father and son,' he told me. The son Huby died in the County Home and left the farm to this monastery. Our Bursar, Father Walsh, found masses of old soggy paper, while he was clearing up around the farm. That was the diaries! He brought them back here in plastic bags and everyone thought he was mad!'

At that point the madman himself appeared, a good-humoured elderly man. He took my particulars and a small amount of money, and I promised to come back next day and spend three nights at Mount St Joseph. As I left, he pressed a copy of his book on me, a *Life of Richard Heaton, First Irish Botanist*.

The sun shone as I walked back to the Pathe Hotel along the country road. It had been hard for me to tell one monk (or Father) from another. All wore brown and cream robes and calm expressions. They had been pleased to talk, equally pleased to stop and very keen to be obliging. While waiting for the Bursar, I had drawn some pictures in my pad of devils playing fiddles while donkeys danced. Very unsuitable for monks, they were intended for any tinker children I might meet.

When I reached the side lane where the trailer caravan was parked, I walked deliberately towards it. Two neat dark-haired girls, of eight and six years old or so, peeped excitedly at me from the caravan door. Was I calling on them? As I passed the caravan, I averted my eyes to the hedge as a countryman does, catching a glimpse of an 'I thought so' expression. Suddenly I wheeled round, made straight for the caravan and loudly asked the girls and their father if they wanted to buy any pictures. The father was an easy-going man in a brown jacket. All three of them looked at my drawings in amazement.

'One pound the lot!' I said firmly, so as to establish myself as sane.

'Please buy them,' the older girl wheedled her father.

'I've got no money right now', he said ruminatively. 'Come back tomorrer. No, wait [a thought struck him], leave the pictures and come back on Thursday.'

So I gave the pictures to the girls, and we parted with many courtesies. Idly, I wondered whereabouts in Ireland they would be on Thursday.

That night in my bedroom, I looked at Father Walsh's book. Richard Heaton (1601–1666) came to Ireland from Yorkshire, and acquired his estate near Roscrea by lending money to the Irish owner, O'Carroll. When O'Carroll couldn't repay, Heaton took his land and changed the estate's name from Ballyskenagh to Mount Heaton. Towards the end of his life, he had the present house built.

Heaton had taken the Royalist side in the English Civil War, and first came to Ireland as a regimental chaplain. During the Stalin-like Cromwellian terror in Ireland that followed the war, he stayed out of trouble in England, returning to Ireland when Charles II gained the throne. He found his Mount Heaton estate intact: many others had been given to supporters of Cromwell. Throughout his career as an Anglican clergyman, Richard Heaton collected, named and catalogued unusual plants, both in Ireland and England. Some were *very* unusual, such as the Hoary Fleabane, whose smell was said to send fleas into paroxysms, and which has never been seen since Heaton recorded it.

Altogether, I thought, as I closed the book, Richard Heaton did not emerge as a wholly agreeable character. His biographer, Father Walsh, came out as the best of the two, for seeing so much good in his subject. Heaton's descendants held the estate until 1818. Various sales followed. The monks arrived in 1878, and the schoolboys in 1905. Now Ballyskenagh/Mount Heaton had become Mount St Joseph. So many monastic estates in Britain have become manors that I could scarcely complain at a manorial estate becoming Church land. It seemed only justice.

Father Walsh's book was full of interesting or horrific snippets of Irish history. My favourite was the account of skins exported from Ireland in 1662. These included the pelts of wolves, foxes, badgers, martens and others, the hides of 'grey stags and black stags', swan-skins and squirrel-skins, the latter sold by the thousand. What a treasury of wild life Ireland must have possessed before this trade began! Now not a squirrel could be seen, but there were plenty of rats.

CHAPTER ELEVEN

☘

In a Monastery Garden

Nobody at the Pathe Hotel seemed surprised next morning when I said that I was going to stay in the monastery. It was seen as quite an ordinary thing to do. However, the taxi driver who took me there seemed surprised to learn that Father Walsh, the Bursar, had written a book. 'Father Walsh written a book!' he echoed. 'There now, I never knew that.' We drove through the gates and along the drive through the park. 'On the centenary of the monastery, in '78, the President of Ireland came here, by helicopter in the pouring rain,' the driver continued. 'He landed in that field over there, and they held Mass on those flat rocks, where they've raised a cross.' He pointed at the prehistoric stones.

At the entrance hall of the monastery, tall Father Gilbert met me, looking harassed. He showed me up the stairs to my room, which was clean and airy, with a glorious view out over the parkland, where chestnut trees were turning gold. The mature chestnut trees were the glory of Mount St Joseph. I opened the windows, dislodging a few small spiders which were the only sign that Mount St Joseph Guest House was not cleaned by women. For the monks, it turned out, lived a Spartan life in a building near the great church. Guests such as myself saw little of their hard-working routine.

Monks in Cistercian orders work hard at practical tasks, such as building their own monasteries. Monastic life, in the Christian tradition, is an attempt to follow Christ's teachings on a communal and organized scale, rather than as an individual alone, giving all to the poor and following Him. There are no individual possessions for monks, but collectively owned possessions are still there. So monks can remain penniless as their monasteries grow rich, and are thus able to help their neighbours all the time. A strict régime of work and prayer prevents the monks from feeling rich and comfortable, for theirs is a life of self-sacrifice. In the Middle Ages and no doubt since, there were many lapses from this high standard, but the standard remains.

Most Englishmen, when they do not confuse monks with Druids, imagine them as fat jolly drunkards, given to overeating and debauchery. Here Protestant propaganda has overreached itself, and made monastic life seem an English Heaven. Apart from the Chinese, the Saxon English must be the most unspiritual people in the world. St Benedictine, who wrote the first generally accepted monastic rules in the sixth century, had no visions of Friar Tuck in mind. (Friars, incidentally, began as wandering holy men, following Jesus as individuals. They too became organized, the better to help the poor.)

According to a booklet in my room, the Cistercian Order began in the twelfth century, at Citeaux in Burgundy. 'Citeaux', in Latin, became Cistercium, hence Cistercians.

When I had unpacked, I set out to explore. Apart from bedrooms, Richard Heaton's old house contained a wonderful old brown library, with busts of eminent Catholics and lots of books by my hero, G. K. Chesterton. There was a shop with a monk behind the counter, selling religious knick-knacks. Only the ground floor, with the great lounge, gave a hint of what the house might have been like when it was a family home.

At half past five, bells rang and I hurried down the steps to the great church, following the other guests. Inside, it was dark and Gothic, with wooden pews and silver-grey pillars. A few countryish people also attended, the women thin with head shawls. Probably they worked on the estate. I sat near the back, so nobody could see that I didn't know how to duck the knee or cross myself. There were two rows of windows on either side of the church, one row of Victorian stained glass and above it, very high up, windows of plain bright blue shading into delicate eggshell hues. No matter the weather during my stay, these windows gave the impression of a blue sky outside.

Thirty monks silently appeared in the dark recesses of the church, from whence doors led to their quarters. Most of them wore white robes, with the hoods hanging back, and some wore brown. They took their places in the choir on the far side of a dais where the priest-monk stood. Mournful, eerie chanting took up most of the service. This was Vespers. After a time, the chanting became restful, soothing and hypnotic. It was in English, and I could pick up a word here and there. Very soon, the service was over and everyone departed, dipping their fingers in holy water as they did so, and dabbing their foreheads. I walked along with a tall, bespectacled old man, with a face of smiling simplicity and rather rickety legs. He seemed to be looking forward to his supper.

Mary, the spirited country girl, showed me to a crowded table piled high with delicious stacks of home-made bread and butter from the monastery bakery and dairy. There was an enormous teapot. Like her counterparts in the Pathe Hotel of old, Mary was adept at brushing off flirtatious men with a joke. My table was not only crowded with eatables, but with other guests, and we all introduced ourselves.

There were two nuns there, one a brisk Irish girl who was on a three-month three-yearly leave from her mission in Gambia, West Africa. The other was a timid, schoolgirlish English gentlewoman who sometimes exclaimed 'I say! How jolly!' Her name was Sister Margaret Merry, and she was on a visit from a convent in Connemara. The tall old man sat on one side of me, and on the other side sat a big, well-dressed imposing man, who said he was a horse dealer and had been a successful businessman in America. He had a slightly abstracted, hunted look, as if he had sold his soul to the devil and time was running out. A nondescript salesman-like man with hair well oiled and brushed sat at one end of the table. At the other end sat a short malevolent-eyed Dublin man named Maher.

Such was Maher's force of character that his end became the head of the table, and he the master of festivities. He had wit spiced with malice, and held strong opinions. Everybody talked as bread, butter and ham and eggs were steadily demolished. Further supplies of bread and tea were called for. It turned out that the tall old man, with his perpetual nodding smile, was called Percy. He had never married and had lived in a single room in an old house in Dublin for the past thirty years. A friend had persuaded him to have a country holiday at Mount St Joseph. Maher, our host, worked for the railways, and came to the monastery each year to see his brother, who was a monk. Sometimes the brother was not allowed to talk or to stop working, and Maher would just wave to him. All the men were Irish. Sometimes the conversation grew surreal, at other times it resembled a Flann O'Brien monologue.

'I've led a worthless life,' mourned the Horse Dealer. 'I need to make a confession.'

In a calming voice, the sister from Gambia told him that he wasn't as bad as all that.

'They've built a New Jerusalem,' the salesman remarked. This was startling news. 'I saw it when I went to the Holy Land. It's just next to the Old Jerusalem. Rich American Jews built it.'

'Jews, eh?' ruminated the Horse Dealer. 'I don't mind them joining the country clubs in America, but they all try and become secretaries and take over. Being Irish and a Catholic, I have been discriminated against in London. They wouldn't let me join the Masons. Is the Masons still where the money is, d'ye know? I try to do my best, but I just haven't lived right. I buy best quality riding horses, but they're all being bought up by the English nouveaux riches. I've made money, but I'm unfulfilled.'

'I was at the seaside once!' the tall old man, Percy, suddenly announced. Everyone looked interested. 'I like to go swimming, but I do be afraid of only one thing – the jellyfish.'

MAHER: To be sure, the jellyfish is bad.

HORSE DEALER: My sister in Dingle was telling me there's a tame dolphin in the sea there, and she was swimming with it.

MAHER: Ah, these creatures, the dolphin, the porpoise, the seal and the penguin, there's no harm in them. There's no harm in the whale. The whale is friendly. Even the killer whale is friendly. I don't know why they call it a killer. The lion, now, is gentle and friendly.

SISTER MARGARET MERRY [tremulously]: I read about a young lady lion tamer who always played with her lion. But one day, when she went into its cage, she heard it growling in a strange way. Then she turned round to get something.

MAHER: And?

SISTER MARGARET MERRY [in a tiny sad voice]: It ate her.

MAHER: Ah, then it was *hungry*. They're tame enough except when they get hungry, so.

After the meal, I strolled out of the back door that had been Richard Heaton's front door into a golden evening, dark shadows barring the avenues of trees. The mansion had lost most of its old castle turrets when the monks had added on a flat-roofed top storey, but it was still an impressive sight. Leaves were yellowing, and I found a hazel tree laden with nuts. On the borders of the woods, meadows where cattle grazed led down to a little stream, with ditches and waterways leading from it, in a series of miniature waterfalls. Two white swans glided by, and chaffinches twittered in the hedges. Now and again, the still, solitary figure of a monk could be seen among the trees.

On the other side of the mansion, near the school, boys wandered about in twos and threes. They wore old-fashioned grey clothes, but no uniform as such. A young man was teaching his eager collie to fetch a stick, watched keenly by a monk and by old Percy, the jellyfish man. I walked up to the gate, and a tinker boy waved to me. As soon as the sun vanished, a large yellow half-moon appeared. Lights began to go on in the monastery buildings. I returned to the church for the last service of the day, Compline.

When I entered people were already kneeling. Grey ghostly monks appeared to the booming of a bell. After a short period of chanting, Compline was over. I returned to the house for the final cup of tea before bed. For most of the monks now it would be the Greater Silence, as they worked and prayed before retiring, ready to be up again at a quarter to four in the morning. Guests could sleep on till seven.

Lingering over my cup of tea, I asked the Sister about her mission work in Gambia.

'Well, we don't have many converts now. Our few converts are all from animist backgrounds. Ninety per cent of the Gambians are Muslims, and they never convert. Once we gave all the children in our school a Christian education, but Koranic teachers now come in to instruct the Muslims. All the children who can, go to our school. Our general education gives a certain amount of moral guidance. But before our policy changed, the Muslims never minded Christian teaching, as they know Christ as a prophet and respect Christian morality.'

That night, from my icon-protected bed, I could hear heavy rain pouring down outside.

Waking with the dawn, I looked out of the window. I had heard the bells ringing earlier, in pitch darkness, and had turned over in bed thankful that I was not a monk. Now I found that the sun was awakening, the soft pink sky fading into blue and mist rising from the dripping wet fields and trees. Wood pigeons cooed and cows lowed far away. Hopping down the steep meadow, beside the great chestnut trees, came a red-brown hare. I could tell it wasn't a rabbit, because it held its body high from the ground like a deer, and hopped on tiptoe. All the same, it wasn't as large as an English brown hare. It was an Irish hare, the first I had ever seen, and I gazed in enchantment as it hopped with ears erect towards the monastery. When it reached the tarmacked path between the trees, it suddenly turned and ran up the drive on long legs, disappearing from view.

I had seen Scottish mountain hares in a zoo, and the Irish Hare was of the same stocky build. Ireland lacks many English animals, and the big brown hare is one of them. When the ice-caps retreated, Arctic hares remained on the Scottish mountain tops, and became grey mountain hares, turning white in winter. Brown hares returned from the south, and occupied the lowlands. However, Ireland became adrift from Europe before the brown hares could get there. So the Arctic hares came down from the Irish mountains and applied for the position of lowland hare. The post was vacant, and they took it, turned brown and stayed that way in snowless winters. In physique, they are Arctic hares still, a perpetual reminder of the Ice Age.

Bells rang once more, and I hurried down to the vast church, the wet flagstones glinting in the sun. Several estate and lay workers kneeled in their pews, eyes closed, muttering in fervour. Once more the monks chanted, the beautiful sonorous sound I had heard in the early morning, outside my room. The day before, a lone chant from an invisible source had surprised me as I went about the monastery. Now I found that these soft stray chants came from the old man Percy, who sang softly to himself as he climbed the steep stairs. Maher gave him an ironic glance.

I looked into the kitchen on my way to the breakfast table and saw baker-monks carrying in huge baskets of home-made loaves, each loaf as light and delicious as the next. Here bread really *was* the staff of life and the glory of the monastery table. Quite unlike the home-made bread of stripped pine households, it could be white or brown, and cut into thin slices. Loaves were loaf-shaped, with round top knots.

Mary, the country girl, hurried in, pink and breathless. She had cycled all the way from her parents' farm. Percy made a gallant effort to flirt with her. 'Get on away out of that!' she laughed. 'I remember when half the Irish girls were like that,' the Horse Dealer said seriously when she had gone. 'Playful, unspoiled and innocent, so that nothing could touch them. What has happened to Ireland? It was better in the days of the great country houses, when people respected those placed above them, and there was order in life. I admire England, and the Anglo-Irish set a standard.'

Horse Dealer himself set a standard, for he leaped to his feet whenever a nun sat or rose, and addressed everyone in clerical garb as 'Father', 'Sister', or 'Your Reverence' as the occasion demanded. Today the Gambian nun and the salesman had gone, leaving only Maher, Percy, myself and Sister Margaret Merry at the table.

'Is it you I hear moaning and chanting about the place?' Maher asked Percy.

'Yes, sacred music is my passion. I love to sing the works of all them classical fellers,' Percy confessed. He took a long satisfying draught of tea. 'Now I'll really begin to talk!'

'Jesus, if that's how you talk before you begin, how will it be after you start? If it's like your singing, I'll have to move out of here altogether!'

Percy was delighted at these sallies, and smiled from ear to ear. 'What a jolly crowd here!' he cried, borrowing the phrase from Sister Margaret Merry. 'And so respectable! You want to hear what people told me about this place, that I'd be on my knees praying from morning to night, attending lectures and singing hymns half the night. Really, the Mass is only a few minutes and you hardly feel it.'

I shared his relief at the Mass, which was even easier for my Protestant self, as I didn't go forward for Communion. Maher, too, had a passion in life, it turned out. He was mad on steam trains, and talked Steam until breakfast was over.

Suddenly I remembered that it was Thursday, so I set out to collect my pound from the tinker family. I didn't really need a pound, nor did I think that the tinkers would still be there, but a fierce insistence on debts paid seemed to be a good way to meet tinkers.

I knew it! The tinkers had gone. So I returned to the gold eagle gate of Mount St Joseph. Not far away, to my delight, I saw another tinker camp, seven trailer caravans parked in a lane that curled away from farm to farm up to the hills on the horizon.

Nodding politely at the tinkers, I strolled past their caravans, noting the strange piles of scrap metal that filled in the gaps between each trailer. The tinkers had neatly stacked their various bits of metal into rows that resembled scrap metal houses, with oddly shaped walls and roofs. From these roofs, wooden clothes props poked like slender chimneys, washing hanging from trailer to trailer like flags at a carnival.

Two tall young men, one with a shock of curly dark hair, were absorbed in a game of hurling rocks into car tyres. Two tyres lay on their sides in the road, with a young man standing by each one. Taking turns in a very deliberate fashion, each man pitched his rock at the other one's tyre. I am not a cricketer, but I think they were over-arm bowling. Rock-chucking seemed a highly organized sport, and you scored a point whenever a rock fell into the centre of a tyre. Wisely, no attempt was made to bat the rocks out of the way.

All the tinkers, including the rock-chuckers, greeted me with polite comments on the weather. They had been tamed by the monks. One trailer, in particular, was beautiful inside, with rows of ornamental china plates on shelves. Children rode up and down on bikes. I walked back to Mount St Joseph along with a kindly weathered-looking lady with a shawl about her shoulders, trying in vain to persuade her small granddaughter to stop crying. She had fallen over while gathering wood and water with her grandmother. Granny pushed a churn of water, surrounded by sticks and branches, on a supermarket trolley, but there was no room for the child to ride.

'Do you know the family who lived there in the side lane of the Roscrea road, and have just moved away?' I asked. 'They owe me a bit of money.'

'I do not,' the granny replied. 'Wait, d'ye mean the man who lives behind the hill, wi' a red-headed daughter in a cartie?'

I didn't, but I relished the description, and wished I *did* know them, even if they owed me thousands. By a 'cartie', I think she meant a simple horse-drawn covered wagon.

Later, at the door of the church, I kept an appointment with Father Walsh the writer and Bursar. He had kindly offered to show me round the monastery. First of all, in the church, he showed me a prayer book hand-written by a nun, with beautiful lettering. It was written in English, but a huge old one, nearby, was in Latin, with metal clasps on the door-like covers.

'We don't do calligraphy here, but we can bind books which the Sisters write,' he said.

The original altar of the church had been replaced by 'something more modern'. 'Vatican II, I'm afraid,' Father Walsh sighed, his merry eyes losing their twinkle for a moment. 'Sometimes I think they threw the baby out with the bathwater.' He was referring to the Second Vatican Council of the early sixties, when it was decreed from Rome that the Church had to 'go modern'.

A door led from the church to the monastery, into a part far removed from the bright airy guest house and the sprightly meal-time conversations. Here were stone flags and dark cloisters, with occasional old monks padding silently by. I was led out to a courtyard, where stone archways led into the former stables, now cowsheds.

'What wonderful ironwork on that door,' I marvelled.

'That was done at the forge. We hardly use the forge now, since the horses have gone.'

I caught a glimpse of an old-world flower garden, then Father Walsh led me back indoors. Cell doorways lined a dark corridor, and in the old dormitory (now disused) strange wooden settle beds stretched from end to end of a lengthy hall. They somewhat resembled bookshelves in a library, with very little shelf-room for sleeping. Hooks on the wooden divisions once carried curtains for privacy. A dusty glass case contained chain mail, helmets and swords, perhaps to complete the medieval image. Bare floorboards and an ecclesiastical window completed the picture. Nowadays the monks had more comfortable quarters.

Father Walsh then took me to the Refectory, or dining room, still in use. Large earthenware water jugs stood in rows along the centre of a long table. A place was laid for each monk along the table, with a cold meal beneath a cloth. Each plate was accompanied by an orange and a banana.

'We are vegetarians,' Father Walsh explained, 'but sometimes meat is served in cases of sickness. Our hospital is upstairs, but there's only one inmate, a senile monk who doesn't know who he is. Look, the Refectory panelling is made up of dismantled wooden beds from one of the dormitories. That was my old bed, that piece at the end.'

I was taken outdoors once more, and shown the carpentry hall, where two old men, one in a cloth cap, were cutting fence posts out of logs. The room resembled a Saxon longhouse, as estate carpentry shops generally do, and the floor was covered in sawdust.

'Now here is the farm,' my guide continued, leading me through an archway.

A stable clock still kept good time. Farm and stables dated, in part, from the days when Mount St Joseph was Mount Heaton. Ideas on farming, however, had leaped ahead to the twentieth century.

'We use some lay people in the farm and the carpentry hall,' Father Walsh said, as Friesian cattle lumbered into the modern milking parlour, hit by men with sticks. I had heard of modern dairy methods in England, and the monastery farm did not seem quite so bad (or so modern), by comparison. Black sockets were clamped over the cows' udders, and the milk was forced upwards through pulsing tubes into glass drums. Part of the stables had been converted into a nursery for sucking calves. Each one stood in a box with its head stuck through a hole as if it had been sentenced to the stocks. Eagerly the calves looked at us, like adorable dark eyed puppies in a pet shop. Where were their mothers?

'These little ones aren't on solids yet, and this way they don't crowd into each other at feeding time,' Father Walsh said uneasily. A new-born calf, still sticky, staggered wild-eyed and motherless in a tiny pen. 'I used to help on the farm, but now it's all mechanized.'

Outside, in the muck-filled yard, a space-age young man in a mask, a paraquat pack on his back and a spray gun in his hand, lurched by, waving cheerfully.

'That's one of our younger Brothers,' said grey-haired Father Walsh with great approval. 'He was the Head Boy at the school and stayed on to become a monk. That's very unusual!'

Away from the cows and the stench of silage, the farm looked more monasterial.

'There's our goat. It leads the cows in to milking, but otherwise it does what it likes. See those henhouses out in the fields? We used to keep hens, but now there's only a few, owned by the old carpenter you saw. They should last his time.'

Last of all, Father Walsh pointed out Mount St Joseph's pride, the bakery. Bread here was not only eaten by the monks and their guests, but by the boys in the school. Extra loaves were sent to nuns and sold to local people. Father Walsh's tour ended near where it had begun, by the weeping beech trees outside the church. I thanked him fulsomely. Never-ending work and prayer made up the life of a Cistercian monk.

Celibacy seemed no more of a hardship to the monks or nuns that I had met that it had been to scholarly bachelor uncles or high-spirited spinster aunts of yesteryear, before we were told that sex was compulsory.

At suppertime in the guest house, the talk turned to politics. 'There's a lot of crewkery [crookery] in politics in Ireland,' said Maher. 'The man I admire is Ian Paisley. I think we should have him for President.'

'I say! Really! Fearful man!' cried Sister Merry.

'He would never accept,' Maher reassured her. 'But that man has got a way with him. He saved a priest's life once. The Republican terrorists had seized an Ulster policeman, so the Loyalist terrorists seized a priest. They said that if the IRA killed the policeman, they'd kill the priest.

'Paisley intervened. He said, "Let the priest go," and they *let* him go. The IRA *did* kill the policeman. So now. Another time, he got a Loyalist terrorist to surrender his weapons. The nuns in Ulster won't hear a word against Paisley. I met some nuns once on the train to Dundalk, and they said how Paisley had helped them, by giving to charity. That's why I say we should make him our President.'

Apart from Sister Margaret Merry, who was English, no one seemed to think this was an unusual point of view. The Horse Dealer, who now seemed more at peace with himself, listened with interest to my description of life in the monastery.

'Have you noticed how few and how old the monks are?' he asked. 'There are thirty here at most, and the rest of the work is done by lay people. This monastery's best days are past. From what you told me, there's only one young Brother here at all. There used to be craftsmen, but now there's nothing but a para-military paraquat-squirter.' The mysterious Horse Dealer rose in my estimation.

At Mass, next morning, a purple-clad priest addressed a large congregation and delivered a homely sermon in English. Years ago, in complete incomprehension, I had attended a Latin Mass in pre-Vatican II days. An Irish girl had dragged me to a church in Brighton when I was in my early twenties. If only I had known that the Latin Mass was going to be abolished, I would have paid more attention. Latin chants would have sounded very fine in this monastic setting.

After breakfast, I set out to revisit the fish farm, taking a side lane around the edge of the estate, past a mill. It was a sunny day, and birds sang in the hedgerows. A path through a dark strip of woodland, over a wooden bridge, led to my destination. The three ponds were larger than I had remembered, with narrow grassy walkway-banks between them, as in pictures of rice plantations. However, only two ponds were full of clear water – the third was a fishless marsh of reeds. Swans with cygnets stood on one bank, and hissed as I walked by. On the ground lay a newly shot seagull, evidently a poacher. A deep-flowing stream was connected to the ponds by various channels, and brown trout darkened the waters. In spite of the constant fresh-flowing water, some trout suffered from fungus, for Nature never meant river fish to live in ponds.

Most of the teeming trout seemed in high spirits, however, and sometimes took it into their heads to sweep across their pond all at once, a swirling, rippling stampede of fish that was most impressive to watch. I was reminded of films I had seen of herds of plain animals, caribou or wildebeest, who suddenly career off in thousands in a sudden whim or panic, leaping and bucketing over the grasslands to the horizon. When the trout leaped, three or four in a row, they looked like porpoises. If the monks ever acquire this fish farm, perhaps they will substitute great carp for trout, and teach their charges to answer to a bell at feeding time, as in monasteries of old.

That afternoon I had an appointment with Father Gabriel, who had promised to show me around the school. I asked him if it were chance that he were named after an Archangel, or if he had chosen a new name on becoming a monk.

'When you come here, you can choose a religious name and propose it to the Abbot, so I chose Gabriel,' he told me. He was a grave man, unlike merry Father Walsh.

We walked over to the school, grey and Gothic at the centre, with pale concrete annexes at the sides, paid for by Government grant. The Cistercial College of Roscrea was the equivalent of a public school in England, and the boys were of public school age, the mid-teens. Lessons were just ending as we arrived at the main entrance, with its baronical staircase and the school coat of arms laid out in tiles on the floor. Boys hurried cheerfully out to the playing fields, dressed in black-and-white-striped jerseys. Teachers in tweed jackets walked out across the lawns.

It soon became clear to me that Father Gabriel regarded the school with pride as something the monks had built with their bare hands ('Father Columban laid that floor'). He proposed to show me buildings, not lesson books, and I would meet no teachers or boys. Throughout his working life as a Cistercian monk, the school had needed constant repair and alteration, and dominated the thoughts of all.

'We made nearly everything in that school, with just a few hired labourers,' he told me.

'Why is it that lay teachers are taking over from monks?' I asked.

'When we were under English rule, the Church provided a Catholic education under discouragement from above,' he replied, leaving me to infer that only Catholics with an extra-special call or mission, such as priests or monks, would then teach in overtly Catholic schools. Protestant discouragement may have fanned their fervour into a fiery, crusading spirit.

'Now that lay people are taking over teaching, this is one of the last monastery schools,' Father Gabriel continued. 'Most, but not all, of the teachers are laymen.'

Once more, as in the monastery, I was in a half-lit world of wooden panels, tiles and stone steps. At first sight, I felt very daunted at the sight of the boys' dormitories. They were not too different from the old monks' dormitories, rows of settle-back boxes stretching along a hallway. Maze-like, they contained ledges for clothes, like the stands at Cruft's.

I was next shown the dining room, library and grimly old-fashioned 'study rooms' for Prep (or homework-at-school). There were several 'study rooms', all large, with old-fashioned desks with holes for inkwells. Sixth-form boys were expected to pass 'Leaving Cert', similar to the English 'A' Level. I had looked at some Leaving Certificate papers in a bookshop, and they seemed of a high standard. Anyway, they were too hard for *me*.

There were no pictures on the wall in the school corridors. A large glass case marked '1916' contained photographs and relics of rebel pupils, exhibited with pride. In my day, we did our rebelling *before* we left school, and got into trouble. After showing me the television room, Father Gabriel led me to the New Chapel, finished in 1945. Most of the monks that I had met had worked on this Chapel.

'Look at those pink marble columns,' my guide said proudly. 'They come from my home, Midleton, in County Cork. There is a lot of green Connemara marble here, but in the sixties, after Vatican II, the whole place was redesigned and the altar moved to the centre. We brought in a redesigning architect, and he painted the green marble white.'

A gifted organist, Father Gabriel patted the instrument fondly, then led me back into the school and along the corridors of classrooms.

'Do the boys change rooms for each subject, or do the teachers come to *them*?' I enquired. I am a great believer in boys staying put, each regarding his familiar classroom as his school home. When my grammar school went Comprehensive and the 'home class' policy ended, I spent the remainder of my school life as a waif and stray, searching half-heartedly for my lessons.

'Boys here stay where they are,' I was reassured, 'except for science lessons and French, as the French room has audio-visual aids.'

Near the science rooms, which were several in number, we at last encountered a group of boys. All greeted Father Gabriel with polite smiles, and went on playing terrible pop music on a ghetto blaster. Further along, we met some more boys gathered round one of their number who sat on the floor playing very prettily on a guitar. Music and sport seemed to be the solace of the boys, and I thought they suffered their captivity bravely. Are public school boys lucky because they are taught so much and can go on to university, or *unlucky* because they are wrenched from the warmth of their homes and taught so much? No two people can ever agree on this, and you will have to make up your own mind.

Last of all, with baffled pride, Father Gabriel showed me the Computer Room, which was brimming with computers. 'I don't know what they do, but it looks very impressive,' he remarked. A crucifix on the wall looked odd in a Computer Room, but perhaps it served as an antidote.

Apart from the hurling and rugby pitches and a swimming pool, that was the end of the tour. I had seen no Art Room. Father Gabriel assured me that the boys had won cups for debate, their favourite pastime, so perhaps their creative powers were stretched in this way.

I shook hands with good Father Gabriel and wandered off into the park, where I surprised an old tinker woman furtively wheeling a trolley-load of broken branches from a wood. Mentally wishing her luck, I reflected that schools are at best a mere substitute for personal tutors, and are not the only way in which knowledge can be conveyed to younger generations. With the best will in the world on the part of teachers and parents, schools have often been the cause of deep unhappiness in the young. I shall now leave this subject open for Debate.

At my last monastery breakfast, the Horse Dealer was absent, but the nun from the mission at Gambia had returned. She told me that the Dealer had spent several hours talking to one of the Fathers and had made confession. He had been assured of God's forgiveness, and whatever had been troubling his mind had been settled one way or another. Indeed, I had seen his nerves recuperating day by day.

So, for the last time, I said goodbye to Percy, Maher and Sister Margaret Merry, and hurried down the steps to meet the taxi that was to carry me back to 'the world', or to be more precise, the Pathe Hotel. I left with happy memories of Mount St Joseph and its hard-working monks.

Roaming round Roscrea that afternoon, glad to be among the shops once more (no ascetic I), I popped into Hartnett's Men's Wear and bought a pair of socks. A comfortable-looking middle-aged man with glasses began to tell me about the wonders of Wales, where his brother had been for a wedding. From the place names he dropped, 'Kendal', 'Windermere' and so on, it became clear that his brother had been not to Wales but to the English Lake District.

'Is that right?' he asked, surprised. 'I've never been across the water, except for changing planes at Heathrow. Oh, I *wish* my brother was here. He only stepped out for a moment.'

His wish was granted, for the brother returned and praised the 'real old-fashioned pubs' of Lakeland. As always when Irishmen talk of England, they marvelled at how cheap everything is over there. National pride had caused Irish money to be severed from British sterling, with unfortunate results.

Lorries rumbled through Roscrea all day long, sometimes carrying enormous loads of straw. Tractors clattered through the town, and cows mooed from bumpy trailers. That night, in the Pathe Hotel, I dined among enormous farmers, raw and red, knives grasped in their gigantic hands as they sawed at huge steaks and set to with a will.

That night there was a concert in the ballroom, starring Eric Bogle, an intensely morbid Scottish Australian singer. Big, bearded and beery, Bogle wrote his own songs in traditional style, though with a left-wing bias that labelled them as 'folk'. He sang with Scottish and Australian accents alternately, and was a great hero with the crowd. His true-to-life song of the Gallipoli disaster, 'The Band Played Waltzing Matilda', had become a Hibernian Hit. For a long time I had tried to get another of his songs, a clumsy piece of satire entitled 'I Hate Wogs', banned from the Shrewsbury Record Library. But they always reinstated it.

The bar closed at two a.m. and I went to bed for my last night in the Pathe Hotel.

It was raining in the morning as I stepped on the bus for Birr. On my previous visit to Ireland, I had walked around Birr on a fine day, surprised at the way the great castle with its high demesne wall dominated the town. Birr Castle is still the home of the Parsons, Earls of Ross. Sir Lawrence Parsons had built the town, on the site of a monastery as usual, in 1620. Park and botanical gardens are open to the public, but the castle is not. This time I could not linger in Birr, as I was catching another bus northwards to Tullamore, 'entertainment capital of the Midlands'.

When it came, the Tullamore bus proved to be the Dublin bus also, and I struggled aboard with my heavy bag behind a large queue. Sharp, spry old ladies showed passes or counted out their money to the driver. The weather improved, and I settled down for an idyllic meander through the Irish Midland countryside. Roadside notices pointed to this saint's shrine and that saint's holy well. We drove through boreens, beside crumbling stone walls, past ruined churches, fields with sheep and cows, more sheep and cows in trailers, black peat bogs, peat on lorries, logs on lorries, industrial sites built on to forgotten historical sites and everything Ireland has to offer except hills. Taylor's Cross, Banagher, Ferbane, Ballycumber, Clara and finally Tullamore. Here I stepped down, and everyone else sailed off to Dublin.

My first impression of Tullamore, gained in the smart main shopping street, was how unpleasant and modish the young people looked. Here was disco entertainment unlimited, with garish posters everywhere. From the local loitering point, well-dressed young men gathered and threw beer-cans into the road. Soon I had taken a room at a glittering hotel near a bridge, the Phoenix Arms.

The hotel was built on to the bank of a narrow river, and my room overlooked the water, with a view of derelict buildings and a bonfire on the far bank. I unpacked and hurried downstairs to explore a hotel that was obviously the Midland Irishman's dream of sophistication. Pictures of brides hung on the walls, beneath fancy lighting, and non-stop country and western music poured from a loudspeaker near the front door.

Obviously, the hotel was a great place for wedding receptions. In fact, one was going on at the moment, in the disco-cum-dining hall where I stopped for a coffee. Lights flashed on and off, and a rock and roll band on a small stage played Irish songs with saxophones taking the place of fiddles. Rows of guests, dressed in bright colours, happily danced round and round in a conga line as I sipped and watched. Dance over, the bride left her husband at the door and scampered around among the guests in her white gown, face flushed with pleasure, chatting animatedly.

Dusk was falling as I finally stepped out into the streets of mysterious Tullamore.

CHAPTER TWELVE

☘

In the Midlands

Wandering around Tullamore, in the blue dusk, I felt like a lost soul in a strange spirit world, or a man in a troubled dream. Bright nightclub advertisements loomed from blank pebble-dash walls, and a aura of dampness and dereliction hung over all. Youths roamed everywhere, intent on their own affairs, ignoring and ignored by old couples on their way home from the bar or chip shop.

Soon I found myself in a gravel and brick-strewn wasteland that seemed part car park, part abandoned barrack square, bounded irregularly by the backs of shops and halls. A yellow patch of light on the puddly ground denoted the open doorway of a shed-like Snooker Hall. Youths from this hall wandered in aimless circles near the doorway, vigorously blowing into tartan Scottish bagpipes. 'St Columcille's Pipe Band', a small sign on the side of the Snooker Hall proclaimed. What a strange, eerie name for a saint!

The fierce, defiant air of the pipes reminded me of the Tartan youths of Belfast, Protestant troublemakers. Not far away, in the main street, could be found an Ulster Bank and a Customs and Excise Office. I could have been in a border town of uneasy atmosphere in Northern Ireland itself, with the Foresters' Hall doing duty as an Orange Lodge. If I had but known it then, the manager of the Ulster Bank had been shot by the IRA in 1922, the same year that they burned the barracks down.

Terraced streets led into the gritty square at forlorn angles, as if former landmarks and corner houses had been demolished. These streets, unlike the square, were lamplit. Some terraced rows were whitewashed, others of lurid orange brick, both starkly illuminated. From a brick terrace I looked back to see the figures of the pipers silhouetted against their open doorway. A country and western group played in the upstairs room of a corner pub, crowds visible through the window and spilling down the steps out of the front door. The street opened out to reveal an immense Catholic church, with lights blazing and queues of people streaming in. All looked most good-humoured.

At each side of the gateway stood a member of The Workers' Party, complete with tin and large placard. Mass-goers good-naturedly dropped money into the tins with the attitude of English pub-goers donating to the Salvation Army: 'Fair enough, not my cup of tea, but they do good work.'

'Yes, we're affiliated to the Socialist Workers' Party in England,' an enthusiastic, bespectacled collecting-lady told me. 'Every year we come here from Kildare – we're going to go in the pubs, stand here for Masses, and tomorrow we go back. I'm a grandmother, you know, with a big family, and I can't be away too long.'

She seemed thrilled by the adventure of it all. Collecting for the Party was her life, and what the Party stood for or intended to do interested her not a whit. A leaflet stated that they believed in 'peace in Ireland and throughout the world . . . we are depending on your generosity. Please give us what you can, so we can intensify the struggle for you.'

'What is your attitude to the Church?' I asked, meaning her Party's attitude.

'Oh, they're *much* better!' she exclaimed. 'At one time they didn't allow us to stand outside at all. In the last few years they've grown more tolerant. We had to get a permit from them to stand outside, and even now they *could* move us on, saying we're in the way, but they seldom do. Yes, lately the Church has made collecting much easier. Mind you, there's not much money about in Ireland at present. It'll be worse next year, when they bring back rates.'

No rates in Ireland! I hadn't known that. Rates or no rates, far too many old houses were falling down, particularly in Tullamore. What Ireland needs are Home Improvement Grants. When rates return, the money might be used in that way. They had not long been abolished, a politician's bid for popularity.

A bearded Socialist Worker came over to hear what we were saying. He seemed an amiable man, but for two pins he might have called me 'comrade', so I left. The quiet happiness of the Mass-going throng impressed me. I had by now discovered, late in the day, that a Catholic service is always called 'Mass'. As the word 'church' is semi-taboo, except for Protestants, Catholics never refer to 'church services'.

Boys in English schools, learning about England's Roman Catholic Middle Ages, wonder how people could have endured it. I remember seeing a twelve-year-old's history essay not long ago, entitled 'The Middle Ages.' 'Life in the Middle Ages was terrible,' he had written, 'with church all the time.'

Although the Irish have not grown noticeably less fond of Mass, or less religious, they *have* become far less eager to become monks, nuns or priests. If they do well at school, they pursue modern careers and expect the priesthood always to be there, as if by magic.

I returned to the square, and watched a full moon struggling from a misty sky to shine on the pipers. A sign on the Forester's Hall stated that the British Army had burned it down, but the Irish had built it up again. I later learned that the huge, impressive Catholic church had been burned down in 1983, and repaired once more. Two young men who had broken into the church on the night of the fire had been charged with arson, but acquitted for lack of evidence. The fire had been officially declared 'accidental' and the interior of the 1902 Gothic church redesigned with lots of wooden beams and pillars, as if to tempt the Fates. Tullamore seemed an inflammable town, but the calm, pleasant faces of the Mass-goers made it seem less uncanny.

Despite the plush-and-aluminium disco-paradise the Phoenix Arms Hotel had become, the hotel had a good pedigree – built in 1768 as the Charleville Arms. My room had a television, so that night, before bed, I watched Ulster programmes. Belfast Shopping Centre was constantly advertised. On Tuesday night the shops stayed open late to give Republicans time to go there and back on day tickets, and shop at British prices.

Breakfast next morning was served in 'Spider's – the Nite Side of Life', with disco lights rippling and music thumping. I felt strangely reassured by a cleaner's broom, propped nearby. On the handle was written, in indelible ink, 'Do Not Touch This Broom. Cleaners Only. Theresa O'Doherty.'

Tullamore had been built up from the village of An Tulach Mhor (the great hill) in the eighteenth century. The hill has long since been covered in houses, but may once have been a pagan sacred site. Nowadays Tullamore seems to consist of one very long street, with shops, houses, and a grand square, the street crossed by a railway line at one end of the town and by the Grand Canal at the other. This street varies in name from place to place.

Many once fine houses stood in sad ruins, with gardens overgrown. Historic sites had been taken over by mills or factories, and then *these* had become derelict, to make double ruins. Cabin suburbs had mostly been cleared away and replaced by council estates, but there were bits of them left. Such was Tullamore.

At O'Connor Square, still fairly smart in spite of its lounging youths, I found an obelisk commemorating the dead of two wars. On it, Tullamore was still referred to as being in King's County, the old pre-Home Rule name for County Offaly. Next door Queen's County, which I hoped to visit by rail, has been renamed County Laois (pronounced 'Leash', as Dermot Rafter had told me).

On my way to the station, I passed the courthouse and jail, side by side, stern reminders of the old régime. The courthouse resembled a Greek temple, the prison a medieval castle. Both had been built in the 1830s. Like practically everything else, the courthouse had been burned in 1922 during the Civil War, but had been repaired afterwards. The prison, also burned, re-emerged in the 1930s as a worsted mill which gave great employment to the town. This had closed in 1982, and it was now something nonsensical called the Kilcruttin Centre. I went in, but a man told me to go out again.

In awe, I stood in the prison grounds, admiring the remaining castle walls, towers and archways. Here, in 1865, took place the last public hanging in Ireland. After that date, hangings continued, sometimes of women, but behind closed doors.

All around the station, a large part of the town had apparently been cleared away and made into a newly landscaped park. Hills rose on the horizon, and out in the fields I could see the lone tower of ruined Sragh Castle, built by an English settler, John Briscoe, in 1588. Where the canal curved round to meet the railway line, there stood a scattering of tinker caravans by the road, and an Official Travellers' Site beyond. Young trees were planted here and there, around new factories and a graveyard. I hurried down through the park, beside a derelict, overgrown watermill and weir, and enquired about a train to Port Laoise, the new name given to Maryborough, Queen's County. It would not leave for some time, so I returned to the Phoenix Arms for a disco lunch.

In the bar afterwards, I met a red-faced world-weary man, who was blearily watching out that his little girl didn't fall down the steps to the dancefloor below. The bar was a gimmicky place, a black-painted balcony above the disco breakfast room.

'How old is she?' I asked him, nodding towards his bright little green-smocked daughter. She looked three, but was only half that age.

'I work for the Bord Fáilte, or tourist board, of a nearby town,' the man said. 'My job is to make tourists like Ireland. Poor old Ireland! Do *you* like this country?'

I said that I did.

'Well, if you lived here, you'd feel different. English who've settled here still feel coldness from neighbours after years and years. This could be a good country, but unemployment is chasing people away, and they've stopped the grant for house repairs. Now half of Ireland's in England.'

'Don't worry, I can report that they're happy enough.'

'They should be!' he cried, in jealous indignation. 'They've got money!'

'When they retire, they might bring it back to Ireland as a nest egg.'

'If they do, more fool them, because all the interest on it will be taxed away by the government. The customs here have huge powers, and seize whatever they like. You can't thrive in this country if you're honest, only if you're crewked and devious.'

'How do you manage in the winter, when there's no tourists?' I asked.

'Ah, I have my own little business,' he said, looking both crewked and devious.

'And I have a train to catch.'

The train pulled in to Port Laoise, with a fine view of the gently sloping Slieve Bloom mountains from the line. A little later, the train pulled *out* of Port Laoise with me on it, for I had not found a great deal to see there. The town is famous for its high security prison where IRA men are sometimes held, but this was situated somewhere out of town. Forlorn bits of ivied towers stood here and there in back yards and decaying industrial sites. Some bits had been churches, others military, but it was hard to say which was which. Dark-eyed secondary school children, freed from lessons at four o'clock, poured noisily into the town's newsagents for sweets, comics or cigarettes. They seemed cheerful, boisterous and aggressive, the boys swearing with every breath.

Not far from the Protestant church, as if placed there as a challenge, stood a statue of the Virgin Mary. It had been unveiled at the beginning of the First Marian Year, a fourteen-month year specially devoted to Mary, in 1953. The Second Marian Year had just ended (June 1987 – August 1988). If I had been a Home Ruler, I would have left Maryborough the county town of Queen's County, and had none of this Port Laoise, County Laois nonsense. Henceforth, I would have explained, the 'Mary' of Maryborough would be the Virgin Mary and the 'Queen' of Queen's County would be the Queen of Heaven. With this pious thought, and the feeling that at least I'd seen part of a new county, I consoled myself as I rode back to Tullamore in Offaly (or King's County).

Irish railway stations are soothing places, as a rule, suffused in dreamy melancholy. People arrive early for trains, settle down on seats and chat to one another. I was pleased to see Tullamore station once more. Although it was a long way out of town, the town itself had obviously lost its spirit in the devastation of the Irish Civil War. Tullamore's rebirth as an Entertainment Capital for the spendthrift disco-crazed children of wealthy farmers had not improved the atmosphere. Tullamore station was near Sragh Castle, so I set off for Sragh, passing the Travellers' Site and the tinker caravans by the road.

I looked down from the steep roadside bank at the permanent Travellers' Site, and liked what I saw. A path led through the middle of the site, towards the raised towpath of the canal. On both sides of this path stood rows of white trailers, each one in a garden compound with a wash house attached. One large trailer, obviously belonging to the most prominent family, was covered in glittering chromium strips. It was at least twice as large as the others. There were no horse-drawn wagons at all, but the tinker village made a pretty sight, the back wall overhung by large trees.

Unofficial trailers had been parked on the edge of the road where I was standing, with washing lines and delicately stacked scrap metal half concealed by ragged blankets and sacking. From a packing-case kennel, a dog watched me with ears erect. Families were at tea, or mending cars, and there was a peaceful atmosphere.

Distant roars from a field near the model village indicated that something was afoot. Burly tinker men, in black dusty suits, jackets hanging open and falling off, were standing in a huddle at the edge of a wood, greatly agitated. Latecomers ran towards them. I had seen such sights in London, and knew that they were throwing pound notes on the ground in a heap and then tossing a die for them. There was a terrible bellow as a big shirt-sleeved man flung himself down on the grass, beating the ground with his fists as he bewailed his bad luck. He seemed a poor loser.

'Serve him right!' said a bright-looking boy of ten or so to his friend. Youngsters from the camp were drifting along the side of the road in groups. The boy noticed me, and asked, 'Are you German?'

'No, I'm English,' I said. 'Can you get to that castle from here, do you know?'

'It's hard to get to, right enough, as it's on the other side of the canal and railway line.'

'I'll leave it then, as it's getting dark and I don't want to see a ghost.'

'Oh, it hasn't got a ghost, it's got a giant,' he said seriously.

While talking, I had been rooting about in my plastic bag and now produced pen and paper. Very quickly I drew a devil playing a fiddle to a dancing donkey, and handed it to him. His young friend wanted one too, and soon I was surrounded by children. Some came scrambling and running up the steep bank from the village. All received devils and donkeys. After a time, girls began to take over from boys. An eleven-year-old girl, dressed in blue, held up a tiny bedraggled child to see what I was doing. Boys exclaimed in rhyme as each new picture appeared. 'Oh gracious, bejasus!' and 'Oh deary, my Mary!' Two of them began to sing a song with the chorus 'Skee-addle, skee-addle, skee-addle – Skee-addle, skee-addle, skee-ay!' Their manners and speech recalled old books about the Irish, and it occurred to me that barefoot tinkers in cabin-like trailers are an uneasy reminder to house-Irish of what Ireland used to be like.

'Have you been to England?' I asked, as well-practised devils and donkeys flew from my pen.

Not only had they all been to England, it turned out, but they all knew the tinker camps I had visited in London. 'The Murphys that were at White City are at the Westway now,' the boy I had first met informed me. 'Do you know a place called Shepherd's Bush?'

'My Uncle Sean's an artist. He draws Elvis,' a girl told me. 'His van is all covered with pictures of Elvis he's drawn, and he's got all the records and medals.'

'I can't draw Elvis, so your Uncle Sean has got me beat,' I confessed.

'Sure, he's a better artist than Uncle Sean,' another girl said gallantly.

On the other side of the road, a pleasant-faced lady and a dignified man walked along together. 'Hello, Miss Dowling!' the children chorused, 'coo-ee-ing' and waving.

'That's Miss Dowling, our teacher. She's ever so nice,' said the girl in blue. 'The man is her husband, he's high up in the Garda. Please draw me another donkey. Oh, I *wish* I was you! I *wish* I was you!'

'Well, you can't be me,' I said regretfully, 'but you can easily learn to draw by copying comics, like I do.'

It was nice to be appreciated, as art teachers and publishers fly into a fury at the sight of my sub-Disney drawings, and almost throw them back at me. True taste, I decided, can only be found in tinker caravans. It was growing dark, and fathers were calling their children home. Soon I found that I was surrounded only by big boys, aged between fifteen and nineteen. They were lean of body and face, with wild hair and sparkling eyes. One young man with thick sandy eyelashes and red hair looked rather sardonic, but he seemed as fond of devils and donkeys as the rest.

'Will you draw me an ass and a divil?' he asked politely. 'Do you like the divil?'

'Ach, what a question! Who likes the divil?' a dark-haired youth exclaimed, spitting politely to one side. Every time the word 'divil' was mentioned, somebody spat to avoid misfortune.

'I'll draw no more devils, as it brings bad luck,' I said.

All the boys agreed. 'Ah, that it does, in truth!'

'Will you draw a poussaint – a mountain goat?' Sandy Eyes asked.

It was my last drawing, as night had almost fallen. When I put my pad away, the boys melted away into the dark with their pictures, and reappeared strolling towards the bawling gamblers. Down in the council-built village, the smaller children were playing in front of their caravan doorways.

On my way back to the hotel, I noticed a small 'inn-sign' on a tiny terraced house. 'Taxi', it read, in red letters. So I knocked and arranged for a taxi on the following day, to take me northward to Mullingar.

☘

'The country's very flat here', I said to the young driver next morning, as we sped to Mullingar, county town of Westmeath.

'We're in the Midlands,' he explained. 'Ireland is like a saucer, mountains all round the edge, and then it dips down in the middle. There was a squire round here a hundred years ago, and he had a beehive hut made out of stone, for his tomb, like. He said he'd be reincarnated as a bee.'

My guide pointed out wide, blue Lough Ennell, a favourite place for holidaymakers with boats. Then we were in Mullingar, a solid, prosperous-looking market town. I dragged my heavy bag into the old-world foyer of the Greville Arms Hotel, a luxurious coaching inn with dark panelled walls and deep carpets.

While I was waiting for my key at the Reception desk, I felt that someone nearby was looking at me. Glancing to one side, I received an awful shock, for there was James Joyce the writer, stuffed, in a glass case, reading a book! Apparently he had stayed in the hotel on his frequent visits to Mullingar. Close inspection revealed that he was not actually stuffed, but a waxwork, though the head had been made from his death-mask.

I eyed my fellow-writer warily. I have never read anything by Joyce, though I've started often enough. My attention wanders after two minutes or so. When people ask me if I've read *Ulysses*, I seek refuge in ignorance and pretend I think they mean the Greek hero. 'Well, there was this giant, see, in this cave, see, with only one eye, right?' That shuts them up. However, I could scarcely try this ploy in the Greville Arms Hotel, which seemed less of an hotel and more of a shrine of Joyceana.

'Did Joyce write anything nice about this hotel?' I asked the Reception girl. She didn't know, and nor did her friend, nor her friend's supervisor.

'He must have done, or they wouldn't have put him in that glass case,' I pronounced, and all agreed.

Joyce could never write like Wodehouse, but he certainly knew his hotels, I reflected, as I unpacked. Then out I strolled to look at Mullingar.

Mullingar, I could see at once, was a cheerful town, and the people had a forceful, good-humoured way of moving and speaking. The town was enclosed on three sides by a loop of the Royal Canal, which used to carry water traffic to Dublin. Now it only carried swans. The sun was out as I walked along the towpath, and I was soon among cows, fields and willow trees. Retracing my steps back to town, I discovered a mansion at the head of a long driveway, a Gothic house surrounded by white statues. It was now a tourist office, and I bought some postcards.

Back in town, I walked along streets of prosperous shops, many of them video stores. At the other side of Mullingar, a bridge crossed the canal once more, near a railway station, a school and the Roman Catholic cathedral. Boys noisily raced around the school playground. Several escaped over the railings, leaped on to the railway line below, scrambled up the bank and ran off into the woods, like runaway slaves. All walks in Mullingar quickly became country walks.

After a while, it began to rain, so I returned to my hotel and explored it thoroughly. A huge brown stuffed pike stared glassily at me from a case in the intricately carved doorway. In another case, halfway up the stairs, a speckled trout seemed, by its expression, to be making the best of things. The sight of Joyce in his case might have comforted it ('Who bagged that one?').

A lounge on the first floor was bright with reproduction-French furniture, covered in stripy cushions, with imaginative sporting scenes on the walls. Downstairs were dark priest-holey snugs and corners, with fringy lampshades everywhere. The staff were cheerful, twenty to every resident, and they shouted out greetings to one another.

In the bar, I stood with my back to the blazing coal fire and eavesdropped on an immensely humorous-looking foxy-faced man of fifty-odd, who had drawn an admiring circle around him. 'Not that I'm speaking ill of him behind his back or anything like that, but . . .' he was saying.

This splendid hotel took its name from a Lord Greville, who had bought the whole town outright, in 1859, for £120,000. Mullingar had previously belonged to an Ascendancy family called Granard. Before Greville's purchase, the hotel had been known first as Wilton's and then as Murray's. Before *that*, the building on its site must have been known by any amount of rude names, for it had been the local prison.

Until Easter Monday, 1916, there had been a large barracks in Mullingar. Where is that barracks now? Once more, the ballad tells the story.

First he went to make his peace with dear old Father Maher,
Then he went out and blew the barracks up, and wrecked half of
Mullingar!
When you read the roll of honour, you will find marked with a star,
Patrick Sarsfield Mulligan, the Man from Mullingar!

I should explain that the common Irish surname 'Maher' is pronounced 'Mar'. So Ireland, with its grocery-pubs, must be the only country where you can walk into Maher's Bar and order a Mars Bar.

During a lull in the rain, I slipped out and had lunch in a Chinese restaurant housed in a rather forlorn draughty cottage. My waitresses, aged nine and ten, were two enchanting little Chinese girls, helped by a brother. Gravely they took orders and served meals, turned on the radiator and brought me a jug of iced water.

'Are you Irish?' I asked them, as their accents were pure Westmeath.

'No, we came here five years ago,' was the reply.

Round the corner to this restaurant, I found a cabin back street, very ramshackle, where most of the tenants (or squatters) seemed to be tinkers. Children played everywhere, and beside a back-yard caravan, a man hammered at a fender. A glimpse into a front room revealed scrap metal décor, orange-box furniture and scattered toys. I wondered if the bright children I had met at Tullamore, who scorned their gambling elders, would become like those same elders when they grew up. Some people are quick-witted and friendly as children, and become surly dullards when adults. In such cases, the childhood self is the true self, possibly resumed in Heaven. Children of slack-witted uncouth parents are often bright because they have to look after those parents. I am not referring specifically to tinkers. The capable Chinese children had an oafish, gawping father.

Back in the main street, flags were being hung across the street, and in the newsagent's near the public library, I learned the reason. 'Did you not know? Tomorrow's the Nissan International Classic Bicycle Race across Ireland, sponsored by the Japanese,' the man behind the counter told me. 'It's the first time such a race has come through Mullingar. There's some good Irish names there represented, some English too, but some good Irish names. Mullingar is a "hot spot", they get extra points here.'

At the hotel, I looked at a map of Ireland and saw that Mullingar was not far from the abbey village of Grange Bective. That was where the Rafter family lived, whom I had met at Ross Carbery, County Cork, where they had been on holiday. On an impulse, I reached for a phone book, rang up the Rafters and invited myself over for tea.

'I'm glad you rang,' Mr Rafter said. 'Come over tomorrow – I've got a business proposition to put to you.'

Rain poured down outside, but there was a farm auction in the hotel, which gave me something to look at. Big genial cloth-capped farmers looked odd in the chintzy upstairs dining room where the auction took place. When the weather cleared up, I returned to the street of tinker cabins.

Despite puddles in the road, the street now looked very cosy, with lights in the open doorways. One front room was lit by candles, and a peep through the curtainless window showed neat, demure children pouring tea, washing up and waiting on an unshaven Dad who sprawled in a chair. Outside the caravan, a boy was feeding a horse, while ducks quacked around his legs.

A red-haired boy of ten showed great energy, running like quicksilver across the road and back and darting all over a piece of waste ground. His friends followed with difficulty. 'What are you doing?' I asked him.

'We're playing "tig". You call it "tag" in England.'

'So you've been to England?'

'Oh yes, to White City, Westway and Parliament Hill Fields. Do you know of a place called Cheadle Heath, near Stockport?'

I did indeed, as I had met Romany gypsies at Appleby Horse Fair who came from a camp at Cheadle Heath. It's a small world, if you're a traveller. Bidding the youngsters farewell, I walked on to the Cathedral of Christ the King. The strange twin towers and huge dome looked eerie against the sad yellow streaks of watery sunset.

'Something odd about this cathedral,' I thought. 'The green dome looks rather wonky, not quite round, and the cup on top looks as if something else ought to be resting on it.' Inside the great building, I read in the guide book that the place had been built in 'Modernised Renaissance' style, in the 1930s, late in the day for good architecture. When I emerged from the cathedral, a full moon had risen over the silvered roofs of Mullingar.

In the Greville Arms dining room, every wall was covered with drawings, silhouettes and photographs of James Joyce. I looked around with interest. A lively young man and woman at the next table addressed one another as 'Cousin'. At the table next to them sat a dry scholastic Irishman with glasses. He looked very like Joyce, and was holding forth loudly about Ireland to two German men. Waitresses, spirited chatty girls, moved talkatively from table to table. Two of them knew the Cousins, and shouted greetings to them over the heads of the diners. Everybody eavesdropped on everybody. When in Rome . . .

'You'll find many red-haired people in Ireland,' the scholar announced.

'That's not so!' the girl Cousin told the boy. 'Hair round here is more mouse-coloured.'

'Aunt Kitty has red hair and a temper to go with it.'

'She has *not* got a temper!'

'She has so!'

SCHOLAR: We Irish have lost our language.

A GERMAN: Not lost it, my friend, *changed* it. English is far more useful, you will find.

SCHOLAR: Yes, if you had a daughter born in England, you'd be pleased to hear her talk English. But what if she never learned German? *Then* you'd be sorry.

BOY COUSIN [fervently]: We ought to have our own language!

GIRL COUSIN: We can remember a few words from school . . .

BOY COUSIN: It's all English, English! They say Ireland has fine writers who write in English, but when you look at them, they're not Irish at all! Shaw, Swift, Goldsmith – all English!

GIRL COUSIN: They're Irish, they're just Anglo-Irish, that's all.

At that moment my roast beef arrived, and I forgot about eavesdropping. Later, over pudding, I thought of the 'native Irish' writers whose books I had enjoyed reading (though I don't know if I could go back to them). Top of the list came Brendan Behan and Flann O'Brien, whom I have already mentioned. Of the former, Ken Tynan's words are often quoted: 'He sends language out on a swaggering spree.' O'Brien too *plays* with the English language. These writers seem as if drunk on a strong, strange heady brew, the English language. Both write in Irish also. I remembered the Biafran writer, Chinua Achebe, who described his childhood joy at hearing the English word 'periwinkle' for the first time.

In one of his throwaway sketches, O'Brien describes the Irish language as if it were a gold standard, a source of wealth to the English language as English can be spoken in Ireland. I say 'can be', because the same Irishmen who complain of losing the Irish language often speak in dull 'standard English', without any of the little Irish frills and curlicues that make a language delightful, so. If the Irish language were to die out completely, its memory would still serve the Irish well for a hundred years. When dialect words have gone, the accent will linger for another century. Or so I predict.

Another O'Brien sketch, *The Jumping Irishman*, features a pre-Home Rule Irishman, loyal to the Crown, who is asked (by a scornful rebel) why he isn't speaking his own language. 'I am. I am speaking English,' the man replies.

Every nation in the world, if it looks back, can say it has lost a language and gained another. Much is spoken of the ancient English habit, in Ireland, of 'planting' settlers with the idea of turning Ireland English. How many know that in the 1930s the Irish government 'planted' Irish-speaking settlers from the West of Ireland in the English-speaking East, not far from Mullingar, to make Ireland Irish? *I* didn't know until recently, or I would have gone to look for them.

That night, in my room, the air conditioning outside my door sounded like the sighing of waves, and I had peaceful dreams of boats.

Morning brought the day of the Bicycle Race. My breakfast waitress, a perky middle-aged woman with quick, dashing movements, grew very animated as she discussed the Race. 'Sure, all the schools are out, to provide children for the waving,' she announced. 'I'll be stuck inside here, but I can see it after on telly.'

'It's a nice day for it,' I said, for the sun was shining. 'Better than yesterday.'

'Sure, you can't tell the seasons apart at all,' she answered. 'It's been cold all summer, and then last Christmas it was a fine day like this one, and you'd want to go out, not stay in at all. I blame the astronauts and all their rockets; they say it isn't so, but it stands to reason now, doesn't it? When I was a girl, winter was winter and summer was summer – seven weeks of glorious sunshine and the children would go out in their feet. You know what I really think? It means the end of the world! The prophecy says "Metal birds shall fall from the sky . . ."'

'Where does it say that?'

'In Colum Cill's prophesies. He lived before Patrick's time, I'll be thinking. "Blood shall flow as far south as Longford!" Oh dear, as long as it flows no souther than that!'

Who was Colum Cill? At least he knew the bloodshed would be in Ulster, to the north of Longford. Suddenly I remembered – Saint Columcille, who ran a pipe band in Tullamore! I had also seen the name spelled as 'Colmcille', and I remembered once meeting an Irishman called Colum. Here were mysteries.

My new friend prattled on, and I learned that she had spent fourteen years as a living-in waitress in a top London hotel, before returning to her native Mullingar. Finishing my breakfast, I hurried out to see the Bicycle Race. However, it turned out that the racers, on their way from Dublin to Galway, would not be passing through the town until noon. Already there was a festive atmosphere, with people looking up the road towards Dublin.

By noon, crowds filled the pavements on both sides of the main street from end to end of Mullingar. Schoolchildren outnumbered adults, but fat old men in cloth caps seemed as excited as the youngsters. Girls aged eight to eleven, in smart blue school uniforms, stood near the railway bridge with their teachers. Not in the least prim, they seemed wildly excited, their faces glowing. Once over the bridge, the cyclists would turn a sharp corner and be gone from Mullingar.

Twelve o'clock, one o'clock, half past one and still no cyclists! By now the crowds were at fever pitch. Everybody cheered, especially the schoolgirls, when a well-known young man cycled by, going the opposite way to the race. They cheered again as a police motorcyclist drove along the cycle route. Now things seemed to be warming up, as police cars appeared and took position beside the already prepared ambulances. Army vans drove slowly by, with soldiers riding shotgun, presumably in case of terrorist attacks on bikes. Then came advertising vans, their roof-racks piled with racing bikes.

A roar from the sky turned each head upward, and there was a red helicopter, slanting sideways to give television cameramen on board a better view. Police cars next, and then ...

In a flash, to a loud cry from every throat, the whole bicycle race went by, the riders bent, with faces and knuckles strained as they turned the corner. A whizz of yellow and white, the colour of their caps and tunics, and the whole bicycle race was over as far as Mullingar was concerned. All that fuss, for two minutes of spectacle!

Boys from the nearby school ran after the already invisible cyclists, swarming through a small park in pursuit and getting on to the railway line and running up and down. I too followed the cycle route, and came across neat cabin suburbs, where old men sat on their doorsteps, as East Enders used to do. Then I had to hurry back to the Greville Arms and ask Reception to find me a taxi for Grange Bective. This they did, and I was soon out on a day's excursion.

CHAPTER THIRTEEN

☘

In Tara's Halls

My driver was a very cheerful, humorous man of around thirty. He told me that he was a part-time fireman and a born-again Christian.

'What do you think of the sightings of the Virgin Mary in Ireland?' I asked.

'It's hard to say. Some may be genuine, but on the other hand, the devil loves to deceive. I took a man to a village once, and he said, "So the tree's gone, then?" '

' "What tree was that?" says I.

" 'Don't you know?" says he. Apparently the Virgin Mary had appeared there a few years before, sitting on a branch of a tree near someone's house. She never did come back, but people flocked there from far and wide, offering to buy the leaves of the tree. So the residents sold every leaf from that tree, and the tree died. People picked leaves from other trees around, and sold them to strangers who did not know any better. But the fuss has died down now.'

A rat crossed our path as we left the farmland behind and entered a strange moonscape of dark brown peat bogs. The landscape had been flattened, furrowed and dug up by peat-digging machines, the peat removed by rail. We crossed an unguarded line, and I looked back to see an orange train, with open trucks and a lorry-like engine, chug slowly through the mournful bog.

'You ought to see the peat-digging machine at work,' said the taxi driver. 'It's bigger than a combine harvester. When a peat bog is not dug up, heather grows all over it. The surface peat is peat-moss, that is what they package for gardening. Below that is peat for briquettes. Sometimes they dig up a bog-oak, the whole tree perfectly preserved.'

He drove along winding roads, between high hedges and below overhanging trees, the bog left far behind. County Westmeath gave way to County Meath. Suddenly we emerged at the town of Trim, where I saw a gigantic column with a statue of the Duke of Wellington on top, looking rather like a Mohawk Indian. A group of boys played round the base, beside an inscription.

'When was that made?' the driver shouted to them, noting my interest.

'It's in Roman – I can't read Roman!' a boy shouted back.

'Sixteen ninety six!' 'Eighteen forty six!' other boys shouted.

No one shouted 'Eighteen seventeen', which would have been the right answer.

I was so entranced by the sight of a vast grey Norman castle, whose ruins seemed to cover half the countryside on the edge of Trim, that I made the driver stop. He went to look at the fire station, while I climbed the stile that led into the grounds of the castle.

Watch-towers of Trim Castle looked out over the modern street outside the high stone walls. I scrambled over steep embankments in my haste to see the largest Norman castle in Ireland. The towered castle rose from amid ribbons of walls that enclosed three acres of land between the town and a meandering river. Bits of ruined wall and tower reappeared in the fields on the river's far bank. Black sightless holes gaped from the central castle, perhaps enlarged from slit-windows by stone plunderers. Archways led nowhere, for much of the castle had fallen down since it had been abandoned in the fourteenth century.

Known as King John's Castle, Trim seems to have been built in the early years of the thirteenth century, the property of the unpopular English monarch. King John had confiscated land for miles around from a Norman baron, De Lacey. In 1215, King John returned castle and land to the De Lacey family, who have remained powerful landowners in County Meath until our day. I knew a branch of the De Lacey family in Brighton, in the 1960s. They had become Communists. (We quarrelled over a banana, as they wouldn't let me take one from a fruit bowl, although I was famished. I was rather young then.)

Meath, in the Middle Ages, was part of the Pale, held by Norman barons for the English Crown. A ditch marked the borders of the Pale, rather like Offa's Dyke on the borders of Wales. Trim had long been the county town of Meath, but had now been superceded by Navan.

I admired the view of the river, gentle green fields and, near an ivied mansion, the fifteenth-century tower of St Patrick's Cathedral. What was my surprise to learn, from the driver, that all the time I had been standing on the Green Grassy Slopes of the Boyne!

So potent a symbol is the River Boyne in Northern Ireland, that I had somehow thought the river itself was there. Yet here it was, in County Meath, and the Battle of the Boyne (1690) had taken place a few miles from where I was standing. It was a Protestant victory over Catholic James II, and Orangemen in Ulster sing to this day, as defiantly, proudly and provocatively as they can:

> On the Green Grassy Slopes of the Boyne,
> Where the Orangemen with William did join,
> And we fought for a glorious de*liv*erance
> On the Green Grassy Slopes of the Boyne.

The slopes were still green and grassy, and I nearly slipped. Back in the taxi, we were off once more, passing the ruins of an abbey and a friary by the river. Having had a taste of history, I wanted more, and persuaded the kindly driver (whose name I never learned) to take me to the fabled Hill of Tara where Irish kings have been crowned in pagan days. Fortunately, Tara was very close to Grange Bective.

Lanes near Tara grew very narrow, winding and curling about hills and between hedges. Rain hissed down, a sudden storm. Just as the weather brightened, in the on-off Irish fashion, we came across a tiny café, incongruously called The Banquet Hall. Near this Hall, a gap in the hedge, with a wooden gate, was signposted 'Tara'.

The Hill of Tara, in Royal Meath, is the Camelot of the Irish, and the Christian driver was as excited as myself to see it. Leaving the car, we walked into the sloping field towards a church. Meath earned its name of 'Royal' long before English kings were crowned at Westminster, so the name-changing Home Rulers have left it alone.

Dark, damp St Patrick's Church, around which grew the only trees on Tara, was closed. In the graveyard, the taxi driver (whom I shall call Christian) called my attention to a strange stone on which a worn carving could be seen, that might have been a cross-legged Puck. I later found that this stone was a centre of controversy, and could have been a pagan symbol mistaken for a headstone and erected among the graves when the Anglican Church was rebuilt in the nineteenth century.

If so, it would be the last feeble, defiant joke of paganism against Christianity, the faith that destroyed Tara's greatness. For the court of Ireland's ancient kings had been sacred to the old gods, the gods who had decreed that the Sovereignty of Ireland should be upon the Hill of Tara, one hill that constituted a Province more important than great Ulster, Connaught, Munster or surrounding Leinster. In their day, these gods had demanded human sacrifice at Tara. Some say the Pooka on the churchyard stone is the horned god of wild beasts, Cernunnos, identified by Christian missionaries as the Devil. That may be so, but there was nothing sinister about modern Tara.

All Tara Hill outwardly contained, as we could see, as we stumped about, was grassy mounds. Here and there a notice declared that such-and-such a mound was really a hall where chiefs, nobles, druids and monarchs had quarrelled or feasted long ago. Tara's glory, for Christian and myself, lay in the imagination, as in our different ways we dreamed of Ireland's legendary heroic past. This hump in the ground suggested golden thrones and cups of mead, in that tussock of grass Ireland's Sovereignty might lie. Whoever ruled from Tara could call themselves High King of Ireland, and High Kings who reigned after Tara had been made desolate by a saint's curse would still add 'of Tara' to their many titles. The name of Tara lent value to their claim. Of course, a High King of Ireland often quarrelled with the low kings, and could never get them all to obey him. He made allegiances with some so as to punish the others.

Sovereignty, to the pre-Christian Irish, was a spirit who must descend, possess or be confirmed upon a king. Sometimes it was imagined as a fairy princess the king must embrace in a mystic bower, sometimes as a mare to be boiled in a cauldron and eaten by the king, and sometimes as a stone on a hill, as at Cashel. One hundred and forty-two known Irish kings have reigned from Tara, a hill positively pulsing with Sovereignty, and before them a long line of chieftains and god-kings go back through the Bronze Age to Neolithic times, the retreat of the Ice Age. But for a quirk of history, a Rome or Athens might have arisen from Tara.

We climbed a large rounded hummock labelled 'Grave of the Nine Hostages'. One of the later kings at Tara was Niall of the Nine Hostages. No one knows who these Nine Hostages were. There is no legend to account for them. Did Druids with banners picket Niall's noble thatch and wattle palace chanting 'Free the Hostage Nine'?

Christian may have been envisaging soaring stone palaces with tapestries in fine thirteenth-century style, as Englishmen dream about King Arthur on bare grassy slopes of Wiltshire. I envisaged a cold West Africa on Tara. Sharpened stockades with human heads a-spike, massively thatched longhouses decorated in swirling patterns, busy craftsmen and metal workers, the fetish house of the Druid with its strange symbols. Tapestries, furs, rich trappings and golden utensils there certainly would have been, and the terrifying majesty of a brooding monarch with powers over life and death.

'Cormac's House', the largest mound was labelled. Sheep grazed peacefully all over Tara, moving aside as we scrambled up and down and staring at us with their knowing ironic eyes, like wise toads' eyes. On top of Cormac's tufty house, thatched by living thistles, stood the centrepiece of Tara, a battered statue of a regal figure on a pedestal. Cormac Mac Art, greatest of Tara's kings, reigned from AD 227 to 266. He is said to have been reared by a family of wolves, as recounted by David Thomson in his masterly *People of the Sea*. All the doings of Tara's people are overlaid in legend, but the people themselves existed, which is more than can be said with certainty of King Arthur. King Cormac caused many of the buildings which now cannot be seen at Tara to be raised.

'That must be King Cormac!' I said knowledgeably, pointing to the statue.

'No, it's St Patrick,' said Christian. He was right. Patrick's bishop-headdress had taken a battering, and now resembled a jagged crown.

Below the statue stood an erect stone, waist high, the Tara Stone of Destiny over which kings had been crowned, to the sound of supernatural roaring that confirmed their Sovereignty. The Stone has been moved, people say, from the circular bank labelled 'King's Seat' and re-used as a gravestone for the Rebels of the 1798 Uprising, killed nearby and buried on Tara. So the Roaring Stone of Irish Kings is now known as 'The Croppies' Grave'. Political attitudes are often combined with hairstyles, and the '98 rebels had stubbly 'cropped' heads.

'Synod', another sheep-cropped mound was named. This name has unfortunate associations for an Englishman, as it recalls the dreaded General Synod of the Church of England, where decree after decree alters the Church as much, or more, than Vatican II alters the Church of Rome. At Tara, St Patrick may have called a synod where the new laws of Christian conduct were framed, argued over and written down. In the year AD 433, Patrick arrived at Tara in dramatic circumstances, and profaned the sacred sites of pagan King Leary by lighting a fire at a time when all lights should have been dimmed. Summoned to Leary's throne, Patrick impressed the monarch by his bold answers, and was given the freedom to preach and the freedom of Tara. Leary died, still a pagan, in AD 458.

Christian had wandered off among the hummocks, sheep and thistles. I ran up and down the mounds, the glory of Tara diminished by the thought that almost any Irish field could have been called 'Tara' and have conjured up the same images. Suddenly I gave a start, for there, at the foot of the Hostage Mound, was the dark entrance to a stone passage grave, barred with iron like a prison window. Neolithic graves on Tara had been broken into by Bronze Age men, and later dug up by British Israelites (AD 1900) in search of the Ark of the Covenant. Department of Works bars prevented any further intrusions, and made the Mound look like a county jail. I called Christian over, and he was very impressed.

'That must be where they kept the Hostages,' he pronounced.

Eventually, we left the mounds, walked past the church, and stopped in amazement at the sight of a long steep-sided gulley, with entrance gaps in the banks every few yards. Until we saw the sign 'Banquet Hall', we both imagined the huge hollowed-out space to have been a triumphal walkway leading to a castle. So the café, which sold such items as packets of crisps, had not been called 'Banquet Hall' as a joke, but in honour of Tara's hall.

Christian warned of rain, and hurried down to the car, but I still sprinted up and down trying to extract every last drop of romance from invisible Tara. I pictured the Banqueting Hall as an immense thatched barn, with beams and cross beams everywhere above, and couches below where slaves poured drinks and proffered dishes. Pagan Ireland had a caste system, and at great feasts, guests would be placed by occupation, the lesser kings, their wives and mistresses grouped around King Cormac.

Every Irishman of legend had been here – Cuchulain, Fin Mac Cool, Dermot and Grania (the Irish Tristan and Isolde) and above all, King Cormac Mac Art.

In the far-off year of 227 (AD, though no one in Ireland yet knew of Christ) a young nobleman named Cormac had wandered into the court at Tara, as King Lug Mac Con sat in judgement. A lawbreaker had been brought before the King, accused of letting his sheep graze on the Queen's pasture.

'Your sheep shall be confiscated and given to the Queen,' grumbled Lug Mac Con.

'Not so!' cried Cormac, and everyone turned to look at the handsome youth who dared to interrupt a king. 'Let the sheep be shorn and their wool given to the Queen, for the grass on the pasture will grow again, and so will the wool grow on the sheep.'

'A true judgement!' the crowd roared, and with that they pulled King Lug off the throne and put Cormac there instead! As if to confirm this action, part of ex-King Lug's house fell down. That is how Cormac became King, as noted down years later by St Patrick's personal scribe, Brogan.

Irish kings were often elected for their good qualities, and more often elected themselves, but always from within the kingly caste. Physical perfection was a kingly quality, and in old age Cormac had to abdicate when his face became scarred in a war. War was a kingly vocation; to this day the British Royal family shows an aptitude for the Services. Among the many innovations Cormac brought to Ireland was the water mill. Until the first mill was installed at a stream near Tara, the grinding of corn into flour had been done by women using heavy querns, or hand millstones.

One of the Tara mill girls, Ciarnait, fell pregnant by Cormac and thereafter, very sensibly, refused to work. So, as many later rulers have done, Cormac sent for a Scottish engineer who rigged up Tara's waterwheel in no time. Alas, Cormac choked to death on a salmon bone at the age of ninety. It was the end of an era, and much later Thomas Moore (the Drawing Room Bard) wrote these lines:

> The Harp that once through Tara's Halls,
> The soul of music shed,
> Now hangs as mute on Tara's walls

As if that soul were fled . . .
No more to chiefs and ladies bright
The Harp of Tara swells;
The chord alone that breaks at night
Its tale of ruin tells . . .

Knowing that Christian would not drive off and leave me until I had paid his fare, I hurried once more to the top of the Mound of the Nine Hostages for a look at the view, for now Tara seemed bathed in magical sunlight. It was the view from Tara, some say, that caused the hill to be thought sacred. All Ireland seemed to spread out below me, so it was easy to see why Tara's King should claim Sovereignty of the whole island. At one point I thought I could see the ocean, but it proved to be fields and woodlands in shadow, strips of blue woodland blurred together by distance. Fields swept up to a ridge of horizon, a line broken only by a single towered church. To one side, I could see the Dublin mountains.

Dark storm clouds rolled across a blue sky, dark clouds in front of white ones, like villains in a melodrama running across a stage with an idyllic backdrop. Strange Celtic sunlight picked out hills, fields and faraway church in soft glowing colours, every outline drawn precisely with a fairy pen. Turning, I saw a hill grow russet gold, crossed by dark hedges, as lights wavered to and fro.

A bright silver cloud nudged the dark clouds, a hole broke through the darkness and a shaft of white light pierced the fields. Now the blue sky had turned whitish grey, smudged with charcoal as rain poured on to hillside farms but spared Tara. Over the whole horizon curved a double rainbow, the Arc of the Covenant, light on darkness. Bright purple glowed on the inner rainbow, the outer one a faded copy. Four ends-of-the-rainbow could be seen on the fields, the top of the bows hidden by clouds.

Yellow, red and mauve lights from the outer rainbow fell across the fields as stained glass windows cast their lights on white church columns. Other fields glowed in the same colours on the inner rainbow's downward path. In the churchyard, the trees bent to form a semi-circle, white light shining between them. Such scenes in Cormac's day would have sent the druids out a-prophesying. As it was, I ran down the field to the car, pausing at the Banquet Hall café for some guide books, and jumped in beside Christian just as the Heavens let loose a sea of rain.

A few hedgy lanes and drenched boreens later, we arrived at

Grange Bective, a scattering of houses by a demesne wall, with a ruined lodge house and a sign pointing to an abbey. I recognized the Rafters' bungalow by young Dermot's description back in County Cork, gave good Christian a golden handshake and knocked on the door.

I was made very welcome, and soon sat down to a hearty breakfast of High Tea. By now the rain had stopped, and I looked out on to a field of stubble. 'Your house backs on to some nice farmland,' I said.

'It looks awful now, with the potato crop still in,' Mrs Rafter said modestly, 'but the corn looked grand before, changing colour from green to gold. A neighbour of ours saw a full-antlered stag out there not long ago.'

Dermot and his brother eagerly asked me about England. They seemed bright, brainy lads. I now felt almost up to spelling Dermot's name in Irish – Diarmaid, or was it Diarmuid?

Mr Rafter, a big practical man with spectacles, now put his business proposition before me. He and his wife ran a sewing machine shop inside a vast new shopping centre at the town of Navan. During the half-term holidays, in about three weeks' time, the manager of the centre would be hiring local bands, clowns, conjurors and other entertainers who would amuse the children while the parents shopped. Would I like to spend two days as resident cartoonist, with free food and board, all expenses paid and a bit over?

'What a splendid idea! I accept!' I cried, and we shook hands on it.

So without more ado, he drove me to the centre to meet the manager, Mr Coary. It was dark when we arrived at Navan, a town newly enriched, I was told, by the opening of a zinc and lead mine nearby. Blinking, I allowed myself to be led into the bright, garish centre, where I met Mr Coary, the manager, in a tiny office hedged in by open-plan shops. A gypsyish side-whiskered man burst in to ask where he could park his lorry, and then manager and I sat down to discuss terms.

We got on very well, as we both liked country and western music, so a deal was struck. Our conversation moved on to Irish ballads, and Mr Rafter sang a few lines of a song called 'Leather Breeches'. I told him how thrilled I had been to hear farmers at Killorglin sing 'Spancil Hill'.

'Everyone in this country can sing "Spancil Hill" if you give them enough Guinness,' he informed me. 'There's "Spancil Hill" deep down in every Irishman, if it takes the Guinness to find it.'

Feeling very much a man of business, just as my grandfather who ran MacNab's Fish Paste had been, I allowed one of my two partners to phone for another taxi to take me back to the Greville Arms in Mullingar.

My new driver was a young man with a moustache. We drove through darkness, then gusts of white mist flew from the hedges into the road towards our headlights, like silent banshees. 'We're going through the bogs now – it's mist off the bogs,' the driver told me.

When he heard I had been to Tara, he urged me to see Slane Hill, 'where Patrick lit the Paschal fire and angered the King and his druids. I can't remember the story now – sure, it's a long time since I been to school.'

This head-on meeting of two religions is well described by Hugh Malet in his historical travelogue, *In the Wake of the Gods.* At one time the story was taught to every Irish child, a vital piece of history-folklore, such as Drake's game of bowls and Raleigh's cloak in English schools. When stuffed with titbits, History can never be boring.

A radio message crackled in the night: 'Manager at Navan says he'll pay the taxi fare.'

Snug in my hotel room, soothed by sea breezes, I opened one of the guide books I had bought, *The Legend of Tara*, by Elizabeth Hickey. From the book's opening words, I could tell that Miss Hickey was a Kerridgean historian. 'This book is not written for scholars. If you are a scholar, shut it up at once.'

According to Miss Hickey, the Christian religion, by the sixth century AD, had undermined the authority of the Irish kings, the hill and stone of Tara only unofficially sacred now. She described a new breed of 'imperious churchmen', far removed from the saintly Patrick.

> Having established the fear of God in the hearts of their countrymen they used the power thus gained to engage in an undignified cat and dog war with the monarchs, trading Heaven or threatening Hell freely to further their own ends. The monarchs with neither Heaven nor Hell at their disposal and with their almost divine rights swept away could only utter unseemly maledictions or impotent threats.

Enter St Columbcille – a new spelling yet again! King Diarmaid sat on the throne of Tara, judging those who brought their disputes before him. Now, St Columbcille had borrowed a copy of the Psalms from St Finian. Without telling his fellow saint, he had the Psalms copied out to make a book of his own. Then, with a careless excuse, he returned St Finian's book. However, St Finian found out and was furious, for he wanted the Psalms all to himself. Books were few and far between in those days. Anyway, St Finian demanded St Columbcille's book, St Columbcille said 'Shan't!' and the matter was brought before the King.

Not caring too much for books, his mind occupied with cattle raids, King Diarmaid pronounced verdict. 'To every cow, her calf.' The copied book was seen as the child of the original, and had to go to its mother, both now the property of St Finian. St Columbcille boiled with rage, but bided his time.

A little later the son of the King of Connaught killed one of King Diarmaid's men, and tried to avoid capture and execution by putting himself under St Columbcille's protection. Ignoring the saint, King Diarmaid had the murderer seized and killed.

St Columbcille went to Connaught, a province to the west of Tara, and preached indignantly to the king and people. A huge army was raised with Columbcille as its spiritual leader. King Diarmaid and his men marched to meet the men of Connaught. The terrible slaughter that followed became known as the Battle of the Books. Three thousand of King Diarmaid's men had been killed, and the king returned to Tara, humiliated and in disarray.

No sooner had he returned, than he fell into worse trouble. Another murderer, Hugh Guaire, had put himself under the protection of another saint, St Ruadhan. King Diarmaid nevertheless had Hugh seized and taken prisoner. In a rage, St Ruadhan sent for all the other saints, St Ciaron of Clonmacnoise, St Brendan of Birr, St Columbcille (of course) and St Brendan the Navigator, with his sailor's roll. With all these saints around, a king's life wasn't worth living. Nobody dared to harm a saint, in case of divine vengeance.

Believing their cause to be right, all the saints sat outside King Diarmaid's door and fasted, in the Indo-European tradition. Believing that *his* cause was right, King Diarmaid sat and fasted too. Finally, when everyone had grown very thin, St Ruadhan could stand it no longer. He loudly rang a bell, and cursed Tara, declaring that no king or queen would ever rule there more, and that court and palace would crumble, and Tara 'be waste for ever'.

It was a self-fulfilling prophecy, like a witch doctor's death curse, for King Diarmaid at once packed his bags, dismantled his treasures, and removed his entire court from the once-sacred Hill of Tara. The year was AD 558. Archaeologists have confirmed that Tara was suddenly evacuated towards the end of the sixth century. For a time, the saints lived there in triumph; then they too drifted away. Early versions of Thomas Moore's lament for Tara were already being written in the tenth century.

What happened to St Columbcille? I put aside Elizabeth Hickey's book, and picked up *The Hill of Tara* by Kenneth MacGowan. There I read of 'the monastery at Iona which had been established by Colmcille.'

Iona? Colmcille – Columcille – Columba! Yes, St Columba, the Dove of the Church, gentle, meek and mild, the saint of Iona described so reverently in the *Children's Encyclopaedia*, steeped in the sea-bound mysteries of the Celtic Church, was one and the same as St Columbcille! Who would have thought that St Columba, claimed by England, had such a fiery Irish past! Filled with guilt over the Battle of the Books, he had fled to the Scottish island of Iona and founded a monastery there in AD 563. Inspired, I leaped for pen and paper and wrote a poem on the spot.

The Harp that once at Tara's Halls kicked up a mighty din,
Has grown so ruddy silent now that you could hear a pin.
For Tara's boys have gone their ways: some are in jail in town,
Some emigrated, some are dead and some have settled down.
But Tara's name is not forgot in London as of late.
As for 'Goodbye' the natives say 'Tara now, me old mate.'

CHAPTER FOURTEEN

☘

I Meet the Ascendancy

Mullingar bus and railway station looked forlorn and decrepit, despite the statue of Our Lady at the entrance. All the ticket and information offices were closed. People sitting on benches or standing beside clumps of luggage looked as if they had been waiting so long that all hope had drained out of them. Buses were supposed to stop in the station forecourt, beside weary 1930ish concrete stands.

To my surprise, one did so, and I dragged my bag aboard. I was off to the town of Longford, which I pictured as an Irish Arundel, overshadowed by the great castle of Lord Longford. Fondly I indulged in daydreams of walking up a long driveway and ringing the castle bell. Years before, I had met Lord Longford on a Tube train in London, and had a friendly chat. He seemed a nice man, if gullible, and I was sure that he would remember me.

I admired the bright flower gardens of the suburbs as the bus pulled out of Mullingar and headed northward. Among Ireland's grey terraces, I had forgotten how lovely gardens could be. Outside town, the bus passed Lough Owel, a bright lake that stretched on for ever, and seemed as long as Lake Windermere. It was succeeded by a long marshy pond, with woods behind, a good place for deer. Swans glided among the rushes. Then came fields with donkeys, and winding boreen-like roads with overhanging trees.

Edgeworthstown, at a busy crossroads, commemorated an Ascendancy family whose most famous daughter was Maria Edgeworth (1767–1849), author of *Castle Rackrent* and other tales of Irish life. *Castle Rackrent* is particularly poignant and funny because the story is narrated by the faithful steward of a frightful landowner, who refers to the ogre as 'my dear old master'. Maria

Edgeworth shares the passionate concern for the Irish poor that shines through the work of the best Ascendancy writers.

And so to Longford Town, where I was mortified to see no castle whatsoever, only an heroic statue to 'the Longford Branch' of the Good Old IRA, outside St Mel's Roman Catholic Cathedral. It turned out that Lord Longford lived at Castlepollard. So he had to do without my company.

Tiring of grand hotels, I had spotted a Bed and Breakfast sign from the bus window, and now painfully dragged my bag back along from the main road to the door of Mrs O'Connor. A bright bird-like widow, Mrs O'Connor lived in a small suburban house with her vivacious punky daughter. Greatly relieved at finding a place to stay after all my toiling, I hoisted the bag up the stairs, the last lap, and into a little bedroom. Then I relaxed over tea and ham sandwiches in my landlady's cosy front room. Wedding photos and golf 'hole-in-one' certificates covered the walls, and golf awards and cups covered the mantelpiece.

'I'm still mad on golf, just as my husband was,' Mrs O'Connor told me.

After a rest, I set out to explore Longford. Soon I was back at the cathedral and statue, where a main street led into the old town. Despite this long busy street of shops, banks, bars and hotels, there seemed to be something awfully dreary about Longford. Perhaps it was because the day itself was grey and overcast. Butchers' shops, I noticed, called themselves 'Victuallers'.

At the top of the main street, a bridge crossed a dark, rapidly flowing river, a tributary of the Shannon. Interesting little streets edged their way between the high walls of disused mills and warehouses. Ahead of me, the main street of the town ran straight to the door of an enormous Army barracks. Behind tall iron bars, a camouflaged tank stood on a pedestal. The Army depot, now used by the Irish Army, looked as if it had been built in the eighteenth century. On my previous visit to Ireland, recruiting posters had been plastered everywhere in small towns – 'Join the Army for the Best Years of Your Life' – but now the Irish Army seemed less important.

I rang the guardhouse bell, and an enormous Sergeant Major with a ginger moustache opened the door. 'The CO's away, and no one can come in without his permission,' I was told brusquely.

Around the corner, near the C. of I. church, where the fields began, a row of shabby Georgian houses had been taken over by firms of solicitors. Longford people must be a litigious lot, so I shall be careful what I say about them. Walls had been clumsily daubed with Northern Irish-style slogans: 'IRA. Up the Provos. Brits Out.'

I walked back to the bridge near the barracks, eager to explore the narrow side streets I had seen. Just then, a car bumped into a couple with a child in a pushchair, and sent them sprawling. Nobody was hurt as yet, for the bump had been fairly gentle, but in a minute another couple jumped out of the offending car and they all began to fight, man against man and woman against woman! Depraved-looking fifteen-year-old boys, on their way home from school, jeered and laughed as wild punches flew. Two Garda arrived from nowhere, pulled the warriors apart and sent both sides sternly on their respective ways. 'There's the pigs!' a boy shouted at the sight of police uniforms.

Leaving such distasteful scenes, I roamed between ruined buildings and boarded-up houses. I noticed the word 'Restaurant' painted in large letters beside a tiny front door. Filled with curiosity, I went inside, and sat down at a table. Three big farmers sat near the fire, heads down as they noisily guzzled brown oxtail soup. A rather bare front room had been made into a café. One waitress, a schoolgirl in a blue jersey, scurried to and fro, looking tired and wan after a day at her lessons.

'I wish I was young – you're enjoying the happiest years of your life,' a white-haired old farmer told her unkindly, unconsciously paraphrasing the old army slogan. Then he went on talking of sheep and heifers with his two friends, a neat skull-faced man and a stout youth with straw hair brushed over his eyes.

'I don't be on the sheep side myself,' the neat man commented.

The old man went on to lament the disappearance of all-round grocery-bars, such as I had seen thriving in County Kerry. 'There you could sit and talk for hours and buy all your tings beside,' he said. 'Ah, but it's the decimals I blame for the rise in prices.'

'I'd say that!' the straw-haired man agreed.

'Yes' is a word that is far too definite, not to say affirmative, for use in Ireland. 'I'd say that' is often used in its place. Why Ireland does not make the most of Independence by refusing to copy England's mistakes, such as decimalization, I cannot say. I finished my meal and returned to the suburbs and Mrs O'Connor's.

There I phoned an Ascendancy family whose address had been given me in London, and invited myself over for tea on the day after next. 'You'll never find the place. Ask for the Old Mill, miles from anywhere,' a gruff voice answered.

I had another romantic vision, of the elderly couple from the Great House banished to a room at the back of a crumbling mill house beside a rubble-clogged stream. There, half mad, they clung to a pretence of gentility, hanging cups on thorny briars that poked through holes in the wall.

Next morning dawned dull, but I was cheered up by Mrs O'Connor's bright remarks as she brought my toast and coffee. Her sprightly, fiery, no-nonsense expression reminded me of Hampstead Thinkers I had met, upper-class Englishwomen who shared the Irish notion that to be a rebel, with strong opinions, is the highest virtue.

I decided to take the train to Carrick-on-Shannon, a town often mentioned in *Woodbrook*. Soon I was speeding through marshy, lightly wooded countryside. For part of the way, the railway ran parallel with the mighty River Shannon. Where the river broadened into Lough Tap, the train crossed over on a bridge, and so into Carrick.

On the platform, I was approached by a tall, thin shabby old man, who tried to whisper in my ear. I could only make out one word, 'car'. Eventually I realized that he was not a beggar but a taxi driver, and that the station was a little way away from the town itself.

'I meet most trains,' he told me, as no doubt he had been telling passengers for the last sixty years.

His car was very old and fragile, and made alarming 'put-putting' noises. Very slowly, at walking speed, he drove into Carrick. The fare was fifty pence.

Unfortunately, as soon as the man had gone, the rain came down, heavier and heavier. So I walked rapidly through Carrick-on-Shannon, in hope of catching the next train back to Longford. I saw a long grey street packed with souvenir shops, and a wide bridge across the Shannon, a river which seemed to join lake upon lake, like a string of sausages. Every inch of the water was packed with white motor boats, just like the Norfolk Broads. Since the reign of the Kirkwoods at Woodbrook, Carrick had become a fashionable marina.

I rushed through the rain, back to the station, along a road well-trodden by the Kirkwoods before me. At the station, I waited on a bench along with a mother and two children. To pass the time, I tried to chat.

'Are you drunk?' the little girl, aged three, asked me solemnly.

'No, not yet. Come back later in the afternoon.'

As soon as I alighted at Longford once more, the sun came out, the rain stopped and the sky turned brightest blue. On an impulse, I jumped into a battered pale blue private bus marked 'Cavan'. I knew that Cavan was in the Irish Lake District, and I hoped to see some spectacular scenery.

'Pay when you get off,' the elderly driver told me. 'There's no bus back, d'ye know that?'

Taxis are easy to come by in Ireland, so I didn't worry. The driver's mate, who did no work whatsoever, was a jaunty young man in blue denim. He was in high spirits, and as soon as we set out, he put his arm around a good-looking girl and whispered in her ear. She stiffened angrily.

'Just *what* did you dream about me in bed last night?' she snapped. 'And how's your wife and children?'

'Ach, *them*! They're all right. You know the fox-hunting round my way ...'

For several miles, until the girl got out, he told hunting stories from the foot-follower's point of view. Needless to say, the rain started up again. Although the windows were soon awash, I enjoyed an Impressionist view of County Longford and County Cavan. The bus filled up rapidly, and had the chatty, relaxed atmosphere of the battered private country buses of Wales. As if through gauze, I peered eagerly at a changing panorama of central Ireland. I saw bogs, marshes, stately homes ruined or otherwise, with high demesne walls and derelict lodge houses, lakes of every shape and size and, near Cavan, mountains. I emerged into busy streets and crowded pavements, despite the steady rain. One pub had a sign in the window that read 'Tuesday: Cards.' It was too wet to look at the lakes, so I dived into the Farnham Arms Hotel and ordered an Irish coffee to dry me out from the inside.

'Is it all right?' the young boy behind the bar asked anxiously. 'It's the first I've made.'

'Excellent,' I said, savouring the cream and the drop of whiskey, so another customer ordered one. John Byers, the young barman, is probably famous for his Irish coffee by now.

At the Reception desk, a girl called Marion phoned for a taxi to take me to nearby Kilmore Cathedral. One of the seventeenth-century bishops there, I had heard, first translated the Old Testament into the Irish language. Like the taxi driver of Mullingar, my driver was also a part-time fireman. A middle-aged genial man, he drove out into the country and stopped outside a shoddy-looking concrete church of modern design.

'This can't be Kilmore Cathedral,' I said. 'It's too modern, and anyway, it's Roman Catholic, not Church of Ireland.'

'It's Kilmore Cathedral all right. That's a fine bell in there in that metal cage ting outside, that's like a tower.'

Inside, my driver dabbled his fingers in the holy water, gestured at the Stations of the Cross and declared that many Protestant churches nowadays looked just like chapels. However, I insisted that he try again. As night was falling, he at last found the driveway of St Fethlimidh's Cathedral, Kilmore. St F. had been the sixth-century missionary to the district. My driver looked delightedly at the ring fences and the mature avenue of trees.

'Just look at all these trees! You can tell this is lord country. Lord Farnham owns all the land round here for miles! He's got a big lake for ducks just a short way from here, and he employs hundreds of people! When he comes here to stay at his Big House, there's loads of security, police everywhere, helicopters in the sky, everything!'

Such lord-worship seemed very English. Like the Duke of Devonshire, Farnham seemed to be almost an absentee from his Irish lands. So many great landlords have been assassinated that absenteeism now seems common prudence.

Kilmore Cathedral looked wonderfully romantic in the dusk, surrounded by dark trees and standing at the edge of lordly fields. A Victorian stained-glass window glowed with soft colours. The main door was shut, but we found the door to the vestry open.

'This must be a Norman cathedral,' I lectured the driver, getting my own back. 'Look at that Romanesque doorway! "Romanesque" means there are stone ridges round the door with zig-zag patterns on them.'

'Why does it say "Cathedral founded 1858"?' the driver asked. He had me there. It turned out that the cathedral had been rebuilt in the Middle Pointed Victorian Gothic style. However, the zig-zagged doorway *was* twelfth century, brought from another church and reassembled.

Maintenance men were tinkering about with the cathedral. We were greeted by a pleasant-faced woman and her young daughter, who were changing the flowers. No one could tell me what had happened to the medieval cathedral. A Bible in Bishop Bedell's translation lay open in a glass case, the Irish script showing great delicacy of penmanship. In the vestry, I was shown a portrait of the Venerable Bedell, a wise old man with a white beard.

Outside on the road once more, I asked the driver to take me to Longford. As he drove cheerfully through the dark, he reminisced on his earlier days.

'I'm one of twelve, ten girls and two boys,' he told me. 'Dad was in the Forestry, and we had a farm. We were all a hard-working family. Our water came from the well, a long way off from the house. If the well failed, it was the river. Lovely and pure, that well water! We'd bring it home in churns.

'Now some of those old houses, a bit like ours, had the animals in a walled-off end-part, under the same roof. It's what we called an End Gable. They reckoned the cows heated the house, you know. People used to go to Mass on Sunday, then come back and bake bread. The door would open on to the kitchen, with a bedroom at each end, and that would be the house.

'Of course, the times have got modern now. My parents are still alive, and the farm is doing well, but they're in a modern house. Now I'm a married man myself. Three children we've got, and that's all we're going to get. Modern times are good in some ways and bad in others. Machines, now. Machines have proved a disaster, throwing people out of work. It's not natural for a man to be at home, for he gets under his wife's feet and they're bound to disagree.

'All the work in Ireland now is "by contract", so as to get round the Unions, redundancy money and so on. You work for a specified time, then the work's over and you try and get another contract. There's no security any more.'

'That's just the same as England!' I cried. 'Laws to make jobs secure have made them *less* secure, and skilled men have to go away on contract and send money home, as migrant labourers used to do.'

Despite being a know-all about cathedrals, nearly as bad as myself, my driver had hidden depths. His description of life in a cabin made me feel nostalgic for a way of life I had never known.

'Ah, it's evening Mass,' he remarked, as we entered Longford. 'There's the light of St Mel's Cathedral. Everyone goes to Mass on Saturday evening now – it counts as the first Mass of Sunday.'

☘

On Sunday morning, the bells of St Mel's could be heard from my bedroom. Apart from a steady stream of Mass-goers, the town was damp and empty. I made my way to the station to look for a taxi, and as I did so, the sun came out.

Just for a change, my taxi driver was of a strong, silent type, and beyond an assurance that somehow he would find the three-house village near Granard where my host lived, he said nothing. Left to my own thoughts, I recalled the exiled Anglo-Irishman who had given me his cousin's address.

'You call yourself an Englishman – hmph!' he had said, looking at me disparagingly from beneath black bushy eyebrows. 'You aren't really English. You don't know what being English means unless, like me, you've sat down to tea on the verandah of your father's house in Ireland, with Union Jacks pinned up and down your jacket for St George's Day. I remember that day at Holford House, the old home in County Donegal. The band of the Black and Tan regiment played "Land of Hope and Glory" while my father entertained the officers. Fenian outrages were plentiful in those days, but my father reassured me. "The English will never leave Ireland!" he said. But we did – betrayed by a German and a Welshman!'

A little mental arithmetic had told me that he meant George V and Lloyd George. He went on to tell me of the day when Fenians (Irish rebels) had raided Holford House while his father was away. 'Don't go in that room, the children are asleep,' his mother had said.

'All right, ma'am,' the raiders had agreed politely. They were after the spears hung on one of the walls as souvenirs of the Zulu War.

'Gleefully they took our Zulu spears and rushed off to kill the English!' my acquaintance continued.

So the slain Zulus may have been avenged by people whose remote ancestors had led remarkably Zulu-like lives! That night there may have been feasting in Valhalla.

'Holford House went to my cousin, but he couldn't afford to run the place after the last war. He sold up and moved – here's his address, "The Old Mill",' my acquaintance had remarked, scribbling on an envelope.

'Here's the townland where your friend lives,' said the taxi driver, breaking into my reverie. 'My partner will meet you here, outside the garage, in five hours' time.'

In a moment I was alone, looking round in vain for an Old Mill. We had passed through beautiful countryside, and the 'townland' (village is an un-Irish word) stood beside a great demesne wall. Entranced, I roamed through avenues of mature beeches, admired *three* lived-in lodge houses, and roamed a few yards into a private park to see, at a distance, white columns of a Georgian mansion. Then I retraced my steps to the garage to ask for directions.

A group of men were now standing in the middle of the road, talking loudly. One of them, a strong elderly potato-faced man, solemnly gave me directions with many a 'sir.' I turned to find that the men were staring me out of sight. 'You're right, sir, go on!' Potato Face roared after me.

Around the corner, a lane wound lazily around the base of a hill. I passed an overgrown boreen, more like a green lane, and eventually came to the gate of a Mock Tudor house with green painted beams. There was a large lawn, an orchard by a stream and a paddock where a chestnut horse grazed. Everything was in apple-pie order. I faltered uncertainly.

'That's the house, sir – go on in!' shouted Potato Face, suddenly emerging from a hedge in the boreen from whence he had been observing me.

'Thank you,' I called back, noticing the name 'Old Mill' on the wooden gate. He vanished instantly.

I rang the bell, and an old-fashioned Major's wife answered, her eyes bright, her voice over-sweet and her swept-back hair elegantly coiffured.

'You must be Roy Kerridge – I am Mrs Harvey-Beaumont. Do come in and have some tea. Reginald is a little deaf, but I'm sure he'll enjoy talking to you.'

Apparently an Old Mill had been removed to allow the present house to be built. The house was crowded with paintings and ornaments meant for more spacious halls. Heavy gilt frames of large oil landscapes seemed to tug at walls meant for flimsier mementoes. All the same, many years would pass before my vision of holes and rubble could become reality.

Reginald Harvey-Beaumont was obviously older than his wife. With some effort, he heaved himself from his easy chair and half bounded forward to shake my hand. Red-faced and tweedy, he had his cousin's eyebrows, augmented by a grey upturned moustache. His eyes looked me over not unkindly, but seemed to register caution: 'Has glasses – an intellectual – therefore a possible Home Ruler.'

'So you're writing a book about Ireland?' he said, eyeing me keenly over the tea things. 'What do you think about a united Ireland, eh?'

'I don't like Republicanism,' I said, 'but perhaps Ireland might be united under an Irish king.'

'A king, eh? Splendid, splendid. The MacDermot has the best claim.'

'Do you think so? Is there a Stuart claimant who might be content with Ireland alone? A Duke of Norfolk might be a good king for All Ireland. He's both a Catholic *and* has connections with our Royal family as Earl Marshal, organizing coronations. That might please the Loyalists up North.'

'Don't say "Catholic", always say "*Roman* Catholic"! I hate the North, both Catholics *and* Protestants. The Protestants up there are Scots Presbyterians, not Anglicans. I mean, the ones who cause the trouble. Northern Catholics don't mind Anglicans – they all liked Captain O'Neill, who used to run the place. Of course, he *was* an O'Neill, line of Irish chiefs and all that.

'Now, as a young man, I wanted to design and make cars, but my father was horrified. He had no time for what he called "the motor trade". So instead he sent me to Harland and Wolff, the shipbuilders in Belfast, as the next best thing. They started me at the bottom, among the men.

'One day a notice appeared in the works, written by someone on the shop floor. "All Roman Catholics must leave by noon", it read. There was a tall man there, a man I liked very much, a Roman Catholic. He was very tall and fierce, with black eyebrows and a black moustache.

' "I fought in the Boer War *and* the Great War, and I've the medals to prove it!" he told them, his eyes blazing. "I won't go unless the boss sacks me."

'The other Roman Catholics simply left. Next day I came in late, and found the men shifty-eyed. I soon learned the truth – the tall man was dead. When he'd come in, early that morning, they had pelted him with bits of metal, the rivetting waste. Then a gang of them had frogmarched him to the River Lagan and thrown him in. He couldn't swim, but he splashed to the edge of the quay and began to climb up the iron ladder. So they dropped an anchor on his head and killed him. No one was charged, and all those men went on working. So now you see why I hate the North.'

This story gave me pause for thought. When the Irish Protestants of 1690 had taken the cause of the Hanovers, and the Catholics had supported the Stuarts, the issue was not an Independent Ireland at all. James Stuart would, if he had not been defeated, have ruled Ireland, England and Wales. Bonnie Prince Charlie, a half-century later, would not have been a 'Home-Rule' King of Scotland alone if his cause had succeeded, as many vaguely suppose today. He would have ruled over a United Kingdom, including London and Dublin. The two religious and racial factions of Ireland would probably always choose different leaders no matter the Cause, just to express the difference they both felt existed between them. One king, or one national flag, could not erase the difference.

I drank up my tea, and Mr Harvey-Beaumont began to show me around his house. Among the many delightful old paintings and prints hung drawings and photographs of his old home, Holford House. One of the sketches showed Holford in its prime, with a meet of foxhounds around the front steps.

'See that dome with windows on top, the cupola? My great-uncle had that put on, to let in the light. Only trouble was, it let in the rain as well. Place cost a fortune to keep up. Here's what it looked like ten years ago. I've no idea what state the old place is in now.'

A modern photograph showed the house roofless, in ruins, the walls and a great chimney swathed in ivy.

'I spent all my holidays there as a boy, learned to ride there,' Harvey-Beaumont continued, deeply affected. 'That scribble in the frame is said to be a poem that Rupert Brooke wrote when he visited my cousin. Some of the family blame me for not keeping the place going. We were there in the 1940s, when rates were terrible. I got in a good stock of cattle, and tried to run the estate and keep the house. It was a great strain, as I had my engineering practice in Dublin, and had to commute to and fro. I'm making no accusations, but our steward grew rich, and we grew poor.

'First we sold all the timber on the estate; fine avenues planted in the eighteenth century came down. Then we sold all our silver, and had to give up entertaining. The servants went, and then we went too. Had to sell the place – a dreadful wrench. A timber merchant bought it, chopped down the few remaining trees, and then chopped up our old house. He stripped away all the wooden fittings; panels, window frames, doors, staircases, the lot. Then he left the place to fall down, never went back. Last time I was there, the steward's family were living in the stables.'

'I tell you what,' I said, filled with pity for the infirm house and vaguely troubled with the thought that I ought to bring it some grapes. 'I'm going to Donegal in ten days' time – I'll have a look at the house and write and tell you how it's getting on.'

Looking pleased, Mr Harvey-Beaumont opened a rosewood writing desk and took out a bunch of folded papers. We sat down.

First of all, he showed me a map of the house in its prime. A former kitchen garden had been transformed by a bygone Harvey-Beaumont into a strange Japanese Gothic extravaganza of secular grottos, bridges over pools, caves, mazes and rose arbours. *Fair Rosamund's Bower*, the italic writing read. Older plans showed that an early eighteenth-century house with an Irish name had once stood on the same spot. Carefully unfolding another piece of paper, my host showed me his family pedigree. His coat of arms was at the top – a lion's paw, well endowed with claws, holding a shamrock and crushing the stem. Two brothers named Harvey had arrived in sixteenth-century Dublin as soldiers of fortune, and made their way inland.

Now the lion's claws had been cut. Although Home Rule could never have been won without the help of passionately idealistic sons and daughters of the Big House, people who were as proud of being Irish as their descendants were now proud of being English, the Home Rule governments had treated all 'old families' as potential enemies. 'Old English', of Norman stock, whose ancestors had resisted the Reformation as best as they had been able, were treated no differently from descendants of men planted by Cromwell.

'All our children live in England,' my host continued, gesturing at framed photographs on top of the writing desk. 'My eldest boy's at the Inns of Court, his brother's an architect . . .'

'Is that your daughter?' I asked innocently. 'What does *she* do?'

'Ha, hrrmph! She knows this door is always open to her!' he blurted out, turning purple, so I said no more. We rejoined Mrs Harvey-Beaumont and talk became general.

'How do you get on with the local people here?' I asked.

'We don't see much of them, but I'm told that we're regarded as "reasonable people",' Mrs Harvey-Beaumont smiled.

'That's because we never mention politics or religion,' her

husband butted in. 'Come to that, I don't *have* much religion. I go to church every Sunday to show the flag. Dam' nuisance, as the services get earlier and earlier and the nearest church is miles away. I had to leave the house at ten to eight this morning.'

'Who lives in the beautiful mansion I saw when I came here?' I enquired. 'A German? Oh. Do you know any Anglo-Irish who still live in big houses?'

'Only Zelda,' Mrs Harvey-Beaumont laughed. 'She's a survivor. If you have time, I'll drive you over to see her.'

'I'm sure Mr Kerridge would rather see the horses,' her husband put in querulously, but Mrs H-B. was already on the phone.

'Zelda says "Come right over!",' she called gaily. 'You have your nap, dear. I'll drive our visitor over and bring him back in time to get his taxi.'

'That's Zelda's lake, and her house is over here. She's still got ten thousand acres, and the locals love her and hate her at the same time, in the Irish manner,' said Mrs H-B. in keen anticipation.

The redoubtable Zelda, I learned, took in paying guests, advertising in America, and was possessed of formidable business acumen. A grand driveway curved towards the steps of a Georgian mansion, a bust of Wellington and one of Disraeli at either side of the entrance. Disraeli seemed to be winking roguishly.

'One of the locals asked Zelda who those busts were, she replied "Patriots",' Mrs H-B. told me, as a rare joke. Nobody in Ireland can be a 'patriot' unless he's a Home Ruler.

An elderly maid, hushed and reverent, showed us in. She wore a white apron over a black dress of thick material, and respectful spectacles. I found myself in a hall, before a splendid chandelier and an Adam's staircase. Or it might have been Eve's. At any rate, it was very old. Classical gods and warriors had been painted in oils directly on to the wooden panelling. Age was turning them brown, so that they seemed to materialize from the grains of the woodwork.

We were shown into an enormous room hung with paintings and immense curtains, the table laden with polished silverware.

'My deahs!' a voice cried, and there was Zelda, a little woman with hair in white ringlets, a floppy jersey and blue trousers. Her archly sophisticated amused expression, with eyebrows raised, suggested that she had vast reserves of humour. Oscar Wilde may have liked her, but I felt uneasy. Ancestors looked down at us. Most of them sprouted noble Roman noses, as did Zelda, but looked more solemn than our hostess. She was curled up in an enormous easy chair beside a blazing fire, like a lap dog.

'Sit down, my deahs! Who's this? You must tell me everything!'

I murmured 'yes' and 'no' to Zelda's queries, and left the talking to Mrs H-B., whom Zelda addressed as 'Bunty'.

'I saw such a *ghastly* play in Dublin last week,' Zelda rattled on. 'It was all in Paddyspeak. My deahs, I couldn't understand a *word*.'

Bunty sympathized, I stared at the mantelpiece on which stood an invitation card from Lord and Lady Granard, and then the maid came in with tea on a tray.

'Put it there,' said Zelda, and the maid silently lowered the tray to a coffee table and left without speaking. Cakes and hot apple pie with cream were pressed upon me.

'So you're going to write about Ireland? Please don't mix us up with those *frightful* Protestants in the North! That Ian Paisley, ugh!'

'We've already told him that,' said Bunty.

'Here's something you may care to put in your book,' said Zelda carelessly, giving me a brochure that advertised 'The Irish Country House Experience'. Bed and Breakfast was seventy pounds a night, which would have surprised Mrs O'Connor in Longford.

'What is the history of this house?' I asked.

'History, uurgh! We've always had it, if that's what you mean. I've had a lot of trouble with the Land Commission. They destroyed Lord ------'s estate, and then they turned to mine. I took them to court! [Her eyes gleamed with satisfaction. The Land Commission, which seeks to divide parts of estates among tenants, was set up by Gladstone, although modern Irish politicians seem to take the credit for it.] I'm keeping my land, thank you very much. When I first started taking in guests, I burnt all the estate papers, rolls, maps, parchments, the lot! They were taking up *far* too much space. At one time, every drawer was full of them. But I forgot this one, and some scholar has asked to borrow it. Here it is, it's my father's sworn oath of office when he became a Resident Magistrate.'

She pulled a document from the side of her chair, unrolled it and handed it to me – spidery writing on yellowing paper.

'I do swear to enforce justice and to prevent in any way Acts of Murder, Treason, Insurrection, Theft, Violence, Witchcraft, Inchantments, Sorcery, Deceit, Trickery ...' I read. The list of crimes seemed endless. I may not have them in the right order.

Evidently the oath dated from Elizabethan times. I wondered if it had seemed as strange to Zelda's father as it did to me. Perhaps not – perhaps he was madly zealous to rush out and prevent incidents of treason, insurrection, witchcraft, trickery and deceit by force if necessary.

Leaving me with the Oath as a child with a toy, the two ladies talked of people they knew and county gossip in general. After some time, the maid entered silently, stood at a distance and gave Zelda an enquiring look. I was reminded of the time I spent in the Deep South as the guest of a plantation owner. There I had longed to escape from my kind hosts and relax in the company of the timid and respectful servants.

'That will do. There's no need,' the mistress said carelessly, and the maid withdrew.

'That was the year the O'Donovans' daughter turned Protestant . . . when *we* were the masters . . . I told them I won't have a Hunt Ball at this place. It's not like the old days – they'd wreck the place. These days they get drunk and vandalize everything. I had some trouble like that before – I took them to court!'

Zelda was in full flow, but Mrs H-B. caught me looking nervously at the clock, and brought the visit to an end.

'Come and see me if you're in Ireland again,' Zelda urged, as I said goodbye. 'Tell all your rich friends to come and stay here.'

Mrs Harvey-Beaumont seemed to grow more girlish when away from her husband, and heaped praise on our recent hostess. However, in many ways, I would have preferred the company of the Revd Ian Paisley, whom I have met, as at least he's very sincere.

'My word, there's your taxi over there, all the way from London,' Mrs Harvey-Beaumont remarked. And so it was – a black London taxi with the orange light on top and a 'For Hire' sign in the window. I had no time to say goodbye to the gruff good-hearted Reginald, but hopped in the cab and was away.

'Yes, this was a London taxi,' said the driver, as he headed for Longford. 'I put a passenger seat in front, as it didn't have one. We're all honest people here. The man who brought you up here, he's gone to a karate contest. Did he not tell you, he's a black belt in karate and a champion at Thai kick-boxing?'

Early next morning I said goodbye to sprightly Mrs O'Connor and set off on my weary way to town, dragging my heavy bag. The suburban road stretched endlessly before me, and every step was agony. I could take three steps, then pant for three minutes, then take three more steps. And people wonder why I prefer plastic bags!

Just as I thought all was lost, and that the Roscommon bus would go without me, a kind man stopped and offered me a lift.

'So you've been staying at Mrs O'Connor's!' he said. 'She's my next-door neighbour. It's seldom you'll find a woman who plays golf as well as she does.'

Rain drizzled gently as the bus pulled out of town. It was full of girl students going home after a weekend in glamorous Longford. Some had hangovers; all were in various stages of disarray.

'Honest to God, it was better than Paris!' one girl exclaimed. (See Longford and die.)

Lough Ree, a vast calm lake lay in flat country near Ballyclare, halfway in my journey.

At the town of Roscommon, I swung the bag off the bus, came safely to rest on solid ground, and stared curiously about me. I was now in County Roscommon, in the Province of Connaught. Oliver Cromwell had intended to use Connaught as a Reserve for Native Irish, rather like the so-called 'Indian Nation' of the USA (now Oklahoma). According to legend, Cromwell told the Catholic Irish gentry that they could 'go to Hell or Connaught'. To this day, Connaught is a very Irish province, where old ways persist. However, Roscommon Town was still Irish Midland in character. Strange civic buildings, some elegant, some gaunt and mad, stood sombrely in the grey dankness I had come to associate with Irish towns. I asked about Bed and Breakfast, and to my horror, a suburban road, straight as a die, was pointed out for me to drag my bag along. Past a roundabout I dragged it, past a farm with models of cows on the gate, and at last, appropriately near a hospital, I came to a row of Bed and Breakfast villas.

A family consisting of solid, dependable father, jolly white-haired mother and pensive grown-up son with a bandaged hand welcomed me in. I lay panting on my bed, in a large genteel suburban bedroom with religious knick-knacks everywhere. Motherly emanations from a pretty figure of Our Lady above my head, encased in blue velvet, seemed to restore my strength.

CHAPTER FIFTEEN

☘

Westward to Galway

Once again I sat down to breakfast surrounded by sporting trophies and medals, many of them won by the young man of the house during his schooldays. As I sipped my coffee, I reflected once more than the Midland Irish were very like the English of the 1950s. They were friendly, but with a suburban reserve; they were mad on sport and thought everybody knew all about it; and they were gaining a glittering net-curtain prosperity against a background of ruined buildings that in England had been bombed in the war (and in Ireland had fallen down). Men smoked pipes, wore roll-neck jerseys and had a stolidly dependable air about them. Imagination was in short supply, and the poverty of yesterday had been banished from their memories, the happy-go-luckiness along with the hardships.

I remember, at the close of the fifties, going to a hairdresser and praying that he wouldn't talk. Unfortunately he did.

'How are we doing, do you know?' he asked.

'What do you mean?' I asked, mystified. I was eighteen years old.

'Eh? The cricket, of course!'

I stammered something about not understanding cricket, totally incredulous that anyone should suppose I *did* understand it, or that I should regard the English side as 'we'. The barber in his turn was equally taken aback – we were all English, weren't we, and wanted to know how England was doing? Rock and roll, which arrived for me in 1958, had completely severed the younger generation from its elders. The elders grew older, and the old Englishness and innocence were lost.

In Ireland I was recognized as English as soon as I appeared on anybody's horizon, and no one in the Midlands asked me how 'we' were doing at Gaelic football, golf, bicycle racing or hurling.

This time with a light plastic bag containing nothing more than a sketchpad and a book (Sleeman's *Rambles and Recollections of an Indian Official*) I set out to have a look at Roscommon Town. As I neared the roundabout outside the old town, I glanced across the fields and noticed an eerie grey ruined abbey standing on its own in flat farmland. Reserving it for later, I plodded on into town. As at Killorglin, a street of dark stone houses climbed a hill. A gaunt building, Roscommon's former prison formed a wall that seemed to seal off the end of the town. Part of the ground floor had become a dress shop.

Later on, I learned that 'Lady Betty', the last woman hangman in Ireland, had her base at Roscommon Jail. Apparently a hooded stranger with a bag of gold had asked if he could stay at her house one night. Overcome by greed, she murdered him while he slept, only to discover he was her own son, who had made his fortune and wanted to surprise her. As a penance, she became a hangman, although I would have thought she would more likely have become a candidate for hanging. The writer of the old guide book whence I gleaned this misinformation had unknowingly quoted a fragment of folklore older than Roscommon Town and its jail. Before becoming a dress shop, the jail had been a lunatic asylum, of the Hogarthian deep-straw-and-goggling-visitors variety.

Round the corner from the old jail, the Royal Hotel boasted a well inside the bar, the top covered by glass and the stone walls curving down into darkness and revealing a tiny gleam of water. Beyond the hotel, the town straggled to an end, and the fields began. In one of them, I could see the broken towers of a Norman castle.

Returning to the main street, I browsed among the many little shops I found there. Despite the grey sky and gloomy weather, the people were unusually friendly, greeting one another and saying 'hello' to me. In one little shop, the lady behind the counter shouted aloud with excitement and joy as soon as she caught sight of my plastic bag. The bag bore the name of my off-the-peg tailor, 'Marcus Menswear, Craven Park, Harlesden'.

'Marcus! Why, that's my wee laddy's name! Marcus! He's five years old! Wait till I tell him his name's on a bag!'

It began to rain, so I dodged into the Roman Catholic Church of the Sacred Heart. There were three altars, one a submarine green. A mosaic of a tree stretched along the whole centre aisle, the branches spreading out before the altars, the birds and beasts of Ireland standing between the leaves. Rampant stags looked odd balanced on twigs among foliage, and so did exquisitely made seabirds, puffins and razorbills. In one of the pews, a woman was fingering her beads, eyes shut, muttering.

When the rain was over, I emerged and strolled back into town along the wide church forecourt, past a heart-shaped flower bed and two Virgins in substantial grottos. Then I hurried down to look at the ruins I had seen earlier, before the next onslaught of rough weather could begin. The path to the abbey ruins was under water, but I managed to keep dry by sidling along the edge, holding on to a fence. Pavements and drains came late to Ireland, and in some cases have stayed away altogether. A notice declared the ruins to be a Dominican Priory. According to a picture I had seen on the wall of the Royal Hotel, this Priory had been founded by King Felin O'Connor of Connaught, whose burial place it became.

Now roofless, the Priory had been tidied up slightly, but with no explanatory labels. This made my delight at finding King Felin's tomb all the more great. There he lay, in knightly stone effigy, with a row of eight knights in stone cartoon-strip below him. These knights were Gallowglasses, twelfth-century mercenaries from Scotland, each in chain mail with a pointy helmet. Each knight was in the act of drawing his sword, the swords a little further from the hilts in each panel, as if the knights were drawings in a moving-picture flick-page book. Having admired the kingly tomb and added the name 'O'Connor' to my list of families who might accept the Irish throne, I wandered off to the Abbey Hotel. A marvellous eighteenth-century folly, this manorlet represented the builder's idea of the Priory gatehouse in all its medieval splendour.

Now the sky grew nearly as black as night, and I galloped into the hotel just as the most torrential downpour I have seen in my life cascaded from the sky as the waters of the Red Sea might have descended on Pharaoh. 'May I stay here for a pot of tea?' I asked the girl at Reception.

'Sure, if you went out you'd be drinched entirely,' she sympathized.

As I drank my tea, I heard her answer the phone: 'Terrible morning, can I help you?' Well, it made more sense than 'good morning'. With judicious use of hot water, I enjoyed four cups of tea, and then found that the rain had stopped. I edged around the puddles in the garden, where belated rain fell from the yew trees, and returned to my Bed and Breakfast house for a soothing sleep.

In the afternoon, I strolled back into town beneath a blue sky. Boys of thirteen and fourteen were stampeding out of school, roaring, jeering and swearing. Ignoring them, I made my way to the Norman castle.

A stile over a stone wall led into a field whose furthest wall consisted of the grey squat towers of the castle. The long grass was so wet that I decided to admire the castle from afar. I walked round the walled field and found myself at the edge of a tinkers' camp. Beyond the seven or eight tents and caravans, the camp ponies grazed, all piebald or skewbald with vivid white patches. Among them, a black and white jackdaw hopped, a magic sign of great portent and possibly the reason why the camp had been pitched there in the first place. Looking hard at the castle, sketch-book in hand, I allowed the corner of my eye to rove the tinker camp.

There were no horse-drawn wagons, but one of the trailers looked very old-fashioned and may have been home-made. It was brown and box-shaped, like a flat-roofed shed on wheels, and had a stove-pipe chimney poking crookedly through the top. A large curved home-made tent, with tarpaulins in different colours draped over it, seemed to be supported by bendy willow staffs. Clinking washing-up sounds came from the shed-like caravan, and the dogs were friendly. All in all, this camp had a peaceful atmosphere.

'Do you want to see the castle?' a plainly dressed girl of fifteen asked me, looking up from her job of sweeping her trailer entrance with a broom. 'Look, there are stone steps into the wall over there.'

When I asked if I might walk through the camp and look at the castle from the other side, Cinderella looked distressed, so I said 'never mind' and made my way back to the stone stile. I had drawn a fairly creditable sketch of the castle when, as I hoped, I heard voices behind me. Two snub-nosed bristle-headed boys were looking over my shoulder in bright-eyed interest.

Looking very solemn and Royal Academyish, I suddenly drew a fiendishly grinning devil playing a fiddle in the castle forecourt.

Both boys drew in their breaths, then began a torrent of pleas.

'Can we have it, mister? Can we have it?'

This was most gratifying. For the next twenty minutes I drew picture after picture of devils playing and donkeys dancing.

I even drew a donkey playing and a devil dancing. It was hard for the donkey to hold a fiddlestick in one hoof, but he managed. Now I had a new mission in life – to ensure that every tinker caravan in Ireland contained a picture of a donkey dancing while a devil played the fiddle.

When I had run out of paper, I bowed to the boys and departed. On my way out, I encountered a dignified, round-faced tinker grandmother, a big lady in a shawl and long dress that swept the ground. She returned my greeting politely.

It was suppertime, so I made my way to the Roscommon chip shop. I found the Italian-Irish proprietor poring over an encyclopaedia of Black Magic while his female relatives served a crowd of hungry teenage boys. 'You see, that's a circle of protection,' he told me seriously, pointing at a drawing.

'You be careful, or the devil will appear one day and ask you to sell your soul,' I warned.

'I wish he would, if I'd get a good price for it,' the man joked.

All the youths seemed interested, so I told them stories of Black Magic in Sussex, a county particularly afflicted by Satan because of all the artistic people who live there, running craft shops or theatrical costumiers.

'On Midsummer's Eve, I walked up to Highdown Hill at midnight, below a full moon. When I saw a fire and capering figures, I ran down again. The grass all around my feet was alive with black toads.'

'Do Black Magic people in England attack you?' a Roscommon chip shop boy asked me in awe.

'No, they just ask you to go with them. In Brighton, the worst place for magic, my sister went to a theatrical costumier. He was dressed as a wizard and the whole place was full of drawings of human sacrifices and magic designs. She was terrified, but he didn't hurt her.'

Back in 1959, I had been sitting one day in a Brighton coffee bar aptly named the Thieves' Kitchen. An upper-class homosexual-looking man with white hair and glittering eyes came up to me and asked if I wanted to go to a Black Mass.

'No fear!' I gulped.

'Ah, I see you're conservative in your ways,' he sneered, expecting that this would goad me into Satanism.

'Is that what you call it?' I replied, and ever after voted Conservative. However, as a compensation, I tend to draw comic devils playing fiddles. Back in the chip shop, I warned the Roscommon boys against trifling with the Black Art.

'One day you'll come in here and there'll just be a burnt patch on the ground and a wisp of smoke where the chip shop man used to be,' I said. 'The devil will take him away in a sack.'

At breakfast, my 1950s landlord told me that Ballinasloe Fair, County Galway, was being held that week. David Thomson and the Kirkwood family from *Woodbrook* bought and sold horses at Ballinasloe, I remembered. Moreover, an emissary from Ballinasloe had attended the Puck Fair at Killorglin. The landlord showed me the way to the railway station and off I went. According to him, it was possible to go to the fair and be back in Roscommon before dark. For a change, the sun was shining.

The train journey southward to Athlone took me through wild flat bogland scenery. Some were heather bogs, some bracken bogs and others were boggy floodlands of marsh grass. Most bogs are full of tree stumps and used to be oak forests, like the Scottish moors. Some of the bogs I saw from the train window had been 'harvested', and rows of beehive-shaped 'peat cocks' stood like haycocks, awaiting collection. These are also seen in Scotland, where they are known as 'peat hags'.

At Athlone I waited in a large modern station for another train to take me to Ballinasloe. The approach to Athlone station was very fine, along a wide bridge over the Shannon. Finally I arrived at Ballinasloe, to find the station a long way from the town. It was a well-manned Victorian station, with dark waiting rooms, a parcels office and a quaint Neo-Gothic shelter with an ecclesiastical window at each end. Outside, in a field, a lively group of boys and girls were piling branches in a heap for their Halloween bonfire.

'Taxi?' said a voice in my ear.

The taxi driver was a sharp-looking middle-aged man who told me that he was the landlord of the Dove bar in town.

'I've come to see the Fair,' I said conversationally.

'The Fair! There's no fair today! Yes, it's Fair Week all right, but the fair is only celebrated at the weekends now, when they sell the horses. Since they've had the marts, they don't be keeping the pig days and sheep days no more. Ah, it was grand in the old days . . .'

Thinking quickly, I asked the driver to take me to Clonmacnoise instead, a famous holy city that stood in ruins scattered over a sloping river bank. I had been to see it years before in a taxi from Roscrea, and had been greatly impressed by the poignant air of haunted melancholy that hung over the ruins. My decision pleased the present-day driver, as the fare would be expensive.

We crossed the River Shannon once more, travelling eastward through open country. A disused stone toll house stood at one side of the river, a ruined mill on the other.

Finally we drove up to the Clonmacnoise ruins. They were spread over a wide expanse of riverbank, back at the twisting, curling Shannon river once more. Here the Shannon resembled a long lake, pale grey in the sunlight. Near the Clonmacnoise entrance, the river had overflowed into the fields, beside a misshapen castle tower that perched on a hummock, balanced at an angle and looking as if it were about to fall over. A broken-off piece of castle lay in the grass nearby. Throughout the centuries, the monks of Clonmacnoise had suffered from raiders sailing up the Shannon to plunder the monastic city. In the thirteenth century, a bishop had ordered the castle to be built and manned as a protection. However, it had been demolished, some say by Cromwell.

To my dismay, the whole entrance to Clonmacnoise had been concreted over in a multi-lane car park that was almost totally empty. As far as I could see, a holy well pointed out to me by my 1973 taxi driver had also been concreted. A young, innocent man, very knowledgeable about ferrets, the driver had led me across a scrubby field that led to the riverbank and had then triumphantly pointed to a weathered stone below a thorn bush. Water trickled from the brown earth near the roots of the bush and traced a dark line through the tall grass. Strips of cloth had been tied to the thorn, as on trees dedicated to strange gods in West Africa, the Near East and India, each strip a supplication.

'Sometimes the priest holds services here – I think on the Feast of St Finian,' the driver had told me.

Clonmacnoise had now become scientific, with a large brick Interpretive Centre where once a motherly woman had sold entrance tickets in a shed. The ticket woman and I had got on famously. Her hair was rather wild, her tongue eloquent. Mrs Kelly, for that was her name, had unintentionally paid me an enormous compliment. 'What part of Ireland are you from?' she had asked, at length.

'Ireland? I'm English – can't you tell by my accent?'

She seemed flabbergasted, but rallied and asked me if I would look in at the Gray Mare in Kilburn and say 'hello' to her son Joe Kelly who worked there. I agreed, but never seemed to notice a Gray Mare on any of my trips to Kilburn. Years later I found it, a tiny pub tucked into a cobbled alley beside a large inn. To my surprise, some of the customers greeted the barman in Gaelic.

'Joe Kelly? He's only just left this pub, and moved to Wembley, but I don't know whereabouts,' the bilingual landlord had told me. So I gave up my quest.

To my chagrin, I found, back in present-day Clonmacnoise, that most of the stone slabs with strange carvings of Celtic saints, reminiscent of Celtic gods, had been taken indoors and put in glass cases under bright lights in the accursed Centre. One of the glories of Old Clonmacnoise was the possibility of seeing a strange stone face staring from a broken column in a randomly-chosen clump of grass.

Half the magic of Clonmacnoise was gone, but there was still some mystery left. There was still the same mournful view across the flooded Shannon from the ruin-studded slopes, with the same toppled tower, arrested in motion, ever-ready to fall. On the inland side of the broken city stood a humpy line of green mounds, perhaps with old treasures or masonry in their innards.

In the mid sixth century, St Ciaran with seven followers had arrived at Clonmacnoise by water and built a wattle church and beehive huts, the foundation of the holy city. St Kevin from Glendalough, and St Columcille-Columba from just about everywhere, were frequent guests. Scholars, disciples, stone-carvers and holy artistic men of every kind taught or studied at Clonmacnoise over the centuries. Until recent times, there was great water traffic on the Shannon and a busy landing-stage at Clonmacnoise. In spite of raiding Vikings, the great days of the city of churches and colleges coincided with the English Dark Ages.

The protection of the local kings, the O'Connors, was not strong enough for Clonmacnoise to withstand disastrous raids by the Norman English in the Middle Ages. A great storm in 1547 destroyed the cathedral. Before it could be repaired, Protestant English troops from Athlone rushed in and looted the place. Bishop and priests left, and Clonmacnoise became a ruin, used only as a burial ground for those who held the site forever sacred.

Just as I had done before, I stumped around Clonmacnoise, surveying each ruined building or ancient cross as I came to it. Stone ruins were dotted about the site, several yards apart, like an abandoned village whose streets had turned to pastureland. Here there was a tall Round Tower standing sentinel over the river, there was a large grey church standing roofless on a rise, its tall end gables resembling towers. The Pope of the day had visited Clonmacnoise in 1979, and a dismal pavilion with throne had been made in his honour. However, it was not too obtrusive. Modern graves with bright plastic flowers sought to take advantage of the saintly dust. A small cemetery plot had been added since my last visit.

I threaded my way between the various broken churches, towers and columns to the entrance-exhibition where posters announced that fibreglass imitations of the stone carvings were soon to be set up outside. There I enquired after Mrs Kelly, only to be told that she was dead! I was very taken aback, as she had not been old, and asked where she might be buried.

'Right here in Clonmacnoise,' the blonde ticket girl replied, and sent for a tall young man who worked in the grounds to show me her grave.

The grave was in the new cemetery plot, with a figure of Jesus crowned in gold on the headstone. With head hung low, the young man looked awkwardly respectful.

'I'm not a Catholic, so could you say a prayer for her?' I asked him. 'In your head!' I added quickly, as the appalled expression of a visitor singled out by a pastor in an evangelical church for 'spontaneous prayer' flashed over his face.

Greatly relieved, he muttered under his breath and crossed himself several times. Now relaxed and talkative, he saw me back to the waiting taxi and told me of his ambitions as a Gaelic football player.

'I went to school with the son Joe,' he added. 'Now he's got a pub of his own at Hitchin, Essex.'

Soon I was being whisked back to Ballinasloe, the driver singing 'Red River Valley' for most of the way. He told me that he had once worked for Lipton's Stores in London, very near my old school, Holloway Comprehensive. Finally he dropped me off outside his pub, the Dove, in a street hung with bunting for the Fair.

'Today would have been sheep day in the old days,' the driver explained, as he hurried in to take over from his wife at the bar. 'I must be careful to lock the car, as youths often steal cars to get home at Fair time.'

Despite the absence of sheep, there was a faint holiday atmosphere at Ballinasloe. A stout middle-aged man sat at a corner playing a red squeeze box and working a pedal with one foot which made a row of wooden puppets dance. Most of the puppets looked rough-hewn and primitive, but two were utterly grotesque, as plastic dolls heads, complete with eyelashes and floppy yellow curls, had been fixed on to their stick-like bodies. In between tunes, friendly loafing policemen (or Garda) chatted amiably with the puppet-master. When the man's shift was over, he was replaced by a shabby flute player.

There were plenty of Garda around, and there ought to have been plenty more, as I saw a group of wild children steal chocolates from a shop and then run off down the road. No one had seen them steal except myself, but they went on running nonetheless.

Unpleasant tinker men with fierce expressions roughly begged from passers-by in the streets. Some of them may have been the fathers of the running children. They too seemed to work in shifts. The off-shift sat scowling on a wall, counting their money.

My train would not leave for over two hours, so I strolled desultorily around the town. Where the fields began, a stream led into the River Suck, and here I found a row of tinker caravans. Children played uproariously with supermarket trolleys, pushing one another around. A surly man stepped from a trailer doorway and asked me for money.

'Certainly not,' I replied primly.

'Jew! You must be a Jew!' he shouted, and turned away.

There is some Jewish blood on my maternal grandfather's side, so this only goes to show the uncanny power of the tinkering race.

Having admired the Roman Catholic church, I retraced my steps to town to see the Church of Ireland, set on a hill. Unfortunately for me, but fortunately for the reader (who may have had enough of churches), it was closed. Suddenly I stared in amazement, for below me, sloping down from the church, was the Fair field, a broad sweep of land entirely covered with tinkers, caravans, and horses. In the distance, ponies in long-shafted light chariots trotted at a spanking pace, the wheels spinning around.

One corner of the field housed a closed funfair, the various attractions packed tightly together. Over the whole plain, the temporary tinker village seethed with life. Grass had everywhere been trampled into mud, well-strewn with waste paper. Dark brown horses roamed freely, nosing round the caravans and grazing midst the rubbish, like black bears scavenging around National Park campsites in America.

Among the great variety of trailers, an enclave of horse-drawn barrel-top wagons formed a circle, like covered wagons on the prairie awaiting Indian attack. Their round roofs were green, the steps, shafts and other woodwork dark red. Old fair hands could doubtless see order in the chaos, the separate camps of the different families within the larger camp. Crooked stove-pipe chimneys sprouted from a hundred roofs, and families could be seen talking animatedly in rows of caravan windows. Children and colts, two of a kind, rushed round and round the field in exhilaration. Bare-back riders tore up and down the slopes, racing one another.

I was reminded of Appleby Horse Fair, a gypsy occasion in Westmorland, but the Irish travellers seemed far less fond of pets and livestock. There were fewer dogs than would be found at a Romany camp, and no poultry at all. Since horse-drawn wagons went out of fashion, both gypsies and tinkers lead a curious, inverted life, buying and selling horses among themselves for sheer pleasure. I suppose stamp collectors and some antique dealers lead similar lives, where dealers deal with dealers, and the public have no place.

Within minutes I was inside the camp, where I hoped to meet the tinkers who had tried to rob me at Killorglin. It's always nice to see a friendly familiar face. An avenue of fortune-tellers' trailers led into the funfair, displaying yellow or red cards in their windows. One woman advertised herself as Madam Homa, an imaginative name. Although most of the 'Lees' were probably Flanellys or Murphies, there may have been some Romanies present.

A scrawny little old lady poked her head from the doorway of a miniature trailer and fervently watched me advancing slowly towards her, moon-faced, a red neon light about my head flashing the word 'Sucker' on and off. Overcome with necromancy, greed and competitiveness, she rushed out and began stroking my jacket in an ingratiating manner. 'Come in and see the crystal ball,' she crooned appealingly.

'No, I'm really looking for the people who told my fortune at the Puck Fair,' I said.

'That was me! That was me!'

'No it wasn't. All right, what happened to me there?'

'You was breathing fire and brimstone!' she guessed, well

knowing the effect a Puck Fair fortune-telling might have on a customer.

'No, I wasn't. 'Bye!'

Ruefully she watched me go. Back in the main street of Ballinasloe, I had to act fast, or I would miss my train. Quickly I bought three chocolate liqueur bottles and a small plastic figure of a stag. These I put inside a paper bag, along with a pound note and a hastily drawn picture of a devil and a donkey. Then I returned to the tinker camp and sought out the same woman.

'All right!' I challenged her. 'Let's see if you can really tell fortunes. If you can tell me the initials of my name, you can have what's in this bag.'

Momentarily staggered, she rose to the challenge, and I could feel her mind racing feverishly. 'You have a nickname and a short name,' she said cautiously.

'Never mind that,' I said, disappointed that she hadn't said 'Rumpelstiltskin'. 'What are the initials?'

The poor woman swayed, appeared to commend her soul to God, and said faintly, 'There's an "M" and a "B" in it.'

'How did you know?' I cried, jumping up in the air in amazement. I had temporarily changed my name to Marvin Brainboxbatterer. 'That's absolutely right! How did you do it? It's amazing!'

The lady looked modest, but said nothing, and I handed her the bag.

'God bless you!' she said with feeling, and shook me by the hand. I was moved to see that she had absolute faith in my goodwill, for she took the bag without glancing at the contents. With that, I galloped off for the train, and even had time for a drink before it left. A tinker accosted me in the bar, asking for a glass of brandy, but I gave him short shrift.

It was a long haul with my heavy bag to the bus stop at the top of town next day, but I made it and set out on a bus journey westward from Roscommon to Galway. There had been heavy rain in the night, and some of the fields were flooded. Sprays of drizzle flecked the bus window, but I could still see out. As we drove westward, the bogs vanished and we were among pastureland enclosed by dry stone walls, augmented with barbed wire. Soon cob and thatch cottages began to appear. Long white cabins with bright thatched roofs are typical of the Province of Connaught, and are known as 'bothies'. They are more often to be seen on Irish calendars than in real life (except as ruins), but many survive as comfortable homes. I wondered if I would ever be able to peep inside one. Whether the thatch on these bothies was old or new, it was always a deep orange colour. Even the haystacks were thatched.

Posters advertising 'Sixties Discos' were stuck to telegraph poles. One pole wore a similar notice which read 'I'm Sick of Sixties Disco Posters.'

We passed two ruined abbeys, one with a tower and one without, and then stopped at a four-house township. A rough-looking man with dark slicked-back hair and heavy eyebrows popped his head into the bus and shouted jubilantly to a friend, 'Come in, there's a funeral wi' free whiskey!'

This man, who was soon joined by three friends, reminded me of the woozily friendly Galway people I had known in Brighton in the late sixties and early seventies. These wild Gaelic-speaking men may have once lived in bothies, but when in Brighton they regarded themselves as raiders in a strange and hostile land. Most of them worked intermittently as hotel kitchen porters, and they slept where they fell. Feeling very daring, I would sit in a circle with them on the grass in Powis Square, and pretend to drink deeply as the cider or barley wine bottle passed around. Sometimes one of them would leap to his feet and dance a jig before falling over.

One of these men had a wife and family, and only joined the Powis Square circle when he was on a spree. Normally he was a model husband and father, kind-hearted and always laughing. When he drank, he grew miserable and would throw every living creature out of the house, wife, children, dog and pigeons, and then rush out himself to Powis Square. Luckily his pigeons were homers and flew back when he was sober.

Most of the Powis Square mob frequented a particular betting shop where their noisy ways were tolerated. They knew very well that the manager kept several pounds of their winnings, but couldn't object, as every other betting shop had barred them. One of these men, named Pat, was going out with my godson's grandmother. He stole a chicken from work, and I watched as he stuffed it and sewed it up with needle and thread in his girlfriend's flat, frowning with ponderous alcoholic severity. He was arrested for theft on the same day as my godson, each in a different part of Brighton. My Bible instruction to the lad had been of no avail.

With these memories, I expected Galway City, my destination, to be a hopeless, broken-down kind of place. As the bus pulled into the depot, just in time before all the busmen went on strike, I looked around in surprise. This seemed a very sophisticated city. With a final burst of furious rain, the sky cleared and I dragged my bag along the road in blinding sunshine. Near the bus and railway station stood a Great Southern Hotel, not too different from the luxurious mansion I had known in Killarney. My purse had grown thin since then, so I struggled on. In the lobby of that hotel, on the following evening, I was to meet a Mrs Knelle, the friend of an English friend, and she was going to put me up at her house in the country. She was an English woman, now widowed, whose husband had come from County Galway. (Irish counties, provinces and county towns can be a bit confusing, so I'll spell it out carefully – I was now in Galway City, county town of County Galway. County Galway itself is part of the Province of Connaught, which contains five counties.)

The front door of the hotel looked out on John F. Kennedy Square, a wide-open space of seats and gardens named after the American President who had visited Galway in 1963. Its real name is Eyre Square. Wearily and painfully, I lugged my bag along the perimeter of the square, past rows of little shops. Before long, I found a Bed and Breakfast, a squalid musty place of peeling lino, connected to a sweet shop. A thin disdainful blonde girl led me up narrow stairs to a room filled completely by a single bed. At the foot of the bed, a window looked out on dip-backed slate roofs. Exhausted, I fell asleep.

I awoke some hours later and, feeling refreshed, went out to explore Galway. Eyre Square, though marred by a mad iron statue put up in honour of Kennedy, was still a fine place, used as a promenade by the young people of Galway. Prosperity seemed everywhere, and I learned that Galway was a university town. A medieval merchant city, unlike any other in Ireland, it had been founded in 1232 by a Norman knight, Richard de Burgo, at the mouth of the River Corrib, facing the Atlantic Ocean. Rich merchants from Spain had traded there, and the young Christopher Columbus is said to have worshipped in the Church of St Nicholas. There was still a Mediterranean atmosphere, as I could see as I walked beneath the Spanish arch along the cobbled quayside towards the harbour. Writers, artists and Bohemians now lived in some of the tiny terraced cottages facing the quay.

One of these houses, with books in the bottle-glass window, advertised Bed and Breakfast. I wished I had stayed there instead of at the sweetshop. A plaque reading 'Michael Walsh was shot by Black and Tans near this spot, 1920', was a reminder of grimmer times. From the harbour, I could see oil installations in the distance, another source of Galwegian prosperity. (Just as Glas-gow-ites are Glaswegians, Galway dwellers are Galwegians.)

Large red and white boats packed the harbour, and I thought at first that they must be private yachts. When I looked more closely, the ropes, winches and heaps of nylon netting showed me that they were superior fishing vessels. One of them was named *Galway Bay*, but of the bay itself, famous in song, I could see no sign. Near here, trips to the Aran Islands were advertised.

One of the Kirkwoods from Woodbrook had told me about these wondrous isles, where fiddlers played Gaelic melodies to fisherfolk who danced on the quayside. At least they did so until the local priest warned them that if they did not stop, he'd say a prayer that would make the dead rise from their graves and walk the length and breadth of the islands. Fishermen went out in curraghs, long Irish coracles, and turf boats named hookers flew in and out of the harbour on wind-filled sails. It was as well that I was unable to visit the Aran Isles, for if they had changed since the 1930s my disappointment might have been too great to bear.

Apparently the Galway and Aran fishermen of those days had the usual fishermen's superstitions. Christianity conquered the land but could never quite conquer the sea. Fishermen would never go out in a boat if anyone who could swim was on board, since the Fates might decide to give the man a chance to do so. A man once fell off the dock, with only one hand reaching above the surface. Nobody would pull him out of the sea. Finally an Englishman did so, to be told by scowling fishermen that 'a drowning man's hand turns against you'. Sure enough, the rescued man later tried to murder somebody with that very hand.

I retraced my steps to the square where Kennedy had been given the Freedom of the City (an empty honour), and explored a network of narrow shopping streets. These were the glittering and opulent reminders of the medieval city. Stone carvings and whimsies had been plastered over in the nineteenth century, but some had now been uncovered. The old grey Allied Bank was decorated with sixteenth-century gargoyles and sculptured animals, some devouring one another. Sophisticated young women, with toned-down Irish accents, tripped in and out of expensive perfume and handbag shops. One or two ruined houses could be seen, but the dreariness of much of Cork and Dublin was absent, as were high-rise office blocks. If you enjoy city life, I recommend Galway.

Kenny's Bookshop, near Buttermilk Lane, seemed to be the centre of civilization in Galway. I just had time for a quick glance into its shelf-ridden depths before it closed, and I saw room after room, opening vistas of eternal reading to my gaze. When it closed, a statuesque elderly lady in curly grey hair, several laps of necklaces and a sweeping gown that may have been bombazine (a word I have often pondered over) showed clearly by her bold carriage that she was a power behind the Kenny throne. I had to restrain myself from running after her and asking who she was – heir to the Austro-Hungarian Empire perhaps?

Emerging from the delightful maze of shops, bars, churches and cafés, I crossed a bridge over the River Corrib. Perhaps swollen by rain, the river rushed into the sea in a torrent of white foam and spray. I found myself in a grey council estate that faced the river. Seeing a Catholic church, I went in, but a huddled family inside looked so shocked at the sight of a stranger that I hurried out again, suspecting a funeral. Cars crawled by, chased by stray dogs.

At one time a fisherman's village had stood not far from here, the Claddagh. It had been a village of thatched cabins, with virtually no other buildings at all, and had been the original Galway town before De Burgo came. The songs, stories and customs of the Claddagh dwellers had set them apart from other Galwegians, and the well-known Claddagh rings originated there. Sad to say, the neighbourhood had been pulled down as 'a slum' in 1927, a council action that had staggered the rest of Galway. There is now not a thatched roof in the city.

I followed a long harbour-wall pathway, then took a gate into a park. All at once I could see Galway Bay. Tall, dim mountains on a curve of horizon, a winking lighthouse and the open sea. There was no prom, and neatly cut grass grew down to the black shiny shore. Seaweed glistened on the rocks, waders large and small ran up and down, and gulls and cormorants bobbed on the waves. A round black head appeared and disappeared – a common seal. The sky was as orange as Galway thatch, overlaid by dark clouds, and the sea also glowed a dull orange.

Dusk was falling as I eventually made my way back into town. I had been right about one thing – an *enormous* procession of funeral guests was making its steady way into the riverside church.

Pensively I roamed through a housing estate, stopped by a bearded man who asked me if I knew where Number Fifty was. When he found I was a stranger, he explained that the houses were numbered at random 'in the old-fashioned way'. In Nigeria, so I had heard, people gave their houses numbers for aesthetic reasons, because a certain number might have a distinguished ring to it. I'd hate to be a Galway postman.

Soon I came to a strange place where the river divided, one part of it compressed as a hurling white torrent between steep artificial banks, the other part let into a tranquil canal that entered Galway from the countryside. A narrow path led between the two waters, the wild and the domesticated. Feeling as if I were under an enchantment, I walked the narrow way, between vivid white hand-rails that shone in the half-light. At one time, this may have been a mill chase with a waterwheel turning. Looming over all was the great green dome of the Roman Catholic cathedral. Beyond yet another bridge, for Victorian ingenuity had been hard at work here, I came across a torrential waterfall labelled 'salmon weir'.

Here it was, I believe, that my hero Frank Buckland, the writer, naturalist and Mayhew-like chronicler of London life, had jumped into the water in order to imagine himself a salmon. Queen Victoria appointed him Inspector of Fisheries, and he took his job seriously, persuading millers to install salmon ladders over their weirs. Floundering excitedly among the real salmon, he had not noticed the water bailiff, who observed, 'Bedad, your honour, you're the finest fish I ever see in this ladder this long time.'

Walking by the riverbank, I came across a W.W. Jacobean neighbourhood of mellow terraced shops, pubs and houses. Seaman-like men in bobble hats or ship caps roamed cheerily around, and the bars advertised 'Music'. Dim lights shone in brown parlour windows and there was a trail of yellow in the purpling sky behind the chimneys. Without knowing how, I found myself in the smart medieval quarter again. Galway was the strangest town I had ever visited, and I felt as if I were in a dream. Strange towns, reached by complicated journeys, are part of my dream repertoire.

In the morning, I paid my disdainful landlady for the use of my room for the rest of the day. Mrs Knelle would not be meeting me until half past ten that night, after the theatre. I was looking forward to being a guest in Ireland for the first time, instead of merely a paying guest. All Irish landladies, however pleasant, seemed to breathe a sigh of relief when a visitor left, and they were able to get on with the intense business of family life without interruption. Bag-dragging had exhausted me so much that I went back to bed and slept until afternoon.

After a second teatime breakfast in a café, I set off without delay for Kenny's Bookshop. What a place! Painted green outside, the inside contained the largest collection of secondhand books about Ireland in the world (I should imagine), going back to the days of Swift and beyond. Framed colour photographs of visiting Irish authors hung between the shelves. I had read none of them, and had only vaguely heard of one, Edna O'Brien.

Seeking to remedy this sad state of affairs, I browsed my way around the bookshop from floor to floor, upstairs and down and in and out of little book-filled rooms that the owners themselves may have forgotten about. My instant history of Galway comes to you by courtesy of Kenny's Bookshop. The shop stocked un-Irish books also, and even the smallest volume was treated and presented with greater care than has ever been known in the bookworm paradises of Charing Cross Road or Hay-on-Wye.

A leaflet near the front door told the history of Kenny's, opened in a former 'crubeen shop' by Desmond and Maureen Kenny. The pair had once been students at the University College of Galway. Not wishing to leave the city when their studies were over, they asked all their friends for unwanted books and opened the shop in November 1940. I realized that the cheerfully forceful woman I had seen the day before must have been Mrs Maureen Kenny herself. As well as running an art gallery in the shop, the Kennys also had a bookbinding business whose services included 'Edges gilt; white handsewn headbands; handmarbled endpapers; full oasis goatskin in differing colours; gold blocked on vellum, oasis circular piece superimposed with antique compass ...'

Such bookbindery had a Biblical ring to it, particularly with all those oases and goats of many colours, and recalled the building of Solomon's temple. Americans frequently sent books to and from Galway to be bound.

Tom Kenny, bearded, bespectacled son of the founders, told me that the shop stocked one hundred thousand books about

Ireland, or by Irish authors. As in George Borrow's day, the booksellers were also publishers, and printed their own catalogue. They were the Irish suppliers to the Washington Library of Congress. Everyone who worked there seemed to be a Kenny.

'Is your father still alive?' I asked.

'Yes, that's him at the back there. Why don't you come back tonight, as it's the opening launch of an art exhibition here?' and he gave me a pamphlet. With that he dashed off on business, so I turned to his mother, who was seated at a table serving customers, a delicate loop of chain attached to her spectacles.

'What does it mean here, where it says that this used to be a "crubeen shop"?' I asked her. 'I don't think they have "crubeens" in England.'

'Of course they do – it means pigs' feet,' she replied decisively.

'You're right, they must do,' I agreed, on thinking it over. 'Otherwise the pigs in England wouldn't be able to walk.'

After another soothing dusk spent gazing at weirs and waterfalls, I presented myself at the Kenny Gallery, behind the bookshop. 'Paintings by Jim Teck', my prospectus read.

'Which one's Jim?' I asked Tom Kenny, edging my way uneasily round all the fashionable people in the brightly lit room.

'It's a misprint for Jill Teck,' he admitted. 'That's her over there.'

Jill Teck was a curly-haired lady with a silvery laugh, and her pictures were bright, swirly and only semi-abstract. Many of them were labelled 'Moondreams'. I introduced myself and chatted to her husband, a sandy-haired man in a huge jersey, who looked like a folksinger specializing in sea shanties. He was in the shellfish business. Both of them were English, I believe.

'Your pictures would make excellent greeting cards!' I complimented Jill Teck. She seemed affronted, but it was the truth.

Escaping from the awkward embarrassment of arty people, in whose company I can never say the right thing, I went for a Chinese meal. Then I collected my bag from the Bed and Breakfast.

To my surprise, instead of the scornful narrow-eyed blonde, I found two frail but good-hearted old ladies in charge, plaid shawls about their shoulders. I spoke to them in the doorway of an old stone-flagged kitchen full of saintly pictures. Both wished me 'Godspeed'. Probably the whole house had been cosy and well-run when these ladies had been in their prime.

Then came a long anxious wait in the foyer of the Great Southern

Hotel. Finally my hostess, Mrs Knelle, and a theatre-going friend, Mrs Molloy, approached me with friendly smiles. Before long we were speeding through the night towards Joyce's Country, County Galway.

The 'merry Joyces' had been one of the fourteen Merchant Tribes of Galway, prominent families who had succeeded to the De Burgos in controlling the city and fighting off the 'wild Irish'. Other Tribes included the 'bloody Bodkins', 'brave Brownes', 'prating Frenches', 'proud Lynches' and the 'litigious Martins'. As for the wild Irish, they had every reason to be wild, for most of them were O'Connors and the site of Galway had belonged to them before De Burgo came. Many of the Merchant Tribes came originally from Bristol.

Mrs Mary Knelle, whose car it was, drove through inky blackness, the headlights sometimes picking out signs stuck to telegraph poles. Instead of advertising Sixties Discos, these were Signs of Unrest.

'No to Licences', 'Save Our Lake' and 'No Fish Farm', I read. Others had rhymed messages, lines of verse which could not be read from a moving car.

'There is a fishing war going on here,' Mrs Knelle explained. She was a calm, pleasant-faced lady with glasses, perhaps in her fifties, with a musical upper-class accent and an air of quiet confidence. 'You see, the people here, around Lough Corrib, have always fished without rod licences, as an ancient right. Then one day, the TDs stayed late at the Dáil – in England you would say "MPs stayed late at Parliament" – and sneaked in a bill about angling licences on the Lough. This came together with the permit for fish farmers to enclose part of the waters. All the local people were furious! They are still refusing to pay for licences, or to pay fines, and they seem quite prepared to go to Mountjoy Jail in a spirit of martyrdom. Their fines were paid by someone unknown. People here say that fish farms will pollute the lake.'

'Farmed fish often get fungus and other diseases,' I said, remembering the trout at Roscrea. Although I could not see it, we were travelling beside the lake where all these controversies were raging.

Mrs Molloy said goodnight at her garden gate, and we rushed onward into the night. Finally we dived into a driveway and continued uphill to the verandah of a large white house. 'This used to be a lord's fishing lodge,' Mrs Knelle told me, with a slight laugh. She seemed to regard the Ascendancy with humour as imperial relics. The late Colonel Knelle had been both Anglo-Irish *and* Anglo-Indian. Like Major Kirkwood of Woodbrook, he had served in the Indian Army. A fervent supporter of Home Rule, he had converted to the Roman Catholic faith. The Knelles had raised their children to feel proud of Ireland.

Kodiak, Mrs Knelle's huge shaggy Alsatian, barked at me excitedly but was soon soothed by his mistress. Scenes of India and Tibet hung on the walls, and I enjoyed a late-night coffee among wicker chairs, potted plants and handwoven Oriental rugs. Clutching a hot water bottle prepared by Mrs Knelle, I finally and thankfully snuggled into bed.

CHAPTER SIXTEEN

The Shores of Lough Corrib

Birds sang outside my window, and when I pulled the curtains back I was astonished to see a vast grey placid lake outside, with no beginning or end; an inland sea. Mrs Knelle's garden – or perhaps I should say 'grounds' – meandered gently down to the narrow lakeside road. Tall beech trees shed leaves over a disused tennis court, near well-kept lawns and bright hydrangeas. I drew the bathroom curtains next, and had another surprise. Wild brown hills of heather and bracken rose up steeply behind the house, just beyond a red-jewelled fuchsia hedge and a grove of mysterious scrub oaks.

Feeling deliciously convalescent, I pottered about in pyjamas, weak yet fortified by the knowledge that I was in a sympathetic house where I could be waited on, and had no appointments of any kind. Kodiak the Alsatian barked at me for a few minutes, and gave up in resignation. Mrs Knelle soon appeared in a dressing gown, and we sat down to a soothing breakfast of toast. What bliss not to have to eat a huge fried breakfast to please a bacon-happy landlady! I explained about my 'baggitis', caused by over-indulgence in books and souvenirs, and Mrs Knelle looked concerned. To my relief, she was not shocked when I asked if I could spend most of my stay at Lough Corrib asleep in bed.

As it happened, a few sweet dozes over the next couple of days was enough to restore my vitality. Meanwhile, over breakfast, we chatted of this and that. Mrs Knelle asked if the huge pair of antlers on the verandah were those of an Irish elk, and I said no, a Canadian moose. She was very keen that I should portray Ireland in a sympathetic light.

'Do write something nice about us! You're not going to the North, are you?'

'No, I've been all over the North, so I'm leaving it this time.'

'Perhaps it's as well. Those Protestants – *ugh*! The Presbyterians, I mean, not the Anglicans, of course.'

'Well, when I was there, I found middle-class Presbyterians who were not very different from Anglicans. They shied away from Orange parades and Paisley rallies.'

'That Ian Paisley – ugh!' she said with feeling. She had a very nice line in 'ughs'. I found that Mrs Knelle regarded the Ascendancy as comic dodos, and took for granted that they were all opposed to Home Rule.

'If it hadn't been for Home Rule in the South, would Ulster have been ruled by Presbyterians in Belfast?' I asked. 'Wouldn't the capital have still been Dublin, where most Protestants are Anglicans?'

'I'll have to look that up,' she said dubiously, unwilling to concede any ill effects to Home Rule. For the rest of the time, we talked only of natural history and local gossip, and got on very well. It turned out that her son was a great friend of the paraquat-wielding monk I had seen at the monastery farm near Roscrea. Mrs Knelle's boy had attended a similar boarding school to the Cistercian college, and had then gone to Maynooth, a prestigious Dublin seminary for priests. From there he had got into Trinity College, and now hoped for a career in the Civil Service.

'Do you mean the Irish Civil Service?'

'Good heavens no, the *English* Civil Service, of course. When my boys first started school, we were aghast at the anti-English propaganda in the history books. But in the last ten years, school history here has grown far more balanced. It was quite an adventure for me to come to Ireland, you know. I met my future husband when he was a colonel in the Indian Army. But I hope I'm not a typical colonel's lady!

'When I was a young girl, I was an army secretary in India. We had to leave the staff headquarters in a hurry at Partition in 1947. Our regiment had a very fine cellar, laid down in Victorian days, and it had to be abandoned. People drank all they could, and I washed my hair in pink champagne. Everybody thought our train would be ambushed, but in the event we got out safely. Perhaps our wine fell into the hands of looters, though we were on the Pakistani side and Muslims aren't supposed to touch alcohol.'

I described the crowning of the goat I had seen at Killorglin.

'Here we have Wren Boys who dress up and go from door to door asking for money, every St Stephen's Day,' she said. 'That's Boxing Day in England. In the old days, they would have a real wren with them, alive or dead, but now I suppose you have to pretend a wren is there. On St John's Day – that's midsummer – people light bonfires.'

Despite the saints involved, both customs derive from Celtic paganism, and are none the worse for that. Later, when exploring the grounds, I met several wrens, as well as titmice, blackbirds and chaffinches. In the words of the Irish ballad, the birds they were singing from tree to tree.

'We used to have strawberry fields, but they were too much work,' Mrs Knelle told me. 'So they turned into jungle. My husband and the boys cleared a path through the undergrowth when we first came here, and they called it the Burma Road.'

She showed me the way to the Burma Road, and I set off up the wooded slope behind the house. Mossy boulders, strangely twisting tree roots and little streams splashing over stones are my delight. I was reminded of North Wales. Here and there, a miniature Halfpenny Bridge of stone curved over the winding brook. Strange moss-covered devices were relics of the house's first electricity system, run by water. Finally I descended the ash and beech slopes to the house once more.

Later that same day, I awoke from a restoring sleep to find rain pouring down outside, the lake nearly invisible. At the back window, the oaks and the steep brown hill looked wonderfully romantic in the deluge. However, I didn't envy the line of white sheep hurrying down the mountain to seek shelter against Mrs Knelle's stone wall.

That afternoon we watched television, which was full of the anglers' strike at Lough Corrib. 'The government has denied that there will be fish-farm cages on Lough Corrib,' said the announcer. 'However, they have not ruled out the possibility of fish farms on streams that drain into the lake, which could be harmful if their waste enters the lough waters. These lakes have never been landlord lakes – the fishing has always been free for the people.The government denies any intention of become a "lakelord" and controlling the waters.'

Mrs Knelle's sympathies seemed anti-government in this case.

'Last week a woman who lives near here was arrested for not

paying her fine, and she was actually put in a police wagon headed for Mountjoy Jail in Dublin,' Mrs Knelle told me. 'She had a helpless husband at home in a wheelchair, dependent on her, but the Garda took no notice. When they had gone some way from here, the Garda received a radio message, stopped and turned around. "Someone's paid your fine, so we're taking you home," they said.

'No one here believes her fine was really paid. They think it was a trick by the Garda or the judges to frighten people and teach them a lesson. But still people won't give in. They say the government insist on fish farms near here, and some hint that there's a "backhander" involved. Now the strike has spread to boatmen, and no local people will take visitors out on the lake. Some fear reprisals if they did so, although tourists have been coming here for years to fish for trout and salmon.'

Mrs Knelle kept in touch with the Irish Catholic grapevine through her friendship with 'Sheilagh, up the mountain in bandit country'. Sheilagh, a farmer's wife, had been widowed at the same time as had Mrs Knelle, and a bond had formed between them. For the most part, Mrs Knelle's world seemed a cosmopolitan one, for well-to-do foreigners from Europe and America were buying houses and bungalows all around Lough Corrib. With the high civilization of Galway City so close, such newcomers had the best of both worlds – wild mountainous scenery with friendly bothy-dwellers and fine restaurants, shops and theatres.

With the huge shaggy Kodiak bounding around me, I plodded down the path next morning in Mrs Knelle's son's wading boots. Telegraph poles along the lakeside road bore warning notices: 'Lakelords Out' and 'No Boatmen'. Sky and water blazed blue beneath a fickle Irish sun. Willows and other small trees grew thickly on the banks of Lough Corrib, fenced off from the road.

Mrs Knelle, however, had a key to her own private gate at the water's edge. I don't know if this made her a lakelady or Lady of the Lake or not. At any rate, in we went, and soon I was happily splashing around the creeks while Kodiak plunged after sticks thrown by his mistress. More than ever he resembled his namesake, the giant Alaskan brown bear, a beast that also rollocks cheerfully through northern waters, sending spray flying with enormous paws. As the bears go after salmon, not sticks, one might make a powerful ally in the Fishermen's War.

Bending and brushing away overhanging thorn branches, I sidled through the water in vain hopes of seeing one of the otters that lived here, according to Mrs Knelle. At length, shielding my eyes against the dazzling ripples, I returned to land.

Later that day, Mrs Knelle declared that she'd take me for a drive, to see Ashford Castle, a local stately home that was now an hotel. Poor Kodiak whined and scratched at the verandah door as we drove off.

First of all, we stopped at Cong, a small town of white houses. There I was introduced to a friendly couple from the North of England, Jack Farrer and his wife Joan. Jack was an artist, and the Farrers had a studio and gallery in a little shop.

I admired bearded Jack's oil paintings of local scenes, and thought him a far better artist than Jim Teck. His work reminded me of that of Kyffin Williams, the Artist of Anglesey. My only complaint was that, in common with the entire Irish tourist trade, he had presented Flann O'Brien's verse 'A Pint of Plain is Your Only Man' in a decorative border as a serious poem. In fact this banal verse, which forms a part of the novel *At Swim-Two-Birds*, is a satire on the cult of imbecile proletarian writers that began in the thirties and later reached its apotheosis under Joan Littlewood.

Over coffee in the studio, amid paints and palettes, we all discussed the Fishermen's War, a war that still drags on as I write.

'People are afraid that the lake will be parcelled out into cages for fish farming,' Mrs Farrer said. 'The locals are very determined, aren't they?'

'Yes, but now some of them are regretting it,' Mrs Knelle put in, scattering fruit from her grapevine. 'There's a new fear, that criminal records will be stamped on their passports, so that striking fishermen and their families won't be able to emigrate or visit relatives overseas.'

Waving goodbye to the Farrers, we sped on to Ashford Castle.

'You see that hideous concrete Roman Catholic church?' Mrs Knelle pointed. 'Well, in order to build that, they knocked down the prettiest little Catholic church you ever saw. It was *tiny*, with lovely windows, like a doll's church.

A ruined monastery reared grey gable ends near the concrete church.

'You see that place, the House of Music?' my guide continued. 'A very forceful woman runs that place. There's no real music there, it's a late-night disco and very noisy, too! Well, a few years back someone else not far away opened a late-night disco and also called it the House of Music! So the woman from the first House went out at night and burnt the rival House to the ground. No one was hurt, but she went to prison, of course. After a while she emerged, quite unchastened, and went on running her House of Music more successfully than ever. Her rival never rebuilt and had to give up.'

Ring fences and tall two-hundred-year-old trees showed that we were approaching a stately home. When the castle came into view, I was stunned at its beauty. Those towers, those gate-houses, the bridges over clear water, the tree-lined avenues, the fountain playing in the forecourt ... it was perfection. As if in a dream, I allowed Mrs Knelle to lead me to the front door. As I stumbled along, she told me that the present appearance of the castle was in part the creation of the hotel people, who had joined two separate buildings together. Originally there had stood a medieval castle alone, then it had been Neo-Gothicized and French Châteaued a bit in the nineteenth century. The Guinness family, the last owners of the estate, had also built a fanciful fishing lodge beside the castle. This had now been soldered to the main building so well that you couldn't see the join.

'As we're not guests, we're not really supposed to go insidc, but let's!' Mrs Knelle suggested mischievously. We tiptoed inside, but no one seemed to mind. No duke or Guinness heir could ever have lived in such opulence. If Versailles is ever to be refurnished in Sun King style, it will have to become an hotel. Only hotels can command fleets of servants now, not so much because their owners are rich, but because there is no stigma of 'domestic service' attached to hotel work. No matter how much of a slavey she might really be, a chambermaid never thinks of herself as a maid.

Polished and carved wood of every kind, fitted or furnished, greeted our eyes. Carved faces grinned at us, reflecting the fires that burned in every grate. We floated around gazing at leather chairs, chandeliers like frozen inverted fountains and embroidered tapestries based on Gould's paintings of Australian parakeets. Finally we floated out on to the porch to admire the lawns and burnished trees, before driving back to relieve pent-up Kodiak of his anxiety. If the Ashford Castle Hotel now wish to give me a free suite in return for this publicity, I shall not demur. As I slept off the last of my baggitis, sweet visions of castles, fountains and autumn leaves drifted through my dreams.

Later, over dinner, Mrs Knelle spiritedly told me of the sensation around Lough Corrib when President Reagan had stayed at Ashford Castle. As Irish people are given naturally to speculating over 'CIA plots', their excitement when *real* CIA security men arrived to safeguard the President can be imagined.

'The countryside round here was simply *crawling* with CIA men!' Mrs Knelle exclaimed. 'One was found on top of a neighbouring castle tower surveying the landscape. The local Garda had been sent to Ashford Castle to protect Reagan, and they didn't get on with the CIA at all. Standing outside the castle, on the edge of the lake, the Garda were dreadfully bitten by midges. So they lit a fire to smoke them away. A CIA man rushed out and roared at them angrily, and they had to put the fire out. The hotel staff felt sorry for the Garda and asked them round to the back door, where they handed out tots of whiskey. Luckily, the CIA didn't know about that.

'One of the CIA men had to phone a message through to Reagan. Whatever he might do, he couldn't get past the postmistress at Cong, who acts as operator, and runs the whole village. Reagan's suite had been given a special phone number for the occasion, but the postmistress didn't believe in such nonsense.

'Again and again she kept repeating, in a stern, calm voice, "The number of the castle is Cong 3. There is no such number as the one you mentioned, and I will not connect you. The number of the castle is Cong 3."

'When she had repeated herself five or six times, the CIA man slammed the phone down in a rage, and Reagan never learned what he had to say.'

On my last full day in her house, Mrs Knelle declared that she would drive me through the mountains of Joyce's Country to the edge of Connemara.

'That should give you some idea of the beauties of County Galway,' she added. 'I have some friends along the way who should be pleased to meet you.'

So off we went. The sky was blue, and the lake and mountains seemed to smile at us. Large houses faced the lake at intervals of miles. Each house stood high on the hillside that sloped down to the lakeside road, with curling or zig-zagging driveways and thick modern stone walls. 'That's a Dutch couple who live there ... those people are Germans ... that's a nice American who lives there,' Mrs Knelle's commentary ran.

One house was so unusual that we stopped and walked around it. It was a small Norman castle keep, with three towers, two with turrets and the middle one with a pointed roof. 'That's Murphy's Castle,' Mrs Knelle told me. 'It's a real medieval castle, that had been a ruin for years, and has now been modernized into a house. Some people complained when the owners painted it white, but it was proved from an old book that Normans often painted their castles.' Maybe so, but the old castle looked to me like a Victorian Gothic lighthouse, looking over the lake.

Now Mrs Knelle drove away from the lake, along a narrow road between green hills where sheep grazed. To my delight, we stopped at a bothy, a long white cabin with a small door in the middle, deep-set windows and a roof of orange thatch. A maze of low stone walls bounded the twisting paths of the front lawn, and one wall of a former next-door cottage had been left standing as an ornament, with glassless windows. A large annexe at the back detracted from the symmetry of the old bothy.

'An unusual couple live here,' Mrs Knelle forewarned me. 'June comes from a well-to-do English family and Pat, her husband, is the son of a poor Galway farmer. The bothy was in Pat's family, and they've made it into a lovely home. June's parents weren't too pleased at the marriage at first, but they accept it now, as the couple seem so suited.'

June, a robust pony girl in short hair and trousers, and Pat, a good-natured sandy-haired young man, made us very welcome. While tea was being prepared, I looked around their bothy home. A turf fire burned merrily in the end fireplace, and roughly-cut brown chunks of turf (or peat) lay in a box nearby. The heat from this fire warmed the whole length and breadth of the bothy, a stone longhouse of one single room. The original bothy had now become a long low front room, with settees and coffee tables, and the beds had been put in the annexe. Although well furnished, the annexe rooms, which led off from the rear of the bothy, lacked cosiness because they were so cold.

'There's nothing like an old bothy for warmth.' Pat told us, as June poured the tea. 'When our two wee ones came along, we had to have the ixtra room, but I prefer the old part of the house. A bothy will keep you warm in winter and cool in summer.'

Mrs Knelle and June discussed turf, which they both used for fuel. Apparently turf was a great talking point in this country, where people greeted one another with 'Have you got your turf in?' instead of commenting on the weather. Most local people cut their own turf from family sites on the hillsides.

'My father used a special spade for digging turf.' Pat put in. 'He called it a "slane".'

'Turf is cut all summer, in dry weather, to prepare for winter,' Mrs Knelle explained to me. 'My friend Sheilagh up on the mountain is very nervy and distraught until she has her turf in. Then she relaxes. When we first moved here, we were very keen to be Irish and we cut our own turf. It was terribly hard work, even with the boys helping. Now I just buy mine from Tommy the Turfman.'

Pat pointed out a castle tower visible from the window, with two ruined churches nearby. 'You see where there's bog – there used to be water there,' he told me. 'The owner of the castle would put his family into a boat and row them across the lake to church every Sunday. But one day his wee son fell out of the boat and drowned. So, in his grief, he had the other church built near the castle itself, so no one need cross the water any more. Now the castle and the churches both are ruins. See where the cintre of the church has fallen in, leaving the two ends, like?'

For Pat, every 'them' was a 'thim' and every 'centre' a 'cintre', pronounced very clearly. 'Simmetry' would be a place for dead people, lending new meaning to Blake's poem about the tiger.

Finally Mary Knelle and I were on our way once more, driving past hillsides where neat black cut-away shapes showed that turf had been extracted. Turf (or peat) is the remains of the ancient Irish forest not yet old enough to be coal.

'Those are turf strips,' my guide informed me in her calm, assured voice that I found so soothing. 'After cutting, the turf is stacked by the roadside until Tommy comes along with his turf cart. For some reason, they always leave three "steps" of turf on the hill, after cutting. Tommy's cart is a trailer on a van now, of course. He simply hurls the turf into the trailer. Someone usually gets in while this is going on, and puts the turf into neat heaps. Then your own turf is delivered to your house. Tommy is a strange man. He walks about at night, and people say he can see in the dark.'

On we drove, and I noticed stacked turf everywhere, in wooden shelters and under tarpaulins, usually by the side of a house. Old style 'African hut' haystacks stood here and there, some with cloth covers on top, others with a single pole poking up through each 'roof'. Small patches of forestry plantation darkened the slopes of some hills.

'Farmers don't care for those plantations,' Mrs Knelle went on. 'They sometimes set them on fire, and you can see hillsides of charred stumps in some places.'

So saying, she pulled up at the gateway of a two-storey farmhouse used as the holiday and weekend home of her friends Mr and Mrs Clay. Sean Clay was a Dublin solicitor with knowing pale grey eyes. He shook my hand heartily, and left us sitting in the front room while he went in search of 'something special'.

'You might have heard of this – potheen!' he said with a smile on his return. A transparent liquid, pronounced 'pocheen', the moonshine, bootleg or Real Old Mountain Dew still-born whiskey swirled around in a lemonade bottle. I backed away in alarm and refused to touch it, so Sean made up for my abstinence.

'Who makes that stuff?' I asked.

'I cannot say,' he smirked.

'How did you get it?'

'I have it.'

'So I see,' I said nervously, watching as he smacked his lips for fire to stream from his mouth, the top of his head to fly upwards on a jet of steam or his eyes to turn into Catherine wheels. None of these things happened.

'If I ever go to a funeral in an out-of-the-way place, I always get pushed a discoloured glass of potheen. So I've acquired a taste for it,' he explained modestly. 'Wakes round here are not what they were. Once they lasted three days, now it's only one.'

I had heard Hindus in London say exactly the same thing about weddings. Celts and Negroes love funerals, Orientals of every kind love weddings, while for inward-looking Saxons the big days are family holidays.

'You see those broken clay pipes on the mantelpiece?' asked Mr Clay. 'We found them behind the house when we moved in. There was a custom here until the fifties of giving people new clay pipes at a funeral. When the guests had gone, all the pipes would be broken at once, and then thrown away.'

'There was a custom here until the fifties.' How often is that sad refrain heard all over the English-speaking world! In the fifties television came along, the destroyer of tradition. Enter the Demon King.

'What killed the old Ireland was not only television, but the motor car,' Sean proceeded, as if reading my mind. 'In the old days of walking and bicycles, you would walk down from your house to the village and stop at every house on the way for talk. Now you just drive straight there and back, with no time for stories.'

However, Mrs Knelle seemed to be driving from house to house to exchange news, and I thought the old Ireland persisted around Lough Corrib as well as might be expected, or better. Some might call Connaught the Real Ireland, but I don't see why turf-cutters are any more or less real than Midland golfers who cut a different kind of turf when they swing their clubs. The Midlander has the better claim for the title of Typical Irishman.

Mr Clay went on to tell of his visits to a bone-setter, who successfully healed him after an accident. Bone-setters were regarded as witch doctors by orthodox Irish medical men, but were never without a clientele, human or animal.

'The man I went to cured my hip just by stroking it,' Sean said. 'Farmers brought animals along to the same waiting room as human patients. There were rows of cars outside when I went, and you had to take a ticket with a number when you sat down.

' "There's two sheep ahead of you," I was told.

'When I went in, the man was very gentle. He could tell what was wrong by magic, without needing to ask. Nearly everyone who saw him was cured. Gaelic footballers were his best customers, as the sport's so rough. The bone-setting power is often handed down from father to son. In this case, the man's grandfather had been a well-known bone-setter for his gentle touch, but the *father* had been a bone-cracking bone-setter. He could heal, but with sharp movements and loud cracking sounds that frightened people away. But his own son, the man I saw, had the gentle gift once more.'

Major Kirkwood of Woodbrook, according to a member of the family, always sent for the bone-healer *and* the vet whenever a horse became lame. He would see that the two rival practitioners never met. Apparently the healer would tie a black thread round the horse's ankle, and it usually worked. Or so the people on the estate said, for it was the Major's aim to please them and keep things running smoothly.

After a little more gossip, we said goodbye to the friendly Clays, and set off on our tour of the countryside. As we left, a herd of cows wandered into the solicitor's garden through the open gate and were shooed out again with loud cries.

My magical ride took me from lake to lake, from Lough Corrib to Lough Mask and then to a third lake that seemed smaller than the last two inland seas set among high mountains. But this 'lough' turned out be an arm of the sea itself, an Irish fjord at Leenane. Soft lights glowed on the mountains as if reflected from stained glass. Bog grass on lower ground shone orange, emerald green or gold. Cumulus clouds rolled majestically through the blue sky, casting shadows or releasing light as they did so.

Some mountainsides were chequered with tall stone walls that cast slanting shadows over the fields they enclosed. The hill country had once been far more populous. Ireland's Highland Clearances had been made not by Man but by Famine. Mary Knelle pointed out to me the green ridges on almost perpendicular fields that showed where potatoes had been grown before 1847.

Here and there were strange unexplained heaps of stones on high places. My theory was that these were 'deer roasts' left by hunters in historic times, when the game would be cut up and cooked on the hill where it was slain. Stones would enclose the fire, and the meat might also be cached under stones. On the verge of Connemara, we passed through a steep valley of rocks poised as if to roll down upon us. High on a mountain we paused and I looked down on Lough Nafooey, a lake lying far below us. From a cloud that hovered over the lake, a rainbow emerged, arching down to the water, suffusing it with fairy gold and mauve. The other end of the rainbow was presumably curled up inside the cloud.

Mary Knelle knew every road between the mountains. I saw a 'table mountain' and rugged peaks of every kind, although with no snow on the tops as yet. Bracken and heather made rufous brown the most typical colour. High over Lough Corrib once more, she pointed out a 'ruined castle' on a wooded island. From that distance it did not look ruined at all. Grace O'Malley, the Pirate Queen of Connaught, might still have been living there. Like Shane O'Neill, another robber monarch, she had made her way to Queen Elizabeth's court in England. There she bargained with the Queen, and in return for not harrying the English ships that were pursuing the Spanish Armada, O'Malley was allowed a free hand in Connaught.

As Mrs Knelle descended from the mountains, she told me

stories attached to various landmarks. 'That's the "witch's house". Until she died a few years ago, a wise woman lived there, a strange being who wore outlandish brightly-coloured clothes and had feathers in her hair. She could cure sheep of all ills, and if anyone cut themselves, she would bind cobwebs into the hurt.

'Over there is where they killed Lord ——, nearly a hundred years ago. There had been an unpopular decision made at the Lords in London, so gunmen here decided to shoot a lord, to set an example. Lord —— was a harmless man, with hardly any land, so they decided it would have to be him. One day, when the lord was stepping down from his carriage, which he drove himself, he was shot dead outside his gate. The murderer thought nobody else was there. But unknown to the gunman, a little boy had been stealing a ride on the bar under the carriage, and he saw it all. He ran home and told his mother, and soon the whole district knew.

'I know both families – the little boy's family and the murderer's family. They both still live round here. Officially the case has never been cleared up, as not a soul reported the man to the authorities. He was never brought to justice, and since he has long since died himself, we shall leave the matter there. If a more powerful lord had been shot, with a vast estate, many men might have been thrown out of work and so have borne a grudge against the gunman.

'Strange things happen round here. Lately the government has taken to giving grants to Swedes to create industry. Two Swedes came to a town near here with a grant, and started a factory that made micro-electric parts or something – anyway, it would supposedly employ hundreds of local people.

'Now the Swedes were of two sizes. One was a little short jolly man of five foot, called Sven Svennsen. The other was a tall man, seven foot high, called Yon Yonson. Well, Yon Yonson took to drink and stayed in the pub until he'd drunk up most of his grant. So regretfully Sven Svennsen had to go back to Sweden.

'After a while, Yon Yonson grew lonely. He shocked the post-mistress in town by asking "Can you get me a woman?" Eventually he met a rather feckless man who had seven children. The two went into a long drinking session, and the end of it was that he bought the man's seventeen-year-old daughter outright, with the last of his grant.

'He took the girl home, and they lived by selling off all the furniture in the factory, bit by bit. By that time the girl was pregnant. Yon Yonson married her in an evident attempt to qualify for the Irish dole. This didn't work, so he took the girl back to Sweden and nothing has been heard of them since.')

Zimbabwe and other African countries are now making the same mistake, and inviting Swedes to come over and do progressive things to their economies. So if Robert Mugabe, Prime Minister of Zimbabwe, is reading this: beware of Yon Yonson. Mind you, I'm not saying a word against Sven Svennsen.

As we drove up to Mrs Knelle's house, we passed a man in dark clothes, with tousled grey hair, walking unsteadily beside the lake. 'That's Tommy the Turfman,' Mrs Knelle told me. 'He lived in a bothy until the roof fell in. His parents kept it spick and span, but when they died, he lived there alone until it went to rack and ruin. He's the one I told you about, who can see in the dark. Sometimes when I take Kodiak out at night, I see Tommy staring at the house.'

Mrs Knelle gave a shudder, and in that moment she reminded me of a Karen Blixen figure in Kenya, who has stayed on after Mau Mau to make the best of life in a new Republic.

CHAPTER SEVENTEEN

☘

The Woodcarver of Sligo

Despite all Mrs Knelle's entreaties that I go westward into the wilder parts of her beloved Galway, I stuck to my original plan. 'Could you please drive me to Tuam?' I asked. 'From there I can get a bus to Sligo Town, in County Sligo, up in the north of the province of Connaught.'

'Tuam! Whatever is there to see at Tuam?' she complained mildly, as we set off.

Kodiak barked a farewell, the moose antlers seemed to wave and the ripples on Lough Corrib frowned at me reproachfully. One day I hope to return and spend several weeks exploring County Galway.

We drove through placid scenery, past a ruined castle and so into Tuam. Once a holy city and (from 1049) the seat of the O'Connor Kings of Connaught, Tuam now resembled a relaxed, fairly prosperous market town in Sussex. Mary Knelle looked around approvingly. 'It's just like an English town of the 1950s, with hardly any traffic,' she said.

With time to spare, we looked at the two cathedrals of Tuam, Roman Catholic and Church of Ireland. The former, a dignified nineteenth-century building, reminded me of St Peter's at Brighton. Most of the Church of Ireland cathedral was nineteenth century also, including the tall spire. However, in the twelfth century corner, I found a place where I could look through four archways at once, a soothing occupation. Part of the cathedral had been roped off as a theatre, a very Sussex touch.

A little later, I stood nervously beside my bag, hoping that I was at the right bus stop for Sligo. Patient as ever, and too kind just to leave me, Mrs Knelle stood by my side, allaying my fears.

Suddenly a small single-decker bus appeared at a corner not far away. Within minutes I was safely on board with my bag, leaving Mrs Knelle waving and asking me to give her good wishes to her friend in England.

Outside my window, the sun slowly set behind mournful evening scenery, fields and bogs, with cows everywhere, sometimes on the road itself. Rivers flashed by, and mountains appeared on the horizon. We were crossing the Plains of Mayo, in the county of that name. Big men with big grins slumped half-sideways on their seats, shouting remarks to their neighbours.

I was suddenly startled to see that we were entering the town of Knock. All over Ireland, posters advertise pilgrim coach tours to Knock, a town famous for apparitions of the Virgin Mary. Our Lady first appeared in Father Cavanagh's chapel in the summer of 1879.

Opening my bag, I managed to unearth a pink magazine I had bought, *The Curate's Diary*. 'Knock Apparition Saved Father Cavanagh from Having Ears Cut Off', the sensationalist headline proclaimed. Inside, the story told how the people of Knock, unable to pay their rent, faced hunger and eviction. Once more the potato crop had failed. Secret societies sprang up, some with the enmity towards the Roman church noticeable in IRA writings today. One such society, the Ribbonmen, decided that Father Cavanagh must be punished for preaching non-violence, and swore a solemn oath to cut off the priest's ears. Few of them were old enough to remember the first Great Famine of the 1840s, when Father Cavanagh had worked tirelessly to help the starving. A day or two before the crime was to take place, the Apparition of Our Lady shone forth, changing bitterness to religious awe and causing the Ribbonmen publicly to repent. Prosperity came to Knock, as pilgrims came from far and wide; and Father Cavanagh kept his ears.

Concluding the entry on Knock, the Curate next confided to his diary the tale of Father Vianney, a priest persecuted by the devil, who kept banging on the walls and throwing furniture around.

> Often Satan, entering Father Vianney's bedroom, would actually cry aloud. 'Vianney, Vianney, thou eater of potatoes, we shall have thee yet! We shall have thee yet! We have thee! We have thee!' ... Continued in next month's issue of *The Curate's Diary*.

Poor Father Vianney must have thought his sacrifices and self-denial in becoming a priest had scarcely been worthwhile if this sort of thing was going to happen. I never learned how he escaped.

Posters advertising Knock pilgrimages that I had seen nearly always mentioned 'matchmaking' as part of the attractions. In pagan days, when Celtic pilgrims journeyed not to Knock but to the Sacred Feasts of Tara, matchmaking played an important part in the celebrations. Some things never change.

Pilgrim prosperity had brought startling modernity to Knock. A grey, unsightly concrete church with a steeple like an upraised sword stuck through the roof stood beside a futuristic glass pavilion with rows of outdoor benches for apparition-watchers. White statues of saints, angels and the Holy Family added a traditional, if sepulchral, touch. Could they not have been painted? Bed and Breakfast houses jostled one another in rows, and a huge shop advertised tawdry 'Religious Goods'. The bus stopped outside gaunt St Mary's Hostel and several girls got out.

'Medieval England managed this sort of thing so much better,' I thought smugly. Then I remembered – the word 'tawdry' comes from 'St Audrey', whose English feast and fair was notorious for vulgar souvenir stalls in the Middle Ages.

Continuing northward, the bus arrived next at Tobbercurry. On the village green stood black life-size silhouette figures of fiddle and accordion players, apparently cut out from thin sheets of iron. I was reminded of the black iron horse silhouettes which decorate the Wolverhampton to Shrewsbury railway line in England. Between Cloonacool and Coolaney, beside the River Moy, the bus passed beneath the rocky peaks of the Ox Mountains. Then came Ballysadare, with its roadside mill and view over the bay. Finally, in the dusk, the lights of Sligo came into view. Overshadowing the town, a massive round-shouldered hill loomed, like Ayer's Rock, Table Mountain and the Wrekin all rolled into one. It was Benbulbin.

Dismounting at the railway station, I cast envious looks at yet another Great Southern Hotel, and dragged my bag to a terraced street Bed and Breakfast nearby. A cheerful, freckled young woman showed me to a small seedy room and I began to unpack.

A straw St Bridget's Cross hung over the door of the dark little room in which I was eating my breakfast next morning. I remembered seeing similar crosses in other Irish homes I had visited, always above a door. St Bridget is supposed to have quickly twisted some dry reeds into the form of a cross, so that a dying pagan could see the symbol of Christ and perhaps enter Heaven.

Curiously misshapen, the straw Bridget's Cross rather resembles a swastika, the ancient Hindu symbol of fortune. St Bridget's affinity to the old goddess Bridget can be seen in the wording of long-ago prayers to the Abbess: 'Bridget, our torch and our sun' . . . 'Bridget, the sun above the stars, the Queen of the South, the Mary of the Gael.'

My meditations on St Bridget were cruelly interrupted by the radio, which bore the news of a policeman shot in Belfast. A lively group of beefy youngsters at the next table gave a loud cheer, and a girl exclaimed 'Great!'

'He escaped with chest wounds and is expected to recover,' the announcer continued.

'O-oh!' the youngsters groaned in disappointment, and went on discussing a blasphemous film they had seen. I was amazed at first, for most Irish people *never* carry on like this, and those that do have first to be *very* sure of their company. Enlightenment soon came – the youngsters proved to be *Australian*. In a moment, the freckled landlady came in with the morning bacon, greeting us in the slightly questioning accent typical of Sligo. Australians too raise their voices querulously at the end of a sentence, only in harsh tones no doubt derived from their country's past. All that their unfortunate ancestors had to say probably came in questions: 'When are you going to let me *out* of here?' and 'Can I go *home* now, please?'

The weather was dull as I stepped out into Sligo. Grey rows of grim houses, three storeys high, led into the town centre. Far from being a one-street town, Sligo turned out to be a city, the centre criss-crossed with bright, lively shopping streets. I sauntered along attractively named Wine Street, then came to a bridge over the rushing River Garavogue. From a seat on the verandah of the Silver Swan Hotel, which overlooked the river, I was able to admire the white foamy torrents hurtling over a weir and beneath the bridge, black and sleek as they sped on their way. At first white-maned monsters, they plunged forward as dark shiny hump-backed whales, each wave a living being. The name 'Garavogue' means the Rough Malignant One.

A little further on, I found a marvellous public library, with a mural that showed the Battle of the Books, the war stirred up by

St Columcille (or Columba). This had taken place at Cul Dreimne, now in County Sligo. St Colum seems to have attracted legends around himself wherever he went, for as Columba he used to be well known to every Scottish schoolboy for converting the King of the Picts, banishing water horses and other praiseworthy acts. While evangelizing Scotland, the saint seemed able to keep his Irish temper under control.

Around the walls of the Sligo library hung framed pages of a magazine named *Broadsheet*, dated 1903. Ballads and rhymes, some by Masefield, were illustrated in black and gold by Jack Yeats. 'He was the brother of W. B. Yeats, the great poet,' the librarian told me.

'Well, I think he's really good,' I enthused. 'I like his drawing of the Fiddler of Dooney. That's the only poem by Yeats I can understand.'

'W. B. Yeats never wrote the "Fiddler" – 'twas his *father*.'

'Oh, that explains it.'

Next door, in a small art gallery and museum, I saw more drawings by Jack Yeats, all excellent. His oil paintings, however, seemed to grow more splodgy over the years. A few strokes of his pen brought out all the Irishness of an Irishman; proud lean faces were a speciality. In the museum, a case was devoted to the Phibbs family, whose Sligo mansion, Seafield House, has been long demolished. The firm of solicitors, Argue and Phibbs, still have an office in Sligo.

Retracing my steps to the town centre, I came upon a street named Harmony Hill, the title of a book of short stories by the late Richard Phibbs (Curlew Press). I was once privileged to meet Richard, father of the Conservative journalist Harry. *Cockle Button, Cockle Ben*, a children's book he wrote in the 1930s, has remarkably good illustrations. In honour of Richard Phibbs, I walked up and down Harmony Hill, although there was nothing special to see there.

In between the bright little shops of Sligo, the dank ruinous atmosphere of Ireland's Everytown intruded. Picturesque 'yards' (courtyards) behind the shops all too often petered out into demolished nothingness, with scraps remaining of stone walls, closed workshops, industrial debris and boarded-up cabins. One cabin had been made into a pottery, others had council murals daubed over them. I should have liked to have seen Sligo at the turn of the century, or failing that, in sunny weather.

As at Tuam, Sligo boasted two cathedrals, Anglican and Roman Catholic. Strange to say, at Sligo they stood side by side, obvious rivals. Inside the former, I read a strange inscription beside the early-seventeenth-century tomb of Sir Roger Jones, Knight, formerly Governor of Sligo Castle: 'This tomb has been restored by Past Masters of "Light of the West" Lodge, this Year of Our Lord 1922, and of Free Masonry 5922.' A nearby plaque stated that W. B. Yeats' mother Susan had been 'married here on Sept. 10th, 1863'.

In the Roman Catholic cathedral next door, I found a baffled couple from Pennsylvania, who turned out to be in the wrong cathedral. 'Why are Catholic churches here not so good as Church of Ireland ones?' the man asked me.

I told him about the Reformation and about nineteenth-century Catholic Emancipation.

'You mean the Anglicans didn't give their churches *back*?' he echoed incredulously.

'No, they held on to them, and the newly free Roman Catholics had to build new ones,' I explained, 'What denomination are you, by the way?'

'We don't have one,' the woman said.

'You *must*. This is Ireland!' I remonstrated. 'How were you brought up?'

'As Roman Catholics, but we've given it up.'

'Then you're Catholics,' I informed them, thinking back to my days in Northern Ireland. 'You don't have to actually believe it, just *be* it.'

All the same, the Catholic cathedral of the Immaculate Conception, built in the 1870s, had many good qualities that the Pennsylvanians seemed not to appreciate. Parts of the outside walls curved in and out like waves of stone, altar and stained-glass windows were awe-inspiring in gold and blue, and the chimes from the clock could be heard all over town, even in my stationside boarding house. There was a wonderfully prejudiced guide book, which referred to Protestant bishops as 'pseudo-bishops' and made no mention of the rival establishment next door. According to this book, the new cathedral's strategic site had been hard to acquire. A private citizen, secretly acting for the clergy, had pretended he was buying the land for non-religious purposes.

For the next few hours, I walked in and out of Sligo, beside the swollen, roaring river, its many weirs, ruined mills and unexpected bridges. Raw council estates spilled over the fields at the edge of town, marring the views. In other places, grey old houses stretched into the distance, merging with the grey mountains, wall-like Benbulbin and mysterious Knocknarea with its stone cairn on top.

Other walkers greeted me as we passed, saying either 'hello' or 'good morning'. 'Hello' is a far more soothing greeting than the English 'All right?' In Ireland, 'good morning' lasts until two o'clock in the afternoon, and then becomes 'good evening' until five, when 'good night' starts to set in.

It was getting on for 'good night' time when I fell in with an old lady who complained that the naughty children of Sligo pulled her ivy down and swore at her. 'And me all alone in the house since my son went to England. I went to see him once, in London, but there were black men everywhere! I was looking around, seeing where to go, when a black man took my arm. "Are you all right, darling?" he asked, and led me along to my son's house! I thought to myself, "If anyone sees me from Sligo, my reputation is lost." You can't walk with a black man here.'

Probably this was no longer true, for I had seen an African in town who seemed very much at home. I humoured the old lady, who soon went on her way.

By a quarter past five at night, the streets of Sligo were full, with people pouring out of workplaces and standing talking on pavements everywhere. Students from a college hurried to the roads leading out of town. Spreading themselves out, they began to hitchhike, just as English students had done in the sixties. One tall girl with curly hair only hitched for two minutes before a smiling family picked her up.

Soft lights glowed from the windows of the shops in Wine Street. I stopped outside Quirke the Butcher's, and noticed with surprise that all the joints of meat were made of wood. In fact, they were not joints of meat at all, but pagan gods and goddesses, grotesquely and beautifully carved from roughly-cut haunches of woodland trees. Bloodlessly they rested on white slabs where mince and chops had once reposed. Books on Celtic mythology lay among them here and there, like garnish. Metal hooks for meat still hung in rows, some with carvings dangling from them. Wonderingly, I walked inside.

A meat saw roared, scattering sawdust, worked by a butcher in a white tunic. The man turned and gave me a friendly nod, before taking up a small piece of wood with pencil markings on it. A few minutes' whittling caused a fairy cobbler to emerge from the tree in which his spirit had evidently been imprisoned. Pagan gods, birds and beasts sacred to the Celts of old stared at me sagely from every hand. Branches lay across the bacon slicer, ready for lopping.

'Excuse me, sir, but could you tell me one thing?' I asked. 'Are you a woodcarver or are you a butcher?'

'I have been a butcher. I was brought up to be a butcher,' the man replied, looking me cordially in the eye. With his tousled hair and humorous expression, he reminded me slightly of Michael Heseltine, the English politician. He was a bit shorter than Heseltine, and his name was Michael Quirke.

'Ever since I was a boy, I've been making models and carvings,' he said. 'I thought it was a weakness I had but it wasn't – it proved to be my strength. Everyone said I was playing when I got out the clay or plasticine, but really I was training myself without knowing it. I felt guilty to be so foolish when I was young, but now I'm enjoying life. At one time, I had a few carvings in a corner, away from the meat, but no one noticed them. Finally I did what I should have done before. On 24 May 1988, the last bit of meat went out the door, and an hour later I felt I'd never seen a T-bone steak!'

My eyes roved around the little shop, taking in the wooden treasures brought to life by Quirke. There was nothing arty or touristy about the old gods – a touch of pagan malevolence, perhaps – and I could see where the phrase 'rough-hewn honesty' had come from. Mr Quirke could have been woodcarver to a pre-Christian Irish King. Banishing an old life and taking on a new life and character when the time seemed ripe was a very Indian thing to do.

Chunks of oak, ash, alder, beech, sycamore and hazel lay here and there, awaiting their miracles. Thick branches of apple, pear and 'whitethorn' lay stacked against the wall.

'I use all native woods, many of them windfalls,' Michael Quirke continued. He was a talkative man. 'This is the Black Boar of Benbulbin. Here he comes, ripping out of the bushes! In Irish legends, the boar kills the hero. Benbulbin, that great hill, acts as a barrier between Ulster and Connaught. There have been many wars here. In 1798, General Humbert of France came over and won a battle near there, but he took so long that the nearby towns had time to refortify. He was the best French leader after Napoleon.

Had he succeeded, Ireland might have been annexed to France, though, mind you, we'd have been no better off than under England. The French were supposed to be "liberating" Ireland, that's the official story.'

The Black Boar had a great crest running from his head along his spine, like the dorsal fin of a fish, the hairstyle of a Mohawk or the rays of the sun.

'Could you tell me what the cairn is for, on the hill outside town?' I asked.

'Knocknarea? That cairn is the grave of Queen Maeve, about whom many stories are told. Here is her likeness! [I inspected a carving of a frightening witch queen, whirled around with strange shapes, a hare and a stag.] Maeve, that malevolent queen and goddess! I've shown her with a March hare, as she can make men mad. Below her cairn on the hill is Tobernalt, a sacred well – the Well of Lunatics. There is a road up to the well now. Don't ask for the Well of Lunatics – that's the old name, and people will be embarrassed. It is a good Christian well now, and the water is said to be curative.

'Maeve is not always wicked. She has three aspects – she can make a man into a warrior. I'll show you how she lies in the landscape, in erotic invitation for those who enter . . .'

Quickly he seized pencil and paper and drew three hills, resembling the breasts and belly of a woman lying on her back, the Maeve cairn becoming a nipple. These are ideas familiar to Indians and West Africans. Maeve could be Kali, or even Mammy Water the lake goddess of Nigeria's Ibo-land who makes beautiful women mad so she can possess their boyfriends. Such a mad girl is termed 'abanji'.

When I told Michael Quirke about Mammy Water, he came right back at me with Finiver, the local Lady of the Lake. Sligo's lake is Lough Gill, where lies the Isle of Innisfree, named after Froech, who took the dragon-slaying sword from the hand of Finiver, his betrothed, raised above the water.

Stories, myths and history poured from the eloquent tongue of Quirke, holding me spellbound. For every character, he had a carving. A Celtic pantheon of gods whirled about my head, and I may have got them a bit mixed up here. As in India, a river, a hill, mountain or lake, in Celtic legend, is personified by a god-like person. Mortals see only a river or a hill, but somewhere on another plane, these natural objects are fierce, lusty or romantic men and women. Sometimes, as in West Africa, a lady arises from a lake, yet she is no lady but the lake itself.

'I've carved Maeve from hazel, as she's sometimes known as the Hazel Queen,' Quirke continued. 'Hazel is the wood of power. Maeve's power drives men mad, not only with lust, but with lust's associate, battle fury, so that Maeve's men fight like demons. Finiver makes a boy into a man, Maeve makes a man into a warrior, but Garavogue, the hag of the river, makes a warrior immortal – that is, she kills him. These are the Three Women of Sligo, Finiver (or Guinevere), Maeve and Garavogue. Finiver is of the rowan, or mountain ash. Alder is the death wood, the wood of Bran. Bran is not a full god here – he is a type of Finn ...'

'Can you make a living doing this?' I interrupted, wondering if the carver was too poetic to survive.

'Yes, I live very well,' he said, as I could see, for at that moment a well-dressed young woman came in and bought the carving of Maeve for twenty-five pounds.

'Now I can carve her again,' Michael said with satisfaction, when the customer had gone. 'I can never repeat a character who is here in the shop with me. Now, where was I? Oh yes, Finn MacCool, the Son of Bright Apple, for he holds the Apple of Immortality. He is carved here with an apple and a boar, for Finn was the Boar of High Summer and his enemy Diarmaid a Wolf. In the legend, you know, Finn has Diarmaid killed by a boar. This log I'm about to carve is alder, a resonant wood, used when making the sound box of a harp ...'

'Have you any lamb chops?' a dark-haired woman enquired. Her voice trailed away, she looked dazed and confused, and said 'Oh no, he's closed' to her daughter. Both left.

'People come in after meat all the time,' said Quirke. 'Yes, Garavogue, or Caravogue, the river, is the Third Woman of Sligo. She confers immortality, as you'd find if you fell in the river, and protects the hero's soul. She is here carved riding in a car drawn by elks. That carving is of mad King Sweeney, a Sligo character. You must have read about him in Flann O'Brien's book, *At Swim-Two-Birds*. In Scotland, they tell of a madman of the woods who sounds like our Sweeney. Lough Doyne is the Two-Birds of O'Brien's book. There Sweeney fought the Hag of the Mill, she who turns a handmill. Sweeney, who was half a bird at that time, whirled round the mountain, he and the Hag, until the Hag dived into the lake, her own navel.'

St Patrick must greatly have simplified Irish thought, a turn for the better, when he introduced Christianity. Animism has its own heady pleasures, however, and I went on listening to Michael Quirke and admiring wooden statuette after statuette. Most of his sculptures in Irish wood were meat size, between eight inches and two feet in length or height. Surviving Celtic figures of pagan imagery are mostly worked in stone or metal, not in perishable wood. Anyone who wished to hoax an archeologist need only buy up Quirke's stock and then sink it in a bog to be rediscovered.

'Those were the good old days, the days of heroes,' Michael Quirke sighed, 'when men didn't fight over politics and religion, but over sensible things like cattle and women! Invaders swiftly became as Irish as the rest of us. The Normans lasted no time at all! In two hundred years, they was Irish. Only the Elizabethan English stayed foreign, as they were absentee landlords, and ruled from over the water.'

Later, I reflected that the Tudors came to Ireland not just as rulers, but as missionaries-by-force, in Islamic style, determined to change the people's religion. When the English upper classes grew too civilized for such ideas, Cromwellians overthrew them and carried on worse than before. Without such a mission, the second wave of English might have become as Irish as the Normans before them.

'We in the west of Ireland have all the old customs that survive in England here and there – the Garland Days, midsummer bonfires and decorated wells. Our old ways have been rededicated to Christianity, the gods turned into saints,' Quirke went on. 'Christians don't know it all. This little shoemaker I'm carving is a leprechaun [he pronounced it "leprehorn"] and the priest will say there's no such thing. Yet an American girl came here, who'd crossed the mountains, and there she had seen a teeny bearded man wearing a black serge suit. Take no notice, it's only the wife,' he added, as a woman looked into the shop from a door at the back. Evidently the Quirke family lived upstairs.

I told Michael Quirke how a heron had once nearly landed on my back in Wales, and he was mightily impressed, taking it as a good luck omen. He called the heron a 'crane', for real cranes, sacred birds to the Celts, have long been extinct in Ireland. From Quirke I learned that the Sligo hares turn red, not white, in winter, as the hills grow fiery with bracken and heather, not white with snow.

'Do you think Ireland should have her own king?' I asked.

'No, that's an Anglo-Saxon idea. We're far too tribal to think of central power.'

Falling under the spell of the story-teller, perched on a stool, I fell into a trance as the woodcarver talked and whittled, whittled and talked.

'That figure of Bres is carved from elm, the tree of Bres. Bres the Beautiful, who told men when to plough and reap. Like Good King Wenceslas, Bres's feet melted the snow when he walked. Leu of the long hand, the beams of the sun, took over from Bres, a shining youth. Here in the west of Ireland, we call him Balor of the Heavy Blows ... Colum Cill, after causing the Battle of the Books, came back to Tara for the Convention of Drumceat at the Hill of Synod, where they discussed what to do about poets. In those times, a poet could descend on you with all his retinue and eat you out of house and home. If you complained, he'd put a curse on you. The issue was finally resolved in our day, as the government have now set up a pension for poets, a license to be lazy. I'm glad I'm a woodcarver ... This happened here at Sligo: Owen Bel died in the River Garavogue, speared by Ulstermen, in AD 500. He cried, "Bury me in the womb, in the mountain, in the belly of the mountain" ... Yes, the plain between Benbulbin and the sea is the place of battles; three rivers and three battles ...'

With a struggle, I broke the spell the woodcarver had cast, and escaped into the lamplit streets, promising to return before I left Sligo. Yet the magical city had not yet finished with me, for I somehow found myself in a dark little wood-panelled bar, with a cosy snug in the rear, and a counter near the door left over from the pub's grocery-bar days at the turn of the century. Drawers for spices and other grocery bygones remained. There was a cheerful, Bohemian atmosphere, the air thick with smoke and the shouts of uproarious women.

'This place has been in the same family for over a hundred years, and it was going strong before that time. Nothing's been changed here for ninety years,' the barman told me.

At breakfast next morning, the son of the house dashed past the open doorway stripped to the waist, shaving cream all over his face, looking very agitated. There was a knock at the door and a man came with a message, causing still more agitation. Doors shut everywhere, and I heard the landlady give a loud 'Shh!' I picked up my plastic bag and walked noisily along the hall, banging the front door behind me. A collective sigh of relief seemed to whistle from every pore of the house as I walked away. It must be hard to have boarders if your family is in a constant case of crisis, as most families are.

I decided to take the bus to Strandhill, on Sligo Bay, and follow the road in a circle around Queen Maeve's hill of Knocknarea. Although very bad at following directions, I might be able to find Tobernalt, the Well of Lunatics.

'I like to get down to the sea and talk to the waves,' one housewife said to another, on the bus.

'Yes, it's good to talk to Nature. Better than being in the house. Nature has so much to say.'

The bus passed directly under the hill of Maeve's cairn, the sea on one side, the hill on the other. A few white houses lined the road, and fields stretched down to the shore. Rain spitting in my face, I plodded along the narrow coastal road, through scenery eerie and desolate, unseen spirits everywhere, conjured up by Michael Quirke. As Strandhill is a peninsula, I could see the hills of the mainland far across the sea. Gulls and waders dabbled at the edge of the breakers, along strands of pale sand. Below the great hill of Knocknarea, brown stark woods, leafless and grim, glowered at me from behind a stone wall. A padlocked iron gateway barred my entrance to the wood, a part of the former estate of the Phibbs family. Open pastureland succeeded the neglected wood as I walked on, and soon I came to a rough circle of boulders on a mound – Lisheen, the little fort, home of fairies.

Before long, Knocknarea towered over me in escarpments of sheer rock, with grassland visible high in the sky. I could not see the cairn from here. A big grey house with a 'Guests' sign stood among trees, so I knocked at the door and asked how to find the holy well. Spaniels frisked around me, and an aristocratic white-haired lady called her daughter Mary to guide me. There was something bookish and appealing about the old lady, but we had no time to get acquainted, for brisk Mary pointed me on my way.

Bungalows began to appear, then a Catholic church at a cross-roads. According to Mary, I was to go straight on.All of a sudden, I came to a place of fairy rings, in fields on either side of the lane. They were spoiled by official 'Historic Monument' signs waffling away about Bronze Age stone heritages. Before I could examine them, I was buffeted by a gust of wind and rain. A car approached, and on an impulse I thumbed a lift. 'Do you know a holy well around these parts?' I asked the driver.

'Indeed I do! Get in!' my rescuer smiled. Clearly he was pleased by my request, for he was a priest, a man for whom the well was a place of Christian worship. He introduced himself as Father Liam Devine, of St Patrick's, Strandhill, and a more kindly and agreeable man I have yet to meet. It was a good thing I *did* meet him, as the Well of Lunatics proved to be a long way away.

We drove up a steep gravel path, and soon beheld the well, Tobernalt. Like most holy wells, it was a natural spring of water, not a man-made sunken well. A park-like path had been laid out around the sacred waters, with stepping stones. Clear fresh water bubbled up from a pebble-filled pool, overhung by rocks. Boulders lay around the waterside, ash trees spreading finger-like leaves overhead. If the well had been in the centre of an ash grove ever since it was discovered, it is no wonder that it was deemed sacred, for ash was holy to the ancients.

A grotto had been hollowed out of the mountainside, with a beautiful figure of Mary. A row of candles stood by the wayside. To my amazement, they were burning brightly as the rain fell and water dripped from the ash trees. I was glad the well had been Christianized, as Michael Quirke himself could scarcely go on his knees and pray to the rascally old gods he so admired.

Below the well, a waterfall tumbled across an artificial rockery. We stepped from stone to stone across the new-born stream, below the trees. Wistfully, I looked back at the haunting beauty of the well. Father Devine beckoned and showed me a huge slab of rock. 'This was a Mass Stone in the Penal Times,' he said reverently.

On we drove, towards Sligo, as I thought. I enquired about Queen Maeve, but the priest doubted if she had ever existed.

'I think the cairn was placed there as a landmark to guide Bronze Age pilgrims to the rings of stone,' he said.'Now let me show you around County Sligo. We don't get many English visitors these days.'

Soon Lough Gill, a vast lake, came into view. Father Devine took a mountain road, and stopped the car. There was a fine spray of rain, and the weather was misty, but I could still see the forested islands on the lake, and the tall mountains brooding all around. One of those islands, half hidden in the mist, was the Lake Isle of Innisfree, of Yeats' poem.

I have often read this poem, starting off jubilantly, but growing disappointed as I go on. To my mind, it begins so well that it could easily be mistaken for a translation of an eighth-century hermit's verse, composed in a beehive hut by a contented holy man of Old Ireland. Then it starts to 'get poetic', and I lose interest. I blame my upbringing! Parents, never teach your children to love folklore, for folklore and high culture can never be friends. Indeed, total illiteracy is an asset to anyone who wishes to acquire folklore.

'I'm in no hurry if you are not. Why don't I show you the place where Mountbatten was killed?' Father Devine suggested. Delighted at the chance to see more of County Sligo, especially as the weather was now improving, I thanked the priest and settled back in my seat. One day cars must be abolished, but not yet.

Mountbatten fell victim to a bomb placed in his yacht. He was never a favourite character of mine, as I do not approve of the British partition and subsequent desertion of India, mismanaged by Mountbatten against a horrific background of massacres. Mountbatten always seemed rather proud of his role in the affair. For a truthful picture of India in 1947, you must turn to fiction. *Train to Pakistan*, a novel by Khushwant Singh, has been a great inspiration for me. Another hitchhiker, a student, raised a thumb in anticipation, and Father Devine slowed down at once. 'People can see my collar, so I must stop,' he told me gravely.

Apparently, in Ireland, stopping for hitchhikers is seen as Christian behaviour. In England it is regarded as 'encouraging wastrels'. In my case, the student proved a welcome recruit to our company, for he too showed great interest in the local landmarks.

Both my new friends pointed out Drumcliff Church (C. of I.) as the place where W.B. Yeats was buried. Moments later we passed the stump of a tower, and the student sang out the date it was built: 1170. Now the sky was blue, and we were bowling along beside the edge of the cliffs, with views across the water to distant strands. A jagged castle appeared on a headland, apparently a ruin. By straining my eyes, I thought I might be able to see Donegal across the bay. Beyond a forestry plantation, the castle appeared again, and closer up it seemed a marvel, with French château-like towers, and a classy name, Classybawn. Near here the student hopped out, waved goodbye and disappeared up a side lane.

Finally the helpful priest drove up to a point overlooking a fine old stone harbour, with a few houses on the quayside.

'Mountbatten used to drink Guinness in the bar down there,

and he was well liked by the locals. Two men worked at night, placing the charge in his boat, leaving a third man on the shore with a detonator. When the two men drove away, the Garda stopped them on a routine check. One of the men was nervous, so the guard asked them the number of the car they were driving. Neither of the men knew, so they were taken to the station and charged with stealing a car.

'It wasn't me put the charge on the boat!' the nervous man cried out. With that, the police gave a jump, and began grilling them, "What boat?" But the men didn't talk. Hour after hour, they were asked "What boat?" until Mountbatten's boat finally blew up. In the end, the nervous man was released for lack of proof. All the people of Sligo feel bitterly ashamed for what happened. Now let's go back and see Yeats' grave.'

We pulled up outside the church.

'Yeats was in a pauper's grave in France, cremated, but he was brought back here to be buried later,' Father Devine explained. 'Some say they brought back the wrong ashes, and that isn't Yeats there at all. Yeats' father had the living here – that white building is the rectory where he lived.'

A sad little grave stood by the side of the church, with some lines by Yeats himself as an epitaph.

> Cast a Cold Eye
> On Life, on Death.
> Horseman, pass by!
> W. B. Yeats – 1865–1939.

'Why did he want people to cast a cold eye on him?' I asked. 'Why not a warm eye?'

'Well, he never meant those lines for his tombstone. Yeats was a complete atheist – he didn't believe in anything. A lady I know who saw his mother's funeral said that Yeats wouldn't go into the church. In fact, he pottered around in *our* cathedral instead!'

'Not many horsemen will pass by nowadays,' I commented. 'Of course, Yeats couldn't have been expected to know that.'

As we drove back to Sligo Town, good Father Devine regaled me with stories of Ireland's literary giants.

'Someone I knew says he saw Brendan Behan in a pub in Dublin once. No one took any notice of Behan, so he got angry and fired a bottle of whiskey at a shelf, breaking all the glasses . . .'

Note the happy use of the word 'fired'. The English only fire bullets, but in Irish speech any missile to hand can be fired, simply by hurling it.

'... And some say that Brendan Behan never wrote the song "Old Triangle", but learned it off another inmate at Mountjoy and claimed it as his own.'

Father Devine went on to speak of his admiration for Shakespeare, but had no fresh gossip about the Bard. He showed me the big green gabled home of Ireland's Minister of Finance. Later I heard that Irishmen outside Sligo nurtured suspicions that the Minister used the Finance of All Ireland just to favour his home town with a new bridge, a new hospital and other luxuries. Sligo deserves them all and more, as for friendliness and conversation its sons cannot be beaten. My priestly friend set me down outside the two cathedrals and I bade him a fond farewell.

CHAPTER EIGHTEEN

Woodbrook

My bus next morning set out for Ballina, westward to County Mayo, to the place where General Humbert of revolutionary France had landed with his soldiers to help drive the English out of Ireland, in 1798. David Thomson's vivid account of these goings-on, in *Woodbrook*, had aroused my curiosity.

The bus took the coast road, around the tall grey Ox Mountains, beside dark sea cliffs with grassy rounded undulating contours, dropping down to Sligo Bay. On the inland side of the bus, cattle grazed on the flanks of the mountains. Silver plumes of snow lay across the peaks. A grim building of thick stone walls stood alone in high-walled grounds in the middle of nowhere, filling me with foreboding. It was Dromore Workhouse, a passenger told me, built for the relief of victims of the Potato Famine. Dirt encrusted on the bus window gave a grainy texture to the scenery. Fiddler's Elbow, a large pub by the wayside, was advertised by a giant wooden carving of a fiddle.

At the coastal town of Easky, two life-sized statues of cloth-capped old men appeared as if turned from flesh to blue-grey stone on the spot, one wheeling a bike, the other resting on a seat. 'God Bless You As You Leave the Town of Easky', a sign proclaimed.

The mountains had now been left behind, and we were in flat, windswept country, the bare trees all bending one way. Easky's spire could be seen from the back window from many miles away. Small cabins were dotted about at the side of fields, mostly ruined or used as farm sheds, but in some cases inhabited. Green grass sprouted from the mouldy, neglected thatched roofs. One lived-in cabin also had a grassy roof, as if the craft of thatching had died out locally. Men with sacks were lifting potatoes, in furrowed fields, behind the cabins.

At Inishcrone, near Ballina, I could see the coast of County Mayo across wide Killala Bay. I was amazed to see a gigantic black statue of a pig, made of plastic and very life-like, standing in somebody's front garden. It was an advert for a fair.

Finally we arrived at Ballina, where the rushing River Moy joined the sea. I would have to take a taxi back to Sligo once I had seen the sights, for there was no return bus. There was little to see, for Ballina seemed to be the usual uphill-shopping-street Irish town. Bunting and Irish flags made a bright display, still celebrating the bicycle race of weeks earlier, the one I had seen at Mullingar. There was a good bookshop, and a large ruined building, gaunt and flaking, the Hibernian Hall. Not far from the river stood a statue to General Humbert, with Irish words underneath, and verses from a ballad. Humbert had landed at Killala, just across the bay.

Wolfe Tone, the aristocratic eighteenth-century Irish nationalist, had secretly arranged the arrival of a French invasion fleet. However, the arrival of the French did not quite coincide with the national uprising of '98. For a time, Humbert controlled part of the countryside, and his soldiers armed, clothed and fed the Irish peasants who flocked to join their banner.

David Thomson in *Woodbrook*, quotes extensively from the diaries of an Ascendancy-class bishop whose sympathies lay with the Irish poor. Dr Joseph Stock, Bishop of Killala, describes how men ragged and barefoot fell on French army uniforms with whoops of delight, putting the clothes on wrong, holding guns upside down and so on. Many of the French laughed at such antics, or felt disgusted at being allied with so 'primitive' a people. The Irish bishop did not laugh, but looked on the behaviour of the peasants as a tragic folly that could lead only to their doom.

How right the bishop was! Eventually Humbert was forced to surrender, handing his sword gravely to the English commander and being treated with all the honours of war and politeness of diplomacy. Meanwhile, the English soldiery hunted down every Irishman suspected of helping the French and put them to death in a variety of ingenious fashions. Corpses hung from gallows, heads were spiked on railings. More people were put to death in Ireland than died in the French revolutionary Terror of the time. However, the aftermath of the French Revolution suggests that

Ireland's fate might have been equally unpleasant had Humbert succeeded in his mission. The Royalist Roman Catholic French would probably have made better conquerors of Ireland, if Ireland had to be reconquered once more.

By now, rain had begun to fall, and I took refuge in the Imperial Hotel. After a leisurely tea by a coal fire, I asked the clerk to phone for a taxi. My driver proved to be a very spirited young lady in her thirties, with blond hair and blue jeans. Her name was Mrs Mulhooley.

'Could you take me for a spin through the country, and then on to Sligo?' I asked, as the rain had stopped and I wished to see more of Killala Bay.

'I'll take you to the town of Killala and back, and me husband will take you to Sligo', she promised. 'Have you been to Ireland before? Look, that's what we call a "goat".'

'We have goats in England, too,' I explained.

Outside Killala, many fields were flooded. A gentle sun now emerged, the sea became blue, and low dune-shaped hills appeared on the far horizon. Near Killala harbour, where the French had landed, I saw a pointed Round Tower, obviously very old. Mrs M. parked the car in a street of stone houses, where steps led up to the tower. However, a locked gate barred the way.

An elderly man was kneeling on the pavement, sawing a slice from the bottom of his front door, to prevent it from jamming. 'Is it the tower that you want? I have the key,' he said, producing it. 'That tower is eleventh century. There's one like it at Glendalough, where St Kevin used to live. Did you ever hear about St Kevin and that Kathleen? Chasing him everywhere, she was. He evidently didn't like women, hee hee hee. Now I've got a key to the Protestant Cathedral also. Would you like to see that, too?'

Young Mrs M. looked shocked at the thought, so she waited outside, while I sprinted in for a quick glimpse at Bishop Stock's former domain. It was an old dark church, full of leftovers from the Harvest Festival, such as cabbages, turnips, sprays of wheat and petal-shedding flowers. An American lady from Boston also looked in. To my surprise, she had never heard of harvest festivals. More of interest were the many memorials to well-known Ascendancy families, the Carys, the Kirkwoods and the Shaws. Joyce Cary, one of my favourite writers, came from an Anglo-Irish background. In his novels, the Carys became the 'Corners'.

I gave the old man a tip, and soon Mrs M. and I were speeding back to Ballina. On the way, we passed a whole family, mother, father, and five children, busily digging potatoes from a field. By and by, Mrs M. stopped the car in a lonely place, and urged me to look at St Patrick's Well.

'This is where St Patrick preached in the olden days!' she declared, eyes shining with enthusiasm. 'Have you heard of the Penal Times? That stone is where they used to say Mass in thim days.'

The well bubbled into a tributary of the Moy, but unfortunately it had been hemmed in by modern concrete and so had lost a great deal of its charm. A former pool had silted up and was turning into a miniature reed marsh. Mrs M. darted around the waters with great vivacity. There are as many Patrick Wells in Ireland as there are haunts of Robin Hood and King Arthur in England. I once knew a man who had been brought up beside a Patrick's Well in County Limerick. He told me that the sacred water was bottled and sold to Irishmen all over the world for its healing powers.

Skirting a tinker camp, Mrs M. eventually put me down beside the fast-flowing River Moy at Ballina. Her husband was out with a fare in another car, and she radioed him to stop and pick me up on his way. With that, Mrs M. gave a wave and vanished. Several misgivings later, I was relieved to see a car stop, and so made the acquaintance of Peter Mulhooley.

A good-natured sandy-haired man, he welcomed me into his car with a smile, and then went on talking to the family sitting in the back, a young couple with a baby. The father was a wild-haired rough-looking young man, very cheerful, and with such a strong local accent that at first I thought he was speaking Gaelic. After a while, I kept catching the word 'lottery'. Shouting and laughing, the family disembarked at a broken-down council estate covered in rubbish.

'That couple are not really married,' Peter M. told me in wondering tones. 'A few years ago you would niver have heard of such a thing.'

'It's the same in England,' I said primly, trying to recall if any of my relatives there had ever bothered to get married.

'I was in London once, with another feller, and we got lost on the Underground,' Peter said. 'The other man had pretended he could use it, but he could not. My brother-in-law's English, a kinder man you never would meet. I was ashamed when he came here and walked in a bar. As soon as the people heard his accent, they all began speaking in Irish, so. Near here is my farm – we have sheep and cattle.'

We were driving along the coast road to Sligo, beside flat fields. All at once, Peter M. slowed down beside the entrance to a narrow lane, or boreen. 'May we just have a look down here?' he asked appealingly. 'There was an apparition down that road two or three year's ago, and they've got a shrine there now. Our Lady was seen by many people, and they call it the shrine of Our Lady of Carns. My wife's very religious now, she goes there to pray a lot.'

'Has she ever seen anything?' I enquired, as we drove down to the shrine.

'She thinks she saw some lights in the sky once. I've never seen anything myself.'

Suddenly, while driving reverently along, a thought occurred to Peter M. and he threw back his head and roared with laughter. 'I've never heard anything so funny as Paisley accusing the Pope of being the Anti-Christ,' he gasped, shaking and holding his ribs. 'That Paisley, he's a terror! He was an IRA man once, and learned all their secrets. They dasn't shoot him, or he'd be a martyr. I don't hold with what's going on up North – if Britain ever left, there'd be another Civil War.'

Soon we reached the shrine, a car-park-like space beside the road in which stood a large glass tank containing a painted figure of Mary looking with pity on Jesus crucified. Rows of benches with damp kneeling pads stood before the display. While I admired the figures, Peter kneeled and prayed with his eyes shut. Finally he drove back to the main road.

'When Our Lady appeared, the Church at once offered to buy the field,' Peter told me. 'The farmer wouldn't sell, but then his cattle got ill. Still he wouldn't sell for them to build a shrine, so the cattle began to die. With that he gave in and sold. At once, all the sick cattle got well.'

'What are those black tarpaulins for, in the fields there?' I asked, when we had returned to the main road.

Black shiny mounds of tarpaulins were weighed down near the ground by rows of large stones.

'I call them "whales", 'cause that's what they look like. They're to cover and protect the silage, made of spoiled hay.'

Two very smart policemen, in caps and polished buttons, stood in the middle of the main road, stopping each car and questioning the driver. I was reminded of the priest's tale of the Mountbatten murder. 'Everything in order? they asked. Peter nodded, and we were waved through.

'That's funny. I never saw them two fellers before, they're new to me,' Peter told me. I never learned who they were looking for. Peter M. began talking about farm animals. 'It's useful to know a good bone-setter,' he said. 'The seventh son of a seventh son can heal both beasts and men.'

We drove into Sligo, where Peter shook my hand warmly and wished me luck. As a parting gift, he gave me a copy of the *Mayo Post and Advertiser*, a sprightly, humorous and well-written paper. I was glad I had met the Mulhooleys.

On my last full day in Sligo Town, I decided to take a taxi south-easterly into County Leitrim, and if possible see Woodbrook, the house brought to life by the able pen of David Thomson. My driver was a cheerful young man named Adrian Scanlon, who boasted a curly moustache. He told me of a visit he'd made to California. While over there, he had gone into Mexico for the day. On his way back into the USA, he found himself faced by a stern row of Immigration Officials.

'It was so easy going *out* of America, I never realised it would be hard to get in! And me with my passport in California, miles and miles away! Luckily, the Immigration Officer who chose me turned out to be a Sligo man! After askin' how everything was doing back home, he waved me through with a laugh. After that I found that if I iver was in trouble far from home there'd always be a Sligo man somewhere to help me.'

He drove along the Arigna Valley, beside the river of that name. It was a sunny day, and the rolling hills smiled peacefully down at us, some wearing dark beards of conifer plantation.

'My grandmother remembered when those trees were planted,' Adrian told me. 'She died not long ago, aged ninety-three. When she was ninety, I gave her a surprise birthday party in a pub near here, on top of a hill.'

Adrian seemed very fond of his grandmother, and spoke of her kindly as he drove from lough to lough, through enchanted countryside. Little Lough Shean led into middle-sized Lough Meenagh, until finally we faced an inland sea, Lough Allen, one of the bigger bulges in the River Shannon. Where the great lake joined the river, at Drumshanbo, we headed directly southward and soon were in neat white Leitrim Village, a row of houses up and down a hillside street.

A corner shop was being repaired, the owners and workmen outside talking animatedly. Adrian asked them the way to Woodbrook, then came back and told me that there was a ruined castle behind the shop. I went over to see, and a girl from the shop pointed eagerly towards a stone wall and a tree in which two boys were climbing. 'That's Rourke's Castle. There's not much left of it, but its history is all in this magazine,' she said.

I bought the magazine, *Shannonside*, and found it to be very interesting. As I looked at the few stones that remained of the castle, I learned from the magazine that the Irish-built castle of the local kings, the O'Rourkes, had once towered over the local countryside. Brian O'Rourke, the builder, had intended the castle as a war fortress for his use when plundering neighbouring kings and chieftains. That was in 1540. Thirty years later, the castle had become the O'Rourke stronghold against the encroaching English. Other O'Rourke castles had been demolished to prevent the English taking them over, for they had stood too close to the Elizabethan English garrison at Sligo Town.

Finally, Leitrim Castle was destroyed by the English in 1603. Part of the remaining walls became incorporated into a police barracks in the nineteenth century. By a strange twist of fate, an O'Rourke was the leader of the local branch of the IRA in 1920. He led an attack on what ought to have been his own castle, and blew it up with dynamite! So much for Leitrim's Castle.

The most romantic episode in the strange history of the castle had taken place in 1588, the year of the Spanish Armada. Storms had wrecked the Spanish fleet on the shores of West Ireland, and the refugees had been welcomed and cared for by the Irish people. Such kindness outraged Sir Richard Bingham, nominal English governor of Connaught. All Spaniards, and all those who sheltered them, he declared, were to be put to death. Nevertheless, the O'Rourke of the day offered hospitality and refuge to Captain Francisco de Cuellar and his crew, survivors of the wrecked galleon *San Pedro*. It must have been a strange sight in a land of Celtic war chiefs, dressed in Highland-type garb, to see the proud, aristocratic De Cuellar in fine Spanish attire, pulling a face as he sipped the O'Rourke potheen and thought of his native wine.

De Cuellar returned safely to Spain, where he wrote an account of his Irish adventure. Like Humbert's French of later times, he regarded the Irish as well-disposed 'primitive people'. According to *Shannonside*, he described 'Señor de Reurque' as follows: 'Although this man is a savage, he is a very good Christian and an enemy of heretics, always carrying on war with them.'

After some zigging and zagging, Adrian Scanlon and I reached the golf course outside Carrick-on-Shannon, said to lie on the old Woodbrook estate. There was no sign of a mansion, so I knocked at a cottage door and enquired.

'Woodbrook is just at that gate with the lodge house – keep right on straight,' the housewife pointed. 'That was a wonderful book David Thomson wrote about it – I'm so sorry to hear he died. He and his wife Martina came here to Woodbrook not long ago.'

'I once had a drink with David Thomson at Camden Town in London,' I said, 'and I know Martina slightly.'

'Are there lots of writers in London?' the housewife asked excitedly, then grew wistful. 'When you go back, tell Martina that Molly Maxwell is in the nursing home now. You remember the Maxwells from the book? My name is Rose Mannion, but I don't think Martina would remember me. Since that book was written, people come to see Woodbrook all the time.'

The wooden gate was broken and the hedge overgrown. Most of the beeches that had been a feature of Woodbrook had been felled. Half hidden by brambles and long grass, the little Gothic lodge house, almost a fairy dwelling, looked at us sadly with a black eye or poked-out ecclesiastical window. I think this had been the former jockey's house, for the Kirkwoods of Woodbrook survived into the middle of the twentieth century by breeding racehorses.

Adrian Scanlon insisted on driving up to the front door, once I had opened the gate. A friendly orange dog came to greet us, but no human was visible. The present owners seemed to be living around the back of the house, beside junk-filled stables. Part of the mansion had been demolished, but the front door still looked impressive, a large window on either side. Now painted an off-cream colour, the house had a forlorn air of sagging decrepitude, the paint flaking. I peeped through the two windows. One room was furnished scantily, in suburban style. The other was used as a store room, a pathetic fate, since the tall window and high ceiling spoke of better days. A step-ladder, cans of paint, a sack of potatoes and assorted rubble lay where Kirkwoods once had frolicked.

I had been expecting this, for David Thomson had written of Woodbrook's fall from splendour once the Maxwell family had succeeded in buying house and grounds from the former landlords, the Kirkwoods. Living in a stately home is an art, acquired by upbringing. Nobody who was not born in a manor house should aspire to one, for if he gets his wish, what a mess that manor house soon will be! According to Rose Mannion, the Maxwells had now sold the house to someone else.

A man of simplicity and goodness, as I have said earlier, David Thomson took many of the remarks made by disgruntled locals too seriously, and so was perhaps a little harsh on the Anglo-Irish, or Ascendancy. Whatever he wrote about Kirkwoods of past ages, no one could have written a better tribute to a family than did Thomson when he described Major Kirkwood and the rest of the present-day family. They come across as a splendid reminder of the days, only just past, when the English and Irish upper class had not become embittered and still looked on their poorer neighbours with sympathy and kindly humour. As the Kirkwood tutor, young David seemed as anxious as his employer-friends that the estate should survive. Major Kirkwood is depicted in the book as a nobleman and a gentleman in the best sense of both words.

It was unfortunate, perhaps, that Thomson should have written so ardently of the love he felt for Phoebe Kirkwood, his pupil, when he was eighteen years old and Phoebe only twelve. Nothing came of this love, but it might have been more tactful, in the aftermath of Phoebe's tragic death, for Thomson to have used pseudonyms. However, had he done so, I would not have known how to find Woodbrook. As it was, I felt thrilled to be walking on the same ground that young Thomson had trodden long before.

'Whenever we came back to Woodbrook after a long absence, the servants would always have a fire and a meal ready to greet us,' Phoebe's sister Antoinette once told me. 'When we asked how they knew we were coming, they would solemnly say that they had seen the Little People lighting candles in all the windows. There was a ring of thorn trees that we never cut, d'ye see? for they said 'twould annoy the Little People.'

I looked back at the house as Adrian drove away. There were no candles burning in the windows. Today the new Little People, those who dance nightly on the television screen, have ousted the old.

We drove through Boyle, a town whose hill had proved agonizing to the bicycle-racers, and around yet another wide lake, Lough Key. The high tops of the Curlew Mountains loomed in the distance. Nearing Sligo, we passed Collooney, where General Humbert and his French-Irish army had defeated the British.

At Ballysadare, just outside Sligo Town, Adrian grew excited. 'That's my father's house, the one with the black roof!' he cried. 'My other relatives live over there. You see the old mill?' Once more I glanced at the large flour mill, temporarily closed, despite the addition of a new silvery turbine engine to take the place of water power.

'Yes, I see it.'

'Long before my time, when my great-grandmother was a young girl, she would bring the men at the mill their dinners hot under a covered tray,' he said earnestly. 'One day she had brought the dinners and started home, when for some reason she looked back. The whole mill was afire, with sheets of flames! A man leaped down from a window five storeys high and drowned in the river. Terrible, it was! There was a ballad composed on the event. My great-grandmother taught it to her daughter, my grandmother, and my grandmother taught it to me. Shall I sing it to you?'

'Yes, please.'

Come all ye loyal heroes
Wherever that you be,
Come and pay attention
And listen now to me.
Concerning this sad accident,
A burning now beware,
And pray for those who lost their lives
In the Mills of Ballysadare.
It was on a Thursday evening
As quick as you could hear,
After coming from their dinners
With neither dread nor fear . . .

'No one knows how it happened!' Adrian burst out in his normal voice. 'It's still a complete mystery! Well, I'll get on with my rhyme . . .'

And eight or nine of those young men
Were bur-ned in their prime.

There was a man on the top loft,
For mercy he did cry.
He was mangled in the river rocks
After lepping five storeys high.
To hear those weeping widows
From your heart would take a tear,
We may cry and weep in sadness
Round the Mills of Ballysadare . . .

'. . . that was taught me by my grandmother, Annie Scanlon. Well, here we are at Sligo.'

'Let me out at Wine Street,' I asked the balladeer, as I prepared a silver handshake.

There is said to be a grandmother at Ross Carbery who can sing the whole of 'The Battle of Ross Carbery', another local ballad. If more men like Adrian would listen to their grandmothers, then Irish songbooks would be a lot fatter than they are.

There was still a light in the window of Michael Quirke's shop, so I called to wish the woodcarver goodbye. On the morrow I would be off to Donegal. Somebody had broken the glass door of the shop, but Michael wasn't worried.

'There's a piece of teak I've carved into a hex sign up there,' he pointed out. 'That means "Keep away from me door".'

He had now completed the leprechaun shoemaker, whose hammer could be taken out and replaced at will. Even as we spoke, a young lady came in and bought the little creature for fifteen pounds, hammer and all.

'So you've been to Woodbrook? The wife wanted David Thomson to address the Literary Society here, but the committee shot her down in flames. Thomson's not Irish, you see.'

Just then Michael's wife and a teenage person stole quietly into the shop from the rear and began working on the lettering of a 'Fiddler of Dooney' carving. 'This must be Mrs Quirke and your daughter,' I said brightly.

'No, *son*', I was corrected, and the poor boy blushed bright red. 'Yes, this is my wife, Eithne. You know, Eithne was the mother of Sigurd the Fat of Orkney . . .'

The present-day Eithne laughed. She was a good-looking dark-haired lady. 'I suppose you know this is all heresy!' she said, gesturing at the Irish gods, who stared back impassively. 'We've gone back to the old gods, in defiance to the Church.'

'Don't you go to Mass?' I asked Quirke, who shook his head. 'What do your parents think?'

'My father approves of this – he never really believed all he heard from the priest.'

It seemed to me that the Quirkes gloried in the poetry of paganism, but were not true pagans, eager to propitiate feared gods with flame and sacrifice. Nor did I see how gods worshipped in days of continual tribal war and plunder could adjust themselves to the world where Peace is an ideal – the Christian world. Gods whose ways co-existed with farming and nature now functioned all the better in the guise of saints. I brought the conversation back to David Thomson.

'When I told the Society I wanted to ask David Thomson over to address one of our meetings, no one said a word,' Eithne told me. 'They didn't want to admit they'd never heard of him. So I lent out some of his books, and they straight away came back and said, "He's not Irish, he's Scottish." If he'd been Irish, they would have paid his fare over. And now he is no more.'

After murmuring words of consolation, I asked her how she'd felt when her husband gave up being a butcher and devoted his life to carving the gods.

'I was pleased, and I still am!' she said, beaming round at the wooden gods. They all made a jolly family.

My bus driver, in the morning, spoke in a guttural Derry accent. The coach was the Dublin to Derry Express. I was glad to hear the accent, for it reminded me of my exciting days in Northern Ireland, recounted elsewhere. Luckily I found a window seat, as passengers with bags were struggling in. Soon we were off, heading northward, along the coastal road.

A sense of something old, strange and eerie came over me as we passed directly below Benbulbin, that strange grey-green mountain, chief link in the chain that guarded Ulster and has made it the most separate of Irish provinces from the beginning of time. Benbulbin ought to have been called Benbulbous, for one end of the barbaric table bulged upward in a great curve, with lesser knuckle-shapes on each side. As the coach swung around the mountain's impressive edge, directly below the vast height, I looked up and seemed to see the grimly laughing face of one of the woodcarver's gods. On a near-perpendicular mountainy field, a flock of seagulls screeched behind a tractor, and men and women raw-handedly filled sacks with potatoes.

Then we continued northward, past Yeats' Drumcliff and Mountbatten's Classybawn Castle out on its headland. Eventually we reached Beautiful Bundoran, a seaside resort overlooking blue Donegal Bay in the Province of Ulster. Cream-coloured Regency guest houses reminded me of Weymouth. Mountains could be seen across the bay.

There is a difference between Ulster and the troubled political entity of Northern Ireland. All of Northern Ireland is in Ulster, yet not all of Ulster is in Northern Ireland. Three counties of the Province of Ulster belong to the Irish Republic – Cavan, Monaghan and Donegal, where I now was. So these three counties are in Limbo. They had more Catholics than Protestants, and so voted for the Republic when Ireland was partitioned. All the same, there are Orange Lodges in Donegal, which you wouldn't see in County Cork.

At Ballyshannon, where a bridge crossed the mouth of the River Erne, we were very close to County Fermanagh in Northern Ireland. When the River Erne reaches Fermanagh, it broadens out into immense Lough Erne, a fragmented inland sea of a thousand islands that bisects the whole county and reaches clear to Cavan in the south. Here, in the 1960s, Hugh Malet rediscovered fierce pagan idols glowering in the undergrowth of Boa Island on the lough. At the wasp-waist of the lough is the town of Enniskillen, scene of tragic murders, yet in itself the most delightful of neighbourhoods.

Meanwhile we were at Ballyshannon, with its tall church spire seen from far away, its 'Old Barracks Bar and Lounge, 1700' and a strange bell-and-weathercock tower that now housed a jeweller's shop. On rolled the coach, around the bar to the estuary of the River Eske, another river that become a lough inland. Here stood Donegal Town, and here I dismounted, with my red, white and blue bag.

I found myself in a smart town square surrounded by glittering bars, hotels and souvenir shops. Without difficulty I found a Bed and Breakfast house, equally smart and highly polished, and settled down for a pre-exploratory nap.

CHAPTER NINETEEN

Ruins in Donegal

Donegal Town square, I discovered, was known as the Diamond. I hurried across the Diamond, down to the shore, where the River Eske meets Donegal Bay. A giant anchor, embedded in concrete, ornamented a small jetty. There was no sandy beach, and as this part of the bay was an inlet, I felt as if I were standing beside a great lake, not the Atlantic Ocean. Three Innisfree-like islands, beautifully wooded, lay out at sea. On my right, across the river, steep forested banks rose up from the water. I could see a white hound running through the trees. A blue-grey heron glided to rest on a pebbly strand, and a cormorant flew high overhead like a goose.

To my left, steps led up to a hummocky cliff edge, on which reposed the fragmented remains of a Franciscan friary. I roamed around archways leading nowhere and windows framed by stone walls standing in isolation. Catholic graves, ancient and modern, occupied most of the ground. A shower of gravel barely missed me, hurled by naughty boys who played among the ruins, ambushing one another. They scooped gravel from the paths and carried it in apron-pouches made from their jerseys.

A green metal notice told me that the abbey had been built in 1474, by O'Donnell, Prince of Tyrconnel, and his wife Nuala.

Back at the anchor vantage point, I met a dreamy-eyed tramp-like man of about fifty. He told me of his travels from one Bed and Breakfast to another, from Galway to Sligo to Donegal. In fact he could have been me, except that he had had the initiative to ask the landladies if he could stay cheaper by foregoing the second 'B' – the breakfast. If only I had his nerve, think of the greasy eggs and tough bacon I could have been spared!

'Do you think I could get a job in London? I can drive a tractor,' he said, and went on to speculate at length on the possibilities of the English dole.

In the end, I could only escape by galloping off, leaving him in full flow, and diving into a shop. Thereafter, I browsed around the shops of the Diamond. The shop people seemed a little sharp. They banged my change down quickly, as if nervous of the English. Donegal folk were dark-haired good-looking people, with a touch of Scottish gravity. A newspaper told the sad story of a six-year-old boy with an incurable illness. 'When we found out, we let him drink, smoke and swear,' the boy's father told reporters. 'We wanted him to experience everything life has to offer. He had a beautiful death. His mother played the recorder, while we all sang.'

A locally printed ballad book contained all-new material composed by a local accordion player. The songs were not very good, with irregular rhymes and metres, but included oddities such as a lengthy ballad recounting the adventures of the characters of *Dallas*. Another song, with no irony intended, celebrated Dole Day in the author's village, evidently the big drinking day of the week for neighbouring farmers.

One of the largest shops of the Diamond was Magee's, the tweed shop, which sold expensive clothes and souvenirs. Later I was to see Magee's huge tweed factory, or mill, on the outskirts of town, a building that resembled a giant Gothic grammar school with stained glass office windows.

Away from the square, near my Bed and Breakfast, I discovered the Roman Catholic Church of the Four Masters, standing on a rise. Apparently the Four Masters were seventeenth-century Franciscans from the Friary, who wrote a pro-Catholic history of Donegal. Built of soft brown stone, the church closely adjoined a tall pointy-roofed Round Tower with a cross on top. This tower was visible from some way away, and with its backdrop of dark conifer-forested hills, it reminded me very much of the tower at Glendalough. I assumed that a medieval abbey had been restored, as at Holy Cross. However, a friendly priest emerged and told me that the whole church had been built, in an old-fashioned style, in 1935. The Round Tower was in reality the church tower. Inside, I heard mutterings from a Confession box, but stifled my curiosity and hurried away.

Almost on the opposite corner to the chapel stood Donegal Castle, its gateway locked, for the ruins were unsafe. The O'Donnells of Donegal had built a stone Tudor mansion on the site of a twelfth-century castle, and the walls that remained were of surprising elegance. Probably rose gardens had flourished here at one time. A tower loomed over the roofless mansion, and beyond it, the spire of the Church of Ireland could be seen. During the Penal Times, Catholics must have thought spires a Protestant invention. Few were built when the nineteenth-century wave of Roman Catholic churches and cathedrals began. All over Ireland, a spire proclaims an Anglican church.

Steps led down to the banks of the river, and from the water's edge, the ruins of the castle dominated the skyline. The name 'Donegal' means 'Fort of the Strangers'. Both Scots and English, acting independently, have made Ulster a province of many races. It was the habit of the Elizabethan English, when dividing the provinces into counties, to name each new county after the town with which the namers were most familiar. Counties Leitrim, Louth and Mayo have been named after towns which nowadays have shrunk to the size of villages.

Damp leaves, moist air and a faint atmosphere of dereliction made my riverside walk feel sadly autumnal. Soon I reached the Diamond once more. It was a Saturday afternoon, and the square was filling up with cars. Young blonde tinker girls begged from passers-by, holding 'babbies' that were obviously not theirs, wrapped in shawls. Posters advertised a local singer, Bluestack Bill.

I headed out of town and found the path through the woods where earlier I had seen the white hound running. Yellow-brown leaves spun downwards from high branches, and the calm estuary waters could be seen below, from between the trees. I could see a heron standing motionless, and a curlew dabbling by the shore. Three pairs of young lovers walked by, hand in hand, whispering dreams of emigration. My path ended in thick undergrowth, just where the estuary widened into the sea. Dark pines and yellow birches lay ahead, as the shoreline curved to meet me. Beyond these woods lay the round green hills of Donegal's farmland, not unlike England's South Downs, the fields bounded by tall hedges.

In the soft evening light, I retraced my steps back to town, soothed by the songs of blackbirds and chaffinches. Wagtails swooped across my path, and from the mouth of the Eske, curlews called shrilly to one another like owls.

Bells rang on Sunday morning, and with some trepidation, I

followed the crowds to the Roman Catholic church for Mass. When in Rome . . .

The bright strip-pine interior of the church (or chapel) was absolutely packed with worshippers, like a Tube train in London's rush hour. This was only one of several Masses that were to take place that day. Nearly everyone in town would be attending at least one service there. I was sandwiched between two big men who joked over my head about how squashed they all were. One of the men fondly dandled his two-year-old son on his knee. Teenagers with sporty slogans on the back of their jackets sat attentively amid the rest of the crowd.

After a song and a prayer, a priest in green vestments came on and preached a long sermon warning us all not to misuse authority. Finally he asked us to pray to be forgiven for the times when we *had* misused our authority. I could not remember when I last had any authority over anyone. However, if anyone were misguided enough to give me authority, I would certainly misuse it, so I prayed along with the rest.

Every word of speech, song and prayer was in English, a great change from the services to which an Irish friend had taken me in 1960s Brighton. There the rise and swell of incomprehensible Latin seemed to have a grandeur that aroused the spirit of poetry in the Gaels, as if they stood on a rocky shore communing with the waves. People in Donegal listened earnestly to the priest, craning forward as if to show him that they were there, but did not seem to be taking in the words.

'When I see the old truck you drive, I'll give it a slap,' the little blond boy on my right said to his father, slapping him heartily in demonstration.'Why have you got a black eye?' the child asked, a moment later.

Probably it was since he last had slapped the poor man. Receiving only whispers for a reply, the boy wriggled down and sat under his father's feet.'When can we go home?' he suddenly enquired, in piercing tones.

'When the priest has finished,' the boy's father muttered, looking very embarrassed.

Holy Communion was taken prior to the end of the service, but to my relief, not all the worshippers took part. So although I sat tight as the communicants went forward, I was not too conspicuously a Protestant.

'Lord, our Mass is over,' the choir sang in sweet, lilting voices as everyone walked down the hill into town once more. Family parties chattered happily, and single people hummed the choir's song to themselves, as they walked.

During my travels round Ireland, I had been reading Sleeman's *Rambles and Recollections of an Indian Magistrate*. Sleeman's Indian journeys, his great interest in local customs and religious beliefs, his explorations of temples and ruins wherever he went in pre-Mutiny India, helped me to see the Irish as an Indo-European people. I sensed that the people of Donegal felt faintly disappointed at having such a rational church service. The return of Latin would make them feel as if they were experiencing something mysterious and exalted, something greater than themselves. Hindu worshippers gather round a holy man in order to absorb Goodness from his aura. They don't expect to understand anything he says. If he is completely silent, they are more than satisfied, if only they can see him. Something of this attitude survives in Ireland.

I made my way to an hotel lounge in the Diamond, where I sat and read a leaflet I had picked up in the church. It concerned the appearance of Our Lady of Fatima, in Portugal, who appeared to a group of peasant children, sitting on top of an oak tree.

The day was still dank and moist when I emerged, but I called a taxi from the rank outside, and asked to be taken to the ruins of Holford House, once the home of Mr Harvey-Beaumont. This visit was to be my last tribute to the Ascendancy.

'I'm thinking I know where that is,' said the driver, an elderly man. There was but a touch of the harsh, ironic but humorous Ulster accent that I knew, in the tones of his speech.

Soon we were driving alongside Lough Eske, the waters below me on my left, shining in the mist. Wooded islands, in pastel shades of orange, yellow and brown, appeared and disappeared in the soft vaporous whiteness.

Bold and clear, on my right and ahead of us, stood the craggy Blue Stack Mountains, rearing their heads in strange volcanic attitudes. Bluestack Bill, the singer, must have come from these damp Colorado badlands.

'I'm seeing that white bothy down there,' the driver informed me, pointing out a delightful cabin with a golden thatched roof. 'That's a German family live there. Ah, what fine people they are, the Germans! They try their hardest to fit in here, and now our two countries are growing together, I'm thinking. Irish pop groups are forever going to Germany now.'

Fortunately the driver made up for this heresy by roundly cursing the French, whom he disliked for the same reason that most Englishmen do – the way they clutter up the place, never get out of the way and can't speak English.

'Holford House . . .' the driver mused. 'Now which one is that? It's all ruins here. See down by the water, that big house is empty. It used to be a hotel. There's a gateway over at that forestry plantation, and there was once a castle there. The O'Donnells had a castle hereabouts, I'm thinking. There is a bar by the roadside, further on, and I'll enquire there, as I think the landlady used to work for the Harvey-Beaumonts.

'I'm seeing my way right now,' the driver told me, as he came out of the bar, followed by the landlady. The old lady ran up to me fervently, her hair wild.

'Are you one of the young Harvey-Beaumonts, from over in England?' she asked excitedly.

'Good Heavens no! I have met some of them, that's all.'

'I was a maid there in the Big House when I was a girl,' she continued, obviously still thinking I might be a modest Harvey-Beaumont in disguise. 'Great landlords they were – wonderful people! You should have seen the house in the old days! Oh, so beautiful inside! The Mulverins have a farm there now – they used to be the stewards when I was a girl. Old George Mulverin has died, and it's his son you'll find there. It's all a ruin now, the famous Bower and all.'

I promised to remember her to the Harvey-Beaumonts 'over the water', and we set off once more, along a road that ran beside a demesne wall. A large iron gateway sagged permanently open, beside a lodge house and a cattle grid. Beyond the grid, the grounds had become pastureland, the curving driveway a tractor-rutted swamp.

'You wait here, while I pay my respects to my friend's house,' I told the driver, and galloped in.

Nervously, I edged past the lodge house, which had been flashily restored, and was evidently lived in. No one stopped me, so I followed the edge of the path round to the house. A most curious maze of ruined stone walls covered in ivy emerged from a mass of brambles. I went over to have a look, but found the jungle impenetrable. Artificial ruins had now become real, and secular grottos and Gothic-whimsy hermitages were impossible to distinguish from caved-in summer houses and heaps of fallen masonry 'mid the briars. This was the site of Fair Rosamund's Bower, once a rose garden, Japanese garden, maze, hermitage and Folly, a trysting place for young people who thought the days of dancing and fox-hunting would never end.

A small roofless house nearby now played host to a large tree growing out of the middle of the floor. Another tree, recently felled, lay by its side. I returned to the tractor-path and in a few moments saw Holford House standing before me on a rise. Grooves in the pastureland showed where the drive had swung round to the front door. The tractor ruts led straight on to a farm gate.

Abandoned in 1947, when barely a hundred years old, the mansion still looked imposing in its new guise of romantic ruin. Holford House now had a knobbly look, the immense chimneys standing inside roofless walls, covered in thick blankets of ivy. The stonework was pale orange in colour, and jutted out in ridges and patterns around the empty frames of doors and windows. Wide-eyed in reproach, those windows must once have been the glory of Holford.

Heart filled with pathos, I slipped through one of the windows, and stepped gingerly around the saplings and splintered tiles, afraid I might crash into the cellar.

Ivy grew around the columns left between doorways and windows, and turned them into foliated columns. These were twisting, turning ivy trees, with thick trunks. New windows with odd shapes had been created in draping curtains and walls of ivy. A ceiling and first floor had vanished except for lines of ledges along the wall. Bushes grew in the arched front doorway, and a wintry wind whistled round the peaks of the Blue Stack Mountains and the chimneys of Holford House. Stepping over a ridge along the floor, I found myself beside an immense open fireplace, all trace of grate and mantelpiece removed. A window-hole looked out on flooded pastureland below, a ruined stable, a kitchen garden that now contained a newly built bungalow, and a working farmyard with a tractor and cows. The former stewards, the Mulverins, were obviously in residence.

Crossing the humpy floor, I looked out of a doorless doorway and saw, half hidden in the grass, the red tiles of the porch where the young Harvey-Beaumonts had sat, celebrating St George's Day by tapping their feet to the brassy music of the band of the Black and Tans. No wicker chairs could be seen there now, only a rusty harrow baring its teeth in the long grass like a man-trap. Names of infant Mulverins had recently been scratched on to the wall. To give the children a surprise on their next visit, I took a small toy lion from my plastic carrier bag and pressed it into a hole in the edge of the doorway. Then I hurried back to the taxi. So that was the last roar of the English lion at Holford House.

To my consternation, I found the taxi was empty. Looking round, I found the farm entrance, where my driver and young Mulverin the farmer both greeted me cheerfully. A jovial, curly-headed man, Mulverin was squelching around in a muddy yard outside the cowshed, mucking out with a spade. Friesian cattle snorted and frothed behind a railing.

'Me mother said one o' the Harvey-Beaumonts came back not long ago, and prised the name of a horse long-dead from the top o' the stable door!' he bellowed. 'I'm sorry the house is so spoiled! It's the rates what did it!'

'Yes , the rates! More than a pity!' my driver agreed. A light rain began to fall, so with a wave to Mulverin, we were off.

When we neared the outskirts of Donegal Town, the driver told me that the former maid suspected young Mulverin of pillaging the Big House for building material.

'What's more, she said it was haunted after the living members o' the family moved out in 1947,' he added. 'George Mulverin had to get the Jesuits in to exorcise the house.'

Musing on all I had seen, I hummed an old Eileen Donaghue song, 'The Homes of Donegal'. Seeing the look of pain on my driver's face, I asked him what had become of Eileen, 'The Girl from County Donegal', possessor of one of the purest ballad voices I know, with a hint of Irish mischief.

'Eileen, is it? I'm thinking she should o' been called the Girl from County Tyrone, as that's where she's from in reality. Her son plays football for Tyrone. Bridie Gallagher, now she's a Donegal singer.'

'Yes, I like her, too. Remember "Home to Mayo"? What about Bluestack Bill?'

'Bluestack Bill!' He began to laugh. 'He's one o' the singers who work for Radio Glencoe right here in town. That's our very own pirate radio. Do you want me to take you there? They'll be going on the air, soon.'

'Have they got a secret hideout?' I asked.

'No, they're in a room behind the cinema,' he said, pulling up and showing me a light in a doorway, up some steps. 'Everyone knows where they are. If you want to know about Donegal music, they're the boys to tell you.'

Thanking the kindly driver, I knocked at the door of Radio Glencoe. A Reception lady showed me into a tiny broadcasting room full of switched-off microphones. There I met Peter Cannon, the youthful Pirate King. He was a friendly, freckled young man of eighteen, with shoulder-length hair. Peter shared the dingy three-room studio with sixteen other disc-jockeys, working in shifts.

'The music we play is country and Irish,' he told me. 'We can be heard all over Donegal and Northern Ireland, and now we're getting fan letters from the west coast of Scotland. All pirate stations, such as ours, have to close at the end of December. After that we can apply for a licence and hope they let us "go legal".'

'Why are you called after Glencoe, a horrible place in Scotland?'

'Well, we originally started at a place outside o' town, called Glencogh. It somehow got turned to Glencoe. During the week, I work in a music shop, and my ambition is to be a professional guitarist. We promote local artists – there are some of their pictures.'

'Do musicians ever play here in the studio?' I asked.

'Yes, when we have a traditional music show, that's all-Irish, they bring the instruments in here. That corner's reserved for accordion players. Here's one of our most popular singers – Bluestack Bill. He's named after the Blue Stack Mountains outside town.'

He pressed a button, and I heard B. B. singing in a voice midway between high-pitched Irish balladeering and smooth country and western crooning, able to leap in two directions. He played sweet hillbilly guitar and sang lilting modern Irish ballads such as 'Summertime in Ireland' and 'At Home in Old Kilcar'.

'Kilcar's a little town further west along the coast,' Peter Cannon explained.

'Last question coming up – what are your hopes for the future at Radio Glencoe? All this is going in a book.'

'Well, we'd like more adverts, so we can make more money and expand a bit. Can't you think of anything else to ask me?' he appealed.

'No,' I confessed, so we parted, and I wandered out into the night humming 'Summertime in Ireland'.

CHAPTER TWENTY

☘

Enniskillen Interlude

On Monday morning, I stood in a queue at the Diamond, and waited for the Dublin coach. It came at last, a huge long-distance coach, with high steps in the doorway. Soon we were off, heading south on the coastal Sligo Road. When we crossed the River Erne, at Ballyshannon, we turned inland, driving between hilly green fields and wet woodland, near the banks of the river. There was a long halt, as a traffic jam piled up ahead.

I thought no more of it, and stared vacantly into space, wishing that the weather would improve so that I could have a better look at the scenery. All at once, I sat up as if electrified, for we had driven into a large corrugated iron compound, and there were British soldiers everywhere! I remembered such clearing-compounds from my 1982 trip around Northern Ireland. We were at the Border, about to cut across County Fermanagh in British Northern Ireland, the better to get to Dublin on time. No one else on the coach seemed surprised.

A tall muscular Lance-Corporal (I think) in a red beret and camouflage suit stepped into the doorway of the coach, gave us all a knowing look, and stepped out and nodded us through the outer gate. How my heart leaped to see a red pillar box once more, on the other side of the compound! I was now back in Britain, in the official as well as the geographical sense. Donegal post office had a 'suggestions' service, and I had suggested that all Irish pillar boxes be repainted red once more, instead of bureaucratic green. Doubtless the authorities would not heed my plea, but here in County Fermanagh I could feast my eyes on red pillar boxes to my heart's content.

Our whole zig-zag through Northern Ireland followed the

western shores of Lough Erne, Ireland's inland sea. There was Boa Island, of the baleful idols, for we were staying on the inward side of Ulster's wall, the Dartry Mountains and the great haunted head of Benbulbin. The lake grew narrow and we were at Enniskillen, where once I had spent many happy days at the Railway Hotel and Irish musical nights at the Cove Bar. How strange again to see the grey château-like castle overlooking Lough Erne, and to recall a boat ride to a ruined monastery on one of the thousand islands! We waited a long time at Enniskillen, an RAF helicopter buzzing above the castle. I caught a soldier's harassed glance, and suddenly remembered a modern Ulster saying: 'There were more helicopters than at Crossmaglen.' (Crossmaglen is a rebel-held town in County Armagh, only nominally a part of Britain. As the entry roads to Crossmaglen are often mined, soldiers go in and out by helicopter.)

Northern Ireland is a very interesting part of the world. Although the shops are richly stocked compared to those of the Republic, Northern Ireland may bear a slight resemblance to a Communist country. People cannot openly speak their minds or be quite at ease, in case they are being spied on – *not* by the KGB or the government, but by 'patriot' or 'loyalist' terrorists.

I remembered buying an 'Orange' Protestant newspaper in Enniskillen and reading the editor's lament that no English literary type had a good word to say about Presbyterian loyalists. As I know that many Presbyterian loyalists are decent, courageous Christian men and women, I wrote to the editor and begged to be excused from his dictum. Then I ran into a snag – the newspaper had no printed address. So I took my letter, sealed in an envelope, back to the newsagent.

'The man that makes the paper just brings it in, on foot,' the newsagent said, beginning to sweat.

'Well, when he comes in, could you give him this envelope?' I asked.

To my surprise, the newsagent seemed too afraid to speak, shaking, sweating and holding his palms up in refusal of my letter. He was a big man, twice my size. Patiently I told him what was in the envelope, bending it to and fro to show that it wouldn't explode. In the end he reluctantly took the letter, though I don't know what happened to it.

In my blunderings around Enniskillen, I may have inadvertently done some harm, as foreigners do in Communist lands by innocently befriending natives who are then shadowed by the secret police and later imprisoned or shot. I had contacts in Enniskillen through Ulstermen met in England. Following these up, I went into a chemist's shop, introduced myself to the tall lady assistant and said that I was a friend of her future husband's brother. She, a Catholic, was about to marry a Protestant policeman, a 'mixed marriage'. When I congratulated the poor girl, she almost fainted. Later I learned that the wedding had nearly been postponed, as the two families thought I might have been a terrorist uttering a veiled warning against the nuptials.

Still, I had happier memories of Enniskillen: of the Horseshoe Lounge in the Railway Hotel (now an hotel without a railway) and a group named 'Country Comrades', who played Irish, Scottish and hillbilly tunes fast and slow, while the crowd whooped and danced merrily; of hillside fields and haycocks; of the Bronze Age burial chamber said to be a giant's grave; and of tales of the local footpack's exploits among the Ulster foxes. I befriended a family named Armstrong, who told me that their ancestors had been deported to Northern Ireland from the Scottish borders in 1610. Certainly the Armstrongs had been famous Border Reivers, or cattle rustlers, in the Debatable Land of Border Ballads and Sir Walter Scott's romances. The Fermanagh Armstrongs seemed peaceable enough. Some Reiver families went further afield, to America's Wild West, where their cattle-rustling instincts were once more allowed full rein.

Ulster Protestants have much in common with their close relatives, American cowboys and hillbillies. Like Southern Baptists of Tennessee, many Northern Irish Presbyterians believe that the wine enjoyed by Jesus and His disciples must have been grape juice, since Christians do not drink alcohol. Consequently, some Northern Irish restaurants serve bottled unfermented grape juice in place of wine. 'Orange songs', a body of fine traditional music ignored by left-wing folklorists, usually celebrate Protestant victories of the seventeenth century. Hotheaded youths often sing them in order to provoke Catholics and start a fight. It is as if cowboys besieged in forts on the Western plains were to compose endless anti-Apache ballads to Irish-Scottish traditional tunes. In England, football hooligans have learned Orange songs, and are adapting them to their own purposes.

My Enniskillen reverie came to an end as we moved out of that city at last, and continued southward beside the great lough. Below

Enniskillen, the lough kept appearing and reappearing, interrupted by birch woodlands. A map of Lough Erne resembles a giant spoonful of quicksilver emptied over Ireland to form and re-form in myriad fluid blobs.

Near Belturbet, we reached the Border once more, and drove into a small enclave. A tiny fair-haired boy in army uniform walked jauntily up and down the bus with an air of chirpy innocence, holding a gun nearly as big as himself. I suppose the lad may have been fifteen, sixteen or seventeen years old. Everyone looked surprised. A moment later we entered the Republic and County Cavan.

Between Belturbet and Cavan Town (where I had been before), Lough Erne fragmented into a series of lakes, with strange names such as Lough Parisee. We crossed the River Annalee at Butler's Bridge, then stopped a while at Cavan, before continuing south-east to Kells, on the River Blackwater, where monks had once preserved the sacred Book. I chatted to a Dublin-bound nurse in the seat beside me, and looked out as lakes, rivers and deeply-furrowed potato patches flashed by.

'Navan!' called the driver, and I jumped up and reached for my bag.

CHAPTER TWENTY-ONE

Working in Navan

As I struggled with my heavy bag at Navan, a strong old man ran to help me. We wobbled down the road holding a handle apiece. A few readers may remember that I had long ago arranged to spend two days drawing cartoons for children in the Navan shopping centre. That was the reason why I had left the Dublin coach in County Meath, before reaching the city. Now I had to reach the shopping centre and meet Ray Coary the manager, who would find me accommodation.

'Why are there Irish flags everywhere?' I asked my kind helper.

'There's been a Gaelic football game. Now, you go through that gap an' you'll see the centre, so.'

Navan consisted of an attractive brick-and-tile shopping street, with a four-pronged C. of I. church that nobody used and a bridge over a river. In short, it was Every Irish Town. However, as I could now see, a vast area behind the shops had been cleared of housing and turned into an enormous shopping centre. Two rival supermarkets faced one another across a tarmacked acreage of car park. Behind the furthest supermarket stood the gigantic glittering indoor shopping centre where I was about to work. In a sense, this huge construction had made the whole of Old Navan redundant, a quaint fringe on the edge of Shopping-Centre Land.

The old man went on his way, and I put my bag on a supermarket trolley and wheeled it off to look for Mr Coary. In the entrance of the shopping centre, I stopped to examine a taxidermist's display. A big brown otter, cleverly mounted, looked up at me with bright eyes. (In England, taxidermy is considered a Victorian vice.) Tropical plants with bright leaves and flowers made a colourful display, and the whole shopping centre was luxurious in the extreme, stuffed with goods and shoppers. I met Mr Coary and Mr Rafter of the sewing-machine shop, and once the back-slapping was over, I set off in the manager's car for my new lodgings.

We drove out of town on the Dublin road, then swung up a lane, beside a Round Tower and monastic ruin. Soon we arrived at Tower House, a suburban-style dwelling with a large front garden. I felt like an invited rather than a paying guest, as I shook hands with Mr and Mrs Noone. Mrs N. was a brisk youngish lady in a green track suit, and her husband was a detective in the Garda, a big gentle friendly man. I was shown to my room, which had a view of the back garden and the Noones' paddock, where three sheep were grazing as the sun went down.

'We hope for more sheep before long,' Mrs Noone said.

Once I had unpacked, I set off down the lane to have a look at the Round Tower before dark. Glancing up, I saw a beautiful yellow bird perched on a telegraph wire, looking like a prize long-tailed canary. It was a yellow wagtail, seen from below, where its colours are finest. After admiring the wagtail for a while, I went on until at last I reached the Round Tower.

All that was left of the monastery founded by St Patrick was a large stone Gothic doorway standing up on its own surrounded by grass and modern graves. Donaghmore Tower, with a dark entrance halfway up, stood undamaged, pointing silently to the Heavens whence cometh our help. Both looked eerie in the twilight. I rejoined the lane, and walked back a little way towards Navan.

Near a tombstone-memorial by the wayside, I gazed on a crowd of boys. They were busily heaving full potato sacks on to the back of a lorry parked in a field of stubble, beneath a bright half-moon. Rows of sacks stood like dark harvest sheaves. I am no farmer, or perhaps I could understand how wheat and potatoes can be grown at the same time in Ireland.

Back at the Noones', I enjoyed a snack in the front room, in the company of the good-looking teenage Noones, curly-headed Martin (or 'Murt') and his pink-cheeked sister, a wholesome girl who played guitar at the Folk Mass. 'I want to be a fighter pilot when I leave school,' said fourteen-year-old Martin.

'Are you going to England, then, to join the RAF?'

'No, I doubt if I could pass the exams.'

So saying, he slotted a video into the telly and began to watch old films of air fights in the Great War. After a while, he took out one of his father's old police notebooks and started to draw aeroplanes. Taking this as my cue, I produced my own drawing pad and began to draw google-eyed rabbits and donkeys, with great speed. This endeared me to the young Noones.

'Do many cartoonists stay here?' I asked Martin.

'No, you're the first one. Usually we just have salesmen.'

With a groan, he took out his homework, which consisted of French and Irish.

'We're lucky in England, as we don't have to learn Irish,' I said.

'You are that, so!' he answered with feeling.

Bright and early next morning, I set off down the lane to work, my drawing pad and pens in my jauntily swinging plastic bag. It's not often that someone can get paid for doing what they enjoy most. Fiery gold and orange trees shed leaves which drifted down before a bright blue sky. At breakfast, I had been given freshly home-made bread, and I felt at peace with the world.

Soon I reached the tombstone-memorial, possibly that of a person killed on that stretch of road. Below the name and date of demise, the following lines had been engraved.

> Well, he's walking through the clouds with a circus mind that's running wild.
> Butterflies and zebras and moonbeams and fairy tales.

If anyone puts a verse like that on my headstone, I'm warning them right now that I'll get up and haunt them for ever. I mean, why zebras?

Before long, the fields ended and Navan began. I hurried down steep Flower Hill, a flowerless road of grey terraced houses and shops that led down to the bridge and the weir. For a time I leaned on a rail and watched the rushing waters where the rivers Boyne and Blackwater combine. I had met both rivers previously on my travels, and felt glad to be present at their marriage.

In the shopping centre, I was gratified to see my name up on the Day's Attractions board, and I sat down at a prepared place by the side of the stage. Goods of every kind were piled around me, waiting to be raffled – giant toy animals, television sets and a stuffed pheasant donated by the taxidermist. Shoppers were already milling around, for the centre opened at nine in the morning and closed at nine at night, when late shoppers had to be shooed out like errant sheep. Mr Coary gave me some enormous sheets of paper and I began to draw.

As a small boy, I devised my own set of cartoon animals, and they now stood me in good stead. So I drew them one by one – Skippetty Rabbit, his wife Gillian, Brownie the Bear, Prowler the Wolf, Fido the Pup, Sly Fox, Piney Cone the Pine Marten, Longtail and Short Tail the Mice, and Bill Mouse with his wife Sue. Other characters – swordfish, manatees, king penguins and Canada geese – had no names that I could remember.

When I was twelve, a boy at school had asked me, 'Are you one of those people who can turn scribbly lines into pictures?'

'I don't know. Try me,' I said, and I found that I was.

Although my efforts would make Mr Walt Disney cringe, they were popular enough with the children of Navan, and I was soon handing out picture after picture – all free, courtesy of Navan shopping centre. My meals came free also, at the nearby cafeteria, and I had an hour off to walk around the town.

All morning, as I drew, musicians played behind me.

'These are all local bands,' Mr Coary said casually.

Although the music of south-east and middle Ireland lacks the depth of music in the magic west, being somewhat derivative, it is still far better than most Irish pub music heard in England. It was hard to concentrate on google-eyed creatures when musicians were animatedly sawing fiddles, caressing accordions, flailing guitars and blowing down flutes.

Mr Rafter looked over my shoulder while I drew a request item for a small boy – a picture of a witch jumping over a bonfire. He returned with a Man from Mullingar, a newsagent who wanted a Halloween witch to hang up in his shop. I obliged with iron-toothed Baba Yaga, and the newsagent asked how much he should pay me.

'See Mr Rafter – he's my agent,' I said loftily.

He took the witch and left. I later learned that he hadn't seen Mr Rafter at all, but had hot-footed it back to Mullingar.

Over a hasty meal, I glanced at the *Official Guide to County Meath*, a gift from the manager. A chapter on famous people, I was amused to see, devoted only a paragraph each to renowned saints, scholars and patriots, but devoted nearly a whole page to Collier the Robber (1780–1849), a noted highwayman. Some of his exploits read like folk tales. Apparently, like Robin Hood, Jesse James and legendary robbers of every land, he had met a weeping widow who faced eviction. 'Collier gave her the necessary sum, and when she had received a receipt of payment from the agent, he duly robbed the agent of the money . . .' Michael Collier's mistake was to have survived into prosaic Victorian times, whereupon he was arrested and sent to Australia.

Closing the book, I went back to my cartooning stool, where a small circle of children awaited me. Parents were parking children next to the cartoons and musicians, and going about their shopping. A snag soon became apparent. All the children wanted pictures of Mickey Mouse. Nothing else would do, all other mice were imposters.

Now Mickey Mouse is Walt Disney's creation. I can't draw in other people's styles, and I turned out particularly inane Mickey Mice. He is not one of my favourite Disney characters, and I soon grew thoroughly sick of him. I punished him in every way I could think of – I married him to Minnie, gave him children, got him bitten by a vampire so that he grew fangs and finally had him turned into a rat by a wicked witch, a great improvement. Still the customers called for Mickey Mouse (with the blessed exception of mischievous tinker children who asked for horses and donkeys). All that day and all the next day, I was doomed to draw Mickey Mouse again and again. So my job did turn out to be work after all. If only they had asked for Donald Duck, a character I hold in great respect!

Some children came back repeatedly. My favourite of these was a boy of ten or so, called Clint, with a black greasy quiff of hair. He had great force of character, and had become a legend in his own lifetime. Long before he appeared I had heard children saying 'Clint' this, and 'Clint' that.

'I don't care about a queue, I just want a picture!' he announced himself, throwing other boys out of the way impatiently. When he received a Mickey Mouse, he swelled triumphantly, and asked for another. I duly and mechanically began another Mickey, and Clint seemed hardly able to believe his luck.

Ages later I saw him listening to the band and clutching his fistful of Mickeys. Needing fresh air, I strolled out into the town.

In a corner of the car park, against a wall, a foreign-looking man exhibited clumsy oil paintings on pieces of wood and played a banjo, his hat on the ground. 'We're in the same business,' I said, and told him about my Mickey Mouse job. His pictures had price tags.

'I am a Belgian,' the shabby middle-aged man told me. 'First I stay in hotel at Paddington, London; now I stay here at Navan.

No, I do not sing. I let my banjo do the singing.'

I felt the pathos of this remark, as all he could do on the banjo was strum 'plunk plunk plunk' over and over again.

After an invigorating gaze at the rushing rivers, I returned to the Mickey Mice. Business was brisker than ever. During a pause between Mice, I noticed a poorly-dressed woman pick up a twenty-pound note in surprise. Anxiously, she handed it in, her face full of pity for the loser. As closing time drew near, the children grew less. Lounging teenagers appeared, using the centre as a rendezvous. *They* all wanted pictures of Mickey Mouse, too! The customer is always right, so I obliged.

Eventually I was driven back to the Noones' house by a blue-clad security man.

News travels fast in Navan, and next day there were twice as many children as before, all demanding Mickey Mouse. As nearly all the children had freckles, I felt as if I were seeing spots before my eyes, and drew Mickey Mice in a trance, my hand and pen moving mechanically through a misty ocean of freckles, wave upon wave, every freckle asking for Mickey Mouse.

At interludes, visitors from my past came in to see me: Mr Rafter and his son Dermot, the Belgian artist, who wished me 'Happy drawing!', and black-quiffed Clint, who eagerly dragged his whole family along. They didn't know what he was so excited about, and his father was disgusted to find that I couldn't draw a footballer (an unKerridgean species). Martin, the Noone boy, also looked in. These kind visitors received animals that were not Mickey Mouse. Apparently, a day or so before my arrival, the children of Navan had been entertained at the centre by a man dressed-up as Mickey Mouse.

At some time during my second afternoon at the centre, a Bonny Baby competition was held, but I missed it all in a blur of Mickeys. One event, however, made my day. Two old countrymen, oblivious of my pack of children, began a friendly argument, raising their voices and ending each sentence with 'Begor!' an abbreviation of 'By God'. Finally one of them clearly pronounced, 'It is that, so! Begorrah!'

It had happened. I had heard an Irishman say 'Begorrah' and now I could die happy.

In England the stage country yokel accent, as mimicked by Londoners for over two hundred years, comes from Buckinghamshire, just outside London. So in Ireland, the stage country Irish accent, full of 'begorrahs', must come from County Meath just outside Dublin.

When the shopping centre was locked up that night, Ray Coary the manager praised my work, and tried to press an envelope on me. Eventually I gave in and accepted it. It was the kind of envelope that crackled. Since he had paid for my food and lodgings, this was an additional kindness I had not expected.

As he lived in the city, Mr Coary drove me up to the Noones' for my bag and then took me all the way back to O'Brien's Hotel in Dublin, where I had stayed long before. Fireworks were going off in the city, in advance of Halloween. There is no Guy Fawkes' Night in the Irish Republic.

It was good to be in O'Brien's Hotel, and to meet the proprietor Maureen O'Sullivan, her tall soft-spoken brother and their Kerry Blue terrier once more. Soon I was in my old room, with its creaky Victorian furniture, looking out of the tall window at the Dublin traffic. I could hardly wait to explore the city once more.

CHAPTER TWENTY-TWO

☘

In Dublin's Quare City

Glad to be in Dublin once more, I roamed around the shops, noticing that many bakers had 'Brack Loaves' on display, with rings placed on them. The loaves resembled barm cakes, and the rings looked like wedding rings. One shop advertised a gold ring inside one of each batch of Brack Loaves. After the shop girl stopped giggling at my enquiry, she explained, handkerchief on mouth, that Brack Loaves with rings inside are a Halloween tradition. She had not realized that everyone in the world does not celebrate an Irish Halloween.

In Perth, Scotland, I have tasted Halloween Buns, which have smiling faces, made of eating-paper, stuck to them. Bakers in England content themselves with Hot Cross Buns at Easter.

Still reflecting on buns, my favourite food, I called a taxi and in lordly tones asked to be taken to Lansdowne Road, home of *Jazz News* magazine. The editor had kindly accepted an article I had written about West Indian gospel music, so I thought I would go to the head office and introduce myself. A sudden cloudburst set the taxi windscreen wipers to work. Meanwhile, the driver, a great newspaper-reader, spoke to me in headlines.

'What Are the Royals Up To Now?' changed abruptly to 'Will Soccer Violence Spread to Gaelic Football?' as he turned a mental page. At Lansdowne Road, I struggled through blinding rain to the *Jazz News* office, the basement of a big house with a garden.

'Pleased to meet you – we're not taking your piece after all,' a lady sub-editor smiled, trying to put me at my ease. 'The editor thought it was now a bit out of date.'

Stunned, I wobbled outside, where fortunately I found that the rain had stopped falling. It was a blow, but I would survive it. In a mood of bitter-sweet melancholy, I walked back to the centre of Dublin. It was an interesting walk, past once-grand Victorian houses divided into flats, past ruined buildings with caved-in roofs, past grey monumental 'British rule' edifices now put to various purposes and past modern office blocks that had already become decrepit.

Pavements gleamed, as I walked towards the sunset, along a narrow street of dark, shabby houses. Lights began to go on in the dark houses, and I relished my melancholy to the last drop. I felt like Max Zillion, a cartoon strip character devised by Hunt Emerson. Max is a jazz musician, a black cat with Negro features, who owns a talking saxophone, his Alto Ego. Although Max is a jazz genius, fame always eludes him, he always loses his fee and ends each episode walking down a lonely street into the sunset, consoled by his friend Alto Ego who loudly plays a mournful tune. I knew exactly how Max felt.

(There is a happy ending to this tale of woe, as shortly afterwards *Jazz News* accepted another article I wrote, this time about blues.)

Cheered up by a Chinese meal, I walked along Wellington Quay by the side of the River Liffey. The Ha'penny Bridge had been illuminated, and shone green in the darkness, rocking whenever a group of people crossed over. I was in the Bohemian quarter, where cobbled alleys full of bars and bookshops met the quayside. Next day, I promised myself, I would come back and explore these streets by daylight. Lights still burned in the musty old Marxist–Leninist bookshop, with its icons to Stalin on the wall. Inside, the elderly English upper-class proprietor told me that true Communism only survives in Albania. Who wants true Communism anyway? Not the Albanians, I'm sure.

All of a sudden, I found myself in a festive gathering, as I had absent-mindedly gatecrashed an exhibition launch at the Gallery of Photography. Wriggling through the crowds, I sidled around the walls, admiring black and white photographs of old men in cloth caps playing fiddles, while children looked on wonderingly. These pictures had been reprinted as a book, *A Time that Was*. Somewhere in the smoky crowd the authoress and photographer, Jill Freedman from New York, was holding court. I didn't meet Miss Freedman, but I read a statement she had typed out.

> I sing of simple pleasures: making music, dancing, friendship, work and fun. Young and old sharing their lives the way they

always had, before television shrunk the world ... It is an older, gentler Ireland I am documenting ... I want to get it down now, while there are still people who remember a time that was.

A worthy aim, well achieved by the camera. She did not sing at all, as it happened, but there were plenty of singers there. Intellectual Dublin seemed no longer to consist of writers, but of folk singers, bearded or otherwise. Faces aflame with drink, grotesque moustaches, pot bellies ... I seemed to have stumbled into a painting by Hogarth. One of the pot bellies was mine. Liam Clancy, a fellow Hogarthian, told me that he was one of the Clancy brothers, a group which has found success in New York with its romanticized versions of Irish songs. Liam sprang on to a table, raised a glass and began to declaim a speech. Now was the moment for Jill Freedman to take a photograph, for he made a picturesque sight – a tall slender man in blue denim, with a new white cap and a bright pink face.

Much later, I arrived back at O'Brien's Hotel, carefully avoiding a straggling pack of wild young boys, who seemed about to fight among themselves.

It was a grey, wet Sunday morning when next I walked through deserted streets to the River Liffey. At Crown Alley, beneath the archway facing the Ha'penny Bridge, a tinker lady was begging as usual, her baby peeping from a plaid shawl. In pensive mood, I explored the Liffeyside Bohemia, stepping carefully around puddles and over cobbles, past closed bookshops and open recording studios. A corner pub, the Norseman, had been packed with arty young people on the Saturday night. A clumsy mural of a Viking adorned one of the windows, the bright colours looking strange in the surrounding drabness.

I rambled around Temple Bar, Temple Lane, then into Eustace Street; dark, narrow thoroughfares of some antiquity. Record studios outnumbered bookshops, and the atmosphere was Liverpudlian. Dublin is in great danger of acquiring a world famous Beat Scene, the Liffeyside Sound. (Let us pray that this fate may be averted.)

Temple Lane Studios, Roadshow Rentals and several other music factories seemed open for business. I entered a studio at random, and spoke to a young man behind a battered desk. The hallway was sleazy in the extreme, plaster falling from those portions of walls that did not have posters holding them together.

'English groups are coming here to make records – they say the Liffeyside rocks!' the young man told me enthusiastically.

He was of Italian stock, as was the proprietor of a blues recording studio I had met in the Deep South of America. Blues singers do well in Ireland, as Celts have a feeling for Negro music. Against my better judgment, I asked the record man if he were able to bring impoverished blues singers over to Ireland. He was all for the idea, and we exchanged addresses. Then I saw a gaggle of youths arriving with guitar cases for a recording session, and I changed my mind. The faces grinning from the tatty punk regalia looked so depraved and hollow-eyed that I could not bear to think of my American blues friends calling them 'sir'. So I strewed the pieces of the Italian's card over the cobblestones.

Blues-lovers such as myself face a dilemma. Should we help blues singers to find a wider audience, outside the coloured quarters of Southern towns, or should we leave them where they are, that the blues may thrive? Each singer who gets rich, learns to play for white people and then settles in Paris, is a loss to the blues. Cut off from his inspiration, he endlessly rehashes songs from his American era. On the other hand, he at last gains well-deserved riches and a life of comfort.

Just as I was about to pick up the pieces of card once more, I stopped transfixed. A glorious Irish voice rang out in song, a manly tenor that equalled the most impassioned of blues. I ran across the road to the open door of another tiny studio, and saw a grizzle-bearded hobo-like man singing into a microphone, his mouth wide open and his eyes half closed. As he sang, he strummed a guitar.

> Oh, Mary of my heart's delight,
> My pride and only care,
> It was your cruel father
> Would not let me stay here . . .

I sidled into the room, scarcely daring to breathe lest I harm the recording. A shiver ran up my spine and into my scalp, as I realized he was singing 'Mary from Dunloe'. This old ballad contains lines that may have inspired a blue-grass ditty of the Kentucky mountains, 'Roll in My Sweet Baby's Arms'. To my surprise, the singer gave me a friendly nod before throwing his head back and tackling the last verses.

I wish I was in sweet Dunloe
And seated on the grass,
And by my side a bottle of wine
And on my knee a lass.

I'd call for liquor of the best
And I'd pay before I go;
I'd roll my Mary in my arms
In the town of sweet Dunloe.

'You needn't keep so quiet, I'm only testing the microphone, not recording at all,' the singer told me with a smile. Watched by an Italianate studio owner, Tony Verrechia, he told me his story.

'My name's Allan Scuffle, and I've been a full-time singer for only four years. If you'd seen me five or six years ago, you wouldn't recognize me now. Most of my adult life I've been a salesman over in England. I've been a life insurance salesman and I was in the deep freeze business for ages. In those days I wore suits, and I was very clean-cut.

'More and more, as years went by, I began to frequent Irish singing pubs, until I was totally immersed in the music. I gave up work so I could practise singing and playing, and went on the dole in England. At first I played the bodhran drum [he pronounced it 'bowran'] and then I took up the guitar. I'm totally left-handed, but eventually I learned the bottleneck style used by blues singers. Back in Dublin, I sang and played in pubs, living for music day and night. At one time I was in a group called "Skin the Goat".'

'Oh, after the cab driver in Phoenix Park!'

'You know your history!' he complimented me.

'It's not mine, it's yours. Well, go on.'

'With practice, my style developed, and there's stacks of work for me now. I've been busking round the bars of Torremolinos in Spain, and at Tenerife, in the Canary Islands. I spent three months in the Canaries, and since then I've been travelling between England and Ireland. Slattery's the travel people, have given me an open ticket, so I can cross the water any day I feel like. I've never made any records yet.'

'I hope you'll be famous one day, as you deserve to be, with that voice,' I said. 'Then I can say, "I knew him when..."'

Allan Scuffle (or scuffling Allan) gave me a frank grin and handshake, and I wandered back down to the Liffey. Just like

Michael Quirke, the butcher turned god-carver, he had totally changed his life from Commerce to Art, in middle age. I was reminded of Kipling's story, *The Miracle of Purun Bhagat*, a tale of a Western-dressed Indian statesman who suddenly becomes a hermit and holy man, living on a mountain, at one with nature. Dublin's brand of rock music merges at times with traditional music, and the studios are used for both styles. So perhaps they have their uses.

At the great Adam, Eve and Immaculate Conception church near the river, I stood with others in the marble hallway and listened to beautiful female solos soaring praises up to Heaven. A monk in brown robes sold religious Christmas cards. Wandering on, I found myself among dreary council flats, improved by a figure of Joseph holding the Baby high on a wall. Although the flats looked poor outside, I glimpsed some well-furnished interiors.

Masses were ending everywhere in Dublin, and I walked back to my hotel through streams of home-going worshippers. The great bells of the Immaculate Conception chimed the hour.

Before leaving Dublin, I decided I ought to see something of County Louth. This uneasy county lies north of Dublin and south of the Border. Like most Border counties in the Irish Republic, it has a name for harbouring gunmen. Louth's county town, Dundalk, is very near Belfast.

As I boarded the Belfast train, at Connolly Station, a guard stepped forward and ran a buzzing metal detector over my plastic bag. Finding the bag innocent of any crime, he waved us both on our way.

It was a beautiful journey, northward along the coast, past Dublin's harbour. Near Balbriggan, there was a wonderful view of sea and river. Thereafter, the coastal scenery reminded me increasingly of lowland Scotland, fields and hedges lying close to the shore.

Dundalk station, with its lovely garden, stood at the edge of town, close to the enormous Harp Lager brewery. I walked down to the town centre, which reminded me of an English country town, with shops of every kind. People smiled a lot and greeted one another. Although Dundalk is supposed to be a seaside town, I could find no trace of a harbour. Red-brick houses, in Belfast style, vied with grey stone dwellings. There was a large temple-like town hall, eclipsed by a gigantic white modern Tourist Information

Office with a mighty fountain playing in the triumphal forecourt. Inside, the usual bored girl presided over a collection of postcards and tea towels.

I wandered into the wholesale office of a big tobacco factory, and found myself in a dark panelled Victorian world of snuff counters, old polished scales for weighing out ounces of baccy and a snug with settle chairs. Pictures of eminent tobacconists graced the walls. Browsing on my way, I dipped into shop after little shop.

A record shop had a large display of 'Rebel Song' cassettes. However, in a nearby café the jukebox sang a peaceful song of a neighbouring town, 'The Village of Ardee'. Crude murals on a hoarding illustrated the legend of the hero Cuchulain, who killed a fearsome hound and then himself became known as the Hound of Ulster.

Away from the shops, the Roman Catholic church faced a wide tree-lined eighteenth-century street. A vast Gothic structure, with strange ornamental spirelets, the church dominated the town. Crossing mosaic floors, and pausing to admire stained glass windows, I reached a little shrine to St Bridget. Instead of candles, a panel of electric light bulbs awaited the saint of my choice. I put some money in the slot, pressed a button, and lit a bulb for St Bridget.

Outside the church, I found a taxi rank, jumped in a taxi and asked to be taken to the village that gave County Louth its name. Soon we were bowling along a narrow road, through a gentle countryside of green fields, with dim mountains in the far distance.

'Those mountains are in Ulster,' the driver told me. He was a middle-aged man named Gerry Matthews. 'The Border's only four miles away. We go up there to get cheap cigarettes, petrol and groceries.'

Gerry told me that he had once run a showband, and played bass guitar. 'Like all the showbands of the sixties and seventies, we had a trumpet, trombone, sax, guitar and drum line-up. The best time I had playing was in Africa, out in Zambia. We played for the British ambassador and some Irish teachers and workers who were out there. It was a St Patrick's Night dance. Would you believe it, the Africans there had formed a brass band and played all Irish tunes! They were fantastic! We had a really good time.

'Before the Vatican II reforms, there would be no dancing in Ireland over Lent. We'd go over to England then, to London and

Birmingham. I've only ever made one record, a Christmas song called "Tonight for Santa Claus". It's been out on a Christmas LP, among lots of other songs, every year for six years running. Yet I haven't heard a word from the record company, and haven't received a penny!'

Soon we were at the village of Louth, which Gerry pronounced 'Lowth'. Noticing a tiny oratory-style church standing alone in a muddy field, I went over to have a look, leaving Gerry in the car. Heifers ran out of my way, taking shelter behind a piece of wall and peering after me.

'St Mochta's House', a plaque on the church announced. 'Built in one night to give shelter to the saint, who died in AD 534. Rebuilt in twelfth century.'

Puzzled, I returned to my musical driver. He was talking earnestly to a road-sweeper, who was at work in front of some English-style cottages with flower gardens. A kind, gentle-looking man, the sweeper had wispy hair and soulfully expressive eyes. 'That was a monastery, where that field is now,' he told me. 'That little building you saw came about like this. One of the monks was a beer man, always on the beer, you know. He fell asleep on the grass outside one night. When he woke up in the morning, the building was raised over him! So he never suffered from cold or dampness. It was a miracle!'

The road-sweeper's eyes shone at the wonder of it all, and then he went on. 'It was a huge monastery in them days. You can see a piece of the walls still standing, just. The road I'm sweeping wasn't here then – it ran right over those fields instead.

'But if you're interested in the old days, you ought to ask the man who lives in the house over there. He's a TD (MP) and he's writing a *book* about Louth.'

After a long genial conversation between Gerry Matthews and the road-sweeper, we were on our way. Gerry offered to be my guide, and show me the sites of the county. The sweeper's story reminded me of a tale told at Ross Carbery, County Cork. St Fachtna, in the olden days, left his precious prayer book in the grass, where he had been sitting reading it. When he reached his church, he missed the prayer book, and hurried back. It began to rain, and his heart sank, for the book was a valuable one, laboriously copied out by inspired monks. In the field he found his prayer book, protected from the pouring rain by a dove that sat upon it with wings outspread.

Back at Louth, we found the TD to be out for the day, to my secret relief. I was afraid I might lose my train back to Dublin.

'I'll take you to Cuchulain's castle,' Gerry promised me. 'Cuchulain was big round here, not just in Ulster as some think. We all learned about him in school, how he was attacked by a savage hound and killed it by knocking a hurley ball slam into its mouth.'

Gerry pronounced the hero's name 'Cahoolin'. The Hound of Ulster is supposed to have lived at the beginning of the first century AD. Whether he really existed or not, he stands as a type of the most bloodthirsty and battle-frenzied of Celtic warriors. When the blood haze was on him, he could not stop killing and might turn on his friends once his enemies had been slaughtered. To prevent this, his friends would soothe him with music, cool water and adoring maidens until at last he would 'come to himself'. Stories of great battle frenzies once featured in legends told by Red Indians on the western plains. Cuchulain legends, written down by monks in the early Middle Ages, are full of taboos broken with dire results, totem animals and other Apache touches.

Once, when a messenger brought bad news to Cuchulain, the hero let him go in peace. Later, the hero's temper flared up, and he fired an arrow after the messenger, which killed the poor man from afar.

'So it was not altogether true that Cuchulain did not kill messengers,' a monk dutifully recorded. 'Sometimes he did so.'

Leaving the car, Gerry Matthews and I walked up a steep hill, past an eerie standing stone, and eventually reached a mound at the hilltop ringed by a deep moat. Mature beech trees were growing from the dry moat's bed. Evidently a medieval castle had been built on the site of an Iron Age fort. A stone tower remained, repaired by later comers, for forts can never be redundant in Ireland. Gerry Matthews took a deep breath, obviously imagining Cuchulain himself stalking down the steps of his tower, one hand on the war axe in his belt.

We retraced our steps to the car, and Gerry next drove me to a field near Dundalk where he said he could show me an altar used in the Penal Days. We squelched across the field, finally reaching the altar, a single slate slab mounted on stones, on the side of a bank overlooking a tangle of briars. A modern shelter had been raised over it, and the ground about the stone had been paved. Here the faithful had once met, safe (I hope) from prying Protestant eyes.

'That's a pool table,' Matthews cried. He examined it carefully. 'No, it's a snooker table,' he finally pronounced. 'Look, there's the holes where it was unscrewed before they brought it here for an altar. They often used slate table tops for snooker in the old days.'

In the town of Dundalk itself, Matthews pointed out a strange hill enclosed in a public park. 'That's called Ice Hill, and it's got tunnels in it,' he said. 'I used to play there as a boy, and people told us the tunnels went all the way to Cuchulain's castle. We would crawl into them. They were hollowed-out places, but always came to a dead end.'

'You were probably crawling into prehistoric graves,' I remarked. 'You ought to have been frightened. Maybe people later put ice in the tunnels, so it wouldn't melt.'

There was no more time for sight-seeing if I were to catch my train, but the helpful Matthews told me of martyr Sir Oliver Plunkett's head, preserved in a church at Drogheda. 'It's a skull really, but the saint's skin has never rotted away,' he informed me. 'Outside Dundalk here, there's a shrine to St Bridget where they hold Novenas. That's nine days of continuous Mass-going.'

'I'll see all that next time,' I promised, wishing him a hasty farewell and lolloping rapidly into the station.

Now it was dark, and the smell of lager hung heavily on the air. My Belfast–Dublin train soon came in, but no passengers were allowed to board it until the customs men had searched the carriages for contraband.

Came the sad morning when I had to say goodbye to the crimson walls, white statues, giant mirrors and piped music of O'Brien's Hotel. Dragging my red, white and blue bag, I stepped into a taxi bound for the Liverpool ferry at Dun Laoghaire (pronounced Dunleary), on the outskirts of Dublin.

We passed a pleasant seaside resort on the way to the harbour. According to the driver, it was to be redeveloped as an industrial site, despite protests. 'James Joyce the writer used to live here,' he added. 'Joyce wrote a lot about Dublin, but unfortunately never said anything nice.'

Staring straight ahead at the road before him, the driver went on talking, telling me of his boyhood ambition to be a footballer and of the Mafia-like behaviour of the modern IRA. As he spoke, his language grew rougher and rougher, as if a Jekyll and Hyde transformation were taking effect. When he turned towards me at

Dun Laoghaire, he looked the complete tearaway. I swear his nose hadn't been broken when I first stepped into the car!

There were not many passengers on the ferry – a handful of English and Irish, with one nun. I stood on the deck, watching the two spires of Dun Laoghaire receding into the distance. The Irish skyline grew thin, but the sea was lighter there. All around me the waves looked grey, but far away at Ireland the sea glowed an ethereal soft green, for it ringed a fairy island.

Sprawled on a chair in the lounge, trying to sleep, I thought of Ireland and its vanished Sovereignty. In the Celtic sense, Sovereignty means more than mere exercise of power. It is a mystic quality, a marriage to the land. There now seemed a gap, a missing dimension to Irish life. Everywhere an unspoken question seemed to hang heavily in the air: Would we have been better off without Home Rule?

I thought of the shoppers' day trips to Northern Ireland in search of cheap goods, and tried enumerating the benefits Ireland might receive from a Reunion with the rest of Britain. Marks and Spencer's, Sainsbury's, W. H. Smith's, Home Improvement Grants... Then I turned to the other side of the coin – the Civil War that might break out, even if Reunion were voted in by a majority and approved by the Dáil. Ideals can be stronger than economic interest. If Dublin were razed to the ground, what would it matter if some of the ashes belonged to Marks and Spencer?

From old Elizabethan days to New Elizabethan days, writing Constitutions for Ireland has been an English hobby. Every such Constitution has been ignored or resisted by the Irish, but still the English persist. I pondered and pondered. After a while, I remembered an article in the *Hot Press* magazine. With tongue in cheek, the writer had suggested that a deal be struck with Britain over the Six Counties in the North. With great fanfare, Britain would hand the Counties over to the Republic, and 'a little later, we quietly slip them Tipperary, Laois and Offaly. Think about it. We don't use Counties Tipperary, Laois and Offaly. They're just there.'

Pondering on, I wondered how Ireland could be prevented from copying every harmful change in English life as soon as it occurred. Why should the nonsensical Nationalization–Privatization ping-pong of English politics be copied in Ireland? Why decimalization? Could Ireland only be prevented from copying England by English rule, or could she somehow rediscover her pride, her lost Sovereignty?

My other idea for a healthy Ireland, an Irish king, had been proved yet another alien English notion, for pre-Ascendancy Ireland boasted not one but many kings. Not *one* Sovereignty has been lost, but a thousand. Yet Republics are deeply repugnant to me. A Parliament without a monarch is like a tail without a dog. Parliaments thrive best where they have not been created suddenly from scratch, but have evolved from a monarch's Council of Elders. In England, Wales and Scotland, most people love Royalty but hold elected politicians in scorn. Ireland has plenty of scorn for its leaders, but where is the love?

At this point I fell asleep. Suddenly I awoke, inspired, and jotted down a complete Constitution for Ireland. Here it is.

The Irish Monarchy must be restored, but on an Irish, not an English plan. A king would not be an hereditary monarch, but would be elected from a small cohort of princely and chiefly families, in the ancient Irish manner. (In the Kerridgean World Order, the Monarchist League, not the United Nations, would be the arbiter of world affairs.) Ireland's traditional Provinces, Connaught, Leinster, Munster and Ulster, would rise to their ancient pre-eminence. Each province would select a candidate for monarch, and then the four would-be monarchs would put their cases before the People of Ireland. How would monarchs be selected? I am not presumptuous – I would leave that to the People. Perhaps by tests of physical skill, at hurling, football or wrestling. In true Celtic fashion, physical strength and absence of blemish would be the qualification of a king. When the King of Ireland reached a certain age, he would have to step down and a new king be chosen. The King of Ireland would take over the ceremonial duties of the Irish President, who is now nominally set over the Irish Prime Minister. The office of President would be gradually phased out.

You can imagine the intrigue, the excitement and gossip that would accompany the selection of a king! Such selections, at provincial level, might be going on most of the time, the cause of much happiness, honest pride and scheming malice! Ireland would be given something new to think about. For the first time in centuries, outdoor Coronations would take place at Tara. A Georgian mansion, as near to Tara Hill as possible, could be restored and used as the Royal palace.

As always, Ideal Constitutions for Ireland must wobble a bit when they come to Ulster. It is imperative that Ulster be united once more, whether under an Irish Crown or the Crown of the United Kingdom. Counties Donegal, Cavan and Monaghan (at present in Republican Limbo) must be a part of Ulster in legal fact as well as by tradition. Now, ever since the emigrations and plantations of past ages, Ulster has been Scottish in character. Ought Ulster not be ruled by the monarch of Scotland? In other words, should the Republic slip Donegal, Cavan and Monaghan to the United Kingdom, whose monarch is also the monarch of Scotland?

Plenty of people in Donegal, Cavan and Monaghan would be delighted, as they would not have so far to go to buy drinks, groceries and cigarettes. They would already be on the right side of the Border for shopping. However, others might be furious, and my Constitution is at its weakest here. It may be that the Protestants of Northern Ireland would acquiesce in the new kingly order. Many of the chiefly families of the other Provinces are now Protestant, and a Protestant High King might be a possibility now and again. If Scotland should one day become independent, with its own monarch, then union with Ulster might seem more acceptable to all. So I'll blur over the consequences for Ulster and hurry on to my next point – the re-establishment of an Irish House of Lords, the first since 1801.

An Irish House of Lords, in my view, should not only consist of Anglo–Irish peers, but of clan chiefs and both Anglican and Roman Catholic bishops. Of course, each King of Ireland would have the right to confer hereditary peerages on heroes and contributors to the public good. Anglo-Irish lords might be entitled to sit both in the Irish *and* the United Kingdom House of Lords. Or they might be asked to choose between one or the other. If they chose Ireland, as I believe most of them would, then the Ascendancy could once more be drawn to the heart of Irish life and be given a high-minded function. Roman Catholic bishops and clan chieftains would even up the balance, and Ireland might boast a Second Chamber that would be the envy of England and the world. At any rate, it would be a lively place! How much power the Lords should enjoy, I leave to the People of Ireland.

Refreshed, I went up on deck and looked at the waves. Of Ireland there was no sign whatsoever. Yet I seemed to hear the distant cheers, as each Province selected its king and the champions of Ulster, Leinster, Connaught and Munster set out for Tara and the kingship trials. I seemed to hear trumpets and see colourful flags and standards fluttering in the sea breeze. When the band plays Four Nations Once Again, then I shall return to Ireland.

The Adastral Hotel
Westbourne Villas
Hove
Sussex

Index